"Dr. Garner's *Sons in the Son* is a f[a]
minimized doctrine of the believ[e]
not need to agree with Garner at every point to recommend this profoundly theological and practical work. In terms of exegetical, biblical, systematic, historical, and experiential theology, *Sons in the Son* is a ground-breaking book that thoroughly mines the field of adoption from Scripture itself all the way to twenty-first-century treatments of the subject. All future work on this subject, which is so precious to the minds and hearts of Christians, should reckon with this masterful treatment."

—**Joel R. Beeke**, President, Puritan Reformed Theological Seminary, Grand Rapids

"David Garner's *Sons in the Son* is to the theology of adoption what John Murray's *Redemption Accomplished and Applied* is to an explanation of Christ's work for us and in us. After having immersed myself in the theology of adoption for a decade, I'm convinced that Garner's book will be considered a theological classic of the Christian faith just as Murray's is today. My hope (and full expectation) is that *Sons in the Son* will be widely read by scholars and pastors for the great good of the church. Garner has served the church exceedingly well with this book. To say I absolutely loved it would be an understatement."

—**Dan Cruver**, President, Together for Adoption; editor/ co-author, *Reclaiming Adoption: Missional Living Through the Rediscovery of Abba Father*

"*Sons in the Son* serves the church well by showing that nothing is more ultimate, nothing more at stake in the salvation of God's elect, not only for them but for Christ himself, than their adoption (Rom. 8:29). Garner explores this key, often insufficiently valued doctrine in its full scope and in considerable depth—in a way that stimulates readers to a fresh appreciation of adoption with its important implications for life in union with Christ. I commend this book most highly."

—**Richard B. Gaffin Jr.**, Professor of Biblical and Systematic Theology, Emeritus, Westminster Theological Seminary

"J. I. Packer and John Murray have told us that adoption is the apex of the Christian's privilege. All Reformed pastors agree that to pray 'Our Father' is holy delight. Yet what is adoption's place in the *ordo salutis*? Many students ask why we speak of justification and sanctification, but say little about adoption. With impressive scope and careful attention to exegetical detail, Professor David Garner explores adoption as the master benefit of faith union with the exalted Christ. To be a believing son of God is to be one with the eternal, now 'adopted' Son.

"Without reducing the importance of application, Garner patiently roots the *ordo salutis* in Jesus' once-for-all history. The eternal Son took on flesh, met the double demand of the broken covenant of works, was himself made 'Son of God in power' by his resurrection (Rom. 1:4), and gave his Spirit to the church. What Christ attained—adoption as Son—is what he confers by his Spirit on the church. This is the full flowering of the covenant.

"Unfortunately, the word adopted will not be easy to grasp as describing the resurrected Christ. It has too many associations with heresies old and new. But Garner's Nicene orthodoxy is impeccable. This book develops yet another important way in which Scripture proclaims that the acts of the triune God in redemptive history, 'for us and for our salvation,' express what is blessedly true of him eternally.

"Dr. Garner's book may well reset the Reformed church's thinking about the relationship of its doctrine of salvation and its doctrine of Christ. Garner firmly challenges the shortchangers: salvation cannot be reduced to justification, nor to sanctification, nor to ecclesiology. Instead, all these cohere in Christ himself. David has given a gift to the church, both for its doctrine and for its piety. It is a pleasure to recommend it."

—**Howard Griffith**, Academic Dean and Associate Professor of Systematic Theology, Reformed Theological Seminary, Washington, DC

"Reading *Sons in the Son* is like putting on a new set of glasses that enable the reader to see the glistening beauty of God's grace of adoption throughout the entirety of his salvation plan. Garner clearly and convincingly traces the adoption of God anchored in his loving purposes from eternity past, enacted through the adoption of Israel, assured by the ascension of Jesus as the adopted Son of God in power, and anticipated by all sons who are joined to the Son. This book both challenged my mind and melted my heart."

—**Nancy Guthrie**, Bible teacher and author of the Seeing Jesus in the Old Testament series

"*Sons in the Son* is a scholarly, faithful exposition of the doctrine of adoption that demonstrates adoption's crucial character in the drama of redemption. It's a valuable resource for any Christian wanting to exult in God's purpose in making us sons and daughters and joint heirs with Christ."

—**Russell Moore**, President, Ethics & Religious Liberty Commission, Southern Baptist Convention

"The jazzy-looking, though admirably apt, title of Dr. Garner's treatise proclaims him to be following, indeed reinstating, John Calvin's exact insight into Paul's account of adoption as a central category in both Trinitarian Christology and covenantal soteriology. This is something that post-Puritan Reformed teaching for three centuries, strangely, has not always made fully clear, and it is high time that the record be set straight. Though at times heavy sledding (after all, a doctoral thesis went into its making), this book is a gem: a precious mind-clearing, heartwarming achievement that I cannot commend too highly."

—**James I. Packer**, Board of Governors Professor of Theology, Regent College

"In this volume, Dave Garner has gathered up with biblical fidelity and captivating clarity the glorious doctrine of adoption, affirming both the privileges of believers as 'sons of God' in Christ and the experiential blessings enjoyed by the sealing presence and power of the Spirit of adoption—a must read."

—**Harry L. Reeder**, Pastor/Teacher, Briarwood Presbyterian Church, Birmingham

"The Scripture's teaching about adoption has enjoyed a renaissance in recent evangelical reflection. Long overdue is a work that not only synthesizes and analyzes recent studies of adoption but also exhaustively surveys the relevant biblical, theological, and historical materials. David B. Garner's *Sons in the Son* is just such a work. Far from merely restating what others have said about adoption, *Sons in the Son* sends readers back to the sources to think about the doctrine in fresh and challenging ways. Garner has performed a great service to the Reformed church; I expect that *Sons in the Son* will quickly establish itself as the standard treatment of adoption for years to come."

—**Guy Prentiss Waters**, James M. Baird Jr. Professor of New Testament, Reformed Theological Seminary, Jackson, Mississippi

SONS

in the

SON

SONS

in the

SON

The RICHES *and* REACH
of ADOPTION *in* CHRIST

DAVID B. GARNER

P.O. BOX 817 • PHILLIPSBURG • NEW JERSEY 08865-0817

Printed in the United States of America

ISBN: 978-1-62995-072-3 (pbk.)
ISBN: 978-1-62995-073-0 (ePub)
ISBN: 978-1-62995-074-7 (Mobi)

Library of Congress Cataloging-in-Publication Data

Names: Garner, David B., 1965- author.
Title: Sons in the Son : the riches and reach of adoption in Christ / David B. Garner.
Description: Phillipsburg : P&R Publishing, 2016. | Includes bibliographical references and index.
Identifiers: LCCN 2016019051| ISBN 9781629950723 (pbk.) | ISBN 9781629950730 (epub) | ISBN 9781629950747 (mobi)
Subjects: LCSH: Adoption (Theology) | Bible. Epistles of Paul--Criticism, interpretation, etc.
Classification: LCC BT165 .G37 2016 | DDC 234--dc23
LC record available at https://lccn.loc.gov/2016019051

To Minda with joy

Contents

Foreword

Sixty years ago, Dr. David Garner's predecessor at Westminster Seminary, Professor John Murray, published his small but widely influential book *Redemption Accomplished and Applied.*[1] It included a brief chapter entitled simply "Adoption." He probably had little idea—and indeed, it has been relatively rarely recognized—that those few pages would mark the beginning of a new epoch for this doctrine. For a variety of reasons, it had been almost entirely absent from the way in which twentieth-century evangelical Christians thought about their salvation. Regeneration, justification, and sanctification took central place. By contrast, John Murray stressed that adoption is "the apex of grace and privilege."

The intervening decades have seen a small bookcase of publications on the theme of divine adoption and sonship. Some have been scholarly works dealing with the biblical background and including detailed technical exegetical studies of the relevant New Testament passages; others have been more pastoral, focusing on the privileges of believers' adoption into God's family and being able to call him *"Abba*, Father." As a direct result, many Christians have discovered a new freedom, joy, and security in Christ.

It is very fitting, therefore, that one of Professor Murray's successors at Westminster Seminary gives us this new and multidimensional treatment of this theme. In these pages Professor Garner lives up to his name, for he has garnered many of the best fruits of the church's meditation and exposition of this great theme.

1. John Murray, *Redemption Accomplished and Applied* (Grand Rapids: Eerdmans, 1955).

But more than that, Dr. Garner presents the biblical teaching on divine adoption in the spirit of Scripture and standing on the shoulders of the Reformed fathers of the church who have best expounded it. Here, then, a line of thought that was almost ubiquitous in Calvin, and first given confessional status in the Westminster Confession of Faith, but that has often been marginalized in both theology and pastoral ministry, is brought to an abundant harvest. And in keeping with his Reformed forebears, Dr. Garner weaves together exegetical, redemptive-historical, systematic-theological, and pastoral-theological concerns so that his exposition possesses a multivalent character that will serve scholars, students, and pastors equally well.

Two qualities in this book underscore its value.

The first is that many readers attracted to these pages because of their focus on adoption may to their surprise discover that they are receiving a much broader theological education. But of course! For if, after all, adoption turns out to be the "apex of grace and privilege," then, pyramidlike, it is undergirded and sustained by the entire structure of biblical theology. Like a good steward, as David Garner takes us deeper into the theme of adoption, en route he brings out many good things old and new from the biblical larder. In this sense, *Sons in the Son* provides even more than its title might at first seem to promise.

The second is that while characterized by wide-ranging and objective scholarship, Dr. Garner's writing overflows with a faith-fueled pastoral passion. Clearly for him the importance of careful exposition is its life-changing subjective appropriation. As "Rabbi" Duncan said of Jonathan Edwards, here doctrine is all application and application is all doctrine. This approach wonderfully enhances these pages. It will also help some readers who might fear that they will be in above their heads with the weight of scholarship represented in these pages by many informative footnotes. For this is scholarship with a high cash value for both the church and the individual. Like James Denney (but with a more resilient commitment to biblical teaching), David Garner is interested in theology that can be preached, and at the same time he believes that all truly biblical theology can be. This is immediately evident in the title he has chosen: adoptive sonship is ours only *in the Son*. Adoption is not treated here as an abstract doctrine but as a personal reality. The flow of all redemptive history, exegesis, biblical theology, and pastoral application always derives from and leads to Jesus Christ. We have no sonship without him or apart from our union with him.

We all need books that instruct us, cause us to meditate more deeply, and lead to the transformation of our lives into the likeness of Christ through the renewing of our minds. *Sons in the Son* belongs to this category. I am reminded of a sentence from my far-off days when young Scottish teenagers were expected to memorize parts of the elegant essay of Francis Bacon (1561–1626) *Of Studies*: "Some books are to be tasted, others to be swallowed, and some few to be chewed and digested; that is, some books are to be read only in parts; others to be read, but not curiously; and some few to be read wholly, and with diligence and attention."[2] David Garner's *Sons in the Son* fits into this last category. Read "with diligence and attention," and this work will enhance your understanding of and appreciation for the riches of God's grace in our adoption as sons in his Son, Jesus Christ.

Sinclair B. Ferguson
Professor of Systematic Theology
Redeemer Seminary

2. Francis Bacon, "Essays of Francis Bacon," http://www.authorama.com/essays-of-francis-bacon-50.html (accessed July 4, 2016).

PREFACE

In the late 1990s, I literally stumbled on Douglas Kelly's "Adoption: An Underdeveloped Heritage of the Westminster Standards."[1] Having previously read with no minuscule appreciation the salient content of chapter 12 of the Westminster Confession of Faith, I agonized over Kelly's assertion that "Reformed Christians have failed to work through the doctrine of Adoption."[2] This claim triggered further investigation, and the more I read, the more convinced I became that, if anything, Kelly had understated the scope of the neglect.

The failure to advance and celebrate adoption was—and *is*, in fact—not the sole province of the Reformed. Yet because of the adoption-rich theology of Calvin and the pastorally vibrant statements in the Westminster Standards, one could surely affirm a higher degree of accountability for those whose confessional standards are Westminsterian. But more important than the "Who's to blame?" question is "Who will correct the problem?" Never swaying from my own personal sense of responsibility, I simply could not leave the matter alone. That I am confessionally Reformed in the Westminster tradition certainly escalated the sense of responsibility. That I am a redeemed son of God and student of his Word left no option.

Captivated by its peculiar Pauline use, I pored through the Greek text, the church fathers and the Reformers, volumes of Reformed, liberal, and evangelical systematic theologies, historical and contemporary commentaries, and the writings of the Westminster divines. I soaked in

1. Douglas F. Kelly, "Adoption: An Underdeveloped Heritage of the Westminster Standards," *Reformed Theological Review* 52, 3 (1993): 110–20.
2. Ibid., 111.

biblical theology, from Irenæus to Calvin, and from Geerhardus Vos to Richard Gaffin. I then worked through key Pauline studies, historical and contemporary. At the end of it all, I found myself compelled by a thesis, which was distilled in my Ph.D. dissertation in 2002, entitled "Adoption in Christ."[3] The dissertation probed the scope of adoption and its relationship to union with Christ, but urged others to answer pressing questions that remained.

More than a decade passed, and a number of works on adoption surfaced in both academic and popular writing. Much in these writings contributed usefully, and while some interacted directly with my thesis (e.g., Trevor Burke,[4] Joel Beeke[5]), the systematic theological questions that my own dissertation asked remained *unanswered*. For the sake of Christ and his church and in view of the treasures housed in adoption, I could not leave these questions as moot. They simply matter too much.

With explicit focus on the essential interrelationship between Christology, pneumatology, and soteriology, *Sons in the Son* extends, refines, clarifies, and solidifies my original thesis on adoption and union with Christ. It builds on the earlier exegetical work, engages more recent contributions about adoption, more fully probes the doctrine's biblico-theological character, and then specifically advances the systematic theological implications for this sweet, filial grace.

Many years in the making, *Sons in the Son* offers a fresh look at the rich and far-reaching doctrine of adoption. The title of the book and an oft-repeated phrase in it, *sons in the Son* serves as theological shorthand to capture the vital relationship that the redeemed share with the resurrected Son of God. By virtue of Spirit-wrought union, the redeemed truly are sons of God only *in* and *through* the beloved Son, in whom the Father finds perfect pleasure. In other words, adoption draws on the Redeemer-Son himself, whose own life-giving

---

3. David B. Garner, "Adoption in Christ" (Ph.D. diss., Westminster Theological Seminary, Philadelphia, 2002).

4. Trevor J. Burke, *Adopted into God's Family: Exploring a Pauline Metaphor*, NSBT 22 (Downers Grove, IL: InterVarsity Press, 2006).

5. Joel R. Beeke, *Heirs with Christ: The Puritans on Adoption* (Grand Rapids: Reformation Heritage Books, 2008).

resurrection as *Son of God in power* demarcates our adoption as sons of God. How that is so is simply breathtaking and worship-generating, if not paradigm-shifting.

Soli Patri Gloria. Soli Filio Gloria. Soli Spiritui Gloria.

ACKNOWLEDGMENTS

Two figures deserve first mention in this book. Dr. Richard B. Gaffin Jr. has made particular impact; his peerless scholarship has shaped every facet of my theology, preaching, teaching, and writing. His corresponding piety, churchmanship, and missionary zeal have sculpted my own evangelical, ecclesial, and spiritual commitments. This volume self-consciously trails Dr. Gaffin's (and therefore Geerhardus Vos's) penetrating biblical and systematic theology. Continuing the Vos-Gaffin course, this book blazes new trails concerning the filially framed contours of Christology, pneumatology, and soteriology.

The second figure is Dr. Sinclair B. Ferguson. Several years ago he enthusiastically encouraged my pursuit of the theology of adoption in Christ. His interest in my early research and writing ignited a fire in my soul, fueling a fifteen-year study of this filial grace. In addition to this particular inspiration, Dr. Ferguson's studies in Calvin's theology, the doctrine of the Holy Spirit, and the theology and history of the Westminster Standards have electrified my thinking.

I am most grateful for the exegetical rigor, theological competency, pedagogical skill, and pastoral graces that distinguish these two men. In whatever ways this book proves useful, it does so in their debt, as the fruit of their contagious compulsion to probe and to articulate God's Word faithfully to *and* for Christ's church. At the same time, I issue this customary, nearly compulsory, caveat with full sincerity: this work is mine, and any blame for its blunders belongs on my shoulders. Neither these men nor any others can be held responsible for any of this project's weaknesses or lacunae.

Though I (obviously) have never met Geerhardus Vos, Herman Ridderbos, or John Calvin, their respective theological projects have rewarded me richly and influenced me roundly. Their pens have formed and fed my relentless compulsion to contemplate the lush, mutually informing disciplines of biblical and systematic theology. As they have shaped my theology of the sons in the Son, I count them as genuine brothers in the Son. I only wish I could thank them personally and, though unable to do so now, could not with integrity release this book without their mention. Calvin's handling of adoption, in particular, resides squarely behind this project. Compelled as an adopted son of God himself, Calvin soaked in the far-reaching scope of this gospel privilege; adoption's permeating and parameterizing function played like a rapturous concerto in his soul. In poring over Calvin's "gospel of adoption,"[1] I have found this same filial symphony playing in my own heart so as to resonate onto each page.

In the writing of this manuscript, special thanks go to Bob LaRocca, Dr. Dwight Singer, Dr. Robert Berman, Dr. Carlton Wynne, Dr. Gabriel Fluhrer, and Jared Oliphint. Their hours of input and feedback have supplied needed suggestions and corrections along the way. Thanks to P&R Publishing, to its president, Bryce Craig, and to John J. Hughes for proofing, promoting, and publishing *Sons in the Son*. Sincere thanks to Karen Magnuson for her remarkable copy-editing work; her hawklike skill in spotting and correcting even the tiniest of errors exceeds that of anyone I know. Chase Daws took on the arduous task of perfecting the index of subjects and names, and I greatly appreciate his carefulness and diligence. I remain very grateful for P&R's value to the church in its publication of biblically rigorous, confessionally loyal, and churchly edifying theology.

Finally, my own family's encouragement sustained this work to the end. Though at times they might have genuinely believed no end would come, let it be noted that this book is bound with a back cover. The *not yet* has indeed become the *already*. No quantity of thanks could adequately convey the depth of my gratitude to my wife and children.

---

1. Brian A. Gerrish, *Grace and Gratitude: The Eucharistic Theology of John Calvin* (Edinburgh: T&T Clark, 1993), 89.

INTRODUCTION

When hearing the word *adoption*, most envision a once-orphaned child now legally joined to a new set of parents. A previously forlorn soul flees a loveless past and enters the permanent embrace of a welcoming family. For the child, life changes dramatically, with changes only slightly less marked for the parents and for the siblings. With legal status now wholly changed, the child takes on a new name, a new identity, and a new address, along with a new set of formal and formative relationships. The legal change effects relational changes. Adoption intercepts the probable destiny of heartache, and exchanges almost certain tragedy for rewarding care and provision. Virtually nothing remains the same for the adopter and the adoptee.

Adoption starts with the parents. A dream conceived turns to conversation and prayer, which in turn give birth to the pursuit of a particular child. Legal, administrative, logistical, and financial processes ensue, and after navigating the often-complex and costly journey, the parents receive the child legally as their own. For the child, newfound stability trounces previous insecurity, settled wonderment replaces sad wandering, and cruelty gives way to compassion. Narratives of this sort drip with altruism if not romance, compel us with their merciful transformations, and offer enthralling narratives to counter the harshness of our world.

With such emotive appeal, the parallels between divine and human adoption seem ready-made, supplying a cache of cognitive capital for appreciating the gospel's redemptive familial conceptions. But the leap from human perception to theological insight easily misrepresents the truth. This distortion happens in at least two ways. First, although some adoptions feature joy and success, not all human adoptions flourish. Onerous problems, including keen mental and emotional traumas, plague many families—both for the adopted children and for their adopting parents. These all-too-common darker sides to human adoption, some of which last a lifetime, can get lost in the sentiment of noble narratives. Just ask myriads of adopting families. Human adoption experiences do not produce the gripping theological analogies quite as neatly as they might first seem to do.

But a second and even more foundational problem persists—not arising from any negative underbelly of human adoption experiences, but from the theological method that moves *from* common social conceptions *to* theological ones. Unscrupulous simplicity combined with bottom-up extrapolation is the mother of illegitimate theologizing, and a theology of adoption shaped by social-to-theological inference writhes in methodological error. Concepts of biblical adoption birthed largely out of contemporary practices or out of compelling altruistic analogies may brush with points of biblical insight, but at best suffer from truncated theological expression and at worst distort the theological riches of the believers' adoption in Christ.[1] The radical distinctions between divine adoption of sinners and human conventions—both in this age and in ancient society—must receive rigorous assessment according to careful hermeneutical and theological analysis.

In short, unlike human convention, divine adoption is mediatorial and redemptive—it comes through the divine Son, Jesus the Messiah. Divine adoption does not proceed from dissatisfaction in God, in which he pursues a family because he is incomplete or longs for something he lacks. Divine adoption moves from heaven to earth by sovereign grace, and transforms the children of wrath into the glorious and radiant possession of the heavenly Father. Divine filial grace is effectual in a way that human initiatives, however blessed they might be, can never attain. Divine adoption never disappoints. The children of the heavenly Father persevere by his grace, and none is lost by the sway of self-centeredness, dissatisfaction, rejection, or discontent. United to the perfect Son of God by faith, the children

---

1. An example of this approach is Jeanne Stevenson-Moessner, *The Spirit of Adoption: At Home in God's Family* (Louisville, KY: Westminster John Knox, 2003).

of God will know no ultimate eschatological distress! As the apostle Paul affirms, drawing from several Old Testament texts:

For we are the temple of the living God; as God said,

> "I will make my dwelling among them and walk among them,
>> and I will be their God,
>> and they shall be my people.
> Therefore go out from their midst,
>> and be separate from them, says the Lord,
> and touch no unclean thing;
>> then I will welcome you,
> and I will be a father to you,
>> and you shall be sons and daughters to me,
> says the Lord Almighty." (2 Cor. 6:16b–18)

Divine pursuit and presence are stark and stunning. By *grace*, the Creator of all becomes the Father of his elect, transforming spiritual orphans and rebels into his blessed and holy children. The intimacy and efficacy of such redemptive grace simply stagger, making any rags-to-riches story of a human orphan rescued by altruistic parents pale in significance.

Notably, the nature of divine adoptive grace exceeds the human plane not only in degree, but also in scope. Human adoption is marvelous, but its customary strictures do not shape gospel adoption. To be specific, forensic and relational categories plainly do not exhaust biblical adoption. The power of the heavenly Father among his people changes their stubborn filial hearts even as it reverses their guilty filial state. Adopted sons of God enter radically different conditions *and* possess radically different constitutions. Because it breathes with spiritual vitality beyond a single soteriological aspect (the forensic), biblical adoption suffocates if relegated to legal categories.

To be clear, important similarities exist between biblical adoption and human adoption,[2] but the theological parallels move from heaven

---

2. The parallels, in fact, may be richer than what appears from the bottom up. Dan Cruver

to earth rather than from earth to heaven. The gospel may compel human adoption and *should* compel various acts of gospel mercy. But divine adoption, a blessing in a category all its own, as accomplished by the death and resurrection of the beloved Son of God, outshines and outwarms all human rescue efforts. When God takes those who are not his people and makes them his people, when the Almighty makes those who are not his children his sons and daughters, the benefits consume, overwhelm, and transform. Those once-spiritual orphans become the favored ones of the Almighty, objects of divine affection, recipients of privilege and security, and benefactors of new hearts and resurrected bodies! All these blessings come in and through the beloved Son in whom the Father is well pleased.

There is a yet even more stunning feature to Pauline adoption. In his commentary on Romans, German Reformer Philipp Melanchthon insisted that *adoption* differentiates the redeemed from the Redeemer. "The fact that he calls them adopted sons distinguishes the other saints from Christ, and this distinction must be held fast in order that we may know that Christ is the Son of God by nature, both equal with the Father and of the same essence, as it is written: 'We beheld his glory, like the glory of the only-begotten of the Father. . . .' [John 1:14] But the saints are sons by adoption, because they have been received of Christ, and have been given the gifts of Christ, namely the Spirit, and new life, wisdom and righteousness, etc."[3] On the one hand, Melanchthon is spot-on. Christ's sonship is eternal and inimitable. That Christ is eternal Son made flesh is assumed and proclaimed in Pauline

---

helpfully probes the theology of adoption by distinguishing *vertical adoption* (divine adoption) from *horizontal adoption* (human adoption). Driving toward faithful gospel response, Cruver insists that we think about human adoption *by* divine adoption, rather than in reverse. This orientation shapes life mission according to divine grace in God's self-disclosure and redemption. "I believe that a biblical understanding of God's fatherhood will cause us to be better able to look outside ourselves in service to others." Dan Cruver, ed., *Reclaiming Adoption: Missional Living through the Rediscovery of Abba Father* (Adelphi, MD: Cruciform, 2011), 7, 18.

3. Philipp Melanchthon, *Commentary on Romans*, trans. Fred Kramer (St. Louis: Concordia, 1992), 174–75. Much more recently, Todd Billings makes a similar point. Though Billings commendably appreciates the vast scope of adoption for Paul, he makes adoption a point of distinction between the Redeemer and the redeemed. Jesus is "the only 'natural' child of God . . . . All the rest of us need to be adopted." J. Todd Billings, *Union with Christ: Reframing Theology and Ministry for the Church* (Grand Rapids: Baker, 2011), 24.

theology. But adoption moves in a different orbit than Melanchthon assumes. For Paul, adoption concerns human sonship in its mature and resurrected state—that of Christ Jesus first and then that of those united to him by Spirit-wrought faith.

The believers' adoption, as we will see, does not serve to distinguish redemptive sonship from that belonging to the Redeemer, the Son of God, but quite contrarily (and astoundingly!) celebrates the filial realities fully *shared* by and with Christ Jesus. Believers, united to Christ in his resurrection, enjoy the full bounty of benefits, the panoply of spiritual blessings attained by their Elder Brother. The motivation to preserve the uniqueness of the sonship of Jesus Christ is biblical and noble. He is the divine Son eternally, and this sonship remains unique to him. He alone is the Mediator, whose identity, nature, and work distinguish him from all other humanity. But we must not allow this proper impetus to exalt the Son of God to receive improper application, and thereby compromise the way in which believers are understood as sons and daughters of God—adoption "*in and for . . . Jesus Christ*," as WCF 12 puts it. What Christ attains in his exalted state of sonship comes to the redeemed in full. Adoption, in its Pauline usage, establishes and accentuates the filial character of Spirit-wrought faith union—the historical, theological, and familial solidarity of the redeemed with their Redeemer. Adoption, then, does not serve to *differentiate* believers from Christ; rather, it serves to *expose* the crowded graces of our salvation, secured in our union with the resurrected, exalted, perfected, and *adopted* Son of God! The believers' redemptive adoption comes by the *adoption of the Redeemer*. His adoption is our adoption, his holy sonship our holy sonship.

With such solidarity of the sons of God with the Son of God in view, this book comes as a plea—a plea to reassess the theological meaning, place, and function of biblical adoption; a plea for a method that moves from divine revelation to theological reflection, rather than from social and cultural reconstruction to theological conclusion; and simultaneously a plea to reexamine key biblical texts within their historical and cultural context. At the end of it all, it comes with a prevailing plea to appreciate the munificent theological reaches of this filial conception. Biblical and theological care is in order, and an exploration of this doctrine requires attention to etymology, exegesis, biblical theology, and systematic theology. As will become clear, according to divine Word and deed, adoption cloaks the gospel in filial array, and weds the doctrine of Christ (Christology) and the doctrine of the Holy Spirit (pneumatology) to generate the doctrine of salvation (soteriology). Spirit-wrought filial solidarity—the gracious placement of the redeemed sons in the Son of God by adoption—actually *structures* biblical soteriology for the apostle Paul.

In one way, the following argument urges renewed reflection on the biblical concept of *adoption*, because theological forces of various sorts have historically squeezed this doctrine from its theological prominence, shrunk it from its expansive theological scope, and thereby relegated it to a subsidiary theological classification rather than giving it the prominence it deserves. Freeing adoption from forensic-only strictures and affirming its legal *and* transformative filial features are not simple tasks, but for the sake of biblical fidelity and theological integrity of the sons in the Son, such articulation is essential. This book seeks, in part, to dismantle the misallocation, misappropriation, and misunderstanding of theological adoption. That is its deconstructive task.

More fundamentally, it seeks to construct a biblically faithful theology of adoption in Christ, one that appreciates the full spectrum of filial grace embraced by this eschatologically, and therefore existentially, vivid soteriological term. The case argued here offers nothing overtly novel, and to be sure, novelty is not the goal. Rather, the subsequent examination flows in direct continuity and sympathy with historic Reformed Christology and soteriology, and simply seeks to express with fresh clarity how the essential interrelationship between the life, death, and resurrection of Jesus Christ and the redemption of sinners wholly informs adoption.

A final word here expresses the prayerful goal of this work. WLC question 113 asks, "What is required in the third commandment?" The answer: "The third commandment requires, that the name of God, his titles, attributes, ordinances, the word, sacraments, prayer, oaths, vows, lots, his works, and whatsoever else there is whereby he makes himself known, be holily and reverently used in thought, meditation, word, and writing; by an holy profession, and answerable conversation, to the glory of God, and the good of ourselves, and others."

As I reflect on Scripture concerning the doctrine of adoption, I pray that this writing treats the name of God, his titles, his attributes, and his Word in a holy and reverent fashion, with the filial fidelity incumbent on one adopted in Christ Jesus. To that doxological end, I, an adopted son in the Son, turn to an examination of adoption in Paul and his theology.

Abbreviations

AnBib	Analecta Biblica
ANF	*Ante-Nicene Fathers*
BECNT	Baker Exegetical Commentary on the New Testament
CTJ	*Calvin Theological Journal*
ESV	English Standard Version
EvQ	*Evangelical Quarterly*
FV	Federal Vision
IBS	*Irish Biblical Studies*
ICC	International Critical Commentary
JBL	*Journal of Biblical Literature*
JETS	*Journal of the Evangelical Theological Society*
KJV	King James Version
MNTC	Moffatt New Testament Commentary
NASB	New American Standard Bible
NICNT	New International Commentary on the New Testament
NIGTC	New International Greek Testament Commentary
NIV	New International Version
NPP	New Perspective(s) on Paul
NSBT	New Studies in Biblical Theology

NTC	New Testament Commentary
RExp	*Review and Expositor*
SBET	*Scottish Bulletin of Evangelical Theology*
SP	Sacra Pagina
TNTC	Tyndale New Testament Commentary
VE	*Vox Evangelica*
WBC	Word Biblical Commentary
WCF	Westminster Confession of Faith
WLC	Westminster Larger Catechism
WSC	Westminster Shorter Catechism
WTJ	*Westminster Theological Journal*
ZEC	Zondervan Exegetical Commentary Series on the New Testament

PART I

ADOPTION: HERMENEUTICS, HISTORY, AND ETYMOLOGY

1

Adoption: Scope and Point of Entry

Important Principles for Interpreting *Huiothesia* ("Adoption")

Cursory enquiry of *huiothesia* ("adoption")[1] in the New Testament might lead one to downplay its theological significance. Only five times does the term *huiothesia* appear, always in the Pauline corpus, ostensibly defending a cursory treatment based on its infrequency and Pauline exclusivity. If adoption is so important, why does the term *huiothesia* draw so little ink? As more careful analysis of the term in its particular usage reveals, simplistic conclusions do not satisfy. Quantitative analysis of vocabulary serves as no adequate determiner, because the word *huiothesia* widely embraces multiple theological foci and vast pastoral treasure. Before giving attention to the sweeping manner in which Paul employs *huiothesia*, critical hermeneutical principles concerning the theological weight of biblical terms warrant mention.

Before we defend or deny a word's importance on the basis of its etymology and regularity, other biblical, contextual, and theological criteria must take precedence. Scholars across the hermeneutical and theological spectrum discern methodological problems with noncontextual word studies.[2] Even one whose Christology suffers

---

1. Throughout this volume I will use transliteration of Greek terms. The term *huiothesia* is typically translated "adoption" or "adoption as sons" (see, e.g., the five instances of *huiothesia* in the ESV, NIV, and NASB). The only exceptions to the use of transliteration are selected quotations and any lexical references.

2. Faulty assumptions about words, including overtechnicalizing, root fallacy errors, and

3

from damaging, unorthodox formulations, James Dunn, astutely warns of faulty conclusions stemming from the rarity with which Jesus is called God's Son in the Pauline Epistles (only seventeen times). Such infrequency renders feeble rationale for determining theological inconsequentiality: "word counts are an uncertain basis on which to build . . . a conclusion."[3] As Dunn asserts, the weight of a theological concept cannot be determined by mere quantitative analysis. Such a simplistic approach would suffer from the word-concept fallacy and ignore the more important questions of *how* a word is employed and of *how* a concept can explicitly and implicitly shape an entire paradigm.[4]

Vulnerability surfaces here for two types of interpretive error. On the one hand, there is risk in overlooking key contextual and exegetical considerations because a particular term appears rarely. In this way, brute quantitative analysis can invalidly curtail emphasis on important theological themes. On the other hand, there is a risk of importing foreign concepts into Scripture because one can presume on a particular theme, make interpretive decisions out of an imposed thesis, and force conclusions into a word, a biblical text, or even the canon of Scripture as a whole. Desire for new insight and the temptation to promote hobbyhorses can cloud interpretive judgment. Avoiding errors in either direction mandates exegetical and biblico-theological care, including the upholding of the interpretive interdependence of Old and New Testaments, particularly in their organic, covenantal structure. WCF 1.9 offers considerable wisdom with its pithy hermeneutical parameters: "The infallible rule of interpretation of Scripture is the Scripture itself: and therefore, when there is a question about the

---

quantitative analysis, can lead to faulty theological conclusions. See D. A. Carson, *Exegetical Fallacies*, 2nd ed. (Grand Rapids: Baker, 1996), 27–64. Cf. Moisés Silva, *Biblical Words and Their Meaning: An Introduction to Lexical Semantics* (Grand Rapids: Zondervan, 1983); James Barr, *The Semantics of Biblical Language* (Oxford: Oxford University Press, 1961).

3. James D. G. Dunn, *Christology in the Making: A New Testament Inquiry into the Origins of the Doctrine of the Incarnation*, 2nd ed. (Grand Rapids: Eerdmans, 1996), 37.

4. A related application of this principle is the *hapax legomenon*, a word used only once in the New Testament. The selection of an unusual term can actually indicate a *critical* theological concept, such as *theopneustos* in 2 Timothy 3:16. See Edwin A. Blum, "The Apostles' View of Scripture," in *Inerrancy*, ed. Norman L. Geisler (Grand Rapids: Zondervan, 1980), 44–48.

true and full sense of any Scripture (which is not manifold, but one), it must be searched and known by other places that speak more clearly." Shared intertestamental theological themes evidence the Spirit's consistent voice in Scripture, and the church's understanding of them. Such themes, it is important to affirm, originate by "good and necessary consequence" (WCF 1.6) and not just by explicit statement.

Sometimes a theme functions so predominantly, its explicit statement is unnecessary, and even tautologous. The covenants and their formative structure in Scripture offer a prime example. In fact, because of their permeating presence, the historical, hermeneutical, and theological significance of the biblical covenants renders an essential guide to the interpreter.[5] By the manner in which it recognizes and appropriates the historic covenants (e.g., Abrahamic, Mosaic, Davidic) and then integrates these covenants into a single covenant of grace (Gal. 3–4), the Pauline corpus substantiates this conclusion. For the apostle Paul, the biblical covenants frame biblical revelation in the Old and New Testaments, providing the structure of biblical history and theology, including Christology and soteriology.

The two-Adam covenantal paradigm organizes Paul's entire understanding of history (Rom. 5:12–21; 1 Cor. 15:45–49; cf. Rom. 8:18–39),

---

5. This conclusion, of course, does not receive unqualified acceptance in biblical and theological studies. In keeping with historic Reformed theology, however, I believe that covenant, in its permeating and paradigmatic functions, remains at the core of biblical revelation. This conviction renders an interpretive grid that shapes the entirety of this volume. Though the term *covenant* is not always used, the contents and the theme of covenant actually serve as the architectonic principle of Scripture, providing coherence to the pretemporal, prelapsarian, postlapsarian, and consummate eschatological contexts. For discussion of the Reformed doctrine of covenants, see, for example, Francis Turretin, *Institutes of Elenctic Theology*, ed. James T. Dennison Jr., trans. George Musgrave Giger, 3 vols. (Phillipsburg, NJ: P&R Publishing, 1992–94), 1:574–89, 2:169–269; R. L. Dabney, *Syllabus and Notes of the Course of Systematic and Polemic Theology*, 2nd ed. (St. Louis: Presbyterian Publishing, 1878; repr., Edinburgh: Banner of Truth, 1996), 292–305, 429–99; Charles Hodge, *Systematic Theology*, 3 vols. (Grand Rapids: Eerdmans, 1979), 2:117–22, 354–77; Heinrich Heppe, *Reformed Dogmatics Set Out and Illustrated from the Sources*, ed. Ernst Bizer, trans. G. T. Thomson, rev. ed. (Grand Rapids: Baker, 1978), 301–19, 371–447; Louis Berkhof, *Systematic Theology*, 4th ed. (Grand Rapids: Eerdmans, 1949), 211–18, 262–301; Peter A. Lillback, *The Binding of God: Calvin's Role in the Development of Covenant Theology*, ed. Richard A. Muller, Texts and Studies in Reformation and Post-Reformation Thought (Grand Rapids: Baker Academic, 2001); O. Palmer Robertson, *The Christ of the Covenants* (Phillipsburg, NJ: Presbyterian and Reformed, 1980).

from creation through redemption unto consummation.[6] In short, the first Adam upon obedience to the covenant of works was to enter "life"—that is, a new quality of life, one of confirmed righteousness and divine blessing.[7] Failing to obey and forfeiting these covenantal blessings, the first Adam established the historical and theological necessity for the covenantal ministry of the last Adam. Accordingly, Christ's redemptive work as last Adam was exhaustively covenantal, and by faithful covenant-keeping and by enduring the covenantal curse as the chief Sin-Bearer, Christ inherited those promised eschatological blessings. The covenant Head, he secured eschatological life for all those whom he represents.[8] Further, the new covenant, though named explicitly by Paul only in 1 Corinthians 11:25 and 2 Corinthians 3:6, features prominently for the apostle,[9] and the epochal/theological transition from the old covenant to the new covenant entirely frames his theology and that of the entire New Testament. Paul's attention to the historic covenants in the life of ancient Israel and the realization of the new covenant in Christ exposes his covenant-hermeneutical

6. Recognizing biblical revelation as covenantal, the authors (divines) of the WCF structure the theology of the document around the covenant of works and the covenant of grace. See WCF 7. Westminster's theology rides on the "architectonic principle" of the covenant. Benjamin B. Warfield, *The Westminster Assembly and Its Work*, vol. 6 of *The Works of Benjamin B. Warfield* (Grand Rapids: Baker, 1981), 56.

7. Though the term *berith* ("covenant") does not first appear until Genesis 6:18, the covenant concept undergirds the Pauline biblico-theological story line from Genesis 1 and 2. Concerning the absence of the word *covenant* in the Adam and Eve narrative, Beale contends, "The argument that the word 'covenant' is not used in Gen. 2–3 does not provide proof that there is no covenant relationship, just as Adam and Eve's marriage relationship is not termed a 'covenant' in Gen. 2:21–24 but expresses covenantal concept and, in fact, is identified as a covenant elsewhere." G. K. Beale, *A New Testament Biblical Theology: The Unfolding of the Old Testament in the New* (Grand Rapids: Baker, 2011), 42. Cf. Grant Macaskill, *Union with Christ in the New Testament* (Oxford: Oxford University Press, 2013), 103–10, 127.

8. Beale, *New Testament Biblical Theology*, 918; see also ibid., 174. Cf. Noel Weeks, *Admonition and Curse: The Ancient Near Eastern Treaty/Covenant Form as a Problem in Inter-Cultural Relationships* (London: T&T Clark, 2004), 8. Even John Murray's much-debated "Adamic administration" operates according to the *themes* of covenant, though he ardently (though unnecessarily) resists the employment of the term *covenant* in a pre-Noahic context. See John Murray, *The Collected Writings of John Murray*, 4 vols. (Edinburgh: Banner of Truth, 1976–82), 2:47–59.

9. See Herman N. Ridderbos, *Paul: An Outline of His Theology*, trans. John Richard DeWitt (Grand Rapids: Eerdmans, 1975), 335; Macaskill, *Union with Christ*, 227–28.

orientation. Faithful hermeneutics must always appreciate this intertestamental continuity and interpretive reciprocity.[10]

In Romans 9:1–5, Paul explicitly draws out this Old to New Testament covenantal development as it is integrated by the rarely appearing word *huiothesia*.[11] Seeing the gospel of the New Testament drawing on the Christ-centeredness of the Old Testament (Rom. 1:1–7; Gal. 3:8; cf. John 5:39–47), Paul understands the Old Testament itself to anticipate the coming New Testament, new covenant revelation; in turn, the New Testament draws on and fulfills the Old Testament, the old covenant(s).[12] As will grow increasingly clear from the coming treatment of Romans 9:1–5 (in chapter 6), Christ secures the benefits of redemption for those whom he represents, including the benefit of adoption, which is listed first in this Pauline summary of God's covenantal faithfulness to his people. Old Testament adoption anticipates the coming New Testament adoption, and the New Testament fluidly draws on and fulfills its old covenant form. Old Testament events and theology, then, *are* the context for Pauline and New Testament theology: "Paul's letters have their origin, their integral place and their intended function within the organically unfolding history of revelation."[13] Methodological marginalization of this organic intertestamental and covenantal structure will ensure theological misunderstanding, and will effectively compromise any proper appreciation for the origin, scope, and meaning of *huiothesia* in Pauline thought.

Exegetical and theological care is indeed in order. Paul's permeating familial and filio-Christological focus combined with his variegated yet sweeping use of *huiothesia* begs for penetrating consideration of its meaning. Short on recurrence, *huiothesia* is long on import. Adoption appeals to grand biblico-theological and covenantal themes, making

---

10. For study on the biblical concept of *covenant* in its hermeneutical and theological import, see, for example, Geerhardus Vos, "The Doctrine of the Covenant in Reformed Theology," in *Redemptive History and Biblical Interpretation: The Shorter Writings of Geerhardus Vos*, ed. Richard B. Gaffin Jr. (Phillipsburg, NJ: Presbyterian and Reformed, 1980), 234–67.

11. More on Pauline covenant theology follows in chapters 7 and 8.

12. See, e.g., G. K. Beale and D. A. Carson, *Commentary on the New Testament Use of the Old Testament* (Grand Rapids: Baker Academic, 2007).

13. Richard B. Gaffin Jr., *By Faith, Not by Sight: Paul and the Order of Salvation*, 2nd ed. (Phillipsburg, NJ: P&R Publishing, 2013), 10.

its theological function noteworthy, even paradigmatic.[14] Accordingly, as will be surveyed in the following chapters, *huiothesia* shoulders substantial theological weight, since it supports the filially framed resurrection of Jesus Christ (Rom. 1:3–4) as the basis for the whole range of gospel graces bestowed on those united to him. The term *huiothesia* embodies a covenantal, Christological, pneumatological, and soteriological construction for the apostle Paul, countering the temptation to underestimate the term's value; its infrequent appearance ought not to eclipse its theological reaches or its pastoral riches. Richard Sibbes most appropriately exclaims, *"All things* are ours by virtue of adoption, because we are Christ's and Christ is God's. There is a world of riches in this, to be sons of God."[15]

Sibbes considers adoption here in terms of its pastoral value, and rightly so. But the primary concern in this study is to probe the bottomless theological gold mine from which these pastoral marvels draw. To change the metaphor slightly, adoption's subterranean roots take us beneath redemption applied to the accomplishment of redemption itself in Jesus Christ, who is adoption's "cause and root."[16] For the redeemed sons of God, adoption's comprehensive benefits come by participation in the resurrection/adoption of Christ, and no other way. Only with a full appreciation of the Christological and covenantal contours of biblical revelation, and in particular the mutually informing role they play in *huiothesia*, will we begin to apprehend the world of riches embedded in this Pauline theme.

Approaches to the Study of *Huiothesia*

The study of *huiothesia* offers a variety of launching points. We could commence by examining familial terms and themes of the New Testament or in Pauline theology particularly, and move then

14. Though beyond the scope of exhaustive study in this volume, other Pauline familial terms, such as *sons, daughters, children*, and *inheritance*, share theologically vital real estate with adoption.

15. Richard Sibbes, *Works of Richard Sibbes*, ed. Alexander B. Grosart, 7 vols. (Edinburgh: Banner of Truth, 1983), 4:502 (emphasis in original).

16. John Calvin, *Commentaries on the First Book of Moses Called Genesis*, trans. John King (Edinburgh: Calvin Translation Society, n.d.; repr., Grand Rapids: Baker, 1989), 138.

to consider *huiothesia* within that litany of familial terms.[17] Since the concern here is *huiothesia* itself, however, it is more appropriate to commence where the term itself appears. The scarce occurrences of *huiothesia* limit the options for an entry point into this exegetical and theological analysis, and it might seem imprudent to demand one text as the only legitimate option. Yet in view of the multidimensional way in which *huiothesia* functions in the Pauline corpus, and in particular the vast theological horizon entailed by the term, the chosen pathway of study does both expose theological commitments and reflect a theological method. Therefore, to make explicit my operating presuppositions and theological method, I list the five passages here within their immediate contexts, provide an introductory analysis of the texts, and then suggest the rationale for the particular launching point in this study of *huiothesia*. An exclusively Pauline term in the New Testament, *huiothesia* appears only five times: Romans 8:15; 8:23; 9:4; Galatians 4:5; and Ephesians 1:5.

The Epistle to the Romans
Romans 8:15–17:

> For you did not receive the spirit of slavery to fall back into fear, but you have received the Spirit of adoption as sons, by whom we cry, "Abba! Father!" The Spirit himself bears witness with our spirit that we are children of God, and if children, then heirs—heirs of God and fellow heirs with Christ, provided we suffer with him in order that we may also be glorified with him.

Arriving at a culminating point in Romans, the eschatological implications of Christ's life, death, and resurrection come squarely into focus. In this first use of *huiothesia* in Romans, Paul draws on the redemptive-historical contrast to deliver a soteriological point. Believers in Christ Jesus have received the Spirit of adoption—whose outpouring certifies and seals consummate filial grace. Recipients of the Holy Spirit,

---

17. See, e.g., Trevor J. Burke, *Family Matters: A Socio-Historical Study of Kinship Metaphors in 1 Thessalonians*, Journal of the Study of the New Testament Supplement Series 247 (London: T&T Clark International, 2003).

adopted children traverse the Christ-blazed pathway from suffering unto glory, and the outpoured Spirit of adoption enables them to echo Jesus' own Gethsemane outcry to his Father. The Spirit-uniting of the sons of God with the Son of God resounds with filial grace: in this eschatologically inaugurated age, adopted sons and daughters enjoy the same love and fellowship with the Father as does their Elder Brother (Rom. 8:1–39).

Romans 8:22–23:

> For we know that the whole creation has been groaning together in the pains of childbirth until now. And not only the creation, but we ourselves, who have the firstfruits of the Spirit, groan inwardly as we wait eagerly for adoption as sons, the redemption of our bodies.

Building these resplendent filial themes and then drawing them to an eschatological climax, the apostle Paul in this particular section of Romans 8 affirms that the recipients of the Spirit of adoption—those who have the "firstfruits of the Spirit"—will enjoy full filial transformation in this Spirit at their resurrection (Rom. 8:18–21), when they conform perfectly to the image of the Son par excellence (v. 29). For Paul, the Spirit of Christ renders final and realized adoption certain, but adoption's consummation awaits resurrection on the final day (v. 23). In fact, this eschatological manifestation of the sons makes adoption and resurrection more than concurrent. The theologically sated terms actually serve in an interdependent, mutually informing manner, making adoption and resurrection inseparable features within Pauline soteriology. Resurrection grace is filial grace. Adoption is resurrection.

Romans 9:3–5:

> For I could wish that I myself were accursed and cut off from Christ for the sake of my brothers, my kinsmen according to the flesh. They are Israelites, and to them belong the adoption, the glory, the covenants, the giving of the law, the worship, and the promises. To them belong the patriarchs, and from their race, according to the flesh, is the Christ who is God over all, blessed forever. Amen.

Having described in Romans 8 the Spirit-wrought adoption through Jesus Christ in its inaugurated and consummate manifestations, in chapter 9 the apostle Paul addresses the question of God's covenant faithfulness. How is it that God can remain faithful to his old covenant promises and the gospel come to the Jews and *Gentiles*? The answer? The very adoption that Paul has described in this new covenant reality relies on its historico-genetic ancestry in the old covenant adoption of Israel. Typological adoption in the Old Testament is of one substance with the eschatological adoption rendered by Jesus Christ himself. That is, Old Testament adoption finds its eschatological fulfillment in the resurrected Son of God, in whose resurrection the typological filial promises come to fruition.

God's provision of filial grace to Jews and Gentiles by faith manifestly draws the nascent adoption of Israel to its intended denouement. Despite the contentions of some first-century Jews, adoption in Christ Jesus, then, does not evidence God's abandonment of his promises, but precisely the opposite. God's covenant and adoptive promises attain their fulfillment for believing Jews and Gentiles in Jesus Christ, the Son of God. God is faithful to his covenant promises, and adoption in Christ evidences this faithfulness.

Romans as an Entry Point into the Study of Adoption

The eschatological thrust of adoption in Romans 8 and 9 protrudes prominently, and does so in a manner consistent with the primacy of covenant eschatology in biblical revelation. Pithily capturing eschatology's thematic hegemony in biblical revelation, Geerhardus Vos writes:

> There is an absolute end posited for the universe before and apart from sin. The universe, as created, was only a beginning, the meaning of which was not perpetuation, but attainment. The principle of God's relation to the world from the outset was a principle of action or eventuation. The goal was not comparative (i.e., evolution); it was superlative (i.e., the final goal).[18]

18. Geerhardus Vos, *The Eschatology of the Old Testament*, ed. James T. Dennison Jr.

Working according to sovereign plan, eschatology governs the very contours of universal history broadly and redemptive history more particularly. Eschatology is not just final reality but, more properly, ultimate reality—a reality anticipated in creation and, in the wake of the sin of the first Adam, delayed for generations, and then inaugurated in the last Adam, and brought to consummation in him at the parousia.[19]

Because of its theological and historical role, divinely determined eschatology precedes and wholly informs the substance of soteriology.[20] Only by appreciating this foundational and informing role of eschatology will soteriology be properly understood. Put a bit more simply, God's ultimate purpose to secure holy children unto himself does not get thwarted by the entrance of sin. Instead, because of his sovereign and infinitely kind intention, God secures his final purpose to claim a people for himself despite sin and its consequences. God's purposes for history overwhelm even his archenemies: Satan, sin, and death. These purposes to overwhelm his enemies and to create a holy family come about through the completed work of his Son, Jesus Christ.

As will become clearer in what follows, all redemptive benefits (justification, sanctification, etc.) therefore possess realized (*already*) and unrealized (*not yet*) dimensions. Furthermore, since the final (parousia) character of soteriology is in organic continuity with its inaugurated character, explicit consummative soteriology fully informs each stage of its redemptive-historical realization and, perhaps most strikingly, its pretemporal ordination. Vos insists that "the shaping of soteriology by eschatology is not so much in the terminology; it proceeds from the actual realities themselves and the language simply is adjusted to that."[21] This permeating eschatology shapes adoption.

In fact, taking the comprehensively significant nature of adoption's climactic moment in bodily resurrection and the theologically

(Phillipsburg, NJ: P&R Publishing, 2001), 73.

19. "The ultimate is in a very important sense the normative, that to which every preceding stage will have to conform itself to prove the genuineness of its Christian character." Geerhardus Vos, *The Pauline Eschatology* (Princeton, NJ: Princeton University Press, 1930), 42.

20. Vos, *Eschatology of the Old Testament*, 73–75.

21. Ibid., 46.

important way in which consummate eschatology determines the present experience of adoptive sonship, the eschatological thrust of Romans 8:15 and 23 could well serve as a proper starting point for investigating *huiothesia* in Paul. But since two of the five occurrences of *huiothesia* appear in Romans 8 and since the third occurrence of *huiothesia* in Romans 9 invokes a robust covenant and Israel-as-son typology, it seems less than optimal to make either Romans 8:15 or 23 the entry point for a study of adoption. Such an approach could risk illegitimately extricating adoption from its thematic development in Romans itself and the Pauline corpus as a whole, thereby robbing the term of its fullest meaning.

With his eye squarely on redemptive history, James I. Cook suggests Romans 9:4 as "the logical place to begin an exegetical inquiry into the . . . content of the Pauline notion of adoption."[22] Here Paul employs the adoption motif for describing the distinct privileges of Israel in the old covenant, and thereby sees the old covenant as the historical/theological basis for understanding *huiothesia* realized in Christ. At the core of Paul's argument in Romans 9 is that Israel's *huiothesia* anticipates the coming *huiothesia* realized in Christ, wherein filial grace increases expansively and intensively from old covenant shadow unto new covenant fullness.

Moreover, it is of no little consequence that Paul places Israel's adoption first in his list of spiritual blessings on the Old Testament people of God (Rom. 9:4), underscoring its foundational redemptive-historical significance for his people.[23] Cook summarizes, "We may say, then, that the concept of adoption in the theology of Paul belongs to the history of salvation, inaugurated at the naming of Israel as God's son, and continued and perfected in the adoption of men

---

22. James I. Cook, "The Conception of Adoption in the Theology of Paul," in *Saved by Hope: Essays in Honor of Richard C. Oudersluys*, ed. James I. Cook (Grand Rapids: Eerdmans, 1978), 137. Others take the same approach. Cf. Matthew Vellanickal, *The Divine Sonship of Christians in the Johannine Writings*, AnBib: Investigationes Scientificae in Res Biblicas 72 (Rome: Biblical Institute, 1977), 69–87; Martin W. Schoenberg, "*Huiothesia*: The Word and the Institution," *Scripture* 15 (1963): 122–23; Allen Mawhinney, "*Yiothesia* in the Pauline Epistles: Its Background, Use, and Implications" (Ph.D. diss., Baylor University, Waco, TX, 1982), 134–210.

23. Cook, "Conception of Adoption," 138.

and women into the family of God through the work of Christ and the Spirit."[24]

Cook's point merits attention. Surely proper investigation of adoption's theology entails this Christologically and eschatologically rich typology within Paul's theology. But Cook fails to consider the even fuller filial context for adoption not only in the Pauline corpus, but even in Romans itself. The creation-to-consummation argument in Romans 8 and the two-Adam paradigm in Romans 5 bear on the *huiothesian*[25] concept. In other words, as a more expansive consideration discloses, Paul's theological perspective on adoption derives not first from Israel's redemptively rich sonship, but rather from the covenantal sonship of Adam himself. In Pauline theological construction, Adam anticipates a filial state of glory beyond his provisional Edenic context, and the eschatological filial (adoptive) realization secured by Christ Jesus corresponds to and completes this final state of sonship anticipated by Adam. Accordingly, though still oriented here to the creation-to-consummation construct expressed in Romans 8:18–30, because of the concern to address the Jew/Gentile question, Paul selects the Israel-to-Christ epochal transition in Romans 9, rather than the broader landscape of redemptive history from first Adam to last.

Making Romans 9 the launching point for adoption would force a regressive thematic analysis, considering Israel's sonship in advance of or even to the exclusion of Adam's. On the basis of the flow of Pauline thought in this epistle to the Romans,[26] such a decision seems difficult to justify. Moreover, with the more expansive redemptive-historical and Christological contours entailed by adoption in its other appearances, the approach could isolate adoption from its fuller biblical and Christological scope. And since Pauline soteriology rests squarely on the person and work of Jesus Christ, the most dominantly Christological *huiothesian* passage warrants serious consideration as an entry point for its study.

---

24. Ibid., 142.

25. For the sake of efficiency, style, and grammatical evenness, at various points in this volume I will use *huiothesian* as an adjective. This is not to be confused with a Greek transliteration of the accusative singular form of *huiothesia*.

26. Including Romans 1–2, creation; Romans 5, Adam and Christ; Romans 8, creation (Adam) to consummation (Christ); Romans 9:1–5, Israel to Christ.

The Epistle to the Galatians
Galatians 4:4–7:

> But when the fullness of time had come, God sent forth his Son, born of woman, born under the law, to redeem those who were under the law, so that we might receive adoption as sons. And because you are sons, God has sent the Spirit of his Son into our hearts, crying, "Abba! Father!" So you are no longer a slave, but a son, and if a son, then an heir through God.

Having summarized the dramatic redemptive-historical script at the hand of the God who established his covenant with Abraham and Moses (Gal. 3–4), the apostle Paul centers the grand climax of redemptive history on God's sending his Son. Here the apostle gives *huiothesia* remarkable redemptive profile with equally remarkable brevity. The goal of God's sending his Son is expressed in two contiguous purpose clauses, with the second clause drawing out the final purpose of the first. In short, in the sent Son of God, redemption attains its goal in *adoption*.

With pregnant redemptive-historical focus, the apostle Paul locates the provision of Christ Jesus in the unfolding purposes of God as the singular means of redemption for those shut up in sin. The divinely designated purpose of God's sending his own Son was to adopt those "imprisoned . . . under sin" (Gal. 3:22), "held captive under the law" (3:23), and "enslaved to the elementary principles of the world" (4:3). Those whom God the Son delivers in his redemptive work, he *makes sons* so that they share in the eschatological privileges he personally secured. Tersely yet grandly, the apostle profiles redemption's filial finality. As the sons of God in the Son of God, believers possess the Spirit of the Son and enter the Son's full inheritance. The same God who sent his Son also sent into the hearts of believers the Spirit of his Son. This Spirit's outpouring marks the climax of redemptive history and applies the soteric, familial benefits for those redeemed by divine grace.

With the scope of redemptive history in view, Galatians 4 envisions the promised redemption realized in the Son of God sent by the heavenly Father. Galatians 4 expresses adoption as the culmination of that divine sending of the Son who faithfully carried out his incarnate, filial duty. Redemptive-historical and existential features of adoption converge in this Pauline text, which displays the Father, Son, and Holy Spirit in their mutually informing roles of planning, securing, and affirming adoption. The sons of God echo the Son of God when the Spirit within them declares, "Abba, Father." The verbal reverberation manifests the spiritual identity. Adoption arrives in and through the Son of God.

Galatians as an Entry Point into the Study of Adoption

Galatians not only chronologically precedes the other Pauline Epistles containing the term *huiothesia*,[27] but also marks the place where adoption's Christological center becomes most perspicuous redemptive-historically, and thereby could surely render the most fitting launching point for exegetical and theological investigation. The development of redemptive history in Galatians 3 and 4 puts on display the grand analytical, soteriological, and eschatological scope that Paul has in view; the *historia salutis* ("history of redemption") wholly structures his outlook. The Father sent the Son to accomplish adoption in his own redemptive work, and poured out the Spirit of Christ on the redeemed sons. This outpouring attests to the Christ-centered, filially charged, corroborative, and applying ministry of his Holy Spirit. Adoption is exhaustively Christological, pneumatological, redemptive, and eschatological.

Yet Galatians' consideration of adoption operates in a still broader theological context, where Christ's redemptive accomplishment as Son of God occurs as a fulfillment of divine pretemporal purpose, the antecedent to the epochally determinative Spirit-wrought realization of adoptive promise (Rom. 8:15–17, 23). Galatians 4:4 actually identifies the extraterrestrial and divine context for the accomplishment and application of adoption: from heaven "*God sent* forth his Son, born of woman, born under the law, to redeem those who were under the law" (Gal. 4:4b–5), marking a protological backdrop to the redemptive-historical concerns of Galatians. In the Pauline framework,

27. Cf. Russell Radoicich, "'Adoption' in the Pauline Epistles" (unpublished paper, St. Vladimir's Orthodox Theological Seminary, Crestwood, NY, 1999), 26.

the redemptive-historical depends on the protological: without divine pretemporal purpose, there is no divine temporal fulfillment. Thus, since the fulfillment and realization of adoption in the argument of Galatians presuppose the *prior* purpose of God, investigation of adoption better commences from its antecedent (protological) launching point. This implicit archetypal orientation in Galatians becomes explicit in the opening doxology of the Pauline epistle to the Ephesians.

The Epistle to the Ephesians

Ephesians 1:3–6:

> Blessed be the God and Father of our Lord Jesus Christ, who has blessed us in Christ with every spiritual blessing in the heavenly places, even as he chose us in him before the foundation of the world, that we should be holy and blameless before him. In love he predestined us for adoption as sons through Jesus Christ, according to the purpose of his will, to the praise of his glorious grace, with which he has blessed us in the Beloved.

This opening passage to the church in Ephesus begins with an extended hymn of praise (Eph. 1:3–14), which situates the ontological and motivational basis of Christ's redemptive work in eternity past. Adoption appears here in a position of soteriological prominence, manifesting the express filial purpose of divine predestination through Jesus Christ the beloved Son. The theological doxology celebrates adoption, a purposed blessing given to those predestined "through Jesus Christ," the Son whom God the Father has declared as the "Beloved."

The appearance of *huiothesia* here draws us behind redemptive history into eternal and pretemporal mystery. Here in the opening of Ephesians, the apostle Paul transports his readers into the invisible and humanly inaccessible recesses of intra-Trinitarian counsel, where God determined and commenced the gracious plan of redemption. In the loving wisdom of this intra-Trinitarian counsel we find *huiothesia*, the realization of which eventuates *in* human history precisely because it lies divinely predetermined *before* human history. Put otherwise, redemptive adoption takes place in history because God intended divine adoption before creation. Adoption begins in heaven before it comes to us on earth.

Ephesians as an Entry Point into the Study of Adoption

In his revealed yet impenetrable plan, the triune God determined to exercise his grace through the Son of God for the sons of God. The adoptive grace typified (Rom. 9:5; cf. Ex. 4:22–23), attained (Gal. 4:1–6), appropriated (Rom. 8:15–17), and consummated (Rom. 8:23) is the adoptive grace predestined by the triune God (Eph. 1:3–6). Without this pretemporal context, there would be no temporal and eschatological realization of adoption. For the sake of grasping the redemptive and eschatological substance in its fullest contours, it seems most appropriate to begin with the revealed mind and purposes of the Father, Son, and Spirit in eternity past, for it is there and then that adoption truly begins.[28] The divinely gracious placement of the sons in the Son draws from eternity past, finds its historico-theological traction in the work of the Son of God in history, and by the Spirit of the risen Christ delivers the filially rich and comprehensively transforming eschatological promises of God upon his people, his children—his redeemed sons and daughters.

The Selected Approach

Pauline adoption has in its purview creation and redemption, encompassing pretemporality/protology (Eph. 1) and consummate eschatology (Rom. 8:22–23) and, within that massive framework, bonding covenant and typology (Rom. 9:4), Christology and soteriology

---

28. I should make brief mention here of the philosophical complications concerning time and eternity. Despite the mystery involved, Scripture does not make divine transcendence a barrier to divine immanence and participation in chronology: "there is a point, therefore—call it 'before the foundation of the world'—when God determines to condescend and to create." K. Scott Oliphint, *God with Us: Divine Condescension and the Attributes of God* (Wheaton, IL: Crossway, 2012), 105. Whatever consternation is created by our attempts to grasp the time/eternity relationship, we must accept that time language for eternity is itself biblical. As Oliphint puts it, "We should remember that 'time language' with respect to eternity is not only necessary for us as creatures; it is the language that God himself uses in Holy Scripture to indicate things that take place in eternity. See John 17:24; Eph. 1:4; 1 Peter 1:20; Rev. 13:8." Ibid., 105n42.

(Gal. 4:4–5), and pneumatology and eschatology (Rom. 8:15–17). Though the term itself appears so infrequently, *huiothesia* and its familially rich concepts expose a critical Pauline theological substructure, in which *huiothesia* serves as a metaconcept for expressing the contours of the gospel. Securing a family of adopted children occupied the mind of God since before the world's origins, and comes to pass on the stage of history according to divine timing and effectuation. God purposed adoption, God accomplished adoption, and God applies adoption. With this filial grace drawing from divine counsel, its faithful exploration must always acknowledge its heavenly source.

With a view to these vital theological connections between redemption purposed, redemption accomplished, and redemption applied and to the parameterizing function of adoption in Christ in drawing these features together, I commence the theological exposition of the *huiothesian* texts with Paul's letter to the church in Ephesus, move to Galatians, and complete it with the threefold appearance of the term in Romans. Before we get to this essential theological exposition, the following two chapters set the stage for doing so by summarizing the historical and etymological matters associated with *huiothesia*.

2

ADOPTION IN HISTORICAL THEOLOGY

Adoption's Riches

"Adoption through Propitiation"

"The *huiothesia* [adoption] of the believers is the climax of the redemptive process,"[1] writes Thornton Whaling in 1923. Fifty years later, J. I. Packer, blending theological insight and doxological exultation, celebrates the gospel's filial grace in three simple words: *"Adoption through propitiation . . .* [:] I do not expect ever to meet a richer or more pregnant summary of the gospel than that."[2] These men are not alone in their high estimation of theological adoption, standing in line behind Irenæus, John Calvin, and some Puritan greats such as John Owen, Herman Witsius, Thomas Goodwin, and Thomas Boston.[3] In varying

---

1. Thornton Whaling, "Adoption," *Princeton Theological Review* 21, 2 (1923): 223.
2. J. I. Packer, *Knowing God*, 20th anniversary ed. (Downers Grove, IL: InterVarsity Press, 1993), 214 (emphasis added).
3. John Owen, *The Works of John Owen*, ed. William H. Goold, 16 vols. (n.p.: Johnstone & Hunter, 1850–53; repr., Edinburgh: Banner of Truth, 1988), 2:207–22, 4:265–70; Herman Witsius, *The Economy of the Covenants between God and Man: Comprehending a Complete Body of Divinity*, trans. William Crookshank (repr., Kingsburg, CA: den Dulk Christian Foundation, 1990), 1:442–68; Thomas Goodwin, *The Works of Thomas Goodwin* (repr., Eureka, CA: Tanski, 1996), 1:83–102; Thomas Boston, *The Complete Works of the Late Rev. Thomas Boston*, ed. Samuel M'Millan, 12 vols. (London: William Tegg & Co., 1853; repr., Wheaton, IL: Richard Owen Roberts, 1980), 7:100–105, 8:209ff., 8:485ff. Cf. Thomas Houston, *The Adoption of Sons, Its Nature, Spirit, Privileges and Effects: A Practical and Experimental Treatise* (Paisley, Scotland: Alex. Gardner, 1872), 124; Robert Alexander Webb, *The Reformed Doctrine of Adoption* (Grand Rapids: Eerdmans, 1947), 17–19; John Murray, *The Collected Writings of John Murray*, 4 vols. (Edinburgh: Banner of Truth, 1976–82), 2:233; John W. Cooper, *Our Father in Heaven: Christian Faith and Inclusive Language* (Grand Rapids: Baker, 1998), 108; Robert E. Wermuth, "The Doctrine of Adoption in Paul's Ephesian Letter" (unpublished master's thesis, Covenant Theological Seminary, St. Louis, 1985), 3–5; Mark Stibbe, *From Orphans to Heirs: Celebrating Our Spiritual Adoption* (Oxford: Bible Reading Fellowship, 1999), 58, 79.

degrees and in varied fashion, adoption has captured these key church figures and convinced them of its worthiness for theological reflection and pastoral explication. Yet despite the healthy exposure given this doctrine by the likes of such men, their theological treatments of adoption represent the exception rather than the rule. In fact, the theological history of adoption evidences perpetual orphaning of this filial grace.

Where Is Adoption?

A survey of the church fathers shows little attention to *huiothesia*, with the notable exception of Irenæus. "It is true that nowhere can we find more emphatic and constant reference to the 'adoption as sons' than in Irenæus."[4] This early father surely stands out because of adoption's frequent appearance in his thought. As a biblical theologian, Irenæus capitalizes on the broad soteric reach of this biblical term. In fact, in his theological construction, adoption serves as the favored motif for the full scope of redemptive privilege.[5] Though in the early centuries of the church adoption did not carry the formative weight given it by Irenæus, associated ideas of God's fatherhood and redemptive sonship through Jesus remained present in the Alexandrian tradition through both Origen (c. 185–254) and Athanasius (c. 297–373).[6]

4. J. Scott Lidgett, *The Fatherhood of God in Christian Truth and Life* (Edinburgh: T&T Clark, 1902), 160. Cf. Daniel J. Theron, "'Adoption' in the Pauline Corpus," *EvQ* 28, 1 (1956): 8; Jacques Fantino, *La Théologie d'Irénée: Lecture des Écritures en Réponse à l'Exégèse Gnostique, une Approche Trinitaire* (Paris: Les Éditions du Cerf, 1994), 211–16. See Irenæus, *Against Heresies* (*ANF* 1:315–567); Irenæus, *The Demonstration of the Apostolic Preaching*, trans. J. Armitage Robinson, Translations of Christian Literature 4, Oriental Texts (London: Society for Promoting Christian Knowledge, 1920).

5. In an unpublished paper entitled "Irenæus: Fountain Father of Adoption Theology" (Westminster Theological Seminary, Philadelphia, 1999), I probed and summarized the prominence of adoption as a comprehensive soteriological concept for this early church father.

6. Origen, as Widdicombe has illustrated, wove a continuing thread of the fatherhood of God and the sonship of believers throughout his work. See Peter Widdicombe, *The Fatherhood of God from Origen to Athanasius* (Oxford: Clarendon, 1994), 7–120; Tim J. R. Trumper, *When History Teaches Us Nothing: The Recent Reformed Sonship Debate in Context* (Eugene, OR: Wipf and Stock, 2008). Cf. Origen, *Against Celsus*, 1.55 (*ANF* 4:453–54); Origen, *De Principiis* 1.2 (*ANF* 4:246). Discussing the believer's relationship to God in Christ, the Latin edition of Origen's *De Principiis* 1.32 (*ANF* 4:379) translates, "As now by participation in the Son of God one is adopted as a son *[In filium adoptatur]*, and by participating in that wisdom which is in God is rendered wise, so also by participation in the Holy Spirit is a man rendered holy and spiritual." Origen also highlights the privilege

Appearing only sporadically, adoption remained essentially hidden until it surfaced again at the pens of certain Reformers.

In sixteenth-century Germany, a now-famous young Protestant monk found solace for his tormented soul in the Scripture's teaching on justification by faith. Martin Luther suffered in his conscience over his sin before Almighty God, and then discovered in the gospel the sweet blessing of justification by faith alone in Christ alone. But that was not all. Luther expressed a measure of appreciation for the familial character of the gospel, too. One can see to at least some measure God's fatherhood and redemptive sonship through Jesus esteemed, for example, in Luther's *Large Catechism* and in his commentary on 1 John: "It is not enough to say that we are friends. No, John says we are called *children of God*."[7] Yet to whatever degree Luther appreciated the filial character of redemption, the supremacy of justification overshadowed any robust consideration of the believer's adoption.

Though the forensic effectively swallowed the filial for Luther, an armchair critique of his understating adoption lacks discretion. "Though some might lay . . . charges, the first generation of reformers is hardly to blame for understating the filial." Indeed, it is the case that the "context of *infusion confusion* [the Roman Catholic denial of imputation and its conflation of justification and sanctification] necessitated the unrelenting articulation of the thoroughly forensic character of justification."[8] Accordingly, Luther's and others' fierce battles for the forensic integrity of justification warrant our commendation, even

---

of adoptive grace in *Against Celsus* 8.6 (*ANF* 4:641–42): "But when we refuse to serve any other than God through His word and wisdom, we do so, not as though we would thereby be doing any harm or injury to God, in the same way as injury would be done to a man by his servant entering into the service of another, but we fear that we ourselves should suffer harm by depriving ourselves of our portion in God, through which we live in the participation of the divine blessedness, and are *imbued with that excellent spirit of adoption* which in the sons of the heavenly Father cries, not with words, but with deep effect in the inmost heart, 'Abba, Father'" (emphasis added).

7. Martin Luther, "Lectures on the First Epistle of St. John," in *The Catholic Epistles*, ed. Jaroslav Pelikan and Walter A. Hansen, vol. 30 of *Luther's Works* (St. Louis: Concordia, 1967), 265 (emphasis added). Cf. Birgit Stolt, "Martin Luther on God as Father," *Lutheran Quarterly* 8, 4 (1994): 384–95; Marc Lienhard, "Luther et Calvin Commentateurs du Notre Père," *Revue d'Histoire et de Philosophie Religieuses* 72 (1992): 73–88.

8. David B. Garner, "A World of Riches," *Reformation 21* (April 2011), http://www.reformation21.org/articles/a-world-of-riches.php (accessed February 6, 2016).

when other features of the gospel did not emerge fully. While some have contended that Luther grasped redeemed filial grace with vigor commensurate to his grip on justification,[9] such a contention remains difficult to sustain. Yet some years after Luther's rigorous expressions of justification had already taken Protestant root, another key Reformer more thoroughly pondered and promulgated the familial cast of the gospel.

Calvin and the "Gospel of Adoption"

The Genevan Reformer John Calvin, following years of medieval scholasticism, "restored the Fatherhood of God"[10] and the doctrine of adoption to greater theological prominence. In fact, though Calvin relentlessly defended the forensic doctrine of justification, adoption plays such a critical role for him that his theology of redemption has been called the "Gospel of adoption."[11] Howard Griffith affirms its role in Calvin: "The adoption of believers is the heart of John Calvin's understanding of salvation."[12]

Not all share such a conclusion about Calvin. Coming up empty in his search for a chapter on adoption in the *Institutes*, Robert A. Webb baldly contends, "Calvin . . . makes no allusion whatever to adoption."[13] Notwithstanding the value of Webb's book on adoption,[14] this assertion

9. Packer, *Knowing God*, 207. Contra Tim J. R. Trumper, "An Historical Study of the Doctrine of Adoption in the Calvinistic Tradition" (Ph.D. diss., University of Edinburgh, 2001), 16–18; Sinclair B. Ferguson, "The Reformed Doctrine of Sonship," in *Pulpit and People: Essays in Honour of William Still on His 75th Birthday*, ed. Nigel M. de S. Cameron and Sinclair B. Ferguson (Edinburgh: Rutherford House, 1986), 81–82.

10. Lidgett, *Fatherhood of God*, 259. For a summary of the place of adoption in Calvin, see Trumper, "Historical Study of the Doctrine of Adoption," 17–18, 37–214; Ferguson, "Reformed Doctrine of Sonship," 82; Howard Griffith, "'The First Title of the Spirit': Adoption in Calvin's Soteriology," *EvQ* 73, 2 (2001): 135–53.

11. Brian A. Gerrish, *Grace and Gratitude: The Eucharistic Theology of John Calvin* (Edinburgh: T&T Clark, 1993), 89. Cf. Griffith, "'First Title of the Spirit,'" 135; Ferguson, "Reformed Doctrine of Sonship," 81–88.

12. Griffith, "'First Title of the Spirit,'" 135.

13. Webb, *Reformed Doctrine of Adoption*, 17.

14. Webb's biblico-theological survey concerning adoption concludes that Adam's original sonship was an adoption and that redemptive adoption restores that very Adamic sonship. While welcomed for its numerous insights, Webb's work fails to consider the eschatological move from provisional glory in the first Adam to confirmed glory in the last Adam. His formulation of adoption flattens redemptive history, and fails to offer an

is untenable by almost any analysis. Calvin in fact uses the Latin word *adoptio* seventy-seven times in his 1559 *Institutes*.[15] That is only a start. As evidenced by the entire Calvin corpus—*Institutes*, commentaries, and personal letters—Calvin offers a filial tapestry for this theology, woven with the threads of adoption.[16] That Calvin's theology lacks a distinct chapter or section on adoption must not generate a false impression. This theological decision represents no theological lacuna or marginalization of the concept. On the contrary, his frequent employment of the term and its expansive function in his thought suggest a permeating place of adoption in his theological framework.

Calvin's references to adoption can be traced back to the first year after his conversion. Subsequently they proliferate throughout his writings, notably (but not exclusively) in his commentaries and his *Institutes*. The evidence of the importance of the motif for Calvin is seen in the rich coherence of these references; in their relevance to an array of other doctrines (such as the fatherhood of God, predestination, covenant theology, the atonement, union with Christ, justification, sanctification, Christian liberty, prayer, assurance, Christian obedience, providence, and the last things, as well as baptism and the Lord's Supper); and in the explicit statements Calvin makes about the motif's importance.[17] Adoption is not a chapter in the *Institutes* because adoption is not reducible to a sequestered chapter in dogmatics. As Calvin saw it, adoption organically exposes the filial cast of the gospel itself, engages the entire scope of redemptive history, and informs the essence of union with the Christ by the Holy Spirit, the Spirit of adoption.[18] Adoption does not reside at a point of logical categorization, but animates his entire theological enterprise.

Any filial fiber in Reformed theology is owed largely to Calvin and his penetrating biblical theology, and this work itself is no

---

eschatologically consummative filial state of affairs. See ibid., 74–78, 92, 167–77, 179.

15. Peter A. Lillback, *The Binding of God: Calvin's Role in the Development of Covenant Theology*, ed. Richard A. Muller, Texts and Studies in Reformation and Post-Reformation Thought (Grand Rapids: Baker Academic, 2001), 141.

16. Griffith, "'First Title of the Spirit,'" 135–53.

17. Trumper, *When History Teaches Us Nothing*, 2.

18. More detailed reference to Calvin's treatment of adoption will appear in chapter 10 of this volume.

exception. Calvin and a few other Reformers in his wake[19] expounded the defining gospel truth that the believer is not merely *forensically* privileged; he is *familially* privileged as he enters Spirit-of-adoption-wrought union with the *Son* of God. The biblical motifs for salvation are not left in the cosmic courtroom, but, by the work of the Son of God and the outpouring of his filial Spirit, boldly and intimately proceed into the *home* and *fatherly heart* of God. God is not exclusively Judge; he is a gracious Father—the believer stands not merely as an acquitted criminal, but as an adopted son in the Son par excellence.[20] The irony strikes bluntly, because "surely no sector of the Christian church has been more vilified as harsh (because juridical) than that spawned by the Genevan Reformer. As we might have suspected, however, Calvin has not deserved the caricature generally portrayed of him. Neither, generally speaking, have the commissioners of the Westminster Assembly."[21]

Adoption in Confessional and Systematic Theology

The Westminster Assembly

Enjoying, then, only minimal attention by the church fathers, and substantial neglect throughout the first fifteen hundred years of the church,[22] adoption surfaced in mid-seventeenth-century England when a group of English and Scottish theologians at the Westminster Assembly illumined some critical distinctions between justification, adoption, and regeneration and, in so doing, brought adoption into summary focus theologically and pastorally.[23] Moving Calvin's filial emphases into systematic expression, the Westminster

---

19. Trumper, "Historical Study of the Doctrine of Adoption," 18–19, notes that Knox (c. 1515–72) and Vermigli (1500–1562), two men most closely associated with Calvin, give adoption consideration.

20. The rationale for maintaining the masculine gender (*son* and *sons*) will be explained in chapter 3.

21. Timothy J. R. Trumper, private correspondence, fall 2000.

22. Trumper, "Historical Study of the Doctrine of Adoption," 11–13; Ferguson, "Reformed Doctrine of Sonship," 81–82.

23. Benjamin B. Warfield, *The Westminster Assembly and Its Work*, vol. 6 of *The Works of Benjamin B. Warfield* (Grand Rapids: Baker, 1981), 110.

divines distinguished adoption from justification and sanctification in a confessional statement,[24] devoting a *separate* chapter to this filial grace:[25]

> All those that are justified, God vouchsafeth, in and for his only Son Jesus Christ, to make partakers of the grace of adoption; by which they are taken into the number, and enjoy the liberties and privileges of the children of God; have his name put upon them, receive the spirit of adoption; have access to the throne of grace with boldness; are enabled to cry, Abba, Father; are pitied, protected, provided for, and chastened by him as by a father; yet never cast off, but sealed to the day of redemption, and inherit the promises, as heirs of everlasting salvation. (WCF 12)

This twelfth chapter of the WCF stands out from among other confessions, because it is the first time in the history of the church that adoption wins a place of its own.[26]

Following this Westminsterian distinctive, five other confessions contain a chapter on adoption: the Savoy Declaration (1658), the Baptist Confession of Faith (1689), the Twenty-four Articles of the Presbyterian Synod of England (1890), the Confessional Statement of the United Presbyterian Church of North America (1925), and the Basis of Union of the United Church of Canada (1925). The Savoy Declaration and the 1689 Baptist Confession of Faith derive their chapters directly from the WCF; the more recent confessions represent

24. Regeneration was also not given a separate chapter in the WCF, but its principal soteriological function is identified in 10.1–3 on "Effectual Calling."

25. WLC 74 and WSC 34 also answer the question "What is adoption?" In an overstated critique, Robert Candlish finds the Westminster statements on adoption "vague and indefinite" and the WSC question/answer simply tautologous. Robert Candlish, *The Fatherhood of God: Being the First Course of the Cunningham Lectures Delivered before the New College, Edinburgh, in March 1864*, 5th ed. (Edinburgh: Adam and Charles Black, 1869), 194. While, as this book will insist, there is *more* to adoption than the Westminster Standards explicitly state, it is historically and theologically misguided to denounce the confessional statements so harshly. See Tim J. R. Trumper, "Adoption: The Forgotten Doctrine of Westminster Soteriology," in *Reformed Theology in Contemporary Perspective*, ed. Lynn Quigley (Edinburgh: Rutherford House, 2006), 96–98.

26. "Of the great creeds in Christendom, none of them contains a chapter, or formal article, on adoption, except the Westminster Confession." Webb, *Reformed Doctrine of Adoption*, 18.

attempts to revive the Presbyterian theology of the seventeenth century and manifestly rest on the theology of the WCF.[27]

When considering the relevance of this particular doctrine to biblical soteriology, arguably one of the most significant contributions of the divines at Westminster to Reformed thought is that, in unprecedented manner, adoption was granted such status.[28] While adoption "struggled to maintain its *locus* in seventeenth-century continental Protestantism,"[29] its treatment by the Westminster Assembly launched hope for a permanent penetration into the life of the church via systematic and pastoral theology. While grouping familial themes in one locus in the Westminster Standards might have actually contributed to further marginalization of adoption, it would be improper "to underplay what mention there is of adoption in the Westminster Standards outside of the WCF 12, [WLC] 74, [and WSC] 34"[30] or to otherwise castigate the Westminster Standards for observing adoption in the manner they do. Blame for adoption's historical marginalization can hardly be cast at those who labored in Westminster's Jerusalem Chamber.

Puritan Theology

In the face of stubborn assertions that Puritan theology evidences little concern for adoption, Joel Beeke traces the Puritans' appreciation of this familial grace, which, as he effectively demonstrates, infuses much Puritan theological and pastoral expression.[31] At the very least, Beeke has refuted critics who would caricature Puritan theology as harsh, vindictive, and lacking the warm, familial graces of the gospel.

27. See Tim J. R. Trumper, "The Metaphorical Import of Adoption: A Plea for Realisation I: The Adoption Metaphor in Biblical Usage," *SBET* 14, 2 (1996): 129–30. Trumper traces these confessions through the historical works of Philip Schaff. Cf. Trumper, "Historical Study of the Doctrine of Adoption," 5–10; Douglas F. Kelly, "Adoption: An Underdeveloped Heritage of the Westminster Standards," *Reformed Theological Review* 52, 3 (1993), 111.

28. Tim Trumper well summarizes the historical and *historic* drawing up of WCF 12. Trumper, "Adoption: The Forgotten Doctrine," 88.

29. Trumper, "Historical Study of the Doctrine of Adoption," 20.

30. Trumper, *When History Teaches Us Nothing*, 5.

31. Joel R. Beeke, "Transforming Power and Comfort: The Puritans on Adoption," in *The Faith Once Delivered: Essays in Honor of Dr. Wayne R. Spear*, ed. Anthony T. Selvaggio (Phillipsburg, NJ: P&R Publishing, 2007), 63–105; Joel R. Beeke, *Heirs with Christ: The Puritans on Adoption* (Grand Rapids: Reformation Heritage Books, 2008).

Placing adoption squarely in their practical sights, the Puritans dwelt prominently on its extensive pastoral benefits. "Above all, the Puritans use the truth of adoption as a source to transform God's needy children through powerful comforts. . . . When oppressed with sin, buffeted by Satan, enticed by the world, or alarmed by fears of death, the Puritans encourage believers to take refuge in their precious, heavenly Father."[32] Such adoptive grace warms the heart, strengthens the weary, and grants confidence in one's relation to God, confirming the familial benefits of the gospel in the Son of God. No doubt gently fathered by the great Genevan Reformer's appreciation for Christ-rendered filial grace, the Puritans did share John Calvin's relishing of adoption and particularly celebrated the incomparable pastoral value of "its greatness, excellency, dignity, and comprehensiveness."[33]

Beeke's fresh digging into the Puritan gold mine has opened our eyes afresh to the appreciation for adoption by these pastors and theologians, leading some to conclude that the claims of adoption's general eclipse are overstated. If it is so neglected, why have the Puritans said so much about it? Beeke, in fact, has urged caution against overstating adoption's disregard. Yet to whatever degree Puritan writers celebrated adoption, that fact ought not to dissuade us from what is more broadly the case. In fact, the uniqueness of these Puritan contributions confirms the very theological delinquency. *Some* theologians and ministers over the last five hundred years have expounded adoption with marked rigor, but it is as much the mention of these theologians as their passion for adoption that draws attention to their treatments of this filial grace.

Disappointingly, after Calvin's affectionate and arguably infectious expressions of adoption as "synonymous with salvation"[34] and

32. Joel R. Beeke and Mark Jones, *A Puritan Theology: Doctrine for Life* (Grand Rapids: Reformation Heritage Books, 2012), 554.

33. Beeke, "Transforming Power and Comfort," 67. In Puritan style, when adoption has received theological attention, its plethora of pastoral benefits is generally enumerated. A few examples: Thomas Manton, *The Complete Works of Thomas Manton* (Worthington, PA: Maranatha, n.d.), 12:124–25; Owen, *Works*, 2:211–22; Boston, *Complete Works*, 1:612–42; John L. Girardeau, *Discussions of Theological Questions*, ed. George A. Blackburn (Richmond, VA: Presbyterian Committee, 1905), 489–521; Robert A. Peterson, *Adopted by God: From Wayward Sinners to Cherished Children* (Phillipsburg, NJ: P&R Publishing, 2001), 27–172.

34. Garret A. Wilterdink, "The Fatherhood of God in Calvin's Thought," in *Articles on Calvin and Calvinism*, vol. 9 of *Calvin's Theology, Theology Proper, Eschatology*, ed. Richard C.

the Westminster Assembly's groundbreaking inclusion of adoption as a distinct locus in systematic theology accompanied by its Puritan embrace in pastoral theology, the doctrine of adoption still suffered gross inattention.[35] Out of the Calvinist trajectory came only two monographs on adoption: Houston's *Adoption of Sons* and Webb's *Reformed Doctrine of Adoption*. Girardeau's section on adoption in *Discussions of Theological Questions* is also worth mentioning. There, as included in the Blackburn Collection (Reformed Theological Seminary in Jackson, Mississippi), he collated a series of papers on the theme.[36]

Other systematic treatment of adoption writhes not only from painful brevity, but also from exegetical and theological ambiguity. When it has found a place in systematic theologies, adoption has typically received diminutive voice, finding itself sequestered into a few sentences or a paragraph and crowded into justification and Johannine sonship. Richard Mueller writes, "The Reformed theologians . . . do not always consider adoption from the same point of view. While some represent it as the fruit of justification, others regard it as coordinate, but subject to regeneration. Rationalism wholly discarded the biblical doctrine of adoption."[37] The liberal dismissal of adoption concerns us little here, since the reasons for dismissing adoption are derived from the outright dismissal of revelation itself.

On the other hand, the historical (mis)treatment of adoption by those genuinely sympathetic to the filial splendor of the gospel discloses some common habits. Besides its brief and sometimes negligible treatment, when appearing at all, adoption gets subjected to justification, becomes a familial appositive for justification, or gets fused so closely with the forensic benefit as to be indistinguishable

---

Gamble (New York and London: Garland Publishing, 1992), 185.

35. See W. B. Selbie, *The Fatherhood of God* (New York: Charles Scribner's Sons, 1936), 63–81; Webb, *Reformed Doctrine of Adoption*, 17–27; Lidgett, *Fatherhood of God*, 142–281; Girardeau, *Discussions of Theological Questions*, 428–30; Packer, *Knowing God*, 181–208; Allen Mawhinney, "*Yiothesia* in the Pauline Epistles: Its Background, Use, and Implications" (Ph.D. diss., Baylor University, Waco, TX, 1982), 2–3, 236–38; Ferguson, "Doctrine of Sonship," 81–83.

36. Girardeau, *Discussions of Theological Questions*, 428–521.

37. John Theodore Mueller, "Adoption," *Christianity Today* 6 (1962): 23. While most subsume adoption under justification, a few identify adoption *with* regeneration or as a fruit of regeneration. See Samuel J. Baird, *The Elohim Revealed in the Creation and Redemption of Man* (Philadelphia: Parry & McMillan, 1860), 646.

from it as "the other part of justification."[38] Others impose adoption into Johannine material, though the term *huiothesia* never appears in John. Such fusion of Pauline and Johannine theology clouds complementary yet distinct emphases concerning the filial cast to the gospel. Such systematic ambiguating and devitalizing tendencies will receive closer examination in chapter 8.

Adoption: Hidden Filial Grandeur

With such a rich treasure of gospel grandeur exposed in Irenæus, penetrated in Calvin, and relished in some Puritan writings, one would expect adoption to receive more careful attention across the church fathers, in systematic theologies, in the confessions of the church, and in biblical theologies. Yet as history indicates, with some exceptions and the small number of developments from the Westminster Assembly in 1647, adoption "has been more often in the dark than in the light."[39] Why is that so?

Girardeau contends that through intense battles for theological truth, "the church's knowledge of the doctrine of the Trinity, of sin, and of justification has been cleared up, matured, and crystallized."[40] This clarification, maturation, and crystallization have protected fundamental doctrines from heresy, and preserved the integrity of the Christian faith for generations. Adoption has had no such bloodstained history. It is likely for this reason, suggests this Southern Presbyterian, that adoption has found itself principally deserted.

Douglas Kelly has suggested that the substantial influence of Francis Turretin on Reformed theology has been the cause of adoption's

38. Francis Turretin, *Institutes of Elenctic Theology*, ed. James T. Dennison Jr., trans. George Musgrave Giger, 3 vols. (Phillipsburg, NJ: P&R Publishing, 1992–94), 2:666.
39. Nigel Westhead, "Adoption in the Thought of John Calvin," *SBET* 13, 2 (1995): 102. Tim Trumper adds, "So substantive has the church's oversight been that it is far easier to document those who have focused on adoption than those who have not. This is especially so, if the list is curtailed in the main to those creeds and volumes that have dealt with adoption *in its own right*. To list those omitting adoption would not be feasible, practical, or interesting." Trumper, "Historical Study of the Doctrine of Adoption," 4 (emphasis in original).
40. Girardeau, *Discussions of Theological Questions*, 428. Cf. Archibald Alexander Hodge, *A Commentary on the Confession of Faith* (Philadelphia: Presbyterian Board of Publication, 1885), 20.

neglect in the modern age, because Turretin subsumed adoption into justification, making it little more than the familial face of a forensic blessing.[41] The problems of subsumption dominate whatever attention adoption has received. Such theological concatenation has provided ample impetus to desert adoption in the alleyways of theological discourse, and blame for their abandonment doubtless rests in part on Turretin's shoulders.

Tim Trumper has provided a more robust analysis concerning adoption's inattention in recent church history, suggesting that following the Westminster Assembly, the confluence of cognitive and social factors, such as rationalism, deism, Arianism and Socianism, Neonomianism and Arminianism, the Enlightenment, Romanticism, and industrialization, stifled theological creativity and "foster[ed] a defensive mindset."[42]

While such causes may plausibly answer questions of post-Reformation adoptive eclipse, the relative dearth of theological exposition on this doctrine will probably remain to a certain extent mysterious. The negligence, as several have thankfully acknowledged, is also intolerable. Until recent years when a "growing *communis consensus* of Reformed Christians [began] calling for the recovery and integration of"[43] adoption, it was only for a brief period in nineteenth-century Scottish theological discourse that adoption received any notable discussion.[44] Now in the

41. Kelly, "Adoption," 112. Ferguson in "Reformed Doctrine of Sonship," 83, shares Kelly's view that the demise of adoption since the WCF may be due in large part to Turretin's influence.

42. Trumper, *When History Teaches Us Nothing*, 31. For a thorough yet concise exploration of the reasons for adoption's historical eclipse, see ibid., 1–32. Trumper's sympathy for so-called constructive Calvinism, a self-acknowledged attempt at a via media between revisionist and orthodox Calvinism (ibid., 36), flavors his analysis in a way that unavoidably (and unnecessarily) criticizes Reformed orthodoxy. Cf. Trumper, "Adoption: The Forgotten Doctrine," 87–123; Tim J. R. Trumper, "Covenant Theology and Constructive Calvinism," *WTJ* 64, 2 (2002): 387–404; Trumper, "Historical Study of the Doctrine of Adoption," 255–81; Ferguson, "Reformed Doctrine of Sonship," 83.

43. Trumper, "Historical Study of the Doctrine of Adoption," 26.

44. I am recalling here the debate between Thomas J. Crawford and Robert S. Candlish in the mid-1860s. See Robert S. Candlish, *The Fatherhood of God*; Thomas Crawford, *The Fatherhood of God Considered in Its General and Special Aspects and Particularly in Relation to the Atonement with a Review of Recent Speculations on the Subject* (Edinburgh: William Blackwood and Sons, 1867).

twentieth and twenty-first centuries, however, as Sinclair Ferguson concludes, "perhaps more than any other influence, the impact of biblical theology on systematic theology has demanded a reorientation of soteriology towards the concept of sonship."[45] Thankfully, then, some in recent years have noted adoption's substantial neglect, and once again some thoughtful contributions on adoptive grace have surfaced in academic, theological, and pastoral writings.[46]

It has become almost annoyingly habitual for contemporary students of adoption to complain about the dearth of attention to it. The more the complaint is followed by an exposition of adoption, the less credible the complaint seems. Yet, however tedious the petulance, a survey of theological literature and even a survey of systematic theologies will simply confirm the inadequacy of the doctrine's treatment. Thornton Whaling's complaint nearly a century ago still wails on: "A complete and well-rounded, and systematic presentation of the Biblical meaning of *huiothesia* or of the theological significance of adoption is still a desideration."[47] Etymological studies (e.g., Scott[48]), historical studies (e.g., Peppard[49]), and now even a measure of biblico-theological analyses (e.g., Burke[50]) have found their way to the presses in recent years, but taking the necessary next step beyond redemptive-historical and etymological-historical analyses, in the final chapter this work draws explicit systematic theological conclusions. The manner in which Christology informs soteriology, redemptive history (*historia salutis*)

---

45. Ferguson, "Reformed Doctrine of Sonship," 84.

46. While some academic work has surfaced, recent monographs on adoption consist primarily of popular treatments—for example, Sinclair B. Ferguson, *Children of the Living God* (Colorado Springs: NavPress, 1987); Mark G. Johnston, *Child of a King: What Joining God's Family Means* (Fearn, Ross-shire, UK: Christian Focus, 1997); Stibbe, *Orphans to Heirs*; Peterson, *Adopted by God*. More recent academic treatments include James M. Scott, *Adoption as Sons of God: An Exegetical Investigation into the Background of* YIOTHESIA *in the Pauline Corpus*, Wissenschaftliche Untersuchungen Zum Neuen Testament 48 (Tübingen: J. C. B. Mohr [Paul Siebeck], 1992); Trevor J. Burke, *Adopted into God's Family: Exploring a Pauline Metaphor*, NSBT 22 (Downers Grove, IL: InterVarsity Press, 2006). For other specific resources, see the bibliography at the back of this volume.

47. Whaling, "Adoption," 235.

48. Scott, *Adoption as Sons of God*.

49. Michael Peppard, *The Son of God in the Roman World: Divine Sonship in Its Social and Political Context* (Oxford: Oxford University Press, 2011).

50. Burke, *Adopted into God's Family*.

informs the application of redemption (*ordo salutis*), and Christ's own filial status informs the blessing of adoption in union with him needs careful reflection for the faithful unpacking of *huiothesia*.

Building on the scriptural synthesis and organic approach to the doctrine by John Calvin, this book employs the insights and methods of Reformed biblical theology in the tradition of Herman Ridderbos, Geerhardus Vos, John Murray, and Richard Gaffin Jr. In keeping with the redemptive-historical framework of these scholars, the attendant primacy of the *historia salutis* for interpreting the *ordo salutis* directs this study.[51] The task, then, is to probe the theological meaning of *adoption in Christ* the Son of God, who at his resurrection was "declared to be the Son of God in power according to the Spirit of holiness" (Rom. 1:4). With careful consideration of the import and power of Christ's resurrection as Son for the salvation of sinners, the primacy of union with Christ governs the interpretation of *all* redemptive benefits, including adoption. Borrowing Hans Burger's clever introduction to his expansive treatment of union with Christ, "To be or not to be—in Christ—that is the question."[52]

Adoption *in Christ*

Sinclair Ferguson has suggested that sonship broadly is an organizing principle for soteriology.[53] While such a position accurately represents New Testament theology, specifically for Paul, it is *adoption* that serves as an organizing principle. Doubtless Calvin likewise perceived Pauline adoption's breadth of significance, as he wove the term throughout his *Institutes*, refusing it locus status in his biblical theology, but granting it prominence not only by its frequency but also by its extensive scope.[54] For this reason, Calvin's "Gospel

51. It is also true that the *ordo salutis* aids in interpreting the *historia salutis*. This theological reciprocity gets fuller attention throughout this volume. From either vantage point, the primacy of the *historia salutis* remains intact, because even when viewing the work of redemption through its application, the work retains theological primacy because it is the source of what is applied.

52. Hans Burger, *Being in Christ: A Biblical and Systematic Investigation in a Reformed Perspective* (Eugene, OR: Wipf and Stock, 2008), 1.

53. Ferguson, "Reformed Doctrine of Sonship," 86–87.

54. More on Calvin's treatment of adoption appears in chapter 10.

of adoption"[55] draws from his attention to the history of redemption (*historia salutis*), in which God's work in Christ the Son of God *accomplishes* and *frames* the nature of salvation. The application of salvation depends entirely on the Son's completed redemptive work.

In addition to the doctrines of justification (legal) and sanctification (transformative), the Scriptures unfold a familial cast to redemption, which for Paul involves a number of terms and concepts, including *Father, Son/sons, brother(s), children (of God)*, and *inheritance*. At the heart of Pauline soteriology is the redemptive-historically charged concept of *adoption (huiothesia)*. For Paul, the entirety of our redemption—from the mind of God before creation itself until its eschatological completion in our bodily resurrection—is expressed by *filial* reality, *filial* identity, and a *filially framed* union. As we will see in the following pages, this filial grace *in Christ Jesus* is expressly and implicitly, in Pauline theology, *adoption*.

While adoption possesses an undeniable forensic dimension, legal and even familial *rights* do not exhaust the scope of this doctrine. In fact, in view of its Christological centrality and the function of the eschatological Spirit of adoption, full moral, constitutive, and bodily *renovation* actually occupy vital significance in adoption's eschatological substance. With this permeating renovative emphasis, Paul extends the term *huiothesia* beyond cultural and etymological constraints, and imbues the term with a full array of Christ-centered and Spirit-rendered biblico-theological content. He masterfully filches the Roman concept of adoption in a way that illumines the full-orbed riches of adoptive grace in the Son of God par excellence. The manner in which Paul adopts this common first-century practice and employs it to explain the gospel of Jesus Christ the Son of God takes center stage in the following chapter.

---

55. Gerrish, *Grace and Gratitude*, 89.

3

What Informs *Huiothesia?*

The Term *Huiothesia*

Significant debate exists among scholars concerning the conceptual backdrop—biblical, cultural, etymological-lexical—to Pauline *huiothesia*.[1] Some suggest that Paul's concept of adoption derives from Jewish practice; others look for the source of adoption

---

1. For investigation and varying opinions on this question, see Daniel J. Theron, "'Adoption' in the Pauline Corpus," *EvQ* 28, 1 (1956): 6–7; Martin W. Schoenberg, "*Huiothesia*: The Word and the Institution," *Scripture* 15 (1963): 115–23; Francis Lyall, "Roman Law in the Writings of Paul—Adoption," *JBL* 88, 4 (1969): 458–66; Francis Lyall, *Slaves, Citizens, Sons: Legal Metaphors in the Epistles* (Grand Rapids: Zondervan, 1984); Matthew Vellanickal, *The Divine Sonship of Christians in the Johannine Writings*, AnBib: Investigationes Scientificae in Res Biblicas 72 (Rome: Biblical Institute, 1977), 71; James I. Cook, "The Conception of Adoption in the Theology of Paul," in *Saved by Hope: Essays in Honor of Richard C. Oudersluys*, ed. James I. Cook (Grand Rapids: Eerdmans, 1978), 133–44; Brendan Byrne, *"Sons of God"—"Seed of Abraham": A Study of the Idea of the Sonship of God of All Christians in Paul against the Jewish Background*, AnBib: Investigationes Scientificae in Res Biblicas 83 (Rome: Biblical Institute, 1979); Allen Mawhinney, "*Yiothesia* in the Pauline Epistles: Its Background, Use, and Implications" (Ph.D. diss., Baylor University, Waco, TX, 1982), 6–7, 10–118, 216–17; T. Scott Franchino, "*Yios* and *Teknon* in the Doctrine of Adoption: Romans 8" (unpublished master's thesis, Grace Theological Seminary, Winona Lake, IN, 1984), 3–30; James M. Scott, *Adoption as Sons of God: An Exegetical Investigation into the Background of* YIOTHESIA *in the Pauline Corpus*, Wissenschaftliche Untersuchungen Zum Neuen Testament 48 (Tübingen: J. C. B. Mohr [Paul Siebeck], 1992); Trevor J. Burke, "The Characteristics of Paul's Adoptive-Sonship (Huiothesia) Motif," *IBS* 17, 2 (1995): 62–74; Ernest Best, *A Critical and Exegetical Commentary on Ephesians*, ICC (Edinburgh: T&T Clark, 1998), 124–26; Robert C. Dorman, "A Study of Paul's Use of *Hyiothesia*: Its Background, Development, and Importance concerning Spiritual Adoption" (unpublished master's thesis, Covenant Theological Seminary, St. Louis, 1997), 7–23, 93–96, 106–8; Sarah Julien, "Coming Home: Adoption in Ephesians and Galatians," *Quodlibet Journal* 5.2–3 (2003), http://www.quodlibet.net/articles/murray-adoption.shtml (accessed February 3, 2016); Michael Peppard, *The Son of God in the Roman World: Divine Sonship in Its Social and Political Context* (Oxford: Oxford University Press, 2011).

not so much in Jewish practice as in the theological themes of the Old Testament. Still others insist that the meaning of this Pauline familial term depends on Roman law and custom and/or Greek law and custom. Naturally, discerning what actually informs Paul's use of *huiothesia* shapes hermeneutical decisions and theological deductions. In the end, the proper conceptual referent will sculpt its pastoral application as well.

What, then, actually shapes proper interpretation of the term in Paul, and what does the *huiothesian* concept embrace in Pauline thought? With the number of Greek familial terms he employs (including *prototokos* ["firstborn"], *teknon* ["child"], *tekna* ["children"], *huios* ["son"], and *huioi* ["*sons*"]), his selection of *huiothesia* is striking. What he means by *huiothesia*, however, requires apposite reliance on driving theological factors and on connotations of the term in its first-century Roman milieu. Understanding how these theological and cultural factors relate to the Pauline concept of *huiothesia* is critical to its interpretation and function. Before building the case for a specific approach, I will first survey the taxonomy of possibilities for the historical and conceptual referent of *huiothesia*.

Greek Law and Practice

An exclusively Greek background to *huiothesia* has enjoyed minimal advocacy. Derek R. Moore-Crispin defends a Greek source for the term,[2] and in Ben Witherington's treatment of Galatians 4:1–7, he insists that the incongruities between Roman practice and Pauline argument suggest a Hellenistic referent rather than a Roman one.[3] "Paul here seems to envision the death of the father and the appointment in a will of guardians and trustees, a normal Greek procedure."[4]

---

2. Derek R. Moore-Crispin, "Galatians 4:1–9: The Use and Abuse of Parallels," *EvQ* 61, 3 (1989): 203–23.

3. Ben Witherington, *Grace in Galatia: A Commentary on St. Paul's Letter to the Galatians*, T&T Clark Academic Paperbacks (London and New York: T&T Clark, 2004), 282–83. Witherington's specific interest in the Galatian use of *huiothesia* highlights the complexity of the question, since one could argue that the conceptual referent for *huiothesia* in one Pauline text might not be identical to another. Yet, as I will argue, the soteriological contours of *huiothesia* for Paul are vast but coherent and mutually informing.

4. Ibid., 283.

Witherington insists that if the southern Galatian theory is true, the letter was not written to a Roman colony anyway, and no evidence in extrabiblical data suggests the existence of a non-Hellenistic inheritance motif in Phrygia. Yet Rome's influence extended well beyond the colony cities, and Paul's Roman citizenship along with the larger Greco-Roman context trumps these limiting contentions.

The Greek-origin hypothesis has gained little traction more generally because most of the data from the Greek world stem from the fourth century B.C., greatly distancing Hellenistic practices from the New Testament context. Moreover, because of the diversity of the Greek culture in its city-state system of autonomous governance, there was no common Greek influence on *huiothesia* from which to draw.[5] By contrast, such widespread Hellenistic variability is not found in the first-century Roman law.

Roman Law and Practice

Francis Lyall, an internationally recognized expert in Roman law and former professor of public law at the University of Aberdeen, argues ardently that the Pauline usage of adoption reflects a Roman legal concept over and against Jewish procedure and Greek law. He states:

> The riches of the concept [of adoption] in Roman law and its weakness in the alternative systems make compelling the suggestion that we must look to Roman law to interpret the notion. Jewish law, the obvious alternative, does not possess the concept, and Greek adoption, existing really as a means of succession, is but a pale shadow of the Roman concept.[6]

With sympathies toward formal legal explanations, Lyall finds the thesis of an Old Testament referent wholly problematic. Witherington concurs: "Neither legal guardianship nor adoption were normal social practices of the early Jews, nor is provision really made for them in the

---

5. Trevor J. Burke, *Adopted into God's Family: Exploring a Pauline Metaphor*, NSBT 22 (Downers Grove, IL: InterVarsity Press, 2006), 58–60.

6. Lyall, *Slaves, Citizens, Sons*, 69. Cf. Samuel G. Shepard, "The Pauline Doctrine of Sonship" (Ph.D. diss., Southern Baptist Theological Seminary, Louisville, KY, 1951), 28–32.

Mosaic Law."[7] Contending that Levirate marriage surfaces as the only plausible Old Testament counterpart, Lyall concludes that the absence of specific laws creates insurmountable doubt concerning any Old Testament practice as background for Pauline *huiothesia*. Lyall queries, "Would Paul, a trained lawyer, writing to Greeks and Romans, use an illustration drawn from an informal practice when by the same words he could be referring to a detailed and well-known legal institution? I do not think so."[8] The lack of Jewish formal referent leads Lyall to affirm a culturally ubiquitous grasp of first-century legal practice as the prime and most plausible fodder for Pauline *huiothesia*.

Adoption existed in two forms in Roman law: *adoptio* and *adrogatio*. Distinguishing the two, Mawhinney writes, "If the person to be adopted was under the authority of a *paterfamilias* the act was called *adoptio*. If the person to be adopted was himself the *paterfamilias* of his family it was called *adrogatio*."[9] If this distinction is sustained, *adoptio* represents the most plausible sociolegal concept behind Pauline *huiothesia*. Arguing, then, for the explicitly Roman context for *huiothesia* (*adoptio* rather than *adrogatio*), Lyall asserts that *adoptio* is "technically a legal *act*, [but] it is also spoken of as a *device*, and is to be thought of as having a continuing effect in the changes it brings about in the statuses of several persons: the natural parent(s), the child, and the 'new' parent(s)."[10]

In certain ways, Roman adoption and contemporary Western adoption appear similar. Yet upon further investigation, stark distinctions surface. In particular, "the issue of inheritance brings into focus the chief differences between adoption in Roman culture and in the modern west."[11] Ancient Roman adoption focused primarily on the continuity of a family name. A trustworthy heir was essential to secure

---

7. Witherington, *Grace in Galatia*, 282.

8. Lyall, *Slaves, Citizens, Sons*, 80. Whatever value rests in these Greco-Roman deductions, Lyall's assertion that Levirate marriage could serve as the Old Testament backdrop for *huiothesia* simply lacks any material defense.

9. Mawhinney, "*Yiothesia* in the Pauline Epistles," 29.

10. Lyall, *Slaves, Citizens, Sons*, 67. Cf. Robert E. Wermuth, "The Doctrine of Adoption in Paul's Ephesian Letter" (unpublished master's thesis, Covenant Theological Seminary, St. Louis, 1985), 19–20.

11. Peppard, *Son of God in the Roman World*, 51.

this destiny, and for this reason, adoption occurred more commonly in adulthood, with time-proven adults rather than untested children. In brief, Roman adoption was tactical, functional, and protective of personal interests. It did not have in view the adoptee's social, emotional, or even spiritual well-being; rather, it served as the means "to pass on . . . wealth, name, honor, and family cult."[12] In the adoption, the adopting father sought to ensure the perpetuation of his family.[13]

From the point of adoption, the father (*paterfamilias*) took the same control over his new "child" as he had over his natural offspring. He owned all the property and acquisitions of the adoptee, controlled his personal relationships, and exerted the rights of discipline. Though not central to the purpose of Roman adoption, substantial benefits came also to the adopted son. The adoptee was taken out of his previous state and was placed in a new relationship of son to his new father, his new *paterfamilias*. All his old debts were canceled, and in effect the adoptee started a new life as part of his new family. The father became liable for the actions of the adoptee, and each owed the other reciprocal duties of support and maintenance.[14]

Lyall notes two stages of the *adoptio* procedure in the Roman legal process. First, the one adopted had ties with his existing legal authority severed, so that the former authority in his life no longer held sway. The second step was to establish the new authority in the adoptee's life by legal declaration.[15] Subsequent research indicates certain distinctions between Roman law and common practice, and that authors in Latin do not cleanly distinguish between *adrogatio* and *adoptio*.[16] Nonetheless, the Roman legal and quasi-legal processes were woven into the fabric of the first century A.D., with certain dimensions of these customs commonly grasped by those living in the Roman world.

---

12. Ibid., 52.

13. "In Roman society, unlike our own, the purpose of adoption in law was not to safeguard the rights and privileges of the child but was exclusively thought of in terms of the benefits and blessings which the adopter received." Sinclair B. Ferguson, *The Christian Life: A Doctrinal Introduction* (Edinburgh: Banner of Truth, 1981), 95.

14. Lyall, *Slaves, Citizens, Sons*, 83. Cf. Trevor J. Burke, "Pauline Adoption: A Sociological Approach," *EvQ* 73, 2 (2001): 121–24.

15. Ibid., 86–87.

16. Peppard, *Son of God in the Roman World*, 53.

Michael Peppard has more recently taken up this first-century Roman imperial context mantle, but considers possible Old Testament references as well. In his analysis of Exodus 2:5–10 and Ruth 4:16–17, he contends that foreign influence and extraordinary circumstances loom large in these passages.[17] When considering other biblical and extrabiblical texts, he concludes:

> We do not have evidence of a codified or widespread system of adoption in ancient Judaism . . . . However, biblical accounts of some key figures (Moses, Joseph, Ruth, David) do portray parent-child relationships enacted not through biological reproduction but through nursing and fosterage.[18]

Peppard argues for a metaphorical use of an adoption motif in the Old Testament, especially in the language of the Davidic covenant in 2 Samuel 7:5–17.[19] He remains skeptical, however, and claims that "the textual allusions are not as strong as they are normally made out to be."[20] Peppard finally rejects reliance on 2 Samuel 7 as a key backdrop to Pauline *huiothesia*, and instead employs a New Testament interpretive paradigm governed by contemporary Roman factors rather than biblico-theological ones.[21]

More greatly influenced by redemptive history than Lyall or Peppard, Trevor Burke also perceives a Roman sociolegal backdrop for adoption, and concludes that adoption conveys a "re-socialisation in conversion" for those who newly enter the kingdom of God; as such, adoption possesses radical *social* and *ecclesiological* implications:

> As a conversion term, Paul's talk of adoption was something which for these early Christians was profound and thoroughgoing—it speaks of a real experience of sharp displacement which many of

17. Ibid., 99.
18. Ibid., 102.
19. Ibid., 105–6.
20. Ibid., 106.
21. James Scott, by contrast, makes 2 Samuel 7:14 *the* backdrop for Pauline adoption in his *Adoption as Sons of God*. Scott's proposal will get further attention shortly.

his new converts would have felt because it brought about a radical change to basic relationships, attitudes, and perceptions similar to those acquired by a child growing up within a family.[22]

The "sharp displacement" from one family to another in Roman adoption proffers fertile ground for Paul to plant the *huiothesian* concept in his theological reflection.

In summary, Lyall, and even more so Peppard and Burke, contributes to the study of Roman *huiothesia* by deciphering a reasonable and informative Roman legal and cultural backdrop to *huiothesia* and unveiling the bearing that such factors might have on investigating the Pauline soteriological motif.[23] Peppard's analysis strengthens the case for the benefit to the *family* that the presence of the adopted son makes, explaining how the adopted son ensures the continuance of the family for the coming generations. Discernible qualifications merit the adopted son's selection, and his inherent and proven excellence benefits the other members of the family. His appointed and then assumed leadership secures the family inheritance and perpetuates the family's existence.

Thus, the first-century context in its well-attested understanding of the Roman practice of adoption warrants attention. Ignoring it risks both importation of foreign ideas into the Pauline concept and missing the fruitful analogies that the common Roman concepts facilitate. The helpfulness of these first-century analogies will surface more explicitly in the coming pages.

Jewish Law and Practice

There is no evidence of specific legal stipulations in the ancient Jewish culture; adoption practice "was known in Israel even though not treated in the law."[24] But lack of explicit laws does not warrant

22. Burke, "Pauline Adoption," 124–25. Cf. Trevor J. Burke, "Adoption and the Spirit in Romans 8," *EvQ* 70, 4 (1998): 324; Herman N. Ridderbos, *Paul: An Outline of His Theology*, trans. John Richard DeWitt (Grand Rapids: Eerdmans, 1975), 201.

23. Cf. Sinclair B. Ferguson, *Children of the Living God* (Colorado Springs: NavPress, 1987), 46, 51–61; Mark Stibbe, *From Orphans to Heirs: Celebrating Our Spiritual Adoption* (Oxford: Bible Reading Fellowship, 1999), 71–72.

24. Z. W. Falk, *Hebrew Law in Biblical Times* (Jerusalem: Wahrmann, 1964), 163. See

the conclusion that adoption was nonexistent. With a view to the New Testament's and in particular the Pauline reliance on the Old Testament, James Scott traces numerous Old Testament texts (including, for example, Genesis 48:5–6; Exodus 2:10; Esther 2:7, 15) as well as extrabiblical sources, and discerns strong evidence of some form of adoptive practice in Old Testament Israel. Scott concludes, "Whether or not Israel had the institution of adoption, several cases of adoption are recorded in the Old Testament, showing that the institution was at least known in Israel."[25] Though no legal strictures were in place, the prominence of the practice could surely have inspired Pauline thought.[26]

But Scott moves beyond general practice to a narrow biblical focus. Second Samuel 7 serves paradigmatically for him, especially verse 14a: "I will be to him a father, and he shall be to me a son." Scott highlights the strong case for an adoption formula here, and argues for adoption as covenant fulfillment of the promised Davidic king, the son of David from whom the filial blessings extend to the covenant people. "The national expectation of divine adoption, converging as it does with the messianic expectation, leads to an appropriation of 2 Samuel 7:14a to the eschatological people of God as a whole, a sort of national identification with the sonship of the *Heilbringer* [Savior]."[27]

Such bidirectional movement between covenant representative and the represented people is not uncommon in the Old Testament canon,[28] and this Representative/represented relationship comes to fullest prominence in the New Testament, poignantly so in the Pauline *in Christ* formulation. For Scott, the Old Testament serves as the primary conceptual backdrop for Paul in his treatment of adoption, and one needs to look no further than the royal and filial convergence

---

ibid., 162–64. Cf. Schoenberg, *"Huiothesia: The Word and the Institution,"* 119–20; Samuel Feigin, "Some Cases of Adoption in Israel," *JBL* 50, 3 (1931): 186–200; Herbert Donner, "Adoption oder Legitimation? Erwägungen zur Adoption im Alten Testament auf dem Hintergrund der altorientalischen Rechte," *Oriens Antiquus* 8 (1969): 87–119; Dorman, "Paul's Use of *Hyiothesia*," 16; Mawhinney, *"Yiothesia* in the Pauline Epistles," 33–51.

25. Scott, *Adoption as Sons of God*, 103. See also ibid., 61–102.

26. For more on adoption in ancient Israel, see *Anchor Bible Dictionary*, s.v. "Adoption."

27. Scott, *Adoption as Sons of God*, 117.

28. See, e.g., G. K. Beale, "The Use of Hosea 11:1 in Matthew 2:15: One More Time," *JETS* 55, 4 (2012): 697–716.

in the Davidic covenant for the redemptive-historical background to this familial and soteric term, realized in Jesus Christ, the Son of God. By the grace of God, the sons of God enjoy solidarity with the Son of God par excellence.

Thus, while adoption is not explicitly a legal act in ancient Israel, analogous laws and parallel practices (see, e.g., Gen. 48:5–6; Ex. 2:10; Esth. 2:7, 15)[29] along with "other terms and formulae"[30] provide a most reasonable conceptual framework for Pauline *huiothesia*. More importantly, with the vital biblico-theological interface between divine kingship and sonship, the kingdom and the church/family of God, the Old Testament renders the core from which the apostle draws to inform *huiothesia* in the wake of the climactic events of redemptive history surrounding Jesus Christ, the King, the Son, and—to borrow James Scott's frequently repeated term—the *Heilbringer* ("Savior"). For Scott, that Old Testament conceptual referent for *huiothesia* is unquestionably 2 Samuel 7 and the Davidic filial/royal promise. New Testament adoption fulfills this Davidic promise and delivers regal and filial blessing on the eschatological people of God. Scott's biblico-theological orientation directs credibly to the apostolic dependence on the organic connections between the ancient Scriptures and the resurrected Christ. The Old Testament backdrop to adoption will become increasingly compelling in the study of Pauline adoption, but not in a fashion that rends *huiothesia* from its first-century imperial Roman milieu.

Huiothesia in Pauline Thought

The Apostle Paul

Trained by the renowned instructor Gamaliel (Acts 22:3),[31] the apostle Paul possessed a remarkable grasp of the Old Testament. Only his undying zeal rivaled his theological credentials. But as he would put it later, the value of academic pedigree became as dung to him

---

29. Scott, *Adoption as Sons of God*, 74–75. Scott defends Pharaoh's taking in of Moses as an illustration of "adoption," something attested even by Philo. Ibid., 75–76.

30. Ibid., 61.

31. F. F. Bruce, *The Book of the Acts*, rev. ed., NICNT (Grand Rapids: Eerdmans, 1988), 114–16, 414–15.

when he met the resurrected Christ Jesus (Phil. 3:4–11). It is not true, however, that his training in the Old Testament served for naught. Having known before his conversion the anticipatory character of the Old Testament, Paul by the grace of God came to grasp the answer to its covenantal expectation in the person and work of Jesus Christ. When Paul encountered the resurrected Christ and received direct revelation concerning the gospel of God in his Son (Gal. 1:11–12), his factually vast yet misunderstood interpretation of the Old Testament became the great reservoir from which his Spirit-revealed and *corrected* understandings concerning Christ surged. In many ways, Paul (Saul) had once been the blinded Israelite for which he later, as the apostle Paul, had "great sorrow and unceasing anguish in [his] heart" (Rom. 9:2).

Converted and commissioned as an apostle, Paul never departed from his grounding in the Old Testament as the Word of God (2 Tim. 3:16–17), because it pointed authoritatively and unswervingly to Christ (Rom. 1:1–4; 16:25–27; Gal. 3:8). But now, illumined in the age of Christ by the eschatological Spirit, Paul for the first time understood the Old Testament for what it really is (cf. Luke 24:13–49; John 5:39–47).[32] He saw and celebrated what had always been present but what he had never before seen—Jesus of Nazareth was the Christ of Scripture. Living at the time when redemptive history attained its cosmic climax in Jesus Christ, by divine revelatory mercy, Paul experienced the dropping of the veil from over his mind and heart as he grasped the Old and New Testament Lord for who he really is (2 Cor. 4:1–6). The arrival of the Son of God in fulfillment of Old Testament redemptive promise, type, and shadow therefore ignited the eschatological fires that informed and warmed Pauline thought and method.

Paul, the Old Testament, and Roman Culture: Possession of Huiothesia

Because of his biblico-theological perspective, Paul's choice of the term *huiothesia*, while vitally connected in particular ways to his Roman cultural setting, must not be interpreted narrowly through

---

32. David B. Garner, "Did God Really Say?," in *Did God Really Say? Affirming the Truthfulness and Trustworthiness of Scripture*, ed. David B. Garner (Phillipsburg, NJ: P&R Publishing, 2012), 154–59.

this first-century *Sitz im Leben* ("contextual setting").[33] Pauline gospel focus derives from the apostle's Old Testament grounding, his thoroughgoing redemptive-historical and theological orientation. It is therefore only proper to consider both explicit Old Testament referents and organically woven Old Testament themes as the *foundational* elements in his apostolic teaching. This interpretive conclusion does not require mere inference, since in Galatians 4:1–6 and Romans 9:4, for example, the saplings of Old Testament biblical theology openly grow to full and fruitful maturity. Behind Paul's use of the term *huiothesia* "stands that broad Jewish tradition of Israel, especially eschatological Israel, as 'son/child (sons/children) of God.'"[34]

Yet bearing theological weight beneath Israel's sonship is Adam's own sonship (cf. Luke 3:38), and Paul's filial-rich theology finds its deepest historical referent in the anticipated glory and inheritance associated with Adam's promised covenantal future as an obedient son (cf. 1 Cor. 15:20–49). The failure of Adam to attain his filial destiny necessitated a second Adam, one promised first in Genesis 3:15 and prophesied throughout Old Testament revelation with mounting intensity and clarity. Covenant history is gospel history: a gospel anticipated and a gospel realized (Gal. 3:8; 1 Cor. 15:1–3). Accordingly, the gospel message—the God-given (revealed) interpretation of the

33. Shepard, "Pauline Doctrine of Sonship," 40, insists that Paul does not "slavishly follow the Roman laws," but that, using the Roman custom, he "pours many of his own ideas into the term." Stibbe, *From Orphans to Heirs*, 41, adds, "When Paul speaks about spiritual adoption he . . . thinks as a Roman, a Jew and a Christian." Cf. Mawhinney, "*Yiothesia* in the Pauline Epistles," 120–21.

34. Brendan Byrne, *Romans*, ed. Daniel J. Harrington, SP 6 (Collegeville, MN: Liturgical Press, 1996), 250. Cf. Byrne, "*Sons of God*"—"*Seed of Abraham*," 13–16; Theron, "Adoption," 7; Schoenberg, "*Huiothesia*: The Word and the Institution," 119–23; Ridderbos, *Paul*, 203; R. Alan Cole, *The Letter of Paul to the Galatians*, 2nd ed., TNTC (Leicester: Inter-Varsity Press, 1989), 162; Scott, *Adoption as Sons of God*, 177; Tim J. R. Trumper, "The Metaphorical Import of Adoption: A Plea for Realisation I: The Adoption Metaphor in Biblical Usage," *SBET* 14, 2 (1996): 103; Dorman, "Paul's Use of *Hyiothesia*," 16–17, 74–75, 90–92; Russell Radoicich, "'Adoption' in the Pauline Epistles" (unpublished paper, St. Vladimir's Orthodox Theological Seminary, Crestwood, NY, 1999), 13–24. "Paul's indebtedness to his Jewish heritage is becoming more fully appreciated—which is helping us to recognise the wealth of connection and interdependence between the two Testaments of the Christian Bible." John Proctor, review of *Adoption as Sons of God*, by James M. Scott, *EvQ* 67, 2 (1995): 171. Vellanickal, *Divine Sonship of Christians*, 69, concurs: "The scholars are becoming more and more convinced of [adoption's] background in Israel's sonship."

biography of Jesus Christ—led to the choice of the term *huiothesia*; "the metaphor (as suggestive and appropriate as it was) did not determine the content of the gospel."[35] Hence:

> The Apostle's concept of adoption is anchored in the supreme expression of God's love and grace, the adoption/election of a people. This in turn leads to the conclusion that the true antecedent of *huiothesia* is for Paul not a legal institution, whether Greek, Roman, or Semitic, but rather a theological confession. All too frequently overlooked is the fact that the Apostle does not use *huiothesia* for what we describe as social adoption, that is, the adoption of one human by another. He always uses it to describe what may be termed theological adoption, that is, the placing of persons into sonship to God![36]

While this observation might appear self-evident, the sustained attempt to make the Greco-Roman character of *huiothesia* its primary or even exclusive informing content makes it necessary to be explicit.[37] So what of the first-century Greco-Roman ideas embedded in *huiothesia*, and how should we think of their interfacing with Old Testament revelation?

No doubt in reaction to overreading a first-century cultural influence on Pauline theology, an opposing error has appeared. Concerned for appreciating the comprehensive coherence of biblical revelation, one might conclude that Pauline *huiothesia* functions in a virtual first-century vacuum, with little to no regard for the contemporaneous

---

35. Mawhinney, "*Yiothesia* in the Pauline Epistles," 149–50. Commensurately, Tim J. R. Trumper, "The Metaphorical Import of Adoption: A Plea for Realisation II: The Adoption Metaphor in Theological Usage," *SBET* 15, 2 (1997): 103, adds, "Having taken hold of a familiar Hellenistic term, Paul applied it in an unfamiliar theological context."

36. Cook, "Conception of Adoption," 139–40.

37. See, e.g., Lyall, "Roman Law in the Writings of Paul," 459; Lyall, *Slaves, Citizens, Sons*, 69; F. F. Bruce, *The Epistle to the Galatians: A Commentary on the Greek Text*, NIGTC (Grand Rapids: Eerdmans, 1982), 197–98; Kenneth S. Wuest, *Untranslatable Riches from the Greek New Testament for the English Reader* (Grand Rapids: Eerdmans, 1942), 90–92; Thomas Houston, *The Adoption of Sons, Its Nature, Spirit, Privileges and Effects: A Practical and Experimental Treatise* (Paisley, Scotland: Alex. Gardner, 1872), 24–25; Burke, "Characteristics of Paul's Adoptive Sonship," 62–74; William Sanday and Arthur C. Headlam, *A Critical and Exegetical Commentary on the Epistle to the Romans*, 5th ed., ICC (Edinburgh: T&T Clark, 1902), 203; Edwin Hartshorn Palmer, *Scheeben's Doctrine of Divine Adoption* (Amsterdam: Kok, 1954), 175–76.

usage of the term. While no one would plausibly contend that Paul's choice of any term occurs with absolutely no reference to his own *Sitz im Leben*, a constraining acceptance of elements within the Old Testament theological backdrop can exercise an overbearing interpretive sway. Illustrative of this danger is James I. Cook, who makes paradigmatic the typological backdrop of *huiothesia* in Romans 9,[38] and largely rends the term from its contemporary setting.

With such an orientation, the historical studies of scholars such as Lyall and Peppard gain no interpretive traction, and leave a term such as *huiothesia* floating in a lexical and cultural no-man's-land. In such an interpretive framework, in order to illustrate gospel reality, Paul borrows a common term but limits its point of contact to vague familial concepts rather than capitalizing on key features of its common understanding. But ignoring these points of Roman contextual analogy short-circuits the understanding of adoption, eclipsing several dimensions of this divine filial grace. Further, while I appreciate the rigorous biblico-theological orientation that Scott applies to his concept of *huiothesia*, limiting adoption to the strictures of 2 Samuel 7:14a and Davidic covenant fulfillment of sonship by the Messiah fails to appreciate the broader influence from the Old Testament.[39] The apostle Paul looks to 2 Samuel 7, Exodus 4:22–23, and, as I will suggest, even to more ultimate covenantal/familial themes from the Pentateuch, including Adam (Gen. 1–2), as he appropriates *huiothesia* for expressing the filial and familial grace of adoption as sons. This appropriation extends *huiothesia* beyond its Greco-Roman constrictions, and even beyond the yet-unfulfilled revelation of sonship in the Old Testament.

38. Cook, "Conception of Adoption," 139–40.
39. James Scott's conclusion that 2 Samuel 7:14 is the *primary* background text for the content of *huiothesia* is conjectural and unconvincing. Cf. Brendan Byrne, review of *Adoption as Sons of God: An Exegetical Investigation into the Background of* YIOTHESIA *in the Pauline Corpus*, by J. Scott, *Journal of Theological Studies* 44 (1992): 293–94; Jacques Schlosser, review of *Adoption as Sons of God: An Exegetical Investigation into the Background of* Yiothesia *in the Pauline Corpus*, by J. Scott, *Biblica* 75 (1994): 287. But we concur with Scott that Paul's dependence on the Old Testament was the primary influence on the adoption motif, and that 2 Samuel 7:14 proffers a vital dimension of that influence. Cf. Shepard, "Pauline Doctrine of Sonship," 27; Proctor, review of Scott, *Adoption as Sons of God*, 172–74; Dorman, "Paul's Use of *Hyiothesia*," 31–32.

In summary, some scholars determine that *huiothesia* draws from redemptive history, making contemporary referentiality essentially negligible. Others determine that *huiothesia* ought to be received according to Greco-Roman contemporary practice, virtually to the exclusion of redemptive-historical considerations. Neither extreme can or should be accepted. Instead, the enriching metaphorical value of *huiothesia* within its immediate cultural context provides appreciable analogies from Roman imperial adoption to inform and enrich Paul's all-informing biblical theology.

Employing this familiar term with a burning appreciation for its fruitful analogies, Paul advances a rigorous Christological and eschatological sonship, the gospel of an affirmed and appointed Son, whose kingdom is not of this world, but whose filial faithfulness to the divine covenant renders a familial and redemptive inheritance of richest proportions to those united to him. Co-opting analogies from its first-century context, the Pauline *huiothesian* concept captures prominent Old Testament themes, and draws together theology proper, creation, covenant, anthropology, Christology, pneumatology, and ecclesiology.

As coming chapters will expose more fully, key factors in first-century Roman imperialistic adoption serve poignantly to deliver these *huiothesian* conceptions. In short, the qualifications of the Son *chosen* for adoption and the responsibility entrusted to him because of his proven and reliable character fortify the dynamic filio-Christocentric soteriology in Paul. Sons of God acquire all their benefits from the Son of God. In gospel-rich shorthand, analogies embedded in the term *huiothesia* link the pretemporal (before the creation of the cosmos) with the eschatological (consummation of the cosmos), and substantiate the filial character of the gospel from Old Testament to New Testament. *Huiothesia* capably transports the full load of redemptive, filial, and eschatological grace in Christ Jesus, the resurrected Son of God.

How, then, does Paul employ *huiothesia*? Speaking of how to deliver the gospel to foreign contexts, J. H. Bavinck (nephew of the well-known Dutch theologian Herman Bavinck) contends for what he calls "*possessio*, to take in possession. The Christian life does not accommodate or adapt itself to heathen forms of life, but it takes the latter in possession and thereby makes them new."[40] What Bavinck asserts for faithful missions echoes Paul's handling of terms such as *huiothesia*. As we will see in the remainder of this study, by the guidance of the Holy Spirit for developing and ratifying the biblico-theological themes, the apostle Paul takes a commonly understood term and *possesses* it. He seizes *huiothesia* from its familiar Greco-Roman context, amasses to it Old Testament messianic and covenantal concepts, and then imbues it with Old Testament and eschatologically realized (New Testament) theological content. He takes a familiar familial term and transforms it to render gospel understanding—in a manner organically connected to Old Testament texts and themes, but reliant also on contemporary concepts of *huiothesia* that effectively expose its particular Christological and eschatological content.

Huiothesia: Etymology and Theology

The noun *huiothesia* is a compound word from *huios* ("son") and *tithēmi* ("to place" or "to put"). "Greek terminology for adoption during the Roman era . . . [used] diverse verbs (such as *poieō, eispoieō, ekpoieō, huiopoieō, tithēmi, huiotheteō*, etc.) and their related nouns."[41] These various related expressions suggest the prominence of the action associated with adoption, so that the translation of the term *huiothesia*, some have argued, should be "adoption" or "adoption as son(s)" and not "sonship."[42]

Contrarily, Brendan Byrne has sought to build a lexical and contextual case for "sonship" as the translation, and then argues that Paul's point is not about the act of entering sonship status (adoption) but rather about the enduring status that filial reality brings (sonship).[43] Byrne's three-point analysis is roundly critiqued by James Scott,[44] who

---

40. J. H. Bavinck, *Introduction to the Science of Missions*, trans. David H. Freeman (Philadelphia: Presbyterian and Reformed, 1960), 178.

41. Peppard, *Son of God in the Roman World*, 53.

42. Scott, *Adoption as Sons of God*, 3–55. Cf. Trumper, "Metaphorical Import of Adoption I," 133–35. Contra Byrne, *"Sons of God"—"Seed of Abraham,"* 80; Ernst Käsemann, *Commentary on Romans*, trans. Geoffrey W. Bromiley (Grand Rapids: Eerdmans, 1980), 227; W. A. Jarrel, "Adoption Not in the Bible Salvation," *RExp* 15 (1918): 464.

43. Byrne, *"Sons of God"—"Seed of Abraham,"* 80–110.

44. Scott, *Adoption as Sons of God*, 175–76.

contends that *huiothesia* should be understood as the act of divine adoption, a fulfillment of Old Testament covenant promises. Scott's rebuttal notwithstanding, it would fail the Pauline scope of adoption to throw out entirely Byrne's concern for a state of sonship acquired by adoption, though his translation of *huiothesia* as "sonship" remains dissatisfactory. The first-century Roman adoptive practices and the theology of the Old Testament render ample resources for Paul to choose *huiothesia* for both the divine act *and* its enduring effects. Paul's selection of the term facilitates his concerns for the redemptive work of Jesus Christ, whose life in humiliation and obedience culminates in a decisive royal and filial declaration, and by whose confirming and crowning sonship believers in him enjoy full filial benefits, forensic and transformative.

Thus, Paul's concern is not only the *act* of adoption, but also the *state* of adoptive sonship, the full change that union with the resurrected Son of God affords. For Paul, adoption carries an eschatological force, in which the sonship entered by adoption differs from any prior earthly sonship. More broadly, Paul conceives of sonship in an eternal and archetypal dimension (the second person of the Trinity) and in derivative dimensions—creation (Adam and his progeny) and redemption (Christ and the elect). This latter redemptive sonship for Paul is an adoptive and covenantal sonship, in which the once-fallen and now-redeemed sons of Adam enjoy the full bounty of eschatologically conditioned filial privileges. Adoption is, then, a transaction, but also a new state of affairs. The believer is *adopted* and then lives forever as an *adopted son*. For Paul, redeemed sonship permanently remains adoptive sonship.

Adoption therefore involves the initiation (initial union with Christ by faith), the dynamic of sanctifying faith (vital union in daily experience), and the eschatological consummation (persevering union for the last day). By accepting Byrne's translation of *huiothesia* as "sonship," the decisive redemptive transition "from the domain of darkness" to "the kingdom of his beloved Son" (Col. 1:13) gets lost. Byrne's rendering leads prematurely to the *experience* of *huiothesia*, without giving sufficient theological credence to the dynamic transaction wrought by *huiothesia*. On the other hand, restricting adoption to the initiation rite itself fails to comprehend the unprecedented and sustained condition that the transaction of adoption secures. Adoption concerns the believer's translation into new filial life *and* the full experience of that new life in Christ, both now and forever.

The Sons in the Son

Redemptive solidarity with the Son of God is at the heart of Paul's soteriology, and the filial terms employed by Paul communicate this Spirit-wrought union. To the point, Paul's *huiothesia* exploits the etymological connections between *huios* ("son") and *huiothesia* to depict the soteric and eschatological solidarity of the redeemed sons with the Redeemer. While the nature of solidarity far exceeds mere etymology, for now, note that Paul's choice of *huiothesia* and the verbs commonly associated with the act of adoption do point to an official, permanent *placing* of sons in a new family (cf. Burke). Adoption is, literally, *son placing*, and this literal rendering tacitly upholds the apostolic intention for appreciating the filial contours of the gospel *in Christ*.[45] The cognate relationship between *huios* and *huiothesia* lexically channels the theological wellspring of filial solidarity.[46]

Thus, for Paul, *huiothesia* occasions Spirit-facilitated gracious *placement in* and perfect *solidarity with* the *huios*. The shared lexicography (*huios* and *huiothesia*) provides apt verbal means for profiling filial gospel grace. All that Jesus Christ, the *Huios* par excellence, is and acquires in his transforming resurrection comes to those redeemed *huioi* united to him. *Adoption as sons*, then, sustains the exquisite filio-Christological connection, and comprises the comprehensive sons-in-the-Son theology of the apostle Paul. To express the Spirit-wrought concatenation of the sons with the Son, the apostle Paul exercises a theological *possessio* of *huiothesia*, and thereby makes explicit the *in Christ* union in all its redemptive-historical, eschatological, and filial

---

45. Cf. Cook, "Conception of Adoption," 139–40.

46. "It may be significant that he chose a word that contains the word (υἱός, *huios*), which means 'son.' His use of a term that invokes adopted *sonship* may have linked the term with other masculine terms in Romans, such as 'seed' and 'circumcision.'" Michelle J. Morris, "Adoption," in *The Lexham Bible Dictionary*, ed. J. D. Barry, L. Wentz, D. Mangum, C. Sinclair-Wolcott, R. Klippenstein, D. Bomar, and D. R. Brown (Bellingham, WA: Lexham Press, 2012–14).

richness. The *ordo salutis*, as we will see, is *salus filiorum* ("salvation of/for the sons") because the *historia salutis* is *salus Filio* ("salvation in/by the Son").

Before we turn to the five *huiothesian* texts that elucidate Paul's sons-in-the-Son gospel, an important contemporary contextual comment is in order. As does modern culture at large, modern academia prefers to neutralize gender whenever possible. It might seem preferable to employ "adopted child" or some other gender-neutral formulation in the translation and derivations of *huiothesia*. As noted already, however, the Greek term for "adoption," *huiothesia*, contains the masculine term *huios*. While in some cases gender-neutral terms may properly convey the meaning and organic (intracanonical) theology in biblical revelation, the use of *huiothesia* is generally not one of those cases.

Because the shared etymology between *huios* and *huiothesia* aligns the redeemed sons of God with the redeeming Son of God, opting for a gender-neutral term in English muddles this verbally poignant Son/sons solidarity. Since Christ is not *teknon*, the chosen conception for filial grace is not *teknothesia*.[47] To preserve this sons-in-the-Son solidarity that shapes Pauline theology, I will normally use the word *son*, while celebrating how the Pauline adoption concept unambiguously indicates privilege for both male and female (2 Cor. 6:18; cf. Gal. 3:25–27). In fact, at times Paul speaks of the *huioi* as *tekna* (e.g., Rom. 8:15–17); we can be assured that Paul's choice of *huiothesia* and *huioi* representing both sexes perpetuates no gender bias and divulges no misogyny. With its etymological composition, *huiothesia* prominently serves his pervasive *in Christ* soteriology in a way that should govern our understanding of both *tekna* and *huioi* as they reference the redeemed people of God.[48]

---

47. Cf. Judith Evans Grubbs and Tim Parkin, eds., *The Oxford Handbook of Childhood and Education in the Classical World* (Oxford: Oxford University Press, 2013), 519–20.

48. Some feminist theologians have complained that Paul's choice of *huiothesia* betrays his male chauvinism: "Paul's affirmation of the special relationship of Christians to God as children and heirs is based on his notion of their 'adoption as sons' (υἱοθεσία [*huiothesia*]), and the evidence suggests that this legal term that he employs had an exclusive, not inclusive, meaning. Paul's use of υἱοθεσία [*huiothesia*] marginalizes women's experience. Since it seems never to have been used to indicate a woman's adoption to insure inheritance rights, the term implies that women must 'become male' before they can become heirs to God

In short, the gender-specific *sons* speaks without an iota of prejudice against the "daughters." In fact, the very opposite is true. Paul will argue that in this *Son*, the sons of God are neither male nor female; all are *one* in the *one* Son (Gal. 3:27–29). Men, women, slaves, and free—all the redeemed are sons in the Son. The selection of "son" (*huios*) or "sons" (*huioi*) serves Paul's purpose to expose the inviolable, indissoluble filial solidarity of the redeemed with the Redeemer. Just as the Pauline label of the church as the bride of Christ (Eph. 5:21–32) does not exclude males, the choice of *huios* does not eliminate or alienate believing females, who are also the sons of God. Though the complaints about sexism might well be gagged purely by calling into question contemporary bias, Paul's gender-indeterminate solidaric theological framework muzzles any perceived male chauvinism on its own.[49]

Adoptive grace extends to both genders, and in contradistinction to the model of Roman *huiothesia*, divine adoption serves to improve not the destiny of the Father (as if that were possible) but rather the destiny of the adopted sons—males and females alike. Furthermore, it is not as though Paul avoids gender-neutral terms such as *tekna* ("children"; cf. Rom. 8:17), which he uses interchangeably at points with *huioi*, but his gospel-union paradigm prefers *huios* and *huioi* because at its core the full redemptive inheritance by the Spirit of adoption (v. 15) comes to the redeemed *sons* (*huioi*) in union with Christ *the Son* (*huios*). These sons in the Son are of both sexes: the sons of God (the *huioi tou theou*) are the children of God (the *tekna tou theou*).

---

and joint heirs with Christ." Cristina Grenholm and Daniel Patte, eds., *Gender, Tradition and Romans: Shared Ground, Uncertain Borders* (New York: T&T Clark, 2005), 29–30. But the cultural presuppositions behind this assessment create a problem not present in Pauline theology. The theology of union for men and women with the Son of God dominates the selection of this term. Paul clearly intends gender inclusivism (Gal. 3:28).

49. Several feminist theologians insist that the maleness of Jesus itself creates gender prejudice and even makes impossible the efficacy of his substitutionary redemptive work for women. See, e.g., Rosemary Radford Ruether, *Sexism and God-Talk: Toward a Feminist Theology* (Boston: Beacon Press, 1983); Rosemary Radford Ruether, "The Liberation of Christology from Patriarchy," in *Feminist Theology: A Reader*, ed. Ann Loades (Louisville, KY: Westminster John Knox, 1990). Addressing this inflammatory and theologically convoluted question goes well beyond the purpose of this volume, but we recognize Scripture's clear teaching about the efficacy of the redemptive work of Jesus Christ for all his people—men, women, and children.

With his redemptive-historical, eschatological framework and his doxological and pastoral zeal, the apostle Paul celebrates the grace of adoption in the Son of God by calling on a feature-rich Roman cultural practice. *Huiothesia*, as will become clear in the subsequent theological exposition, captures the whole scope of filial grace enjoyed by means of the Spirit-wrought union with the resurrected Son of God. To state it otherwise, adoption moves in the full orbit of union with Christ,[50] and offers a comprehensive filial complex, divulging the filially framed forensic and transformative contours of this union. To appreciate this full orbit requires an examination of the vast theological horizons covered by the fivefold *huiothesian* constellation.

50. John Murray, *Redemption Accomplished and Applied* (Grand Rapids: Eerdmans, 1955), 170.

PART 2

ADOPTION: AN EXEGETICAL AND THEOLOGICAL SURVEY OF THE KEY TEXTS

4

ADOPTION PURPOSED:
FATHER, SON, AND HOLY SPIRIT

Blessed be the God and Father of our Lord Jesus Christ, who has blessed us in Christ with every spiritual blessing in the heavenly places, even as he chose us in him before the foundation of the world, that we should be holy and blameless before him. In love he predestined us for adoption as sons through Jesus Christ, according to the purpose of his will, to the praise of his glorious grace, with which he has blessed us in the Beloved. (Eph. 1:3–6)

Ephesians: Paul, the Gospel, and the Church

Francis Foulkes tersely captures the imposing gravitas of Ephesians: "In many respects Ephesians . . . is like a sermon on the greatest and widest theme possible for a Christian sermon—the eternal purpose of God which he is fulfilling through his Son Jesus Christ, and working out in and through the church."[1] With a cosmic outlook, this letter specifies vital connections between redemption purposed, redemption accomplished, and redemption applied. Making the invisible visible, bringing the celestial to the terrestrial, and revealing divine grace on the fallen sons of Adam, Ephesians unwaveringly grounds the work and application of redemption in the pretemporal purposes of the triune God. Elevating the reader from the limitations of human

---

1. Francis Foulkes, *The Letter of Paul to the Ephesians: An Introduction and Commentary*, 2nd ed., TNTC (Downers Grove, IL: InterVarsity Press, 1989), 20.

investigation, the apostle Paul by the Spirit of Christ opens windows into heaven itself. In view of how Paul consistently assumes, affirms, and appropriates pretemporal divine purpose for his explication of all reality (e.g., Rom. 9:10–26; Phil. 2:1–11; 2 Thess. 2:13–14; 2 Tim. 1:9; Titus 1:1–2), such Trinitarian emphasis in Ephesians should come as no surprise. Yet the exposé in the opening chapter of this letter elucidates, more than anywhere else in the Pauline corpus, the interface between heaven and earth. Triune mystery in heaven finds expression in the triune mastery of redemption on earth. Therefore, the only proper orientation for interpreting our world and our place in it is humble receptivity, as we function consciously as creatures who depend on the eternal God and his authoritatively interpretive words about creation, redemption, and consummation. That in grace he reveals himself as a merciful Father to his chosen people situates the entire apostolic message preached and inscripturated.

Before exploring the pretemporal *raison d'être* for the familial cast of the gospel in Ephesians, that is, Paul's placement of *huiothesia* in its eternal context, it is necessary to determine whether the apostle Paul actually wrote this letter. With the contemporary disputes over its authenticity, contending for *huiothesia* in Ephesians as Pauline requires explicit affirmation of Paul's authorship of the epistle. To put it straightforwardly, Pauline authorship of Ephesians finds little sympathy in contemporary scholarship. Employing an assortment of arguments that have garnered cumulative weight, modern scholars commonly reject the epistle's authenticity.[2]

Despite such formidable opposition, affirmation of Paul's authorship remains a legitimate, and in my view the most plausible, option. Contrary to certain scholarly pushback, myriad data afford persuasive evidence to uphold the authenticity of Ephesians. An ardent and informed group of scholars still maintains Pauline authorship

---

2. Ibid., 19–48; Samuel G. Shepard, "The Pauline Doctrine of Sonship" (Ph.D. diss., Southern Baptist Theological Seminary, Louisville, KY, 1951), 2–3. Some authors, such as Best and Lincoln, after weighing the internal and external evidence, choose to remain noncommittal on the identity of the author of Ephesians, leaving Pauline authorship as somewhat plausible but not probable. See Ernest Best, *A Critical and Exegetical Commentary on Ephesians*, ICC (Edinburgh: T&T Clark, 1998), 6–46; Andrew T. Lincoln, *Ephesians*, WBC 42 (Dallas: Word, 1990), lix–lxxiii.

of this letter,[3] which "has the earliest attestation of any book in the NT."[4] Donald Guthrie rightly concludes, "When all the objections are carefully considered it will be seen that the weight of evidence is inadequate to overthrow the overwhelming external attestation to Pauline authorship, and the epistle's own claims."[5] Making the decision a matter of indifference by citing the "authorial fallacy" and distinguishing a "historical" from a "canonical"[6] Paul fails to satisfy.[7] Internal and external evidence warrants confidence in Pauline authorship, the denial of which renders deleterious effects on the self-attesting authority and reliability of Scripture. Nor is the reader spared these consequences. By rejecting Pauline authorship, one positions oneself in a place of injudicious autonomy in the handling of Scripture. Furthermore, Ephesians expands and enriches themes introduced in other Pauline letters, and to rend this epistle from Paul's corpus is to militate against the Spirit-guided preservation of the apostle's teaching. For our concerns, rejecting the authenticity of Ephesians compromises the rich protological-to-eschatological contours of adoption implicit elsewhere in Paul but made explicit in the opening section of this letter.

Received as authentic, this epistle delivers fuller exposure to the Christological, pneumatological, soteriological, eschatological, and

---

3. Harold W. Hoehner, *Ephesians: An Exegetical Commentary* (Grand Rapids: Baker Academic, 2002), 1–61; cf. Clinton E. Arnold, *Ephesians*, ZEC 10 (Grand Rapids: Zondervan, 2010), 46–50; William Sanday and Arthur C. Headlam, *A Critical and Exegetical Commentary on the Epistle to the Romans*, 5th ed., ICC (Edinburgh: T&T Clark, 1902), liv–lxiii; E. K. Simpson and F. F. Bruce, *Commentary on the Epistles to the Ephesians and the Colossians: The English Text with Introduction, Exposition, and Notes*, NICNT (Grand Rapids: Eerdmans, 1957), 18; Charles Hodge, Commentary on the Epistle to the Ephesians (Old Tappan, NJ: Fleming H. Revell, 1980), xv–xvii; William Hendriksen, "Exposition of Ephesians," in *Galatians and Ephesians*, NTC (repr., Grand Rapids: Baker, 1979), 53–56; A. Skevington Wood, *Ephesians*, Expositor's Bible Commentary 11 (Grand Rapids: Zondervan, 1978), 3–9. Cf. Brooke Foss Westcott, *Saint Paul's Epistle to the Ephesians: The Greek Text with Notes and Addenda* (London: Macmillan, 1906; repr., Minneapolis: Klock & Klock, 1978), xxv–xxxvi.

4. Hoehner, *Ephesians*, 60.

5. Donald Guthrie, *New Testament Introduction*, 4th ed. (Downers Grove, IL: InterVarsity Press, 1990), 527.

6. Some scholars who doubt Pauline authorship still recognize Ephesians as a part of the genuine Pauline corpus, so that "Ephesians is already part of the 'canonical' Paul, whatever its relation to the 'historical' Paul." Lincoln, *Ephesians*, lxxiii.

7. Ibid.

ecclesiological rigor of Pauline theology. As the epistle that discloses the most expansive New Testament teaching on the church,[8] Ephesians delves into the deep structures of a Christ-centered ecclesiology and the Spirit-of-Christ-enabled family life of the people of God (Eph. 4–6). With particular focus on the realized dimensions of eschatology (see Eph. 1:15–23; 6:10–20), the letter to the Ephesians insists on gospel living in Christ that corresponds to the cosmic, kingdom-securing, peace-producing, once-for-all dynamic of redemption wrought in the Lord Jesus Christ, the Son of God (1:7, 20–23; 2:6, 14–16; 4:8–10), as applied by the Holy Spirit (1:13–14; cf. 4:3; 5:18) to the redeemed sons of God. God's redeemed people make up a new community, a new eschatological body of Jews and Gentiles, a new *family of adopted saints* united to the Lord Jesus Christ by grace through faith. This redeemed communion of saints enjoys an unprecedented, divinely created familial dynamic of grace, love, holiness, and unity (4:1–6), by virtue of the exaltation of their Elder Brother Jesus Christ in his resurrection power and glory (1:15–23). At the gateway of Pauline thought is how Christ Jesus secured adoption for the fallen sons of Adam, according to the perfect divine *plan*.

The Divine Plan of Redemption in Christ

Divine Counsel and Salvation History

Salvation history unfolds because of divine pretemporal purpose: "salvation is not an afterthought but part of the divine plan from the beginning."[9] The redemption that God ordained in a single pretemporal decree he also works out flawlessly (Eph. 1:11b, *ta panta energountos kata tēn boulēn tou thelēmatos autou*: "who works all things according to the counsel of his will").[10] In the opening of Ephesians, the absolute yet gracious sovereignty of God in salvation comes to the forefront even by Paul's choice of words, *exelexato* ("chose," v. 4),

---

8. "In the whole of the NT literature there is nowhere an ecclesiology which is so extensively structured or which is revealed so effectively as that in the Epistle to the Ephesians." Rudolf Schnackenburg, *Ephesians: A Commentary* (Edinburgh: T&T Clark, 1991), 293.

9. Best, *Critical and Exegetical Commentary on Ephesians*, 51. Cf. ibid., 119.

10. See Francis Turretin, *Institutes of Elenctic Theology*, ed. James T. Dennison Jr., trans. George Musgrave Giger, 3 vols. (Phillipsburg, NJ: P&R Publishing, 1992–94), 1:320–22.

proorisas ("predestined," v. 5), *prooristhentes* ("having been predestined," v. 11), *eudokian* ("purpose," vv. 5, 9), and *thelēmatos* ("will," vv. 5, 9, 11). Because of God's supreme sovereignty, paternal purposes, and covenantal self-binding, no disparity exists *or even could exist* between the free ordination and the free accomplishment of his will: "Our God is in the heavens; he does all that he pleases" (Ps. 115:3). As the pages of Scripture uniformly contend, the work of God in history is for the salvation of his people, something that he accomplishes effectively and flawlessly and, in fact, that brings him glory (Eph. 1:6, 12, 14).

To put it otherwise, as the opening words of Ephesians affirm, without the all-wise counsel and eternal purpose in the mind of God, redemption would never have happened. Following this theme, "Ephesians 3:11 refers to this 'eternal purpose' (*prothesin tōn aiōnōn*) with an adjective in the genitive case, indicating that there was never a time when God's plan with all of its parts was not fully determined."[11] To be clear, the singular divine counsel brings about "all things that exist or will occur,"[12] but Scripture gives specific attention to the purpose of God in redemption. In holy wisdom, the eternal Trinitarian God puts in irreversible motion his gracious, loving, and saving work in Christ Jesus. "There is, in the Godhead, quite apart from creation, a free, voluntary agreement that he—Father, Son, and Holy Spirit—in the person of the Son, will condescend to relate to his creation and to save a people for himself, and all to his own glory. This work began in eternity."[13] The glorious work culminates efficaciously in accordance with his eternal purpose in and through his own Son.

Unique in the scope of its explicit pretemporal contours, Ephesians like the other Pauline Epistles makes prominent the *actualization* of the redemptive plan in Christ. The message of the New Testament centers on the accomplishment of redemption in the Son of God, but as Paul explicates in the opening verses of Ephesians 1, this accomplishment

---

11. Adam Sparks, "Salvation History, Chronology, and Crisis: A Problem with Inclusivist Theology of Religions, Part 1 of 2," *Themelios* 33, 2 (2008): 9. Cf. Herman Bavinck, *Reformed Dogmatics*, ed. John Bolt, trans. John Vriend, 4 vols. (Grand Rapids: Baker, 2006), 3:274.

12. Bavinck, *Reformed Dogmatics*, 2:373.

13. K. Scott Oliphint, *God with Us: Divine Condescension and the Attributes of God* (Wheaton, IL: Crossway, 2012), 109.

fulfills divine purpose for the gracious application of redemption to sinners, a purpose grounded in eternity past. Grace incarnated in history, because before even a blink of world history, God had determined to act in grace for his glory. That sovereign determination set in motion and secured with certainty his gracious purpose on earth.

The Covenant of Grace

Put in more classically Reformed language, God's dealings with his people throughout history occur by his covenant grace or *covenant of grace*. In Christ Jesus, this covenant of grace comes to its eschatological realization, because God ordained the accomplishment of redemption to occur in his covenant Son.[14] Though the term *covenant* is not found in Ephesians 1:3–14, historic Reformed hermeneutics has avoided the word-concept fallacy, and discerned that the redemptive decree of the triune God was accomplished in an intra-Trinitarian covenant— the *pactum salutis* ("covenant of redemption" or "covenant of peace").[15] As Berkhof representatively concludes, "The counsel of redemption [*pactum salutis*] is the eternal prototype of the historical covenant of grace . . . ; [it is] the firm and eternal foundation of the covenant of grace, [and it] gives efficacy to the covenant of grace, for in it the means are provided for the establishment and execution of the latter."[16] Concerning this pretemporal intra-Trinitarian covenant, he continues:

14. See Geerhardus Vos, "The Doctrine of the Covenant in Reformed Theology," in *Redemptive History and Biblical Interpretation: The Shorter Writings of Geerhardus Vos*, ed. Richard B. Gaffin Jr. (Phillipsburg, NJ: Presbyterian and Reformed, 1980); Oliphint, *God with Us*, 106–8.

15. See R. L. Dabney, *Syllabus and Notes of the Course of Systematic and Polemic Theology*, 2nd ed. (St. Louis: Presbyterian Publishing, 1878; repr., Edinburgh: Banner of Truth, 1996), 432; Charles Hodge, *Systematic Theology*, 3 vols. (Grand Rapids: Eerdmans, 1979), 2:360; Heinrich Heppe, *Reformed Dogmatics Set Out and Illustrated from the Sources*, ed. Ernst Bizer, trans. G. T. Thomson, rev. ed. (Grand Rapids: Baker, 1978), 374–82, 411; Peter A. Lillback, *The Binding of God: Calvin's Role in the Development of Covenant Theology*, ed. Richard A. Muller, Texts and Studies in Reformation and Post-Reformation Thought (Grand Rapids: Baker Academic, 2001), 212–14; Thomas F. Torrance, *The Christian Doctrine of God: One Being Three Persons* (Edinburgh: T&T Clark, 1996), 219–20; Robert E. Wermuth, "The Doctrine of Adoption in Paul's Ephesian Letter" (unpublished master's thesis, Covenant Theological Seminary, St. Louis, 1985), 36; J. Mark Beach, "The Doctrine of the *Pactum Salutis* in the Covenant Theology of Herman Witsius," *Mid-America Journal of Theology* 13 (2002): 101–42.

16. Louis Berkhof, *Systematic Theology*, 4th ed. (Grand Rapids: Eerdmans, 1949), 270.

Now we find that in the economy of redemption there is, in a sense, a division of labor: the Father is the originator, the Son the executor, and the Holy Spirit the applier. This can only be the result of a voluntary agreement among the persons of the Trinity, so that their internal relations assume the form of a covenant life. In fact, it is exactly in the Trinitarian life that we find the archetype of the historical covenants, a covenant in the proper and fullest sense of the word, the parties meeting on a footing of equality, a true *suntheke*.[17]

By deducing this intra-Trinitarian covenant in Ephesians 1, we see that a vital connection between God's elective decree and God's fatherhood becomes contextually explicit (Eph. 1:3–5).

Divine decree, election, and predestination actuate by the *Father*, and through the *Son* are lovingly carried out covenantally on the historical stage of creation, redemption, and consummation. The *Holy Spirit* applies this divine covenant to those recipients of elective grace. Covenantal accomplishment and application in history then attain precisely according to the eternal pact, in which the members of the Trinity covenant to the accomplishment and application of redemption. As revealed to the apostle Paul concerning the divine pretemporal counsel, predestination is a family matter—the Father through the Son by the Spirit redeeming people for himself, a people that he creates by his covenantal grace to be his sons and daughters (2 Cor. 6:14–18). This familial work, as expressed in prophetic and apostolic revelation, unveils him as Father, Son, and Holy Spirit. Coerced by none, the triune God works according to his infinite wisdom and by his own kind initiative to create his redeemed family. The perfectly purposed, accomplished, and applied redemption occurs exclusively out of divine pleasure and divine love.

Exploring the comprehensive scope of Ephesians 1:3–14, Westcott identifies a progressive sequence framed entirely by the archetypal *love* of the Trinity: "The work of the Divine love is summarily characterised in v. 3; and then it is analysed in detail as it was wrought beyond time in the eternal order (vv. 4–6), and then historically realised in time

17. Ibid., 266.

in the experience of believers, both Jews and Gentiles (vv. 7–14)."[18] Put somewhat differently, the Trinitarian God works redemption in seamless solidarity:[19] the Father lovingly ordains his eternal purposes (vv. 3–6), the Son willingly and lovingly carries out these purposes on the stage of history (vv. 7–12), and with love outpoured (cf. Rom. 5:5) the Holy Spirit applies the ordained and effected purposes of the Father (Eph. 1:13–14).[20] With no qualification whatsoever, "the atonement in none of its aspects can be properly viewed apart from the love of God as the source from which it springs."[21] Love enacted in eternity past becomes love manifest in history, and a love that triumphs for eternity future. For the apostle Paul, as verbalized in Ephesians 1, the loving purpose of the triune God sustains its integrity in the execution of the covenant of grace, maintaining flawless calibration between the divine plan (pretemporal/protological context) and the divine result (the realized eschatological consummation).

Thus, according to the all-wise and loving plan of God, the *pactum salutis* determines, effects, and procures the covenant of grace. As revelation moves from heaven to earth, its light beams on Christ

---

18. Westcott, *Saint Paul's Epistle to the Ephesians*, 4.

19. "All the persons of the blessed Trinity had a part in this amazing transaction." Thomas Houston, *The Adoption of Sons, Its Nature, Spirit, Privileges and Effects: A Practical and Experimental Treatise* (Paisley, Scotland: Alex. Gardner, 1872), 28. Cf. Herman Bavinck, *In the Beginning: Foundations of Creation Theology*, ed. John Bolt, trans. John Vriend (Grand Rapids: Baker, 1999), 45; Samuel J. Baird, *The Elohim Revealed in the Creation and Redemption of Man* (Philadelphia: Parry & McMillan, 1860), 665; Torrance, *Christian Doctrine of God*, 2; Robert C. Dorman, "A Study of Paul's Use of *Hyiothesia*: Its Background, Development, and Importance concerning Spiritual Adoption" (unpublished master's thesis, Covenant Theological Seminary, St. Louis, 1997), 52–53.

20. "The Spirit of Yahweh is not a self-existent agent operating independently." Daniel Block, "The Prophet of the Spirit: The Use of *RWH* in the Book of Ezekiel," *JETS* 32, 1 (1989): 48.

21. John Murray, *The Collected Writings of John Murray*, 4 vols. (Edinburgh: Banner of Truth, 1976–82), 1:62. Murray continues, "The atonement springs from the fountain of the Father's love; He commends His own love towards us. We must not think, however, that the action of the Father ended with the appointment and commission of the Son. He was not a mere spectator of Gethsemane and Calvary. The Father laid upon His own Son the iniquities of us all. He spared not His own Son but delivered Him up. He made Him to be sin for us. It was the Father who gave Him the cup of damnation to drink. God was in Christ reconciling the world to Himself. Here is love supremely demonstrated." John Murray, "The Atonement," http://www.graceonlinelibrary.org/doctrine-theology/the-atonement/the-atonement-by-john-murray/ (accessed January 19, 2015).

Jesus, the beloved Son of God. According to divine revelatory purpose, the willing and winning work of redemptive history's protagonist, Jesus Christ, becomes the central theme of the gospel (cf. 1 Cor. 15:1–3). Through the work of his Son and by his Spirit, the Father lovingly redeems and gathers Jews and Gentiles unto himself as one family (Eph. 2:11–22; 4:1–6), a family of adopted sons and daughters.

The Father's Loving Purpose and Huiothesia

Within its pretemporal-to-consummation outlook, this Pauline epistle characterizes the New Testament's brimming *familial* orientation. The family motif of choice for the apostle Paul is *huiothesia*. Ephesians gives *huiothesia* its Trinitarian, pretemporal, and substructural parentage, theologically informing all of Paul's other expressions of the concept. In an important sense, this epistle authenticates the redemptive prominence of adoption by showing how it lies squarely in the cosmic and loving purposes of God the Father from eternity past. Hence, while the other *huiothesian* texts place adoption within redemptive history, Ephesians 1:5 overtly discloses its origin in the eternal purposes of the triune God. In his excavation of the divinely predetermined soteriological plan, Paul supplies this supramundane keystone of *huiothesia*, a fact warranting further consideration of its function in Ephesians 1.

The apostle Paul boldly affirms the heavenly rationale for the divine adoption of the sons. According to Ephesians 1:5:

> God has chosen us and has predestined us to adoption "to himself" (*eis auton*). This ties in with love as the basis for his predestinating act and reinforces the idea that he views his people as his own glorious inheritance (Eph 1:18). The final purpose of election then is relational. God is bringing together a people whom he can delight in and enjoy.[22]

Rightly understood, divine enjoyment of his redeemed people implies no desiderata in the self-contained and self-sufficient God of Scripture. Father, Son, and Holy Spirit, of course, need nothing. This love of

---

22. Arnold, *Ephesians*, 82–83.

the redeemed, however, speaks instead of divine covenant purposes to secure this relational and familial grace for the sons in the Son. "Adoption is an act of God's free grace and excludes all human merit; it is absolutely *sola gratia.*"[23] As the self-contained and self-sufficient God, God is compelled by nothing outside himself. His love is pure, self-generated, and perfect; the motive for adopting sons flows from this divine love. God does not need the sons, but he everlastingly loves them, from eternity past to eternity future, by virtue of the promised and accomplished redemption through his own Son.

As Scripture makes clear, God's sovereign decree governs the entire scope of redemption. Some have critiqued Calvin and other Reformed theologians' explication of the divine elective decree, contending not only for an unforgivable determinism but, even worse, for a cold and heartless god. Such criticisms have disastrously (and unbiblically!) failed to acknowledge the indispensable fatherly context of predestination. Despite caricatures to the contrary, the best of Reformed theology has never ripped election from divine love.[24] Even among those who have understated the grace of adoption, cold and loveless determinism does not apply to historic Reformed orthodoxy, let alone to John Calvin himself. Following Paul's lead in Ephesians 1, "Calvin understood predestination to serve as the protological context of *adoption.* This is evident from the regularity with which Calvin mentions predestination in connection with Ephesians 1:4–5 (his *locus classicus* of predestination)."[25] Adoption and predestination function inseparably (Eph. 1:5). Predestination is *unto* adoption, and in Pauline soteriology no element of sovereignty in salvation eludes the filial grace in which this divine initiative is expressed. The origin of *adoption* itself,

23. John Theodore Mueller, "Adoption," *Christianity Today* 6 (1962): 22.

24. Speculation about divine volition and the divine mind has frequently turned treatments of divine predestination into philosophical abstraction, away from its biblical moorings. Concerning philosophy and predestination, see, for example, Margaret J. Osler, *Divine Will and the Mechanical Philosophy: Gassendi and Descartes on Contingency and Necessity in the Created World* (Cambridge: Cambridge University Press, 1994).

25. Tim J. R. Trumper, "Adoption: The Forgotten Doctrine of Westminster Soteriology," in *Reformed Theology in Contemporary Perspective,* ed. Lynn Quigley (Edinburgh: Rutherford House, 2006), 99. For more on Calvin and predestination, see Charles Partee, *The Theology of John Calvin* (Louisville, KY: Westminster John Knox, 2008), 240–49; Paul Helm, *John Calvin's Ideas* (Oxford: Oxford University Press, 2004).

then, lies in the pretemporal loving decree, when God the Father in love[26] ordained lost sons of Adam to become his family through his own incarnate Son. There is no biblical predestination outside biblical adoption; adoption frames predestination within the *love* of God the Father, God the Son, and God the Spirit.

Jesus Christ and the Holy Spirit: Adoption, Holiness, and Inheritance

Adoption and the Work of Christ

Consistent with Paul's Christological focus throughout his theology of redemption (cf. Col. 1:15–20; 2:8–10), Ephesians 1 celebrates the redemptive work of the Son (Eph. 1:3, 5, 10).[27] Paul, in his discussion of the heavenly covenant (the *pactum salutis* discussed above), extols God as *Father* and Jesus as his *Son* (Eph. 1:3), and it is through the Father's own beloved Son (Eph. 1:6) that predestined lost sons of Adam become adopted sons. Christ's messianic work performs on center stage in the unfolding drama of redemptive history, and in his role as messianic Son[28] he efficiently secures the adoption[29] of the sons whom the Father has chosen.

In the final chapters of this book (chapters 7–10), I will consider more fully the way in which adoption actually comes to believers through the beloved Son. For now, I simply note that in this Ephesian doxology, Christ is the source of the believers' adoption, and therefore,

26. Hodge, *Commentary on Ephesians*, 34–35, properly identifies the final phrase *en agapē* ("in love," 1:4) with the preceding clause, rather than with what follows in 1:5. To attach *en agapē* to the clause in 1:5 is manifestly tautological in view of the phrase *kata tēn eudokian tou thelēmato autou* ("according to the purpose of his will," 1:5).

27. In addition to the explicit references to Christ's redemptive work, the repetition of *en Christō* ("in Christ") and variations of *en auto* ("in him") throughout this eulogy (eleven times in twelve verses) demonstrates the Christological centrality. See Hodge, *Commentary on Ephesians*, 30.

28. "The phrase 'God and Father of our Lord Jesus Christ' [1:3] seems to express the double filiation of the Son, His trinitarian Sonship and that of His humanity as the Sent of the Father." Simpson and Bruce, *Ephesians and Colossians*, 24. Cf. Hodge, *Commentary on Ephesians*, 27. Further, the shift of emphasis in the passage from Christ's eternal sonship to his messianic sonship occurs simultaneously with the shift from pretemporal determination to redemptive-historical accomplishment.

29. Cf. Westcott, *Saint Paul's Epistle to the Ephesians*, 10.

apart from him, there would be no adoption. The Son made incarnate answers the call to effect the *pactum salutis*. In short, by divine decree adoption of the sons obtains in the loving, selfless, and all-sufficient *work* of the Son of God. Adoption accomplished relies wholly on him, and in him redemptive grace gains traction on the stage of history.

Adoption and the Eschatological "Heavenly Places"

Enfleshing this eternally purposed divine love (Eph. 1:4–5),[30] Christ came (Eph. 1:7; cf. Gal. 4:4), lived, died, and was raised from the dead. The perfect sacrificing and sacrificed Son, he gave himself for the sake of the corrupted and guilty sons of Adam. In his humiliation and exaltation he accomplished redemption and secured the eschatological *in caelestibus* (*en tois epouraniois,* "in the heavenly places," in Ephesians 1:3; 1:20; 2:6; 3:10; and 6:12) spiritual blessings of salvation for those united to him.[31] In view of the cosmically significant, redemptive-historical thrust of Paul's argumentation,

> the heavenly realms in Ephesians are to be seen in the perspective of the age to come, which has been inaugurated by God raising Christ from the dead and exalting him to his right hand. . . . The blessings can be said to be in the heavenly realms, yet they are not viewed as treasure stored up for future appropriation, but as benefits belonging to believers now.[32]

Care must be taken not to read into this phrase abiblical Greek philosophical dualism. Instead, the "heavenly places" should generally be taken as a temporally conditioned dative of sphere/location, with full tethering to the new order of things brought in the consummate eschatological success of the Son of God.[33] "The resurrection

---

30. This love is not based on some foreseen worthiness in the recipients, but rather based on the worthiness of the Redeemer who is their federal Head. "It is, there, in Christ, i.e., as united to him in the covenant of redemption, that the people of God are elected to eternal life and to all blessings therewith connected." Hodge, *Commentary on Ephesians,* 31.

31. Geerhardus Vos, *The Pauline Eschatology* (Princeton, NJ: Princeton University Press, 1930), 38–40.

32. Lincoln, *Ephesians,* 21.

33. Unique to Ephesians, the peculiar phrase *en tois epouraniois* ("in the heavenly places"),

of Christ is the beginning of the new and final world-order, an order described as spiritual and heavenly. It is the dawn of the new creation, the start of the eschatological age. In terms of the conceptual framework with which Paul view[s] the whole of history, it is the commencement of the 'age-to-come'."[34] With this unique *in caelestibus* concept, Paul underscores the cosmic and kingdom dimensions of Christ's work and the comprehensive impact of that work for those united to him, as they *now* enjoy *to huperballon megethos tēs dunameōs* ("the immeasurable greatness of his power," Eph. 1:19) by Christ's victory over sin and death. The filial face of this redemptive victory pervades the theological landscape of both Old and New Testaments (see, e.g., 2 Sam. 7:8–14; Ps. 2; Rom. 1:3–4; Heb. 2:10–18; 4:14–16; 5:7–10).

By the ministry of the Spirit (Eph. 1:13–14), the believer is united to the victorious Son and thereby drawn into the heavenly places where the already-resurrected Son has ascended (1:15–23; cf. 1:3, 20; 2:6; 3:10; 6:12). The full realization of these heavenly benefits, however, awaits the redemptive consummation. For now, the believer resides in an inaugurated eschatological state, living in the tension between this age and the age to come.[35] But Paul intends in Ephesians to enlighten believers to the comprehensive contemporary relevance of the Son's resurrection and session (1:15–23; 2:6; 6:12). The scope of God's saving purpose in Christ is cosmic and complete: heaven and earth unite (1:10) according to eternal purpose realized in God's saving purpose in his Son (1:5–7). "The summing up of all things in Christ means the unifying of the cosmos or its direction toward

---

according to Westcott (*Saint Paul's Epistle to the Ephesians*, 7), "describes the supra-mundane, supra-sensual, eternal order." Cf. Geerhardus Vos, "The Eschatological Aspect of the Pauline Conception of the Spirit," in *Redemptive History and Biblical Interpretation: The Shorter Writings of Geerhardus Vos*, ed. Richard B. Gaffin Jr. (Phillipsburg, NJ: Presbyterian and Reformed, 1980), 118n50. *Contra* Best, *Critical and Exegetical Commentary on Ephesians*, 117–18. Paul's usage of this phrase demonstrates that the eternally ordained realization of grace was to occur in the incarnate Christ in an unprecedented way redemptive-historically. The incarnation of the Son marks the penetration of the eternal order into the temporal/mundane (cf. Phil. 2:5–11), and effects the redemptive-historical transition from flesh to Spirit.

34. Sparks, "Salvation History, Chronology, and Crisis," 12–13.

35. See Vos, *Pauline Eschatology*, 38; M. M. B. Turner, "The Significance of Spirit Endowment for Paul," *VE* 9 (1975): 57, 60.

a common goal,"[36] the goal of sweet cosmic harmony, a harmony displayed by the Spirit-wrought unity and community of the sons of God in Christ (2:11–22; 4:1–32).

The redemptive-historical force of Christ's work brings ultimate eschatological blessing to bear on believers, the sons in the Son, right now. The eschatological age inaugurated in the Son of God now wholly characterizes the believers' outlook, because the resurrected Christ as Son of God par excellence has already secured adoption for the sons of God. The believers' adoption is both *now* and *not yet*, but by virtue of their union with the resurrected Son, the future determines current existence: familial identity, legal status (a member of the family of God), and filial/constitutional transformation (ongoing renewal in the Son of God by the life-giving Spirit, 1 Cor. 15:45). By pretemporal and therefore redemptive-historical necessity, such realized familial themes dominate the Ephesian letter because of the realized implications of filial grace secured for the sons in union with the Son (cf. Col. 1:13–14). By the Spirit of the resurrected Son outpoured (Rom. 5:5), such *in caelestibus* soteriology is wholly eschatological, wholly familial, and wholly transformational. In the exalted Son of God, the sons of God already taste of the supramundane, eternal order. Heaven has come to earth, the Son of God has ascended to the heavenly places (Eph. 1:15–23), and the sons of God united with him in his resurrection (Eph. 2:6) enjoy the filial blessing, joy, and spiritual victory of *his* exalted state.

Adoption en Christō *("in Christ")*

Pauline soteriology centers in the believers' vital union with Jesus Christ.[37] "The central role of the Spirit is to reveal Christ and to unite us to him and to all those who participate in his body."[38] Variations on

---

36. Lincoln, *Ephesians*, 33. See also Frank Thielman, *Ephesians*, BECNT (Grand Rapids: Baker Academic, 2010), 67.

37. See, e.g., Marcus Peter Johnson, *One with Christ: An Evangelical Theology of Salvation* (Wheaton, IL: Crossway, 2013); Constantine R. Campbell, *Paul and Union with Christ: An Exegetical and Theological Study* (Grand Rapids: Zondervan, 2012); Robert Letham, *Union with Christ in Scripture, History, and Theology* (Phillipsburg, NJ: P&R Publishing, 2011); Robert A. Peterson, *Salvation Applied by the Spirit: Union with Christ* (Wheaton, IL: Crossway, 2015).

38. Sinclair B. Ferguson, *The Holy Spirit*, Contours of Christian Theology (Downers Grove, IL: InterVarsity Press, 1996), 100.

the redundant *in Christ* (*en Christō*) refrain throughout this epistle (and the Pauline corpus as a whole) expose the way in which Paul relishes Spirit-wrought redemptive solidarity of believers with the Lord Jesus Christ.[39] Using this pointed language of solidarity, Ephesians 1:4–5 focuses God's purposed love in the redeemed sons of God in union with the redeeming Son of God. Ecclesiology (union and communion of God's people in Christ) flows from soteriology; gospel vitality for the people of God relies on their solidaric union with the humiliated and exalted Lord Jesus Christ, the Son of God. In short, gospel blessing yields ecclesiological blessing *now*—redemptive, Spirit-wrought *in Christ*, sons-in-the-Son fellowship.

While God could have drawn the redeemed merely, yet gloriously, as slaves to himself,[40] he, according to his infinite love and wisdom, brought fullest glory to himself by adopting them as *sons*. By sovereign decree the Father determined to deliver those whom he redeemed from the kingdom of darkness into the kingdom of his beloved Son (Col. 1:13). This *huiothesia* through Christ the messianic Son (Eph. 1:5) actually serves as the supreme expression of praise (1:6). As Ephesians 2:19 puts it, God has granted believers a new citizenship, and even a new family: the redeemed are "members of the household of God." Adoptive grace is declarative and legal—the redeemed inherit a new citizenship and enter a new household with all the rights and privileges of sonship.

With a closer look, however, the purposes of this eschatological and Christological adoption extend beyond judicial, reconciling decree. The work of Christ as Son of God delivers more to the redeemed sons than legal and relational status. Despite the ostensible legal parameters embedded in common usage of *huiothesia*, biblical adoption's effects exceed the forensic. As an expression of the Father's redemptive purpose in Ephesians 1:4–5, Paul employs adoption in Christ Jesus to capture

---

39. Thirty-six times the epistle to the Ephesians employs such solidaric language: *en Christō* (1:3; 4:34); *en Christō Iēsou* (1:1; 2:6, 7, 10, 13; 3:6, 21); *en tō Christō* (1:10, 12, 20); *en tō Christō Iēsou* (3:11); *en tō Iēsou* (4:21); *en kuriō* (2:21; 4:1, 17; 5:8; 6:1, 10, 21); *en tō kuriō Iēsou* (1:15); *en autō* (1:4, 9, 10; 2:15, 16; 4:21); *en hō* (1:7, 11, 13 (2×); 2:21, 22; 3:12; 4:30). See Hoehner, *Ephesians*, 170–74.

40. For which even basic privilege he also ought to have been praised.

the filial character of transformative and renewing grace. Adoption changes status. It also changes hearts. It changes everything.

Adoption and Holiness

The relationship between election ("he chose us") and purity ("holy and blameless") in Ephesians 1:4 affirms a fundamental theological connection between the decretal/judicial and the transformative moral/ethical. Paul asserts that election involves an irreversible determination for the holiness of the redeemed. Hodge notes that this holiness and blamelessness "may be understood to refer to our justification, or to our sanctification." Though many take this passage only as a forensic declaration, the natural force of the text, as Hodge then concludes, indicates a genuine dispositional transformation: "propitiation is in order to holiness."[41] Westcott reaffirms the transformative force of the Pauline argument: "The use of the simple infinitive (*einai*) as distinguished from *eis to einai* (v. 12) marks the purpose as potentially realised and not simply as aimed at."[42] Use of the *to be* verb here suggests a change beyond that of a legal declaration and its relational implications. Instead, the apostle indicates that the divine pretemporal goal for the elect *is* real holiness. Put otherwise, the final goal of election is neither forensic nor merely aspirational, but actual and essential. The holiness determined is to be realized; the end of redemption for the sons in the Son of God entails *justification* and *sanctification* (*transformation*). According to divine purpose, the sons will become *like* the Son.

John Murray expresses this soteriological point in his treatment of definitive sanctification in Romans 6, and makes reference to Paul's letter to the Ephesians. His insights are worthy of extended quotation:

> The truth is that our death to sin and newness of life are effected in our identification with Christ in his death and resurrection, and no virtue accruing from the death and resurrection of Christ affects any phase of salvation more directly than the breach with

41. Hodge, *Commentary on Ephesians*, 33–34.
42. Westcott, *Saint Paul's Epistle to the Ephesians*, 9.

sin and newness of life. And if we do not take account of this direct relationship we miss one of the cardinal features of New Testament teaching. It is not only in Romans 6 that this comes to expression. It is no less patent, for example, in Ephesians 2:1–6. It is the quickening from death in trespasses and sins that is in the forefront when the apostle says: "But God being rich in mercy . . . hath made us alive together with Christ . . . and hath raised us up together." And again in 2 Corinthians 5:14, 15 this thought is clearly in view—the death and resurrection of Christ insure that those who are the beneficiaries live not to themselves but to him who died for them and rose again. In Colossians 2:20–3:4 the same doctrine is the basis of both rebuke and entreaty.[43]

Murray captures here the efficacy of Christ's redemptive work for the moral problem of sin's power in addition to the legal problem of guilt. Jesus Christ's death and resurrection overwhelm both, and by virtue of union with him, the redeemed possess *Christ's* resurrection power for victory over sin. Though this final victory awaits the final transformation (1 Cor. 15:35–49), the elect sons of God will surely "bear the image of the man of heaven" (v. 49b), Jesus, the resurrected Son of God.

Consistent with Murray's important articulation of "definitive sanctification," adoption occupies theological real estate here in regard to both the juridical/forensic and transformative power of Christ's resurrection. In the subsequent theological exegesis of Romans 8 concerning the Spirit of adoption, I will demonstrate this son-sanctification corollary more fully. For now, note that in Ephesians 1:5 the apostle demarcates the theological goal of predestination: divine predestination is *eis huiothesian* ("for adoption as sons"). Verses 4 and 5 reside in syntactically parallel fashion, creating an appositional relationship between the *election to holiness* ("he chose us in him before the foundation of the world, that we should be holy and blameless before him," 1:4) and *predestination unto adoption* ("he predestined us for adoption as sons," 1:5). Elective decree and predestination surely involve forensic change—God sovereignly determines a transfer of

43. John Murray, "Definitive Sanctification," *CTJ* 2, 1 (1967): 14.

redeemed sons into his family ("He has delivered us from the domain of darkness and transferred us to the kingdom of his beloved Son," Col. 1:13), counting the righteousness of the Son par excellence on their behalf. Once condemned in the domain of darkness, the redeemed sons enjoy a new status and a new familial identity.

But redemption's goal is not merely a judicially determinative placement and familial status change, but an unstinted filial and moral transformation. Redemption "in him" (Eph. 1:4), that is, "through Jesus Christ" (Eph. 1:5), produces *holy* sons (cf. 2 Cor. 7:1; Eph. 4:24; 5:27; 1 Thess. 3:13; 4:3–4, 7; Heb. 12:14; 2 Peter 3:11). In the theological logic of the New Testament, and in particular of the apostle Paul, to stand *katenōpion autou* ("before him," Eph. 1:4) requires filial identity *and* filial purity. Because of the divine goal of perfect redemption, the spiritual power of Christ's resurrection effects such transfer and *renovation* of the redeemed sons.

In sweeping fashion, Paul in this Ephesian doxology exposes the vital connection between *actual* holiness and adoption, concisely yet compellingly disclosing how the beloved Son secures filial holiness for the sons of God. It was the Son of God who secured such a mighty adoption; as Son, he lived and died in obedience, and as Son, he overwhelmed the power of sin and death in his own resurrection from the dead (Eph. 1:7, 20; cf. Rom. 1:3–4). His resurrection as Son delivers the full implications of that resurrection on those in solidarity with him; that is, he secures the resurrection, the full transformation, of the sons. Only in this all-encompassing transformation are the adopted "holy and blameless before him" (Eph. 1:4). The choice of "Beloved" (Eph. 1:6) in this context underscores the filial contours of this holy redemptive efficacy. Fatherly satisfaction in redemption required the Son of God to *obtain* holy sons. In other words, the holy purposes of sovereign election are realized only through Christ Jesus as Son of God, who effectuates and secures believers' Son-conforming adoption. The actual manner in which the biography of Jesus as Son functions as the basis for the believers' holy adoption receives fuller attention in the coming chapters.

A corresponding Pauline formulation is worthy of mention here. In parallel to Ephesians 1:5, Paul asserts in Romans 8:29 that the purpose of predestination (the verb *proorizō*, "predestine," appears in Romans 8:29 and in Ephesians 1:5) is conformity to the messianic Son: "For those whom he foreknew he also predestined to be conformed to the image of his Son, in order that he might be the firstborn among many brothers" (Rom. 8:29).[44] According to the logic and language of Romans 8, predestination unto adoption *is* predestination unto actual Son-likeness. Mawhinney suggests that "predestination to adoption is the 'how', or the mode, or the manner of election to holiness."[45] More than this, the shared adoption/resurrection of the sons in the Son marks the very holy purposes of solidarity with the Son of God. Sons are *made* holy by their union with the consecrated Son of God. Linking holiness and familial identity, Paul places adoption in the purposes of God to ensure a holy seed, whereby the holy sons may dwell in the presence of God their Father. Adoption in Christ ensures family identity and filial emulation; the sons of God are made like the Son of God. Ephesians 1:5 and Romans 8:29 express this filial identity and filial transformation in mutually informing fashion. In the Beloved, adopted sons become holy sons; by the Holy Spirit of adoption (Rom. 8:15), they conform fully to the image of their Elder Brother (Rom. 8:23–30; 1 Cor. 15:12–49). Election and predestination deliver filial transformation—legal and renovative—by filial grace.

Returning to the broader theological outlook, the Father's election of the sons unto purity and holiness precedes creation (*pro katabolēs kosmou*, "before the foundation of the world," Eph. 1:4), and thereby functions compatibly with the intended covenantal goal of adoption in its typological form—of Israel as corporately adopted son. By God's grace, the

> adoptive elective relationship between Yahweh and his people, enacted at the Exodus, is foundational for the Old Testament and, we may believe, was foundational as well for the theology of Paul.

44. This relationship between Ephesians 1:5 and Romans 8:29 is further developed in chapter 6.

45. Allen Mawhinney, "*Yiothesia* in the Pauline Epistles: Its Background, Use, and Implications" (Ph.D. diss., Baylor University, Waco, TX, 1982), 184. Highlighting the ethical implications, he adds, "Adoption is a call to live as sons of God." Ibid., 186.

It is therefore not surprising to encounter *huiothesia* . . . in Eph. 1:5. Here it appears in company with the verb that is crucial to this long sentence, *exelexato*. God chose us for himself, says the Apostle. And if the phrase "in love" is taken with the words preceding it we have the theologically related participle *proorisa*, "having predestined," coming just before *huiothesian*. It is followed by the purpose for which this adoption/election has been enacted, "to the praise of his glorious grace." This can hardly be understood as describing anything less than a life of obedient service, and is a significant echo of Exod. 4:23, "Let my son go, that he may serve me."[46]

Scripture weds covenantal obedience to Israel's adoption, and Israel's failure to obey manifested the necessity of a representative Son yet to come. As will become increasingly clear in the exploration of Romans 9, Paul's sonship/obedience framework tethers Israel's sonship organically and covenantally to the adoption realized in the holy Son, Christ Jesus.

Yet for Paul, as Romans 8 will also expose, Israel's sonship does not exhaust the theological backdrop for filial identity or obedience. Predating Israel's sonship is Adam's (Gen. 1:26–28; Luke 3:38), in its full covenantal and moral contours. Adam's covenantal failure did not abrogate the doxological and moral purpose of his existence; rather, his failure necessitated an alternative means of attaining the purpose for those created as the *imago Dei*. Adam's sons, having died with him through their federal participation in him, are under judgment (Rom. 5:12–21; Gal. 3:1–4:6). But according to Ephesians 1, as was purposed in the pretemporal covenant, God the Father would place this curse and judgment on his Son Jesus Christ in his death (1:7), so that those *in Christ* might achieve the filial goal in divine election. Those in Adam are sons of disobedience (2:1–2), guilty and corrupt in him. Those in Christ are adopted sons, forgiven (forensic) and washed (renovation) in him. Sons in the Son enjoy forgiveness and new status; they further enjoy transforming grace, whereby they are conformed into the image of the redeeming Son.

46. James I. Cook, "The Conception of Adoption in the Theology of Paul," in *Saved by Hope: Essays in Honor of Richard C. Oudersluys*, ed. James I. Cook (Grand Rapids: Eerdmans, 1978), 138.

With an expanding yet organic notion of sonship and obedience, Israel's sonship recapitulated the sonship of Adam covenantally, and typified the eschatological sonship realized in the last Adam. Only in this last Adam does the power of perfect obedience in life and death attain filial perfection—for himself and for those whom he represents as covenant Head.

Adoption, Resurrection, and Inheritance

Son-shaped transformation brings the elective purposes of God to fruition. Because "resemblance is the indispensable prerequisite of personal fellowship and understanding,"[47] such pure resemblance to the Beloved—secured in *huiothesia*—is the indispensable purpose of God in redemptive history. This final and perfect *en Christō* filial affinity awaits the consummation, when the adopted sons receive their *resurrected* bodies (with the completion of moral change met in bodily change). By the perfecting work of the eschatological Spirit of the perfected Son, the redeemed become sons in the fullest sense, with a son's rights, privileges, and immediate access to the Father. These rights and privileges, however, come to completion *because* of the full *en Christō* change that is graciously realized at the consummation— the redemption of the body (cf. Rom. 8:23). There would be no such inheritance (Eph. 1:14) without the receipt of the Holy Spirit, whose presence, as the measureless scope of the language in Ephesians 1:3 (*en pasē eulogia pneumatikē*, "with every spiritual blessing") suggests, applies the totality of *en Christō* ("in Christ") blessing—judicially and renovatively. Or to return to Murray's language concerning sanctification, "the outcome for the believer is self-purification after the pattern of the Father's purity. 'Every one who has this hope in him [i.e., the Father] purifieth himself even as he is pure' (1 John 3:3)."[48]

In the same way, Paul declares, in 1 Corinthians 15:50–51, that the perishable is *changed* to the imperishable and is *thereby* qualified to receive the inheritance of God's kingdom. Constitutive and bodily transformation is the prerequisite for the possession of and inception

---

47. William Hendriksen, *Exposition of the Gospel according to Matthew*, NTC (Grand Rapids: Baker, 1973), 277.
48. Murray, "Definitive Sanctification," 10.

into full eschatological glory. In keeping with the pretemporal divine purpose, adoption, as Paul sees it, entails this somatic transformation (cf. Rom. 8:23). Adopted sons are thoroughly changed, so that on the basis of the perfection of the life-giving Spirit/Son (1 Cor. 15:45), they become ethically righteous, being conformed into the image of their Elder Brother (Eph. 1:12; cf. Rom. 8:29). Without this full Spirit-wrought transformation, from perishable to imperishable, the eschatological realization of familial inheritance would remain eternally out of reach. No resurrection, no adoption. But by the efficacy of the eternally purposed plan "that he worked in Christ when he raised him from the dead and seated him at his right hand in the heavenly places" (Eph. 1:20), God delivers on his predestination unto adoption—whereby the sons transformed in the Son receive "the riches of his glorious inheritance in the saints" (1:18).

Adoption and Doxology

As the interpreter reflects on the conceptual influences on *huiothesia* for Paul, previously discussed in chapter 3, the Ephesian profiling of adoption as grounded in the mind of God forces the interpreter away from simplistic dependence on contemporary or cultural referents. Paul's theology of adoption is not created by familiar contemporary adoption themes, but is driven from a *revealed* theology from above. The gospel is familial because God is Father; his pre-creation love for his Son *and* his covenant love for his people ensure adoption's realization. The protological secures the eschatological, and more specifically, the protological determination (*pactum salutis*) to secure a family of redeemed children puts adoption into irreversible motion and inexorable conclusion. Adoption, in its consummate and transformative splendor, is secure because God is God. It is no wonder that Paul celebrates adoptive privilege with such confidence and jubilance.

In the opening section of Ephesians, Paul's grand summary of divine redemption joins deep theological reflection and doxology: "A gateway, a golden chain, a kaleidoscope, a snowball, a racehorse, an operatic overture and the flight of an eagle: all these metaphors describe the impression of colour, movement and grandeur which the sentence

[Eph 1:3–14] makes on the reader's mind."[49] As these metaphors seek to uphold, the packed theological reflection in Ephesians 1:3–14 exudes worship and celebration over the gracious familial contours of redemption. Attained by God's resounding grace, the priority, nature, and scope of adoption compel worship.

As Ephesians 1:3–14 indicates, the final purpose of redemption on the stage of history is the glory of the triune God: "Blessed be the God and Father of our Lord Jesus Christ" (1:3), "to the praise of his glorious grace" (v. 6), and "to the praise of his glory" (vv. 12, 14). With the view of salvation in Jesus Christ before him, the apostle Paul situates the insuperable power of adoption in Christ with a pervasive scope. Adoption as filial declaration and filial transformation accomplishes the prevailing doxological purpose of God for a holy family, the people of God, his *ekklēsia* ("church"). According to his sovereign plan, securing holy sons by adoption through the dead and resurrected Son delivered the loftiest expression of his glory.[50] Fulfilling this purpose, liberated children of God worship their Father because in Christ these renovated sons are now spiritually transformed, and through the renewing eschatological Spirit, they delight in pleasing the One who has adopted them—now incompletely, but at the parousia in renovated, filial perfection.

By God's astounding grace in his redeeming Son, adopted sons will attain full Spirit-wrought conformity into the image of their Elder Brother, the resurrected Son par excellence. The divine plan for creation involves a filially shaped redemption, so that creation (and the covenant of works) "finds its *idea*, its principle (*archē*) and its final goal (*telos*) in the Triune being of God,"[51] who effects creation's Adamic *telos* through his planning, accomplishing, and applying the redemption in the last Adam, his incarnate *Son*. In this sons-in-the-Son redemption, the created and adopted sons will now truly "be to the praise of his glory" (Eph. 1:12). Put otherwise, Trinitarian purpose gains its redemptive-historical and doxological footing in the Son of

---

49. John R. W. Stott, *The Message of Ephesians: God's New Society*, The Bible Speaks Today (Leicester: Inter-Varsity Press, 1986), 32.

50. Wermuth, "Doctrine of Adoption," 27–28.

51. Bavinck, *In the Beginning*, 45 (emphasis in original).

God sent from the Father. By the Son par excellence, the sons can "walk in a manner worthy of the calling to which [they] have been called" (4:1) and can "be imitators of God, as beloved children" (5:1). By the gracious provision of God in the Son of God, adopted sons are propelled into a life of worshipful obedience and destined for a completed worship-facilitating transformation.

As expressed in the Ephesians opening doxology, *huiothesia* harvests these theological foci. By God's grace, adoption in Christ creates redeemed sons, and these sons constitute the family of God. At the epicenter of this enabled privilege and obligation is Jesus Christ, the *redeeming* Son of God. In Galatians 4, Paul draws us more fully to adoption's essential Son-centeredness, and we address that marvelous Christological core of adoption next.

5

ADOPTION ACCOMPLISHED: THE INCARNATE SON OF GOD

But when the fullness of time had come, God sent forth his Son, born of woman, born under the law, to redeem those who were under the law, so that we might receive adoption as sons. And because you are sons, God has sent the Spirit of his Son into our hearts, crying, "Abba! Father!" So you are no longer a slave, but a son, and if a son, then an heir through God. (Gal. 4:4–7)

Redemptive History and the Sons of God

The redemptive-historical orientation of the apostle Paul, while pervasive in all his thought, is never so explicit in his writing as in the book of Galatians, particularly in chapters 3 and 4.[1] Having in his sights the transtestamental nature of the gospel (Gal. 3:8; cf. Rom. 1:1–4), the move from promise to fulfillment, and the role of the law in the history of redemption (Gal. 3:15–29), the apostle Paul explains the historico-theological continuity between the Abrahamic and Mosaic covenants. Expounding the nature of divine grace in mutually explanatory and telescopic fashion, these two covenants anticipate the divine work of God's grace in his Son.

In Galatians 3–4, Paul either foresees or responds to a perceived conflict between Abraham and Moses. The seeming theological tension

---

1. Cf. Oscar Cullman, *Salvation in History*, trans. Sidney G. Sowers (London: SCM, 1967), 129, 261–65; R. Alan Cole, *The Letter of Paul to the Galatians*, 2nd ed., TNTC (Leicester: Inter-Varsity Press, 1989), 153.

between the two covenants resolves when properly understanding the historico-theological purpose of the Mosaic law; the law did not invalidate the gracious promise (it did not function *kata tōn epaggeliōn [tou theou]*, "contrary to the promises of God," Gal. 3:21), but rather exposed the actual character of covenantal obedience, intensified its obligations, and illumined the need for powerful redeeming grace. The Mosaic law served the ends of the Abrahamic covenant, delivering a subsequent and clarifying explication of covenant life. According to Paul, the Abrahamic and Mosaic covenants actually share an eschatological expectation: a coming Seed, which is Christ Jesus himself ("offspring," 3:16), the Son sent from God (4:4). The Mosaic covenant complements its Abrahamic antecedent, and buttresses the redemptive-historical necessity and clarity of its gracious covenantal promises.

The Covenants and Sonship

The place of the filial and familial in God's purposes stands out prominently in Galatians, as the unfolding of redemption reaches its goal. By the arrival of the promised Redeemer (Gal. 3:24), Abrahamic gospel filial blessing (3:8) comes to fruition: *pantes gar huioi theou este dia tēs pisteōs en Christō Iēsou* ("in Christ Jesus you are all sons of God, through faith," 3:26). The work of Jesus Christ as Son secures the longed-for filial blessings woven into the fabric of Old Testament covenant promises. More specifically, adoptive sonship expressed in Galatians 4:5 constitutes the eschatological realization of the Abrahamic covenant (Gal. 3:7–9, 29).[2] Living under the legal strictures of the Mosaic covenant, those under the law found themselves earnestly yearning for the eschatological sonship promised in the Abrahamic covenant, a sonship typified in the period of the Mosaic covenant (Ex. 4:22; cf. 2 Sam. 7:14) and during that same period apprehended only incompletely—old covenant saints lived as minor sons. In the unfolding of God's filial grace, New Testament adoption explicitly fulfills the Abrahamic promises that prevailed through the Mosaic administration, bringing minority sonship to its full and intended adult maturity.

---

2. These covenants' shared vision for the coming Son is further expressed in Romans 9:1–5. I will consider this passage in the next chapter.

The means of expressing these complementary features of the Abrahamic and Mosaic covenants led the apostle Paul to a complex metaphor. Having described the irrevocability of the promise to Abraham (Gal. 3:22) and the critical tutoring function of the Mosaic law in redemptive history (3:17, 21, 23–25), in Galatians 4:1–2 Paul adds to the custodial motif a concept of minority sonship that awaits its inheritance. "The law has been compared to a prison-warden and a slave-attendant; now its role is compared to that of the guardians and trustees appointed to take care of a minor and his property."[3] The apostle employs this contrast between old covenant sonship (Israelites as minor children) and new covenant sonship (spiritual sons of Abraham, fully grown and in possession of the inheritance), and thereby expresses the redemptive-historical development of sonship from the era of the Mosaic law to the era of Christ's fulfillment of the law. Underage sons are no less sons, but the fullness of their filial benefits awaits the turning point of redemptive history in the mature sonship of the Son sent from heaven.

One point deserves reiteration. Despite its prominent legal character, the Mosaic covenant does not obviate or abandon the sonship motif, but serves it by accentuating the holy character of God's sons. In fact, the Mosaic covenant explicitly (e.g., Ex. 4:22–23) and implicitly advances sonship by making prominent the unqualified demands for holiness of those who are the sons of God. In demanding filial obedience, the law exposes the comprehensive nature of covenantal obedience and, in turn, makes prominent the perpetual perversity of the sons of Adam. The realization of full familial blessing awaited a Son ("offspring") whose obedience satisfied the positive demands of the law and whose suffering reversed its mastery over corrupted sons of Adam.

Accordingly, by divine orchestration, redemptive history pivots on Christ's success as Son, who in his mature obedience secures his filial inheritance and by divine grace shares this inheritance with the redeemed (Gal. 3:29–4:8).[4] By the coming of Christ, the messianic

---

3. F. F. Bruce, *The Epistle to the Galatians: A Commentary on the Greek Text*, NIGTC (Grand Rapids: Eerdmans, 1982), 192.

4. See Hans Dieter Betz, *Galatians: A Commentary on Paul's Letter to the Churches in Galatia*, Hermeneia—a Critical and Historical Commentary on the Bible (Philadelphia:

Son sent by the Father (*exapesteilen ho theos ton huion autou*, "God sent forth his Son," 4:4)[5] at the "fullness of time" (*to plērōma tou chronou*, v. 4), God provides the eschatological substance of Israel's minority sonship (vv. 1–2). Paul describes this realized and mature sonship as new covenant *adoption* (vv. 5–6) in Christ Jesus, the Son of God. Old covenant sons in Christ *anticipated* the full inheritance; new covenant sons in Christ *possess* it.

Acknowledging Paul's redemptive-historical orientation, James Scott divides Galatians 4:1–7 into two parts:

> If the first half of the comparison refers to the redemption from bondage in Egypt and the *huiothesia* of Israel at the time of the Exodus (vv. 1–2; cf. Rom. 9:4), then the second half probably refers to the eschatological redemption (*exagorazein*) and *huiothesia* expected in the messianic time (vv. 3–7). In other words, the relationship between the two halves of the comparison is probably not that between illustration and application (so the currently prevailing view), but rather that between type and antitype.[6]

Seeking to build his case, Scott argues that the typological nature of the exodus from Egypt with a view to the promised eschatological redemption is well known in Jewish traditions, and accordingly should be seen here in the opening verses of Galatians 4.[7] With this

---

Fortress, 1979), 202–4. Cf. Robert C. Dorman, "A Study of Paul's Use of *Hyiothesia*: Its Background, Development, and Importance concerning Spiritual Adoption" (unpublished master's thesis, Covenant Theological Seminary, St. Louis, 1997), 64–69.

5. Cole suggests, "It is tempting to see an allusion to the title *apostolos*, 'apostle', over which there had apparently been controversy between the Jerusalem church and Paul. It is noteworthy that, after the admission of 1:17 (where Paul includes himself in the number), he does not in this letter use the title 'apostle' of the leaders at Jerusalem. The application of the term 'apostle' to Christ would not, of course, be isolated: Hebrews 3:1 applies the noun to him directly as God's unique 'messenger' or 'delegate'." *Galatians*, 160–61. Christ's uniqueness, however, is typified by his unparalleled sonship status, introduced in Galatians 4:1–4. While Paul seeks to express the marvels of eschatologically realized sonship in this new aeon, he does so exclusively through his expression of Christ's inimitable yet graciously shared sonship. Cf. Col. 1:15.

6. James M. Scott, *Adoption as Sons of God: An Exegetical Investigation into the Background of* YIOTHESIA *in the Pauline Corpus*, Wissenschaftliche Untersuchungen Zum Neuen Testament 48 (Tübingen: J. C. B. Mohr [Paul Siebeck], 1992), 149.

7. See ibid., 151–55.

typological function of the exodus from Egypt deserving mention, a typology that Paul appreciates at various points (cf. Rom. 6:17–18; 1 Cor. 5:7), Scott here incorrectly concentrates Galatians 4:1–2 on the exodus event in particular and the bondage in question on the *pre-exodus* Egyptian slavery.

Such interpretations mistakenly pare Paul's argument too constrictively, failing to draw from the more expansive referent lying behind this portion of Galatians. As the context of Galatians 3 cogently bears out, Paul focuses not on the redemption from Egyptian bondage per se, but on the bondage under the law in the extended, provisional, eschatologically anticipatory period after the exodus. "Paul in his letters is not the slightest bit concerned with the *Egyptian* period of bondage but with the period *after* Israel's emancipation from slavery."[8] The burden on the pre-Christ believers, who lived in the age of law, created a longing for release from this extended yet provisional and anticipatory period of legal prominence. Generations of families in the old covenant craved a future spiritual and filial emancipation, and it is this extended historical period of restless anticipation on which Paul builds his filio-soteriological argumentation.

Slavery vs. Sonship

With such focus on this post-exodus epoch, Paul explains old covenant sonship status as ostensibly indistinguishable from slavery.[9]

8. Trevor J. Burke, *Adopted into God's Family: Exploring a Pauline Metaphor*, NSBT 22 (Downers Grove, IL: InterVarsity Press, 2006), 57n17. Burke's important critique extends further: Scott "couches everything in terms of Egyptian typology, where Israel's redemption from slavery (vv. 1–2) is a type of eschatological redemption effected by Christ (vv. 3–7), whom he regards as a second Moses." Nonetheless, the exodus event cannot in any way be justifiably disconnected from the subsequent era, because the redemptive event inaugurated the custodial period of bondage reflected in Galatians 4:1–2. See Bruce, *Galatians*, 194; George S. Duncan, *The Epistle of Paul to the Galatians*, MNTC (London: Hodder and Stoughton, 1934), 125–27. Cf. James D. G. Dunn, *The Epistle to the Galatians*, Black's New Testament Commentary (Peabody, MA: Hendrickson, 1993), 209–14.

9. Much as he does with *huiothesia*, Paul undoubtedly has Roman legal customs of slavery and custodianship in mind, but applies them in his redemptive-historical argumentation. The revealed theology drives the selection of the terms and analogies; the contextual features do not *create* the theological argument. See G. Daan Cloete, "Christmas: Heirs of God, the Father, through Jesus, the Son, Incarnated (Galatians 4:4–7)," *Journal of Theology for Southern Africa* 85 (1993): 53–57.

In fact, old covenant sonship under the Mosaic administration in certain ways appeared so similar to pre-exodus slavery as to perpetuate an appearance of redemptive-historical stagnation.[10] Because the strictures of the law's demands produced palpable (and proper!) fear, like the taskmasters in Egypt, the post-exodus slavery (cf. Rom. 8:15) was no mere illusion. It stood in radical disparity from the promised filial peace and blessing embedded in the Abrahamic covenant and intensified in its Mosaic successor.

Corresponding to the redemptive-historical crisis created by the law, the periods of prophetic revelation during this custodial age pointed forward to a coming Son. In confirming the promises, this prophetic revelation further illumined the provisionality of old covenant stipulations and simultaneously elevated the subeschatological angst. That is, as the old covenant sons awaited the promised satisfaction of eschatological glory, the prominence of legal constraints and the fear in the presence of God created a slavelike context that intensified their longings for filial inheritance. Eschatological release from bondage was yet future. Thus, as a means to exposing the elevated tension, the ostensible indistinguishability between the slaves and sons combines with swelling old covenant restlessness to focus on the eschatologically decisive arrival of the Son of God, Jesus Christ. The entire old covenant custodial and subeschatological epoch stands in stark contrast to the age of realized filial blessing brought by the Son of God and conferred by his Spirit (see Rom. 8:15–17).

While enforcing the redemptive-historical contrast, the apostle resolutely maintains continuity, development, anticipation/realization, and promise/fulfillment between the covenants (cf. Rom. 9:1–5; Eph. 2:12–16). By singular divine purpose (Eph. 1:4–5), New Testament sonship privileges sprout from the minority privileges graciously given Old Testament saints (cf. Rom. 9:4).[11] As Paul argues in Galatians 3–4,

10. Cf. Herman N. Ridderbos, *The Epistle of Paul to the Churches of Galatia*, trans. Henry Zylstra, NICNT (Grand Rapids: Eerdmans, 1953), 152; Trevor J. Burke, "Pauline Adoption: A Sociological Approach," *EvQ* 73, 2 (2001): 131; Herman N. Ridderbos, *Paul: An Outline of His Theology*, trans. John Richard DeWitt (Grand Rapids: Eerdmans, 1975), 198–99; Dorman, "Paul's Use of *Hyiothesia*," 70–71.

11. While Paul argues for corporate, typological sonship in Romans 9, in Galatians 4 he understands individual sonship under the old covenant in unrealized, immature terms.

believers in the Old Testament were sons, but juvenile/minority ones. In a redemptive-historical sense, not until the arrival of the Son par excellence who attains and secures fully mature sonship conditions do the minor sons of God become the fully adopted sons of God. Such a transition requires a clear grasp of what Paul is and is not arguing. In a critical sense, filial grace and blessing in Christ deliver no surprise. In an equally important sense, however, the arrival of full filial blessing exceeds all expectations (cf. 1 Cor. 2:9; Eph. 3:20–21).[12]

Thus, the gospel privileges now fully enjoyed through Jesus Christ (Gal. 4:6–7) fulfill Old Testament sonship anticipation, albeit with a qualitative fullness that cognitively and existentially astounds. "The grace of the New appears in this, that by redemption accomplished and by faith in Christ (cf. Gal. 3:26) all without distinction (cf. Gal. 3:28) are instated in the full blessing of sonship without having to undergo tutelary preparation corresponding to the pedagogical discipline of the Mosaic economy."[13] Now Jews and Gentiles alike—true Israel (Gal. 6:16)—enjoy unprecedented sonship privileges because of the work of their Elder Brother (cf. Heb. 2:10–13), the Son par excellence.

"Elemental Things": The Contrast Further Intensified

The sweeping epochal contrasts that Paul makes in Galatians 4:1–2 intensify by the explicit language chosen in Galatians 4:3–7. Paul

---

In both Old and New Testaments, sonship is never viewed apart from the *family* of God, just as corporate family emphasis never obviates the need for personal faith. Cf. Robert A. Peterson, *Adopted by God: From Wayward Sinners to Cherished Children* (Phillipsburg, NJ: P&R Publishing, 2001), 23–26.

12. The element of "surprise" is often associated with the Christotelic hermeneutic, which insists that the New Testament writers introduce a "surprise" element in the use of Old Testament texts. They employ Old Testament texts in ways that divert from their original meanings, when they relate them to Jesus Christ. See Dan McCartney, "Should We Employ the Hermeneutic of the New Testament Writers?," http://www.bible-researcher .com/mccartney1.html (accessed February 6, 2016). For a response to McCartney, see Lane G. Tipton, "The Gospel and Redemptive-Historical Hermeneutics," in *Confident of Better Things*, ed. John R. Muether and Danny E. Olinger (Willow Grove, PA: Committee for the Historian of the Orthodox Presbyterian Church, 2011), 185–213. The New Testament is *not* without development, nor does it lack an element of pleromic surprise, but the Christocentricity of Scripture (cf. Luke 24:13–52; John 5:39–47; 1 Peter 1:10–12) makes a Christological reading of Old Testament texts not a rereading or a "reading in" but a faithful reading.

13. John Murray, The Epistle to the Romans: The English Text with Introduction, Exposition and Notes, 2 vols. combined. (Reprint, Grand Rapids: Eerdmans, 1997), 2:5.

more poignantly frames the oppressive and condemnatory features of the Mosaic law, which drove its pupils to yearn for promised filial freedom.[14] As he upholds here and in Romans 2:14–15, obligation and condemnation include both Jews and Gentiles; not only were the old covenant people browbeaten by the law, but Gentiles also lived in parallel bondage, equally wanting of the freedom that only the redeeming Son of God could bring.

Paul views all people as *hupo nomon* ("under the law," Gal. 4:5).[15] First, from the vantage point of the old covenant revelation, the law condemns all the sons of Adam—Jew and Gentile alike; both Jew and Gentile were under the curse of the law, which "is the ultimate *reductio ad absurdum* of all religion and ethics."[16] As Paul surveyed the landscape, the desperate spiritual topography was identical: Jews and Gentiles had been cast into the pit of legal condemnation and were uniformly bound in their sinfulness. Effectively, Paul unites all unbelieving peoples, whether Jew or Gentile, revealing the universal necessity for Christ Jesus (cf. Rom. 3:1–20). Their common state of desperation in the age of the law and its curse exposed their need of gospel grace, their need for divinely provided redemption, or, as Paul puts it, their need for an eschatologically realized *huiothesia*. Sinners, whether Jew or Gentile, needed the Savior-Son in order to become sons of God.

Paul further demonstrates the shared condemnation from the vantage point of pagan religions. He situates Jews and Gentiles under *ta stoicheia*[17] (Gal. 4:3, 9), under which they were "slavishly

---

14. Ridderbos, *Epistle to the Churches of Galatia*, 146.

15. "Paul teaches elsewhere that the law condemns both Jews and Gentiles (cf. Rom. 3:9–20) and thus confines them (Gal. 3:23)." Scott, *Adoption as Sons of God*, 173. Cf. Tim J. Trumper, "The Metaphorical Import of Adoption: A Plea for Realisation II: The Adoption Metaphor in Theological Usage," *SBET* 15, 2 (1997): 111–12.

16. C. K. Barrett, *From First Adam to Last: A Study in Pauline Theology* (London: Adam & Charles Black, 1962), 63.

17. The meaning of *stoicheia* has seen extensive treatment. See, e.g., Josef Blinzler, "Lexikalisches zu dem Terminus *Ta Stoicheia Tou Kosmou*," in *Studiorum Paulinorum Congressus Internationalis Catholicus 1961*, vol. 2 of AnBib 17–18 (Rome: Pontifical Biblical Institute, 1963), 429–43; Clinton E. Arnold, "Returning to the Domain of the Powers: Stoicheia as Evil Spirits in Galatians 4:3, 9," *Novum Testamentum* 38, 1 (1996): 55–76; Thomas H. Olbricht, "The Stoicheia and the Rhetoric of Colossians: Then and Now," in *Rhetoric, Scripture and Theology*, ed. Stanley E. Porter and Thomas H. Olbricht (Sheffield: Sheffield Academic Press, 1996), 308–28; David R. Bundrick, "*Ta Stoicheia Tou Kosmou* (Gal 4:3),"

subjected,"[18] in dire need of release from their bondage. In view of its usage in Colossians 2:8 and 2:20,[19] "elementary principles" most likely refers here to unspecified[20] vain religious or philosophical means for providing self-redemption, the folly of which revealed their utterly helpless condition: "in slavery to powers utterly beyond their control."[21] In just a few short words, "Gal 4:3 contains Paul's thought about man's situation before God prior to the redemption in Christ."[22]

While precisely defining the "elementary principles" ("elemental things," NASB) is tenuous, the intent to demonstrate how apart from Christ both Jews and Gentiles dwell in shared spiritual bondage emerges unambiguously. "The revelation God has made in Jesus shows up the ideas of both the Jewish and the Gentile worlds for the elementary teaching they were,"[23] and since the Judaizers had made Yahweh into a national Jewish God in an idolatrous fashion parallel to the regional gods of the other nations, their rebellious construct of religion fails to honor the biblical God. In addition to the complex metaphors at work in the transition from the age of the law to the

---

JETS 34, 3 (1991): 353–64; Eduard Schweizer, "Slaves of the Elements and Worshipers of Angels: Gal 4:3, 9 and Col 2:8, 18, 20," *JBL* 107, 3 (1988): 455–68; Ridderbos, *Epistle to the Churches of Galatia*, 153n5; Cole, *Galatians*, 159–60; J. B. Lightfoot, *Saint Paul's Epistle to the Galatians: A Revised Text with Introduction, Notes, and Dissertations* (London: Macmillan and Co., Limited, 1902), 167; Richard N. Longenecker, *Galatians*, WBC 41 (Dallas: Word, 1990), 165–66; George Eldon Ladd, *A Theology of the New Testament*, ed. Donald A. Hagner, rev. ed. (Grand Rapids: Eerdmans, 1993), 442–43.

18. Ridderbos, *Epistle to the Churches of Galatia*, 154. The *ēmeis* of 4:3 probably refers to both Jewish and Gentile Christians. See Scott, *Adoption as Sons of God*, 156–57.

19. See Lightfoot, *St. Paul's Epistle to the Galatians*, 167. In Paul, *stoicheia* possesses both redemptive-historical and conceptual features, which focus on spiritual bondage—Jewish and Gentile alike. The author of Hebrews uses the same term, albeit critically, in a fashion showing that the semantic range of the term entails immature belief (Heb. 5:12), not only pagan belief or *unbelief*.

20. "We can know relatively little about the religion of the Galatians before they were seized by the Pauline gospel." J. Louis Martyn, *Galatians: A New Translation with Introduction and Commentary*, Anchor Bible 33A (New York: Doubleday, 1997), 395–96. Cf. Betz, *Galatians*, 213.

21. Donald Guthrie, *Galatians*, New Century Bible, n.s. (Greenwood, SC: Attic Press, 1969), 118.

22. Betz, *Galatians*, 205.

23. Leon Morris, *Galatians: Paul's Charter of Christian Freedom* (Downers Grove, IL: InterVarsity Press, 1996), 128.

age of the Spirit, Paul equally denounces all Judaistic perversions of God's covenant grace and Gentile idolatries. Accordingly, Scott points out that these idolatrous *stoicheia* are identified both with the Torah and with nondeities of the pagan Gentiles: "In effect, therefore, Paul classes Judaism with polytheism as enslavement under the *stoicheia*!"[24] As George Howard put it in equally striking fashion, "Paul looked upon that version of Christianity propagated by the judaizers as synonymous with paganism."[25]

Adoption and the Work of the Messianic Son

Redemption and Incarnation

The pre-Christ situation is condemningly bleak. Jews and Gentiles, under the law and its curse, face comprehensive futility and need divine redemption. The problem was shared; the solution was singular. Centering his argument in the Father's Son-sending and the Son's redeeming ministry (Gal. 4:4–6; cf. Rom. 1:3–4; 10:4; Eph. 1:3–23), Paul profiles the specific means of accomplishing the divinely purposed and promised glorious redemption: the Son of God. Christ's arrival occurs in this context of the comprehensive human bondage to the law and the damning qualities of futile religiosity, the "elementary principles"; Christ was therefore necessarily and purposefully "born of woman, born under the law, to redeem those who were under the law" (Gal. 4:4–5a). To release those in bondage, he had to enter the slavery himself.

As Paul builds implicitly here and explicitly elsewhere (Rom. 5:12–21; 10:4; cf. 1 Tim. 3:16), redemption required incarnation.

---

24. Scott, *Adoption as Sons of God*, 158.

25. George Howard, *Paul: Crisis in Galatia*, ed. G. N. Stanton, 2nd ed., Society for New Testament Studies Monograph Series 35 (Cambridge: Cambridge University Press, 1990), 66. Herman Bavinck writes, "When the fullness of time had come, the Jews, considered as a nation, were on the same level as the Gentiles. Together they were worthy of condemnation before God, because they sought to establish a righteousness of their own based on the law and rejected the righteousness that is through faith (Rom. 3:21)." Bavinck further shows how Paul develops this similar line of argument in Romans 11, where he argues that "God has imprisoned all, Gentiles and Jews, in disobedience so that he may be merciful to all (vv. 25–32)." Herman Bavinck, *The Last Things: Hope for This World and the Next*, ed. John Bolt, trans. John Vriend (Grand Rapids: Baker, 1996), 100, 104. Cf. Bruce, *Galatians*, 30.

The covenant-filial curse required a covenant-filial curse-absorber. As such, the incarnate Son fulfilled the law's demands (cf. Matt. 5:17) and took on the law's curse (Gal. 3:13), and in these historical acts he effects redemption. To bring the slave-sons out of their bondage, the sent Son took on human frailty and bondage in the context of the cosmic curse. He came himself *hupo nomon* ("under the law"), that in his filial obedience in life and in death, he might emerge victorious and vanquish the cursed bondage. His curse-reversing life, death, and resurrection as Son of God deliver in full the Abrahamic familial promise (Gal. 3:22, 29).

Employing the redemptive-historically pregnant concept *plērōma tou chronou* ("the fullness of time," Gal. 4:4), Paul has built the argument in Galatians to a theological crescendo. In contrast to Platonic abstract concepts of fullness, *plērōma* in New Testament usage concerns redemptive-historical completion. In this way, divine *telos* ("purpose," "goal"; cf. Rom. 10:4; 1 Cor. 1:8; James 5:11) and *plērōma* combine in biblical revelation to express historico-theological fulfillment moving from type to antitype, shadow to substance. Here in Galatians, the apostle Paul makes this transition explicitly filial: history has awaited the arrival of this Son, because no prior son had put or had even been able to put an end to the law's condemning control.

The history of biblical revelation is the history of promise. From the moment of fatherly redemptive promise in the *proto-evangelium* (Gen. 3:15), the God of creation reveals himself as the merciful God of redemption, the Father who will forgive and restore his people (2 Sam. 7:8, 14; Isa. 43:6–7; Ezek. 37:24–28; cf. Lev. 26:12; 2 Cor. 6:16–18). Forgiveness and purification from sin cost, and because of the corrupting sinfulness of sin itself, the price tag exceeds the capability of the fallen sons of Adam to pay. Salvation must be of God alone; it must be in a Son he provides. God's purposeful redemption centered on those originally made in his image, and the revealed message of Scripture becomes increasingly perspicuous that the goal of the image will be attained by a Messiah/Son who will bring the *imago Dei* to its eschatological goal. As Anselm famously captured in *Cur Deus Homo*, atonement for sin must be of man and of God: though man *ought* to make the needed satisfaction as the debtor, only God *could* make the needed satisfaction; accordingly, it was necessary "for a God-Man to make it."[26] Redemption required the eternal Son of God to become the incarnate Son of God.

Precisely according to promise, the Son was sent by the Father (Gal. 4:4), and he submitted to his redemptive task confirmed in the pretemporal intra-Trinitarian pact (*pactum salutis*). This Son-sending, as the New Testament underscores, happens according to divine orchestration: God appointed the right *timing* of his birth, life, death, resurrection, and exaltation (cf. Rom. 5:6). This timely "pleromafication"[27] work on behalf of the church (cf. Eph. 1:15–23) captures Paul, because it is in the Son's timely humiliation and exaltation (Gal. 4:4–5; cf. Rom. 8:3–4) that he acquires and proffers *adoption* for those in bondage to the law and its curse. The epoch of the law's curse comes to an end in the redeeming death of the Son, and the epoch of the Spirit emerges in this same Son's resurrection on behalf of those united to him, the adopted sons. "The sending forth of Christ marks to him then πλήρωμα τοῦ χρόνου [*plērōma tou chronou*, 'the fullness of time'] (Gal. 4:4), a phrase which certainly means more than that the time was ripe for the introduction of Christ into the world: the fulness of the time means the end of that aeon and the commencement of another world-period."[28] According to God's governance of history, the age of law and curse had run their course. The dawn of the new age was at hand. The One whom Abraham and Moses had longed to see had arrived—the Son of God incarnate.

Thus, while ontological questions regarding the eternal sonship of Christ are theologically foundational and assuredly undergird Galatians 4:4, the redemptive-historical accomplishment of this Son as the Messiah attains gospel prominence in Galatians 4. As Paul

26. Anselm, *Cur Deus Homo* ("Why God Became Man"), in *A Scholastic Miscellany: Anselm to Ockham*, ed. and trans. Eugene R. Fairweather, Library of Christian Classics 10 (Philadelphia: Westminster, 1956), 151.

27. John Jefferson Davis, *Worship and the Reality of God: An Evangelical Theology of Real Presence* (Downers Grove, IL: IVP Academic, 2014), 64.

28. Geerhardus Vos, "The Eschatological Aspect of the Pauline Conception of the Spirit," in *Redemptive History and Biblical Interpretation: The Shorter Writings of Geerhardus Vos*, ed. Richard B. Gaffin Jr. (Phillipsburg, NJ: Presbyterian and Reformed, 1980), 213.

sees it, the believer's eschatologically realized sonship is contingent on the physical birth, obedient life, obedient death, and vindicating resurrection of the messianic Son, whereby the children under bondage (4:1–3) might become the adopted sons of God (v. 5) by the Spirit (v. 6). Adoption in Christ is adoption in history, by the historical Son incarnate, ushering in the new age and bringing the redeemed sons with him—all according to divine *telos* and timetable.

Eschatological (and doxological!) confidence bursts forth here in this climactic section of Galatians. God's work in Christ Jesus, his sent Son, bears cosmic and comprehensive implications for the salvation of God's people—Jew and Gentile. The stranglehold of the law and the power of its curse meet their defeat under the power of Christ and the cross, as the Son's work singularly obliterates the power of sin, death, and the law's curse. As Paul understood, this ministry of the messianic Son did not perpetuate history in the *status quo* or serve as some mere exemplary model of a life well lived (and well died), but marked the decisive ushering in of the eschatological age, long anticipated in every facet of the old covenant. The eschatologically resplendent work of the Son of God crushes any perceived redemptive-historical stasis.

The language employed, in fact, shouts realized biblical eschatology: Christ's messianic sonship that attained its culmination at his resurrection (cf. Rom. 1:3–4) ushered in a new age, securing realized sonship for the true children of Abraham (Gal. 3:29). For Paul, Christ's adoption-proffering work marks the eschatological delivery of divine promise to the old covenant's underage sons, frees them as mature sons from the bondage of the age of the law, and renders the fullness of filial blessing and inheritance on them as the redeemed sons in the post-Christ age. Now free from the law's supervision/tutorship and its condemnation, no longer *nēpioi* ("children," 4:3) and no longer *douloi* ("slaves"),[29] the sons of God now experience "reception of a new relationship with God, which involved primarily the enjoyment of full sonship rights."[30]

29. Galatians 4:7 states the contrast with the singular *slave*: "So you are no longer a slave. . . ."

30. Longenecker, *Galatians*, 172.

Adoption in Its Redemptive-Historical Prominence

The significance of adoption in Galatians 4:5 could hardly be overstated. The grammatical structure (two purpose clauses, culminating with *huiothesia*)[31] makes adoption the very goal of Christ's coming.

> The two ἵνα [*hina*] clauses in v 5 are formally parallel, like the two ἵνα [*hina*] clauses in 3:14, but this time the latter clause is materially dependent on the former, or at least carries on the thought to a point beyond that reached by the former. Those who have been redeemed by Christ from their former life "under law" are the "we" who through him receive their instatement as sons; indeed, it may be said that the purpose of Christ's redeeming them was that they—both Jews and (quite emphatically) Gentiles—should receive this instatement.[32]

In other words, "the purpose for which God sent his Son was in order that Jewish and Gentile believers might receive the divine adoption as sons."[33] *The* stated purpose for Christ's messianic sonship is adoption, releasing those in bondage to the full freedom of Spirit-born or *adopted* sons. The apostle Paul's employment of these consecutive purpose (*hina*) clauses in Galatians 4:4–5 builds the immediate verses to a climax, and the entire logic of chapters 3 and 4. Arguably, the final purpose clause in Galatians 4:5—*hina tēn huiothesian apolabōmen* ("that we might receive adoption as sons")—functions as the climax of the entire epistle.

Notably, Paul's concern to bring the accomplishment of redemption by the Son of God to the forefront here, with all its epochal, eschatological, and existential force, harks back to the legal curse of Galatians 3:13. Bruce understates the point when he avers that "the *huiothesia* is the subject in the forefront of Paul's mind at this point in

---

31. Ronald Y. K. Fung, *The Epistle to the Galatians*, NICNT (Grand Rapids: Eerdmans, 1988), 182.

32. Bruce, *Galatians*, 197.

33. Scott, *Adoption as Sons of God*, 174. Cf. Keith Alan Mosebrook, "The Pauline Doctrine of the Adoption of Believers," (ThM thesis, Dallas Theological Seminary, 1981), 39; Mawhinney, "*Yiothesia* in the Pauline Epistles," 200; Sinclair B. Ferguson, *Children of the Living God* (Colorado Springs: NavPress, 1987), 27.

the argument: the sending of God's Son and his redemption of those who were 'under law', important as these are in their own right, are here means to an end, the end being the *huiothesia* of believers."[34] This assessment draws from the culminating redemptive-historical language in Galatians 4, and aligns seamlessly with *huiothesia* in Ephesians 1, which profiles the pretemporally determined plan of the triune God for redemption. The adoption designed in the pretemporal intra-Trinitarian counsel is the adoption accomplished by the sent Son of God. And in view of the case that Paul builds throughout Galatians 3–4 and the fruit of Galatians 4:5 in the lives of the sons, along with the distinctly prominent place that *huiothesia* plays in the redemptive purposes of God (Ephesians 1 and Galatians 4), the climactic nature of adoption redemptive-historically and soteriologically should receive prominent attention.

In a manner parallel to Ephesians 1, Paul weaves divine redemptive purpose, divine redemptive accomplishment, and divine redemptive application tightly together in this Galatian letter. In the sending of the Son and the Spirit of the Son upon the redeemed sons, everything changes. Everything changes historically and eschatologically. Everything changes for the redeemed judicially (justification) and morally (sanctification/renewal). Everything changes for these sons of Adam *by their adoption* in the Son of God humiliated and exalted. "Believers are now adopted as God's children through the cross-work of Jesus Christ."[35]

The Spirit of the Son(s)

For those united to the resurrected Son by faith, the redemptive-historical attainment delivers immediate eschatological and therefore existential implications. Paul fortifies this eschatological reality by pointing to the work of the Holy Spirit in the adopted sons of God (Gal. 4:6). The Old Testament saints well understood that the promised outpouring of the Spirit represented the ushering in of the eschatological age (cf. Jer. 31; Ezek. 36; Joel 2; Acts 2). Paul grasped, as 1 Corinthians

---

34. Bruce, *Galatians*, 194.
35. Thomas R. Schreiner, *Galatians*, ZEC 9 (Grand Rapids: Zondervan, 2010), 271.

10:11 indicates, for example, that the work of Christ marks the critical transition in history, separating the pre-Christ epoch from the post-Christ one.[36] Thus, Paul affirms the redemptive-historical significance of the outpouring of the Holy Spirit at Pentecost as fulfillment of the eschatological promise in the Old Testament of new covenant blessing. Hence, in Paul's estimation (and that of the entire New Testament), the current historical epoch comes as the eschatological fulfillment of the Old Testament promises and shadows, and all soteriological benefits in the risen Christ possess a necessarily eschatological cast.

Put otherwise, since Christ's messianic work is centrally eschatological in nature, and the Holy Spirit's ministry precisely coalesces with that of Jesus Christ, the Spirit's ministry could be described as nothing less than eschatological. This eschatology is both arrived (*already*) and yet to come (*not yet*). Only with reliance on the hermeneutically and theologically determinative function of the last days in biblical revelation, and the organic harmony of the eschatological *already* but *not yet*, will we properly grasp Paul's understanding of Christ's work and the Holy Spirit's work.

With this Trinitarian, Christological, pneumatological, and redemptive-historical thrust, Paul accentuates the eschatological freight carried by adoption in this new epoch, pointing to the glorious eschatological realization of redemptive sonship, only proleptically and partially experienced by believers whose lives preceded Christ's life and work. He states emphatically to his readers that on the basis of the completed work of the Son par excellence, they who are children of Abraham by faith, and as attested by the Holy Spirit, are now *truly* sons in the fullest eschatological sense (*hina tēn huiothesian apolabōmen*, "so that we might receive adoption as sons," Gal. 4:5; *hoti de este huioi*, "and because you are sons," 4:6; *ōste ouketi ei doulos alla huios*, "so you are no longer a slave, but a son," 4:7; cf. 3:26). The parallel construction of the Father's sending in 4:6 and 4:7 not only underscores the deity of the Son, but accentuates the securing of the promised filial eschatological blessing.

---

36. See Anthony A. Hoekema, *The Bible and the Future* (Grand Rapids: Eerdmans, 1979), 17.

The eschatological Spirit applies and confirms the work of the exalted *messianic* Son, so that the believing sons of this age enjoy the privileges of mature sonship as attained by their Elder Brother. The "decisive difference between old and new covenant believers . . . is the Spirit-worked *union* New Testament believers have with the *exalted* Christ, the life-giving Spirit, the Christ who is what he is, because he has suffered and entered into his glory."[37] Filial grace in the New Testament age reveals full sonly attainment, maturity, and inheritance. As Calvin has put it, "Were not the holy patriarchs of old also held to be among the sons of God? Yes—relying upon this right, they called upon God as Father. But after the only-begotten Son of God was brought into the world, the heavenly fatherhood became more clearly known. Accordingly, Paul assigns this privilege, as it were to Christ's Kingdom."[38] In contrast to the pre-Christ age, adoptive grace is tasted in full now because at his resurrection, the Son of God attains his inheritance and reigns as King.[39]

The Comprehensive Contours of Adoption

Just as in Ephesians 1, where the pretemporal Trinitarian decree grounds the redemptive-historical work of the Son and the Spirit, so here Trinitarian coalescence radiates preeminently. The Father sent his Son (*exapesteilen ho theos ton huion autou*, "God sent forth his Son," Gal. 4:4), and the Father sent the Spirit of his Son (*exapesteilen ho theos to pneuma tou huiou autou*, "God has sent the Spirit of his Son," v. 6).[40] Sent by the Father, the Son accomplishes redemption, that is, the adoption of sons; sent by the Father, the Spirit applies and confirms this adoption within the adopted sons (v. 6). Adoption is Trinitarian

37. Richard B. Gaffin Jr., "The Holy Spirit," *WTJ* 43, 1 (1980): 71–72 (emphasis in original). Gaffin continues, "The covenantal communion with God enjoyed by Abraham and the other old covenant faithful was an anticipatory and provisional fellowship; it lacked the finality and eschatological permanence of our union with (the glorified) Christ, which is the ground and medium of our experiencing all other blessings of redemption." Ibid., 72.

38. John Calvin, *Institutes of the Christian Religion*, ed. John T. McNeill, trans. Ford Lewis Battles, 2 vols. (Philadelphia: Westminster, 1960), 2.14.5.

39. "The fact is . . . that Christ has indeed brought in the new age, the age of the kingdom of God." Hoekema, *The Bible and the Future*, 31.

40. The Father sends the *preexisting* Spirit just as he sends the *preexisting* Son. Cf. Longenecker, *Galatians*, 166–70; Bruce, *Galatians*, 195.

business from start to finish,[41] and fulfills Trinitarian purpose for the creation of a family of God—sons graciously and securely gathered by the Son par excellence.

With redemptive history and eschatology in focus (redemption accomplished), the existential implications for soteriology for the sons of God by faith (redemption applied) surface expectedly but no less poignantly. These *ordo salutis* concerns, though distinct from the *historia salutis* concerns, function inseverably from one another. Paul and the other New Testament writers insist on such theological correlativity. For this reason, the events of Christ's humiliation and exaltation and the associated outpouring of the Holy Spirit of the risen Son provide the historical and theological framework for defining the meaning of the believers' adoption.

The culminating *goal* of the pretemporal plan and of the redemptive work of God in Christ, as noted in the previous chapter, requires a comprehensive transformation commensurate with holiness in the eschatological family of God (cf. Eph. 1:4–5). As sons placed in the Son, they experience the Spirit-wrought filial bond that delivers all that Christ Jesus has accomplished as Son of God. Thus, by the work of the messianic Son, those once under the condemning power of the law (Gal. 4:5) and the distorting effects of sin now live as transformed sons in the freedom of the life-giving Spirit (cf. 1 Cor. 15:45)—a freedom in and for obedience. Filial heart change—desire, motive, goal, and power—stems from the efficacy of Christ's successful sonship.

With this eschatologically completed adoptive work of the messianic Son in mind, Paul transitions into an extended treatment (Gal. 4:8–5:26) of the ethical implications that mature sonship's freedom bears. Israel's typological adoption bore ethical and doxological implications (Ex. 4:22–23; Rom. 9:4–5); so, too, realized eschatological sonship of believers obligates undiluted obedience to the Father. Now in the age of Christ's redemptive work and the outpouring of his Spirit,

---

41. The underlying Trinitarian theology of Paul (i.e., Rom. 1:1–4; 1 Cor. 12:1–6; 2 Cor. 13:14; Eph. 1:3–14; 4:1–6) is cogently articulated by Gordon Fee. See Gordon D. Fee, *God's Empowering Presence: The Holy Spirit in the Letters of Paul* (Peabody, MA: Hendrickson, 1994), 839–42. Cf. Richard B. Gaffin Jr., "'Life-Giving Spirit': Probing the Center of Paul's Pneumatology," *JETS* 41, 4 (1998): 581.

what was out of reach under the old covenant is *spiritually* animated in the new covenant. In fact, the sending of the Spirit into the believers' hearts functions in a "reciprocal relation or correlational"[42] fashion with sonship. To be sons is to be in possession of the Holy Spirit of the Son; to be in possession of the Holy Spirit of the Son is to be adopted, and therefore obedient sons. Adoption entails possession of the holy, sanctifying Spirit of Christ (Rom. 8:9–17).

As the climactic purpose of Christ's work, adoption surely involves a judicial declaration of sonship (Gal. 4:6). But there is more to filial grace than legal pronouncement and resulting relational status. Adoption of sons in the Son of God involves justification *and* sanctification in the lives of the believers; both forensic and renovative elements radiate here. Forensically, the adopted sons are removed from their former kingdom/family, and are placed in the eschatological kingdom/family of the Son of God (Gal. 4:6; cf. Col. 1:13).[43] As those spiritually engrafted into the Son of God resurrected, they enjoy extraordinary intimacy with the Almighty: they actually *nun de gnontes theon* ("now . . . have come to know God," Gal. 4:9). In fact, Paul describes them not only as *knowing* God, but also as being *known* by him, *mallon de gnōsthentes hupo theou* ("or rather to be known by God," v. 9). The adopted sons no longer suffer alienation; they live in an unprecedented state of access to and intimacy with God.

Such intimacy bespeaks the legal privileges of adoption, but it also affirms the transformational efficacy of Christ Jesus' work as Son of God. The sons in the Son enjoy the fullness of Christ's resurrection status and power. While not yet resurrected bodily, the new sons possess the Spirit of the resurrected Son of God, who delivered full resurrection power for their willing filial obedience. For believers in

---

42. Longenecker, *Galatians*, 173. Longenecker continues that Paul highlights "the integral nature of sonship and the reception of the Spirit—not as two stages in the Christian life, but as two mutually dependent and intertwined features in the subjective experience of salvation." Ibid., 174.

43. Noting this kingdom transfer, Girardeau posits this forensic definition of *huiothesia*: "Adoption is an act of God's free grace, whereby, for the sake of Christ, he formally translates the regenerate from the family of Satan into his own, and legally confirms them in all the rights, immunities and privileges of his children." John L. Girardeau, *Discussions of Theological Questions*, ed. George A. Blackburn (Richmond, VA: Presbyterian Committee, 1905), 486.

Christ, solidarity with the risen Son is real, historical, and complete. To be sure, the believers' bodily resurrection awaits a future day; but Paul insists that believers have already been raised with Christ (see, e.g., Rom. 6:1–4). That is, the believers' "*pre-functional* disposition,"[44] that internal aspect of Pauline anthropology, which is distinct but inseparable from the body, *now* enjoys the fullest access to resurrection power. "The past resurrection of the inner man is to be understood as realistically and literally as future, bodily resurrection. Believers experience the ongoing renewal ('day by day') spoken of in 2 Corinthians 4:16, based on the resurrection of the inner man."[45] Possession of the Spirit of the risen Son supplies the full bounty of Christ's provision for each obedient step along the believer's pathway, through suffering unto glory (cf. Rom. 8:15–17).

The admitted complexity associated with reckoning with the inner/outer-man distinction for Paul must not cloud the pervasive Pauline point concerning the sons of God in the Son of God. For Paul, *in Christ* resurrection—inner man and outer man—cannot be separated from redemption's consummate goal, adoption in Christ. By virtue of union with the Son of God resurrected, filial grace renders *already* and *not yet* benefits. This filial grace renders both forensic and renovative privileges: believers' identity and status change, and so, too, does their prefunctional disposition. Adoption in Christ, by union with him in his resurrection, brings familial translation and filial transformation.

Furthermore, the attestation of this eschatologically realized resurrection/sonship is the subjective ministry of the Holy Spirit (the *eschatological* Spirit), who speaks in the heart of each adopted son[46] with the *ipsissima verba* of the messianic Son, "Abba! Father!" (Rom. 8:15; cf. Mark 14:36).[47] "The clear implication of Rom. 8:15f. and Gal.

---

44. Richard B. Gaffin Jr., *By Faith, Not by Sight: Paul and the Order of Salvation*, 2nd ed. (Phillipsburg, NJ: P&R Publishing, 2013), 63 (emphasis in original).

45. Ibid., 77.

46. Note that Paul changes to the singular *you* in Galatians 4:7, personalizing the force of the adoption. We are adopted collectively by grace through faith, each one as a son of God in the Son of God.

47. That Paul is referencing the Marcan tradition of Christ's words is attested by the uniqueness of the phrase. See Scott, *Adoption as Sons of God*, 183–84; Mark Stibbe, *From*

4:6f. is that Paul regarded the *abba* prayer as something distinctive to those who had received the eschatological Spirit."[48] The believers in Christ not only obtain the sonship and inheritance privileges granted them by faith union with the Son of God, but also enjoy the filial *intimate* access that the holy Son of God renders to them. "On the one hand, it [adoption] is a thing of the future, a longed for goal (Rom. 8:23: 'we wait for adoption as sons'); on the other hand, it is a present thing, as is attested by the fact that in the Spirit—that eschatological gift—we cry, 'Abba!' (Rom. 8:15f.; Gal. 4:6f.)."[49]

Summary: Life in the Spirit of the Risen Son

The life of believers launched in this new epoch is life in the Spirit of the risen Son. This new and renewing life in the Spirit functions in whole reliance on the completed work of Christ. "Life in the Spirit has its specific eschatological quality because it is the shared life of the resurrected Christ in union with him."[50] Confirming their realized sonship identity, the Spirit of the Son leads, motivates, and empowers the adopted sons in a redemptive-historically unprecedented way, making a return to moral and spiritual bondage (Gal. 4:9; cf. Rom. 8:15–17) an untenable alternative, and establishing obedience as the essence of their eschatologically conditioned familial relationship (Gal. 5:16–6:10; cf. Rom. 8:14). Redemptive grace in its full contours is *filial grace*, grace in and through the Son of God; adoption as the *telos* of redemption entails *all* that union with Christ by his Spirit entails—the forensic and the renovative.

Thus, the work of Christ the Son introduces an unprecedented state and condition of sonship, producing an unfettered intimacy with God as Father through the Son. The legal demands of the law have been met in the crucified and resurrected Son: the adopted sons are

---

Orphans to Heirs: Celebrating Our Spiritual Adoption (Oxford: Bible Reading Fellowship, 1999), 67–68. Contra James Barr, "'Abba, Father' and the Familiarity of Jesus' Speech," *Theology* 91 (1988): 179.

48. James D. G. Dunn, *Christology in the Making: A New Testament Inquiry into the Origins of the Doctrine of the Incarnation*, 2nd ed. (Grand Rapids: Eerdmans, 1996), 27.

49. Rudolf Bultmann, *Theology of the New Testament* (Waco, TX: Baylor University Press, 2007), 278.

50. Gaffin, "'Life-Giving Spirit,'" 584.

justified. The Spirit of the resurrected Son renews hearts with transforming and renewing filial grace: the adopted sons are sanctified. As evidenced by the subjective confirmation of the Holy Spirit in the hearts of the sons (Gal. 4:6),[51] those adopted *must* and *can* live in the freedom of obedience by submission to the eschatological Spirit (4:9, 31; 5:1, 5–6, 13–26). Therefore, by the faithful work of the Son of God, the divine goal of redemptive history is exhaustively fulfilled: "*adoption through propitiation*."[52] By the faithful ministry of the Holy Spirit, this redemptively consummate adoption takes the sons safely and successfully through suffering unto glory. The rich provisions of the Spirit of adoption in the *now* and the *not yet* surface prominently in Paul's treatment of *huiothesia* in Romans, where the apostle draws the pneumatological, eschatological, and covenantal contours of filial grace. To this magisterial epistle we turn in the next chapter.

51. The "Spirit not only assures us, but also enables us to address God as Father." Peterson, *Adopted by God*, 88. Freedom for filial relationship with the Father comes only by the completed work of the Son par excellence, and the applying and *transforming* ministry of the Holy Spirit who "personally, supernaturally, individually, and inscrutably assures us of our sonship." Ibid. Cf. Robert A. Peterson, "Toward a Systematic Theology of Adoption," *Presbyterion* 27, 2 (2001): 123–27.

52. J. I. Packer, *Knowing God*, 20th anniversary ed. (Downers Grove, IL: InterVarsity Press, 1993), 214 (emphasis added).

6

ADOPTION APPLIED:

THE SPIRIT AND THE SONS OF GOD

For you did not receive the spirit of slavery to fall back into fear, but you have received the Spirit of adoption as sons, by whom we cry, "Abba! Father!" The Spirit himself bears witness with our spirit that we are children of God, and if children, then heirs—heirs of God and fellow heirs with Christ, provided we suffer with him in order that we may also be glorified with him. (Rom. 8:15–17)

For we know that the whole creation has been groaning together in the pains of childbirth until now. And not only the creation, but we ourselves, who have the firstfruits of the Spirit, groan inwardly as we wait eagerly for adoption as sons, the redemption of our bodies. (Rom. 8:22–23)

For I could wish that I myself were accursed and cut off from Christ for the sake of my brothers, my kinsmen according to the flesh. They are Israelites, and to them belong the adoption, the glory, the covenants, the giving of the law, the worship, and the promises. To them belong the patriarchs, and from their race, according to the flesh, is the Christ, who is God over all, blessed forever. Amen. (Rom. 9:3–5)

The Eschatological Spirit

Pneumatology and Eschatology

Using the term *pneuma* ("spirit") only five times in Romans 1–7,[1] Paul makes a dramatic shift in chapter 8, where *pneuma* appears *twenty-one* times.[2] Keeping in mind the epochal transition marked by Christ's humiliation and exaltation, the coalescence of Christ with the Holy Spirit throughout the Pauline corpus and in particular here in Romans 8,[3] and the combination of Old Testament prophecies and the Acts 2 fulfillment, we see that Paul's repeated emphasis on the Holy Spirit here signals the culmination of divine redemptive purposes on the stage of history. Furthermore, his escalating argument in Romans drives the reader to the anticipated eschatological hope promised in the Old Testament and realized in the risen Christ. The vigorous emphasis on the Holy Spirit brings the eschatological thrust of Paul's argument to the forefront, because the Spirit of Jesus Christ is the *eschatological* Spirit.[4] It is not surprising that of these twenty-one occurrences of *pneuma* in chapter 8, at least nineteen of them refer to God the Holy Spirit—and only once does *pneuma* necessarily indicate the human spirit.[5]

---

1. Rom. 1:4; 1:9; 2:29; 5:6; 7:6.

2. Rom. 8:2, 4, 5 (two times), 6, 9 (three times), 10, 11 (two times), 13, 14, 15 (two times), 16 (two times), 23, 26 (two times), 27. See Trevor J. Burke, "Adoption and the Spirit in Romans 8," *EvQ* 70, 4 (1998): 311.

3. Cf. Geerhardus Vos, "The Eschatological Aspect of the Pauline Conception of the Spirit," in *Redemptive History and Biblical Interpretation: The Shorter Writings of Geerhardus Vos*, ed. Richard B. Gaffin Jr. (Phillipsburg, NJ: Presbyterian and Reformed, 1980), 107; Robert Letham, *The Work of Christ*, Contours of Christian Theology (Downers Grove, IL: InterVarsity Press, 1993), 212–13; M. M. B. Turner, "The Significance of Spirit Endowment for Paul," *VE* 9 (1975): 64–65.

4. See Vos, "Eschatological Aspect," 94–125; Turner, "Significance of Spirit Endowment for Paul," 56–61; M. M. B. Turner, "The Concept of Receiving the Spirit in John's Gospel," *VE* 10 (1977): 24; James D. G. Dunn, *Jesus and the Spirit: A Study of the Religious and Charismatic Experience of Jesus and the First Christians as Reflected in the New Testament* (Philadelphia: Westminster, 1975), 310–12; Herman N. Ridderbos, *Paul: An Outline of His Theology*, trans. John Richard DeWitt (Grand Rapids: Eerdmans, 1975), 214–23; George Eldon Ladd, *A Theology of the New Testament*, ed. Donald A. Hagner, rev. ed. (Grand Rapids: Eerdmans, 1993), 407–11; Sinclair B. Ferguson, *The Holy Spirit*, Contours of Christian Theology (Downers Grove, IL: InterVarsity Press, 1996), 176–82; Gordon D. Fee, "Baptism in the Holy Spirit: The Issue of Separability and Subsequence," *Pneuma* 7, 1 (1985): 91–93.

5. The second occurrence of *pneuma* in Romans 8:16 *must* mean "human spirit." See James G. D. Dunn, *Romans 1–8*, WBC 38A (Dallas: Word, 1988), 454. Other occurrences subject to debate concerning the divine or human referent of *pneuma* are 8:10 and 8:15.

The Holy Spirit's comprehensively Christological focus marks the dawn of the end of ages (1 Cor. 10:11). The ministry of the Spirit, as the personal agent who confirms and applies the completed work of Jesus Christ, distinguishes the end of one age (law and bondage) and the beginning of the other (grace and freedom). More specifically, the Spirit's outpouring at Pentecost signals this epochal change, which was secured by the resurrection and ascension of Jesus Christ. This resurrection/ascension marks history's dramatic hinge point, and with its cosmic and epochal significance also swings biblical revelation from anticipation to realization, from shadow to substance, and from promise to fulfillment.

> From his Jewish heritage he [Paul] well understood that the Spirit was part of the promise for the future. The promises of the New Covenant had been put into an eschatological frame by Jeremiah and Ezekiel and had become thoroughgoing in later Jewish expectations on the basis of Joel 2:28–30. This is why the Spirit is so crucial to Paul's understanding of Christian existence. The gift of the out-poured Spirit meant that the messianic age had already arrived. The Spirit is thus the central element in this altered perspective, the key to which is Paul's firm conviction that the Spirit was both the *certain evidence that the future had dawned, and the absolute guarantee of its final consummation.*[6]

This eschatological character of the Spirit's work runs through the eighth chapter of Romans, where Paul makes overt Christological/pneumatological connections (8:2–3, 9–11, 14–17, 26–30). These explicit references frame the section with a comprehensive redemptive-historical orientation, and this Christological/pneumatological solidarity implicitly saturates the entire chapter and the subsequent argumentation in Romans 9–11, even as it does the entire Pauline

---

Since the context of 8:9–11 centers on the ministry of the Holy Spirit, it is best to view its meaning in 8:10 as the Holy Spirit (as indicated in the ESV). Its meaning in Romans 8:15 will be considered shortly.

6. Gordon D. Fee, *God's Empowering Presence: The Holy Spirit in the Letters of Paul* (Peabody, MA: Hendrickson, 1994), 806 (emphasis in original).

concept of the Holy Spirit. The long-promised and long-awaited stage of redemptive accomplishment has arrived in Christ, putting an end to the subeschatological restlessness of the pre-Christ epoch.[7] Precisely as promised, the Old Testament guarantee of the outpoured Spirit coincides with the accomplished redemption in the Messiah.

> As such, namely, as the eschatological gift of salvation, the Spirit is the firstfruits, the temporary share, the *aparchē* [firstfruits] of the new aeon. At the same time He is the pledge, the *arrabōn* [earnest or pledge] of the entire redemption which the Lord will bring about. In this way the Lord and the Spirit belong together. They belong together by virtue of the revelation of the fullness of time. When the fullness of the times had come (Gal. 4), then God sent His Son, but together with His Son also the Spirit of His Son. Therefore, in Paul's preaching the Spirit represents before anything else the stage of salvation which the Church of Christ had reached by the coming of the Son.[8]

Hence, Paul's *Spirit*-focus in Romans 8 affirms the new age, the new creation, and the kingdom inauguration ushered in by the resurrected, exalted Son of God.

The Holy Spirit of Christ, the Holy Spirit of Adoption

Only with this redemptive-historical function of the Holy Spirit in view does one properly understand *adoption* in Christ. These pneumatological/Christological contours contextually situate the *huiothesian* concept in Romans. In short, the combined emphases of sons-in-the-Son resurrection, sons-in-the-Son adoption, and the Holy Spirit of adoption in this section of Romans indicate that a proper grasp of adoption will come only by placing it squarely in a grand filial/eschatological construct and the instructive pneumatological

---

7. See David B. Garner, "Did God Really Say?," in *Did God Really Say? Affirming the Truthfulness and Trustworthiness of Scripture*, ed. David B. Garner (Phillipsburg, NJ: P&R Publishing, 2012), 154–59.

8. Herman N. Ridderbos, *When the Time Had Fully Come: Studies in New Testament Theology* (Grand Rapids: Eerdmans, 1957), 51–52.

already but *not yet* parameters employed in Romans 8–9. The intrusion of the future on the now characterizes Pauline eschatology, so that future glory shapes present life. "In Christ's resurrection . . . the age to come has begun, the new creation has actually dawned; eschatological reality has been inaugurated."[9] Christ's resurrected and exalted sonship establishes the adoption of believers in the age of the Spirit.

Put otherwise, the resurrection life of the Son of God comprehensively shapes the believer's state, nature, outlook, and identity in this world. As Ladd put it tersely, *"the future has created the present."*[10] Because redeemed sons are placed in the Son by the Spirit of the Son, eschatology inaugurated and consummate eschatological realization in Christ define life for the redeemed. In Romans 8, the apostle shows how the Spirit of adoption's dynamic presence bonds the redeemed to the resurrected Son, so that the adopted sons of God enjoy this Spirit's vivifying and purifying work. This Spirit of Christ will transform their bodies on the last day, manifest them as renewed sons, and conform them fully into the glorious image of the Son of God (Rom. 8:29; cf. Phil. 1:6).

In view of the necessity of the Holy Spirit's eschatological outpouring for the realization of new covenant promise, for the conferral of Christ's righteousness, and for effective victory against unrighteousness, Paul caps his discussion of sanctification's necessity and essence (Rom. 6–8) with a vigorous emphasis on the Holy Spirit. For sanctification to occur, the presence of the Holy Spirit is mandatory—he alone brings the believer to victory over sin in his life through his application of the work of the eschatologically victorious Son. In fact, according to Paul's argument in Romans 8, this Spirit-led victory of the in-Son sons provides proof of personal salvation, of genuine sonship. The Holy Spirit is the Spirit of adoption; Pauline pneumatology is filio-pneumatology. Holiness and sonship are mutually informing and mutually inclusive. It is the sons of God who are led by the Spirit; adopted sons are holy ones.

9. Richard B. Gaffin Jr., *By Faith, Not by Sight: Paul and the Order of Salvation*, 2nd ed. (Phillipsburg, NJ: P&R Publishing, 2013), 69.

10. George Eldon Ladd, "Eschatology and the Unity of New Testament Theology," *Expository Times* 68 (1957): 273 (emphasis in original).

The Spirit of Adoption *Already*: What Now?
Filial Freedom and Transformation by the Spirit

In contextual and organic continuity with the culminating eschatology of *huiothesia* in Romans 8:23, verses 12–17 first express the realized eschatological contours of the believers' adoption. Having established, in verses 1–11, the epochal shift brought about by Christ and the transformative implications for believers, in verse 12 Paul transitions with *Ara oun* ("So then"), giving cue that his following argument flows directly from the previous epochal and soteriological discussion.[11] Building on the historical and functional convergence of the eschatological Spirit with the eschatological Son, Paul contends that the Spirit of the resurrected Christ indwells the believer (v. 9), and then moves on to develop the nature and implications of that spiritual[12] and eschatological presence. What is broadly characteristic of Paul's doctrine of the Holy Spirit gets explicit treatment in verses 9–11, as the apostle exposes the implications of the *past* resurrection of Christ for believers to live *presently* according to *in Christ future* reality.

By the Spirit we have already received our "adoption" as God's children, but what is *already* is also *not yet*. Therefore, we "who have the firstfruits of the Spirit" await adoption's consummative glory, in the form of the redemption of our bodies (Rom. 8:23). The first sheaf comes as God's pledge to us of the final harvest. Thus, in one of the clearest passages in the corpus in which Paul delineates his basic eschatological framework, the Spirit plays the essential role in our present existence, as both evidence and pledge that the future is now and yet to be.[13]

The full resurrection "life to your mortal bodies" (Rom. 8:11) that awaits the believer at the eschaton *already* defines and shapes the believer's life by virtue of the Spirit of the resurrected Christ. Paul views Christ's resurrection as the first ("firstfruits," 1 Cor. 15:23; cf. Rom.

---

11. Cf. John Murray, *The Epistle to the Romans: The English Text with Introduction, Exposition and Notes*, 2 vols. combined (repr., Grand Rapids: Eerdmans, 1997), 1:293; C. E. B. Cranfield, *Introduction and Commentary on Romans I–VIII: A Critical and Exegetical Commentary on the Epistle to the Romans* (Edinburgh: T&T Clark Limited, 1975), 394.

12. All sanctification, as Paul sees it, is Spirit-wrought. Though literary convention sadly requires the lowercase in *spiritual*, the Spirit is *personal*.

13. Fee, *God's Empowering Presence*, 807.

8:23) in one whole harvest of resurrected saints, so that the bodily resurrection of the saints is not merely promised and anticipated, but sealed and made certain by the Holy Spirit of Christ (1 Cor. 15:12–58). The Old Testament rich agricultural image (cf. Gen. 49:3; Ex. 34:22; Prov. 3:9; Jer. 2:3; Ezek. 44:30) serves the theological point—there is one resurrection that believers share with Christ. This *in Christ* resurrection solidarity is not merely conceptual, but eschatologically vital and existentially formative. The age to come intrudes on the current age, making the life of the redeemed wholly determined by the eschatological success of the Son of God in his obedient death and his resurrection (Rom. 1:3–4). The condemnation of sin in the flesh by God's "own Son" (8:3) is accomplished so that we might now possess the Spirit and be possessed by the Spirit (v. 9), that we might be made alive in the Spirit and live in the Spirit (vv. 10–11), and that by the Spirit's lively presence we might actually "please God" (v. 8) and have our minds "set . . . on the things of the Spirit" (v. 5). Such spiritual life confirms the organic character of *already* and *not yet* eschatology:

> The renewing and working of the Spirit in believers during their present life can also be understood as a beginning of the resurrection of the body, and be described by Paul in this way (cf. 2 Cor. 3:18; 4:10, 11, 16, 17; Eph. 5:14; Phil. 3:10, 11). So the shining of the glory of the future life illuminates them even now (2 Cor. 3:18; 4:6), a first-fruit and earnest in the present time of their resurrection from the dead (cf. Gal. 6:8; Rom. 8:23; 2 Cor. 5:5).[14]

Final resurrection/glorification constitutes the final act of transforming grace by the Spirit of God, of whom believers now possess the "firstfruits" (Rom. 8:23). The believer's life is Spirit-given resurrection life.

To put it in the particular Pauline filial categories, in view of the underlying *now* but *not yet* eschatological continuity, the ultimate resurrection/adoption that takes place by the Spirit at the parousia (Rom. 8:23) makes essential the *current* filial renovation by the Holy Spirit of adoption (v. 15). Such transformation by the Spirit of adoption does not

14. Ridderbos, *Paul*, 551.

and cannot await the eschaton, but as the last days are inaugurated and the eschatological Spirit of adoption indwells the believer, the reality of consummate adoptive grace comprehensively bears on our present sonship status *and* ongoing filial and moral transformation by the Spirit of the resurrected Christ. By virtue of union with the resurrected Christ, bodily resurrection and final filial conformity require present sanctification by the Spirit of adoption (vv. 11, 15).

The Spirit, Adoption, and Moral Obligation

Moral obligation, as Paul sees it, is a vital component of the gospel and, in particular, concerns the Spirit's vital ministry in the life of the believer.[15] Moral obedience is not a *means* to receiving God's grace, but is a necessary manifestation of it. Paul does not hesitate to express our *familial* indebtedness in the context of the gospel: "So then, *brothers*, we are debtors" (Rom. 8:12a). The Christian life is not one free of obligation, but one free *unto* filial and moral obligation. "Our union with Christ does not free us from obligation to the law, but from its curse. This union does not free us from the weight of the imperatives, but by the power of the indicative (Christ's life, death, resurrection) frees us *for* the imperatives. Gospel freedom is holy freedom, and the Spirit of Christ is the *Holy* Spirit."[16]

While the *debt* concept arises in Romans 8:12, the particular debt owed remains unidentified until 8:13. Before probing what *is* owed, Paul briefly profiles Spirit-given liberty. Because of the resurrection power of Christ indwelling the believer (8:11) and the certain eschatological freedom (cf. 7:24), the living, indwelling eschatological Holy Spirit removes the *present* obligation to the flesh and to sin (cf. 6:11–14). A theme already developed in Romans 6, and carried forward in Paul's current argumentation, is that apart from Christ and the Holy Spirit, the flesh (sin, unrighteousness, death—understood first epochally and

---

15. Mark Jones, *Antinomianism: Reformed Theology's Unwelcome Guest?* (Phillipsburg, NJ: P&R Publishing, 2013), 67, 114. Cf. David B. Garner, "You Just Might Be an Anti-nomian," review of *Antinomianism: Reformed Theology's Unwelcome Guest?*, by Mark Jones, *Reformation 21* (February 2014), http://www.reformation21.org/shelf-life/antinomianism-reformed-theologys-unwelcome-guest.php (accessed February 6, 2016).

16. Garner, "You Just Might Be an Antinomian" (emphasis added).

then existentially, as explained more fully below) retains mastery over one's life. With the presence of the Spirit of the victorious Son in this pneumatological age, however, the mastery of the flesh is overwhelmed, moral/spiritual slavery is abolished, and the slave is emancipated from the tyrannical rule of sin (cf. Rom. 6:15–19; 8:2; Gal. 4:7; 5:1). The cosmic, redemptive-historically decisive work of Christ defines the soteriological and eschatological realities of faith: since the risen Son is Master and Lord, "sin will have no dominion over you" (Rom. 6:14).

The Spirit of Christ, this Spirit who works according to pretemporal intra-Trinitarian purpose (Eph. 1:3–14) and whose outpouring depends on the redeeming work of the incarnate Son (Gal. 4:1–7), indwells the believer and applies to him Christ's resurrection power for his battle against the flesh (Eph. 1:15–23; 6:10–20). Note well that *flesh* is not exclusively, and indeed not even primarily, an existential term for Paul. Rather, it connotes a redemptive-historical concept that places the eschatological/pneumatological *age* in contrast to the former, pre-Christ epoch of flesh. As the *historia salutis* sets the theological basis for the *ordo salutis*, the epochal informs the existential. Ridderbos comments accordingly:

> Flesh is the mode of existence of man and world before the fullness of time appeared. Flesh is man and world in the powers of darkness. And opposing this is the Spirit, the Pneuma, not first and foremost as an individual experience, not even in the first place as an individual reversal, but as a new way of existence which became present time with the coming of Christ . . . . This being in the Spirit is not a mystical, but an eschatological, redemptive-historical category.[17]

And it is *this* historical and theological category that defines the redeemed sons' context.

The work of kingdom transferral is foundationally an epochal/eschatological change, moving one from the ruling epoch of darkness to the new epoch of kingdom light in the messianic *Son*.[18] The Spirit's

---

17. Ridderbos, *When the Time Had Fully Come*, 52. Cf. Ridderbos, *Paul*, 66–67; Anthony A. Hoekema, *The Bible and the Future* (Grand Rapids: Eerdmans, 1979), 30, 58.

18. James Dunn comments on this passage, "There is nothing quite like this claim

outpouring indicates the full vindication/justification of the sons of God in the Son of God. But in addition, in this age of the new kingdom, the believer is subject and indebted to the King/Master (Rom. 6:1–14), and under new covenant blessing also possesses in richer ways *personally and existentially* the real and realized enablement of the Spirit of Christ for obedience.[19] To return to the motif of Romans 8, the believer— who dwells in the age of the outpouring of the eschatological Spirit, that is, the age of *realized* adoptive sonship (cf. Gal. 4:4–7)—now declared an adopted son (the legal), bears an intensified yet now fully empowered sonly obligation to his Father (the renovative). Graciously juxtaposed with this intensified obligation is the dynamic presence of the renewing, eschatological Spirit in the sons themselves.

Continuing with his theme of obligation, Paul proclaims that instead of obligation to the flesh,[20] the redeemed son has a joyful obligation through the Holy Spirit to the mortification of it. Living according to the flesh necessitates spiritual death; mortification of the flesh, by the Spirit, accomplishes spiritual life. "The only way of avoiding the issue of death is to be delivered and desist from the life

---

that believers in Christ Jesus have already (aorist tense) been transferred into the kingdom, like a whole people transported from their traditional territory to settle in a new region." He adds, "The language is . . . the exaggerated expression of rich spiritual experience and full confidence (hope) that what had already been done (aorist tense) would be completed without fail." James D. G. Dunn, *The Epistles to the Colossians and to Philemon: A Commentary on the Greek Text*, NIGTC (Grand Rapids: Eerdmans, 1996), 77–78. What Dunn considers "exaggerated" is more properly understood as *inaugurated* and *actualized*. The kingdom transfer has been accomplished because of the outpouring of the eschatological Spirit and the believers' Spirit-wrought union with Christ in his historical accomplishment of redemption.

19. In chapter 9, further consideration is given to the distinct privileges for believers living in the postresurrection age. Meticulous care is in order here to avoid an unbiblical discontinuity between the spiritual experiences of Old Testament saints and New Testament ones. Yet an equal meticulousness is in order in view of the redemptive-historical significance of the resurrection and the outpoured Spirit of Christ. The veritable intensification of revealed obligation in the new covenant is met with full adequacy by the outpoured presence of the life-giving Spirit. Whatever we say about proleptic ministry of the Holy Spirit in the lives of the old covenant saints must neither flatten redemptive history nor minimize the eschatological significance of the resurrection by understanding the radical existential implications of new covenant blessing. See Richard B. Gaffin Jr., "The Holy Spirit," *WTJ* 43, 1 (1980): 70–78.

20. Paul uses the term *sōma*, which here functions synonymously with *sarx*. See Cranfield, *Romans I–VIII*, 395.

of the flesh."[21] Here, Paul reiterates the critical connection of justification with sanctification (Rom. 8:1–4). Further, he is restating his conclusion of Romans 6 noted above that the believer's obligation to sin's mastery has been removed in the death and resurrection of Christ. This emphasis on Christ's historical work once again features the epochal before the psychological and existential meanings of *flesh* and *Spirit*. The Holy Spirit applies this finished holy work of the risen Christ to the believer.

Here in Romans 8:13, this application by the Holy Spirit gains emphasis by way of a contrast. Without the Spirit, life leads to death; with the Spirit, the believer lives, and in this life engages mortification: "by the Spirit you put to death the deeds of the body." In addition, by the inclusion of *pneumati* ("by the Spirit"),[22] Paul points to the indispensable and preeminent role of the Holy Spirit. To put Pauline thought (in Romans and beyond) in theological shorthand, Spirit-wrought sanctification is not optional, but is the essential corollary of justification, and is a central element of biblical sonship (cf. Ex. 4:22–23). Without sanctification, spiritual death results;[23] and without possession of the eschatological Spirit of adoption, there is no sanctification, and indeed no salvation.

In Romans 8:14, Paul's *debt* argument unfolds yet further. The obligation to mortification in verses 12–13 reflects the newly established mastery of the eschatological Spirit in the believer's life (cf. 8:2–4): "Those who by the Spirit put to death the deeds of the body are led by the Spirit of God."[24] As Paul articulates in 8:14, these who mortify the deeds of the body *are* sons; it is these sons who are *pneumati theou agontai* ("led by the Spirit of God").[25] The mortification of sin by the

21. Murray, *Romans*, 1:294.

22. An instrumental dative. Cranfield explains, "The Spirit of God—and only the Spirit of God—is to be the means of the destruction of the flesh and its activities." *Romans I–VIII*, 394. The placement of *pneuma* in the sentence emphasizes the indispensability of the Holy Spirit in sanctification.

23. Dunn comments, "The repetition of the final phrase of v 12 shows that Paul has in mind no merely hypothetical or unreal possibility. The danger is real for his hearers: the switch to second person increases the note of warning." *Romans 1–8*, 448.

24. Murray, *Romans*, 1:295.

25. The emphatic *outoi* in Romans 8:14b indicates that it is these renovating sons *alone* who are sons of God.

Holy Spirit[26] in the believer's life not only confirms that he is raised spiritually, but also solidifies his new privileged identity transformed by Christ's resurrection. The sonship realized in Jesus Christ and enjoyed by the outpouring of his Spirit is mature, eschatological sonship, because Christ's sonship in his resurrection/vindication marks the attainment of complete and faithful sonship. For the redeemed sons, power to combat the "deeds of the body" (v. 13) comes by union with the fully vindicated Son of God and by the leading of his Spirit (v. 14).

Paul's developing thesis here could be summarized this way: the process of experiential/filial sanctification as a resurrected son confirms and manifests the believer's spiritual and eschatological sonship, shared in and with Jesus Christ. It is exclusively those led by the Spirit that are *huioi theou* ("sons of God"), and the leading of the Spirit is "what differentiates [the children of God] from all others . . . . None can claim the high title of sons of God who are not led by the Spirit of God."[27] Because of the consummate victory of the Son par excellence over sin and death, sonship in the sanctified Son of God and experiential moral renovation remain inseparable: "The evidence of being Spirit-led-sons-of-God (Rom. 8:13) is shown by the Christian continually . . . putting to death the misdeeds of the body. The *ethical* responsibility for God's sons to live circumspectly pervades Paul's thesis of adoption."[28] This ethical responsibility also necessarily reflects the obedience of the Great Son himself, the Lord Jesus Christ, who was led by the Spirit into the wilderness (Luke 4:1), learned filial obedience (Heb. 5:7–10), and committed himself to doing the will of

26. The *thanatoute* ("put to death") and *pneumati* ("by the Spirit") indicate the dual responsibility in sanctification. Believers must mortify the sin, but the Holy Spirit enables them (v. 13) and leads them (v. 14) in the process. Sanctification is preeminently a work of the Spirit whereby the adopted sons walk by his holy, empowering lead.

27. Benjamin B. Warfield, *Biblical and Theological Studies* (Philadelphia: Presbyterian and Reformed, 1968), 545. The leading of the Spirit is not merely divine guidance of *any* sort, but, as Benjamin B. Warfield contends, guidance into righteousness. The "'leading of the Holy Spirit' is revealed to us as simply a synonym for sanctification." Ibid., 546. Cf. Ferguson, *Holy Spirit*, 183; James M. Scott, *Adoption as Sons of God: An Exegetical Investigation into the Background of* YIOTHESIA *in the Pauline Corpus*, Wissenschaftliche Untersuchungen Zum Neuen Testament 48 (Tübingen: J. C. B. Mohr [Paul Siebeck], 1992), 263–64; Burke, "Adoption and the Spirit," 319–20.

28. Trevor J. Burke, "The Characteristics of Paul's Adoptive-Sonship (Huiothesia) Motif," *IBS* 17, 2 (1995): 64 (emphasis in original). Cf. Burke, "Adoption and the Spirit," 320.

his Father (Ps. 40:8; Heb. 10:7–9) according to the Word of his Spirit (Luke 4:4–13). As their Elder Brother walked, so must those walk in solidarity with him—to borrow the Pauline phrase, they must "walk by the Spirit [of Christ]" (Gal. 5:16). Or as John Murray puts it succinctly, "The activity of the believer is the evidence of the Spirit's activity and the activity of the Spirit is the cause of the believer's activity."[29]

By virtue of the Spirit's ministry uniting believers with Christ, the Spirit by his Word also governs the lives of the adopted sons, compelling and enabling Christlike obedience. The Spirit's gracious joining of believers to Jesus Christ the resurrected Son forms a most remarkable familial relationship with the heavenly Father (Rom. 8:15). The change is surely one of state and condition (cf. Col. 1:13), but by virtue of the outpoured personal Spirit of Christ, the change produces new filial motivation and internal transformation (Rom. 8:9–11, 29).

The Spirit of adoption empowers the believer for spiritual renovation by mortification of sin, and he accomplishes this empowerment in the mystical union with the Son by the Spirit, or, as Paul puts it succinctly, by *adoption*. In other words, change by the Spirit for conformity to the Father's expectations confirms adoption by the Father and manifests familial likeness to the glorified Son (cf. Rom. 8:29). The believer is not merely a slave in the presence of a new King; he is an adopted (resurrected) *son* in the household of the *Father*, empowered by the Spirit of the Son to please his Father. He is a son in the Son.

Human or Divine Spirit?

Building on the spiritual renovation of the adopted sons, Romans 8:15–16 develops the argument concerning the sonship of those who are led by the Spirit (v. 14).[30] Paul posits two contrasting and mutually exclusive notions: the spirit (or Spirit?) received is one of slavery *or* the spirit (or Spirit?) received is one of adoption. Determining the proper rendering of *pneuma* ("spirit") in these occurrences has produced some interpretive disagreement. Does Paul speak of a human *pneuma* or of the divine *pneuma*? Or does he speak of a human *pneuma* with *pneuma*

---

29. Murray, *Romans*, 1:295.
30. The conjunctive *gar* ("for") of Romans 8:15 indicates this connection.

douleias ("spirit of slavery"), and the divine *pneuma* with *pneuma huiothesia* ("Spirit of adoption")? Exegetical clues within Romans 8 provide important guidance, but before we consider them, a brief New Testament survey concerning *pneuma* is in order.

Though the term *pneuma* is frequently used of a *human* dispositional complex, spirit, or *habitus* (e.g., 1 Cor. 4:21; 16:18),[31] with arguably *no* exception, when considered as a gift from God in a soteriological context, the term refers to the Holy Spirit. God gives only his Spirit and, in this eschatological age, gives only the Spirit of his Son. Contrary to this assertion, Luther, Dodd, Lenski, Meyer, Sanday and Headlam, Moo, and others take the occurrences of *pneuma* in Romans 8:15 as a human spirit. Yet this rendering does not cohere. In fact, when the New Testament, in a soteriological context, speaks of God's giving (*didōmi*) *or* mankind's receiving (*lambanō*) *pneuma*, it is arguably *always* in reference to the person of the Holy Spirit, not an abstracted impersonal or even a human disposition.[32]

A plausible exception is found in Ephesians 1:17, where Paul prays for the Ephesians, *hina ho theos tou kuriou hēmōn Iēsou Christou, ho patēr tēs doxēs, dōē humin pneuma sophias kai apokalupseōs en epignōsei autou* ("that the God of our Lord Jesus Christ, the Father of glory, may give you a spirit of wisdom and of revelation in the knowledge of him"). Yet the context of this prayer does not suggest that Paul prays for a gift of human disposition, but Spirit-wrought understanding. Paul beseeches the Father to equip the Ephesian saints with spiritual *discernment* and *intimate understanding* of the depths of God's blessings for them through Christ the Spirit (Eph. 1:17–19). This spiritual

---

31. "The character is the *habitus* of the person, the whole complex of desires, of motives, propensions, principles. This may conveniently be called the dispositional complex, and the complex comprises all that goes to make up the distinguishing moral and religious, bent, aim, purpose, and propension. Scripture calls this the heart." John Murray, *The Collected Writings of John Murray*, 4 vols. (Edinburgh: Banner of Truth, 1976–82), 2:61.

32. Cf. William Hendriksen, *Exposition of Paul's Epistle to the Romans*, NTC (Grand Rapids: Baker, 1981), 258. Cf. Turner, "Receiving the Spirit," 25–26. Concerning *lambanō* with *pneuma*, see John 20:22; Acts 2:33; 8:15, 19; 19:2; Gal. 3:14. Concerning *didōmi* with *pneuma*, see Luke 11:13; Acts 5:32; Rom. 5:5; 1 Thess. 4:8; 1 John 3:24; 4:13. Throughout the New Testament, in terms of *soteric benefit*, God gives us only the "Spirit," not a human "spirit." Such a fact remains consistent with the unilateral nature of grace, in which the objective monergistic work of the triune God in Christ is the *efficient* cause of personal salvation.

understanding comes only by the persuading and illumining power of the Spirit of Christ, by whom they are already sealed (Eph. 1:13). The petition for epistemic clarity and genuine understanding presupposes the redemptive presence of the Spirit, who blesses his people with the pneumanoetic effects of regeneration (cf. 1 Cor. 2:1–16). Paul does not pray that believers receive the gift of the Spirit whom they already have, but that they understand and embrace the gift *from* the Spirit of spiritual understanding.[33] Even this passage maintains the personal divinely *spiritual* meaning.

Another use of *pneuma* frequently interpreted as a human "spirit" appears in 2 Timothy 1:7 (NIV, KJV, NASB, ESV), yet in this text, which in many ways parallels the thrust of Romans 8:15, this anarthrous *pneuma* also ought to be translated "Spirit." Paul says, *ou gar edōken hēmin ho theos pneuma deilias alla dunameōs kai agapēs kai sōphronismou* ("for God gave us a spirit not of fear but of power and love and self-control"). Though translation "with a lower case *s* is possible (since the definite article is absent in Greek), . . . it is most highly improbable and quite misses both the relationship of this sentence to verse 6 as well as Paul's own usage and theology elsewhere."[34] Finally, the other apparent exception occurs in Romans 11:8, where God clearly gives a spirit other than his own. This giving is one of *judgment*, however, not of soteriological blessing, and therefore does not alter this consistent New Testament treatment of the divine gift of the divine *pneuma*.

Redemption is not reducible to a philosophy, an ethic, or even a fresh perspective, precisely because God sends the Spirit of his redeeming Son into the redeemed sons. The cosmic and eschatological outpouring

33. In a similar way, in Ephesians 3:17, Paul prays that "Christ may dwell in your hearts through faith." The apostle does not intend us to conclude that the believers *lose* Christ and must ask for him to reenter their hearts. Rather, he prays that the Spirit of Christ would effectively be "at home" in their hearts. As believers, they possess the Spirit. Paul prays, in a manner consistent with Ephesians 5:18, that the Spirit would possess ("fill") them fully. See Harold W. Hoehner, *Ephesians: An Exegetical Commentary* (Grand Rapids: Baker Academic, 2002), 480–82.

34. Gordon Fee, *1 and 2 Timothy, Titus*, International Biblical Commentary (Peabody, MA: Hendrickson, 1988), 226. Cf. George W. Knight III, *The Pastoral Epistles: A Commentary on the Greek Text* (Grand Rapids: Eerdmans, 1992), 371. How the Spirit is the "Spirit of fear" will receive consideration in the following study of Romans 8:15.

of the Holy Spirit at the hinge point of the ages entirely frames the salvific themes that dominate the Pauline Spirit. Without vacillating, Paul affirms that the redeemed receive *this very* eschatological Spirit, who is the agent of redemptive-historical change.[35] Soteric blessing, as the gift of the covenant-keeping God, is personal. The believer is given none less than the Spirit of the Son of God.

The Spirit is the agent of change—cosmic, eschatological, ecclesiological, and personal. Returning to Romans 8:15–17, Paul identifies the *pneuma* of the Son of God as the soteric and filial source of the eschatological age and therefore also as the personal, eschatological blessing given to the adopted sons. God does not merely give the sons a demeanor; he does not dispense a positive attitude or outlook. This *pneuma* bestowal is neither a mystical power nor an impersonal force; *he* is the very person of God, the Holy Spirit of the risen Christ, the Spirit through whom believers receive the adoption. In other words, the gift from God is a person, not a personality; the Almighty and redeeming God personally sends his personal, eschatological Spirit, not merely an impersonal and subjective motivation for improvement or even a positive human response engendered by the legal blessing of justification.[36]

Summarily, what is true in the application of redemption is true because of the accomplishment of redemption. The cosmic, redemptive-historical ministry of the Spirit grounds the soteriological blessing of the Spirit. The Holy Spirit existentially causes the Christ-union, faithfully confirms the union in the heart of the adopted son, and effectively energizes filial obedience consistent with that Christ-union. United to the eschatological Son by the eschatological Spirit, the adopted sons are called, motivated, and enabled unto obedience in this age of the new covenant: this Christological, pneumatological, and eschatological age.

35. Further, the Spirit's functional equivalence with the risen Christ (cf. 1 Cor. 15:45; 2 Cor. 3:17) makes redemptive-historically explicit the *personal* and *divine* gift of the *pneuma*. See Vos, "Eschatological Aspect," 94–125.

36. Cf. Matthew Vellanickal, *The Divine Sonship of Christians in the Johannine Writings*, AnBib: Investigationes Scientificae in Res Biblicas 72 (Rome: Biblical Institute, 1977), 78; Gordon D. Fee, *Paul, the Spirit, and the People of God* (Peabody, MA: Hendrickson, 1997), 22–35.

The Spirit of Slavery to Fall Back into Fear

An even closer consideration of Romans 8:15 underscores the epochal significance of Paul's repeated use of *pneuma* in this chapter. Given the New Testament usage of *pneuma*, the comprehensive eschatological-Spirit emphasis of Romans 8 (including the immediate consideration of the Holy Spirit in 8:9–14 and the subsequent mention of the Holy Spirit in 8:16), the parallel usage of *pneuma* in Galatians 4:6, which indisputably refers to the Holy Spirit,[37] and the immediately proximate discussion of the Holy Spirit's role in sanctification (Rom. 8:12–14), viewing both occurrences of *pneuma* in 8:15 as the Holy Spirit emerges as the soundest option.[38] A seeming theological incongruity quickly erupts. How can Paul in any sense describe the Holy Spirit of God as the *pneuma douleias palin eis phobon* ("spirit of slavery to fall back into fear")?

Though it may seem perplexing for the Holy Spirit to be so named, indeed that ostensibly strange label flags Paul's intended point.[39] Some have suggested that the language functions rhetorically: in pointed fashion the apostle insists that the Spirit given is not one of enslavement, but quite the opposite, one of gracious adoption. In this interpretation, Paul in no way intends the Holy Spirit to be described in such a fashion, but intends that the *pneuma douleias* ("spirit of slavery") in Romans 8:15 functions as a purely "rhetorical foil to *pneuma huiothesia*" ("spirit of adoption").[40] Of course, it is argued, the Holy Spirit does not enslave or produce fear.

Yet while the terms *slavery* and *fear* concerning the Spirit may seem unfitting, the chosen phrase must not be reduced to rhetorical flourish. The language is epochal, not grandiloquent. Both the flow

37. See chapter 5.
38. Contra Ladd, *Theology of the New Testament*, 534.
39. Cf. Leon Morris, *The Epistle to the Romans* (Grand Rapids: Eerdmans, 1988), 314; Murray, *Romans*, 1:296–97.
40. Scott, *Adoption as Sons of God*, 176. Cf. Brendan Byrne, *"Sons of God"—"Seed of Abraham": A Study of the Idea of the Sonship of God of All Christians in Paul against the Jewish Background*, AnBib: Investigationes Scientificae in Res Biblicas 83 (Rome: Biblical Institute, 1979), 99n75; Burke, "Adoption and the Spirit," 315–16. Some see the spirit of slavery as demonic. See, e.g., Mark Stibbe, *From Orphans to Heirs: Celebrating Our Spiritual Adoption* (Oxford: Bible Reading Fellowship, 1999), 146.

of argument in Romans 8 and a comparison with the redemptive-historical outlook of Paul in Galatians 3–4 fortify this conclusion. Beginning the chapter with a bold statement concerning the new epoch introduced by the resurrected Christ and the Spirit of life (Rom. 8:1–2), in 8:18–30 Paul constructs a global assessment of history—from creation to consummation. He emphasizes the bondage and suffering that characterize this age,[41] placing present futility and corruption in stark contrast to the filial freedom of the gloriously transforming consummation (8:19–23). The scope of the futility is comprehensive, and surely harks back to the covenantal curse expressed following Adam's sin in the garden (Gen. 3). The sin of the original son affected not only his progeny, but also the earth over which he was commanded to exercise dominion (Gen. 1:26–28; cf. Ps. 8): "cursed is the ground because of you" (Gen. 3:17b). Adam's sin triggered the divine curse, a necessary consequence of disobedience according to the covenant established by God with man.

In view of Adam's sin, before and apart from the Son's efficacious work, the Spirit's outpouring would deliver judgment. Adam, the first son of God (Luke 3:38), became guilty of sin, and brought sin's guilt and consequences to himself and his progeny. The proto-evangelical promise (Gen. 3:15) does not mollify sin or its curse, but foresees a cosmic battle by the woman's offspring, who would fight victoriously over sin, guilt, and death (Rom. 5:12–21; Gal. 4:1–6; Heb. 2:10–18). Awaiting such redemption, the former epoch is properly characterized by bondage and fear of eschatological wrath, since the presence of God's Spirit in this pre-Christ context of sin conveys judgment. The first son's and his wife's hiding in the garden of Eden exposes this fear before God's ominous presence,[42] making the delay of divine eschatological wrath and the concomitant promise of redemption contextually *and* cosmically striking. With a view to this pre-Christ epoch of judgment and fear, Galatians 3:23 aptly describes the comprehensive bondage: "Now before faith came, we were held captive

41. See Geerhardus Vos, *The Pauline Eschatology* (Princeton, NJ: Princeton University Press, 1930), 24–34.

42. Concerning Genesis 3:8, see Meredith G. Kline, "Primal Parousia," *WTJ* 40, 2 (1978): 245–80.

under the law, imprisoned until the coming faith would be revealed." Galatians 4:1–4 continues to affirm slavery under the law (Gal. 4:5a) and to the *stoicheia* ("elementary principles").[43] The culpability of Adam and his progeny for sin and its consequences continues unrelentingly (Rom. 5:12–21).

These cosmic effects of Adamic sin on the creation require fuller explanation. In the course of describing the "slavery" and "fear" (Rom. 8:15), the "eager longing" and "wait[ing] eagerly" (vv. 19, 23; cf. v. 25), and the "groaning" (v. 22) of the entire creation, Romans 8:20 centers on the ultimate cause of the futility. It comes "because of him who subjected it." The subjection is personal and covenantal precisely because sin is personal and covenantal. Creation was not the cause of its own bondage and futility, and perhaps most remarkably, Paul argues that *neither* were Adam and Eve! As part of the Pauline disclosure of history's beginning, middle, and end, in no uncertain terms he points to God himself as the source of the futility, bondage, and groaning: "the whole of the groaning creation has been subjected to vanity by God himself (Rom. 8:20)."[44]

The nature of God's covenant with man illumines the context and its meaning. God established a covenantal arrangement with mankind, with both curses and blessings divinely asserted, the realization of which depended on man's response. Obedience would bring blessing; disobedience would bring cursing. In the face of Adam's disobedience, the Creator enacted the curse of futility and bondage just as he had decreed (Gen. 3:14–19). Futility exists because God himself decreed and effected it. As Murray judiciously observes, however, just as God imposed the futility, he alone is the One with the authority to terminate it: "Neither Satan nor man could have subjected it *in hope*; only God could have subjected it with such a design. Besides, the context indicates that the hope will one day be realized and, since only by God's action can this be, in like manner God alone could have established the necessity or ground for hope."[45] Divine agency in the imposition of futility also ensures that though futility enters the creation, this futility

43. See chapter 5 on *stoicheia*.
44. Ridderbos, *Paul*, 92.
45. Murray, *Romans*, 1:303.

does not hopelessly define creation. By sovereign determination, futility is overwhelmed by divine eschatological purpose. Because of divine gracious purpose, hope triumphs over futility; resurrection triumphs over corruption; freedom triumphs over bondage. Creation's futility gives way to God's redemptive purposes; the Son of God resurrected triumphs for those elect sons of Adam condemned.

Describing the ongoing effects of this covenantal curse on the earth, Paul has as his primary concern in Romans 8 the culmination of redemptive history, a climax centering on and dependent on the final manifestation of the adopted sons (Rom. 8:19, 21, 23). From this global and historical vantage point, the apostle brings the redemptive-historical and eschatological transition to full relief in his statement about the Spirit of Christ in Romans 8:15. Epochally speaking, the old age was *divinely* subjected to bondage and to fear. By the work of Christ, that curse and its damning futility have been fully countered and fully overwhelmed. As the redeeming Son on whom the sin of the elect of God has been laid and the One who was vindicated at his resurrection (2 Cor. 5:16–21), Christ releases creation from the divine curse, futility, groaning, and bondage. Because of the resurrected and vindicated Son of God who delivered the bound and condemned sons of Adam, the Spirit of God no longer operates as the agent of covenant curse and bondage, but as the Spirit of the resurrected Christ who renders consummate release.

In the language of Romans 8:15, the divinely determined age of fear and futility finds resolve in the divinely determined outpouring of the "Spirit of adoption." In the old age, the presence of the Spirit confirmed and prophesied the coming judgment; he was indeed the Spirit of slavery (*pneuma douleias*). In the new age of the resurrected/adopted Son of God and coordinately the sons in the Son, he is not *again* the Spirit of bondage unto fear. As the eschatological Spirit of Christ, he confirms the cosmic vindication in the resurrected Son and is, for the believing sons, the Spirit of adoption, by whom creation "obtain[s] the freedom of the glory of the children of God" (Rom. 8:21).

Returning to Romans 8:15, we must appreciate the Pauline pneumatological orientation, as the apostle exposes the dramatic change in this new age. A critical flaw with any rhetorical interpretation concerning the "spirit of slavery" is its insufficient treatment (disregard!) of *palin* ("again") in 8:15. This adverb fortifies the redemptive-historical and theological significance of the passage, and simply disallows a mere rhetorical supposition. Paul envisions here the radical historical contrast brought by the *eschatological* Spirit, who as the Holy Spirit in the pre-Christ epoch functioned as the agent of eschatological judgment unto fear. The work of Christ changes the work of the Holy Spirit for the adopted sons. And at the manifestation of the adopted sons conformed fully into the image of the Son on the last day (Rom. 8:23, 29), the Spirit comes in his fullest manifestation as the gracious Spirit of adoption.

Creation once was divinely subjected to futility, bondage, and fear. The Creator of the first son (Adam) interposed his redemptive plan on the bound and corrupted creation. He sent the last Son (last Adam), whose faithful filial obedience lifted this futility, bondage, and fear. By the Spirit of this last Son, this change occurs cosmically and historically (Eph. 1:15–23; cf. Ps. 8); consequentially, by the Spirit of this Son, this glorifying change comes to the adopted sons blessedly—savingly, irreversibly, and incorruptibly (Rom. 8:15–17; cf. 1 Cor. 15:51–57).

The Christological-pneumatological-soteriological interweaving is remarkable. As is common for Paul, he moves seamlessly between the events of redemptive history and the personal implications for believers living in this new epoch: Romans 8 fluidly integrates redemption accomplished and redemption applied. Having established the epochal change brought by the Spirit of the risen Christ, the apostle insists that for those in Christ, the Spirit is not the Spirit of fear *any longer*, but of *adoption*. The filial hope of the gospel rides on the historic success of the Son, and the Spirit whom the Son bestows on those who believe. In the epochal transition from covenant curse to covenant blessing, the Spirit of fear is now the Spirit of adoption for those in Christ.[46]

---

46. In affirming this radical change in redemptive history, we must reject any notion that filial blessing was entirely inaccessible to Old Testament saints. God's grace extends across the epochs to all of his people, as saints of all ages rely wholly and sweetly on the efficacy of Christ's resurrection.

The Spirit of Adoption

Therefore, in this eschatological age of the outpouring of the Spirit, believers do not possess the Spirit of *slavery to fall back into fear*, so that they remain in their condemnation or in a state of sonship indistinguishable from slavery (Gal. 4:1); rather, they possess the Spirit of *familial freedom*, by whom their eschatological sonship is realized in Christ. Expressly, the Holy Spirit given to believers does not perpetuate theological status quo or evidence redemptive-historical retrograde; he is not *pneuma douleias palin eis phobon* ("the spirit of slavery to fall back into fear," Rom. 8:15)—with this existential fear reflecting anxiety created by the divinely given curse of the law under the former dispensation (cf. Rom. 8:2). Instead, he is *pneuma huiothesia* ("the Spirit of adoption"), in whom believers are transferred, transformed, and confirmed as sons in this Christological/pneumatological age.

The *nomos tou pneumatos tēs zōēs* ("law of the Spirit of life") in Romans 8:2 probably anticipates the language in 8:15—that a son, by faith in Christ in the eschatological age, moves from one state (bondage to the law, which brings fear) to another state (adoption into God's family, which brings the freedom and *power* to obey the law). Perhaps Paul here intends an early reference of *huiothesia*, foreshadowing his development of the *law of adoption* under which believers discover filial love, freedom, assurance, and glorious hope (8:15–17). In Romans 8:2, then, the legal bondage of the former dispensation (*tou nomou tēs hamartias tou thanatou*, "the law of sin and death"), in all its restrictiveness and fear, is replaced with the spiritual law of *huiothesia* (*os gar nomos to pneumato tēs zōēs en Christō Iēsou*, "for the law of the Spirit of life . . . in Christ Jesus") in all its energizing, filial, and *renovative* richness. This emphasis is enhanced by the fact that the Spirit of adoption is also the Spirit who in the new covenant enables obedience to the law of Christ (1 Cor. 9:21); the legal declaration of adoption comes to fruition in renovated sonship through the eschatological Spirit. The radical difference in prominence, privilege, and power between slaves and sons[47] accentuates the tremendous privilege granted by God

---

47. Cf. Robert Alexander Webb, *The Reformed Doctrine of Adoption* (Grand Rapids: Eerdmans, 1947), 28–40. Webb delineates seven relevant distinctions between sons and slaves: The son and the servant differ from each other (1) as to their respective *origins*; (2) as

to the adoptee in this eschatological age—a privilege reflected in the sons' Christlike communication with the Father.

In Romans 8:15, Paul attests to the believer's spiritual freedom in terms of his filial access in prayer (*en hō krazomen, Abba ho patēr*, "by whom we cry, 'Abba! Father!'"), a freedom that further manifests the sons-in-the-Son identity. This particular cry, *Abba ho patēr*, echoes the intimacy of Jesus Christ's relation with his heavenly Father, uttered in the garden of Gethsemane at a crisis point in his suffering (Mark 14:36). Undoubtedly, this repetition in the believer's heart of the words of Christ to his Father reiterates the astonishing notion that the believer *shares* in the eschatological and intimate adoptive sonship of Christ. Enabling the *believer's* response to adoption in Romans 8:15, in verse 16 it is the *Spirit* (*auto to pneuma*; "The Spirit himself" is emphatic) who confirms within the human spirit the indisputable reality of spiritual sonship. This familially confirming witness "is . . . given *to* us as distinct from the witness given *by* us."[48]

Change in the human spirit is inevitable because of union with Christ, and such internal change is contingent on the necessarily *prior* presence of the Holy Spirit. In fact, the impact of the Spirit of Christ on the human spirit/heart is attested by the cry of the adopted sons, "Abba! Father!" (Rom. 8:15–16). The human spirit is filled with, governed by, the Spirit of Christ (cf. Eph. 5:18), and therefore the Christo-filial cry (Mark 14:36) comes both from the Spirit in the sons (Gal. 4:6) and from the spirit of the sons (Rom. 8:15). Filling with the Spirit changes the mind, the heart, the *habitus*; the redeemed sons' *pneuma* comes

---

to their respective *natures*; (3) as to the fundamental *forms of government* under which they respectively have their careers; (4) as to the *motive* regulative of their obedience; (5) as to the *ground of their expectation* of reward; (6) as to the design had in their respective *punishments*; and (7) as to their respective *freedom and fullness of access* into the presence of their superior. Cf. Stibbe, *From Orphans to Heirs*, 88–91, 109.

48. Murray, *Romans*, 1:297 (emphasis in original). The question whether Paul means that the Holy Spirit confirms "with" our spirit or "to" our spirit is answered convincingly by Cranfield: "But what standing has our spirit in *this* matter?" *Romans I–VIII*, 403 (emphasis in original). Though the verb *summartureō* means "to bear witness with another," it can also carry an intensive and general meaning, "to bear witness." This latter meaning serves the theological argument more sufficiently in this context, and also imitates the general usage of this term in Romans 2:15 and 9:1. Cf. Morris, *Romans*, 316–17; Douglas J. Moo, *The Epistle to the Romans*, NICNT (Grand Rapids: Eerdmans, 1996), 539–40.

in comprehensive submission to the redeeming Son's *pneuma* (Eph. 5:18–21). Thus, Paul writes in 1 Corinthians 2:12–13, "Now we have received not the spirit of the world, but the Spirit who is from God, that we might understand the things freely given us by God. And we impart this in words not taught by human wisdom but taught by the Spirit, interpreting spiritual truths to those who are spiritual."

That the "Abba, Father" of Christ in Mark 14:36 is repeated not only by the Spirit of Christ himself within the adopted sons (Gal. 4:6), but also by the adopted sons themselves (Rom. 8:15), exposes the comprehensive sons-in-the-Son filial identity wrought by the Holy Spirit in the redeemed. The human heart is graciously, sovereignly, and by divine initiative overtaken by the Spirit of Christ, in whom the adopted sons dwell confidently and irreversibly in their participation with the Son of God par excellence. The believer's adoption in Christ, as given and confirmed by the Spirit, then depends on and derives from Christ Jesus. Attested and applied by the Spirit of the Son, adoption delivers stunning eschatological privilege: the relationship of the Elder Brother to his Father signals and sustains *mutatis mutandis* the adopted son's relationship with his heavenly Father. The Spirit of adoption is the Spirit of Christ; Christ's eschatological sonship—as secured by his own adoption[49]—is given by the Spirit to those who believe, making them sons of God.

Returning to the Pauline emphasis on the Spirit, it is critical to note that adoption comes to the believer *now* in a context of longing and groaning on this side of the last day. Suffering emerges prominently here even as it does for Christ in Mark 14:36; as the adopted sons anticipate their fully realized glory, they do so in a life of suffering—in which they join into the sufferings of Christ (Rom. 8:17–30). Traversing the pathway to fully realized glory comes by sharing first in the last Son's sufferings (cf. Col. 1:24–29) and, as will become more evident in the following section, bears implications not only for the redeemed sons but also for the entirety of creation itself. Creation as a whole anticipates the eschatological transformation and manifestation of the sons (Rom. 8:22–23). Creation anguishes

---

49. See chapter 7 for a full explanation of Christ's own adoption.

because of the fallen sons; it anxiously awaits the full manifestation of the adopted ones.

For now, the adopted sons suffer, not in fear but in the outpouring of the fully gracious filial benefits that belong to them in the resurrected Son of God. They are not slaves under the curse of the law, but sons under the blessing of Christ. And as they await their own bodily resurrection/adoption (Rom. 8:23), they undergo the rigors of learning filial obedience, following in the footsteps of Christ, and sharing in his suffering-unto-glory course. "The Spirit-worked, suffering obedience of the church, which is the fruit of self-abandoning faith that rests in and lives out of its covenant head, is, together with his own obedience, as Murray puts it, integral and necessary to attaining the full possession of the eschatological inheritance."[50]

There is no future glory without present suffering. Or, to put it in the Romans 8 adoption framework, there is no consummate adoption without first a suffering adoption; identifying fully with their Elder Brother, glorified sons are first suffering sons. The Spirit of Christ's sealing and confirming work renders the destiny as certain as the process. Thus, just as for Jesus, suffering on this side of our final resurrection is not antithetical to sonship, but is its concomitant unto mature filial confirmation (adoption). Richard Gaffin has captured this motif of suffering unto glory with his typically precise prose:

> Looking in one direction, we must agree that New Testament eschatology is most assuredly an eschatology of victory, and of victory presently being realized. But, any outlook that fails to see that for the church, between the resurrection and return of Christ and *until* that return, the eschatology of victory is an eschatology of suffering, any outlook that otherwise tends to remove the dimension of suffering from the present *triumph* of the church, distorts the gospel and confuses the (apostolic) mission of the church in the world. The church does indeed carry the eschatological victory of Jesus into the world, but only as it takes up the cross after him. Its

---

50. Richard B. Gaffin Jr., "The Usefulness of the Cross," *WTJ* 41, 1 (1979): 242. Cf. Murray, *Romans*, 1:299.

glory, always veiled, is revealed in its suffering with him. Until Jesus comes, his resurrection glory in the church is a matter of strength made perfect in suffering. The "golden age" is the age of power perfected in weakness.[51]

A primary difference between the redeemed sons and the redeeming Son is that the redeemed now enjoy the full bounty of Christ-attained resources for spiritual victory, all the while traversing life, its sorrows, and its sufferings. Christ attained this mature sonship by his faith and obedience in the epoch of the curse. The adopted sons, while awaiting their Savior's return, walk by faith in the continuance of the old age, yet with the power and efficacy of the age to come. Thus, the sons traverse the Son's same pathway, but under the gracious provisions and the redeeming efficacy of his life well lived and his resurrection power outpoured.

This power made perfect in suffering is for the believer a graciously bestowed filial strength, granted by the Spirit of the resurrected Christ. Appreciating our adoption joy in the context of an *already* but *not yet* eschatology, the verb *krazō* ("cry") in Romans 8:15 indicates bursting emotion, which leaps from the soul of one who grasps his sonly state, leading him to a joyful proclamation of his exalted eschatological relationship with his Father (cf. 1 John 3:1). Calvin, in his consideration of a believer's privilege of prayer, describes with amazement the intimate access to God as Father: "With what confidence would anyone address God as 'Father'? Who would break forth into such rashness as to claim for himself the honor of a son of God unless we had been adopted as children of grace in Christ?"[52] With a similar sense of awe, J. I. Packer comments, "To know that God is your Father and that he loves you, his adopted child, no less than he loves his only begotten Son and to know that enjoyment of God's love and glory for all eternity are pledged to you brings inward delight that is sometimes overwhelming; and this also is the Spirit's doing."[53] Adopted in Christ, the redeemed son is able to cry out to his heavenly Father with confidence (cf. Heb.

---

51. Ibid., 245 (emphasis in original).

52. John Calvin, *Institutes of the Christian Religion*, ed. John T. McNeill, trans. Ford Lewis Battles, 2 vols. (Philadelphia: Westminster, 1960), 3.20.36.

53. J. I. Packer, *Keep in Step with the Spirit* (Grand Rapids: Fleming H. Revell, 1984), 77.

4:16) and with joy, *because of* the leading and enabling of the Holy Spirit in the sufferings associated with the mortification of sin (Rom. 8:12–14). "For to address the true God by the name of Father with full sincerity and seriousness will involve seeking wholeheartedly to be and think and say and do that which is pleasing to Him and to avoid everything which displeases Him."[54]

In Paul's thought, suffering for sanctification by the leading of the eschatological Spirit remains inseparable from his confirming ministry in adoption (assurance); the munificence of the adoption is enjoyed only in the fullness of the Spirit's energizing for familial obedience. As the adopted sons submit to the Holy Spirit's empowering leadership in the mortification of sin, they find themselves subjectively confirmed in the reality of their adoptive sonship. Just like his Elder Brother, the believer finds that it is in his most desperate suffering that he discovers the familial joy of being the child of God. The cruciform life facilitates the filial joy of union with the Son of God, for in the crucible of suffering, the cry of "Abba, Father" surges with eschatological spiritual freedom, spontaneity, and the certainty of glorious transformation into the image of the Elder Brother (Rom. 8:23, 29; cf. Eph. 4:13).

Adoption and the Risen Christ

The Christ-centeredness of this adoption has implicitly saturated this discussion of *huiothesia* in Romans 8:15–17. Risking redundancy for the sake of avoiding misunderstanding, this implicit factor is worthy of fuller statement. Paul makes explicit the thoroughly Christological character of eschatological sonship, by articulating a *now* but *not yet* tension in terms of present *in Christ* suffering and future *in Christ* glory (v. 17). The eschatological Spirit accomplishes his confirming sonship ministry through identification with Christ in his humiliation and exaltation. The reception of future glory by constitutive and bodily transformation (cf. v. 23) is conditioned on progressive conformity to the Son (cf. v. 29) in and through suffering (v. 17; cf. 2 Cor. 1:5; Phil. 3:10; Col. 1:24).[55]

---

54. Cranfield, *Romans I–VIII*, 393.

55. "Both sides of the death-life paradox remain in full force in the believer's experience to the end; he must experience the full outworking of death as well as of life if . . . he is to experience the resurrection from the dead." Dunn, *Jesus and the Spirit*, 334.

Once again, Paul highlights the centrality of the *historia salutis* in his soteriological conception, wherein the believer's participation (union) with Christ defines the character of his adoption. The apostle's choice of vocabulary itself could not be more poignant in conveying this point: the adopted sons are *sugklēronomoi de Christou* ("fellow heirs with Christ," Rom. 8:17) and joint sufferers with Christ (*sumpaschomen*, "we suffer with him,"), so that this suffering provides the divinely appointed means of attaining glory with Christ (*sundaxosthōmen*, "we may . . . be glorified with him"). The prefix *sun* ("with") on the featured words in Romans 8:17 emphatically pronounces the organic Christological contours of adoption/inheritance/glory. Thus (and this point should be appreciated with the verbal force of the text itself), the present struggles of the adopted sons, which are also contextually connected to the moral leading of the Holy Spirit of adoption (vv. 14–15), actually demonstrate the participation of the adopted sons with the Son par excellence, guaranteeing the future glory of adoption consummated (v. 23). The Spirit of Christ, current adoption status, and subsequent emphasis on the resurrection (vv. 18–30) present a powerful and mutually informing complex. Together they manifest unequivocally that the focal point for Paul in Romans 8:12–17 is the renovation of adopted sons through Spirit-provided union with the messianic Son.

It should be remembered here that suffering is not hostile toward adoptive sonship, but is the very means of attaining its glorious resurrection end (cf. Phil. 3:8–11). Just as Christ suffered as Son of God until he was glorified as Son in his resurrection, so, too, believers suffer as sons as they await their final bodily transformation. The pathway to resurrection glory is the pathway of suffering; to be a fellow heir (i.e., to share in the filial attainment of Christ) requires becoming a fellow heir in suffering. The believer's filial identity in Christ receives confirmation and attestation along this Christologically shared pathway; sons of God walk in the footsteps of their Elder Brother, who has successfully blazed the trail for them (cf. Heb. 12:1–3). The familial cry of "Abba, Father" coincides with the crucible of suffering, but a crucible fully defined by the resurrected Son of God, in whom the sons of God enjoy resurrection power and filial joy.

Having attained to culminating filial glory in his own life, death, and resurrection, Christ shares the efficacy of his "firstfruits" resurrection with those in union with him. The power of resurrection in Christ comes to the believers in both this life and the next: in their suffering now and in their glory to come. The adopted sons' walk in suffering has as its destiny the fully realized blessing of their adoptive sonship—a realization that comes at the parousia, at their resurrection, at their revelation as the sons of God (Rom. 8:19; cf. Phil. 3:20–21). Just like that of Jesus Christ (Rom. 1:3–4), the resurrection of believers is a filial resurrection—they are raised *as sons*. As will receive attention next in the following theological exposition on Romans 8:23, adoption, in fact, entails this resurrection. Building on the Spirit-given sonship and spiritual leading unto holiness that characterize the *now* of adoption, the apostle Paul turns to the parousia, when the *not yet* of adoption will come to sweet fruition.

The Spirit of Adoption *Not Yet*: What Then?

Some exegetes of the Pauline *huiothesian* passages have restricted adoption either to an exclusively present forensic reality or to an exclusively future forensic reality. Fitzmyer, on the basis of Romans 8:15–17, argues that Paul commends the *present fullness* of adoption exclusively. Since adoption is a legal act, it is asked, how could an already-adopted son later be adopted?[56] Others suggest that the believer currently enjoys only the "spirit of adoption" (Rom. 8:15), and that *any* realized adoption awaits the parousia. For example, though Buswell finds *huiothesia* the "most significant word which the apostle Paul uses to designate our future inheritance," he restricts adoption to the eschaton: "*Huiothesia* is never said to be our status in this present life."[57]

---

56. Joseph A. Fitzmyer, *Romans: A New Translation with Introduction and Commentary*, Anchor Bible 33 (New York: Doubleday, 1993), 510.

57. James Oliver Buswell, *A Systematic Theology of the Christian Religion*, 2 vols. (Grand Rapids: Zondervan, 1963), 2:213. Cf. Andrew Telford, *Subjects of Sovereignty* (Philadelphia: Berachah Church, 1940), 17; C. K. Barrett, *A Commentary on the Epistle to the Romans*, ed. Henry Chadwick, Harper's New Testament Commentaries (New York: Harper & Row, 1957), 163; Robert Lee Riffe, "A Study of the Figure of Adoption in the Pauline Epistles" (ThM thesis, Dallas Theological Seminary, 1981), 32, 37.

For both textual and theological reasons, neither of these polarized options is sustainable.

Most exegetes rightly recognize both present and future elements in Paul's doctrine of adoption; "neither adoption nor redemption is fully completed in this life in all they encompass."[58] While it is now generally agreed that this future adoption is not a second adoption or even the *actual* adoption, it is often asserted that the future aspect of adoption is reducible to public or final revelation of adoptive privilege. "We have been adopted, but our adoption has yet to be publicly proclaimed,"[59] writes Cranfield. To be sure, the prominence of fully exposed glory (Rom. 8:19; cf. Col. 3:1–4), the cosmic show-and-tell, characterizes the drama of final eschatology. Creation awaits the last-day *manifestation* of the glorified sons of God. As Vos puts it, "Status as sons of God with all privileges attached, such as freedom and heirship, existed before, but had not been openly demonstrated. Not their celestial body, but their supreme sonship was in hiding. It is this *status* that will be revealed, and this revelation will be accomplished, by laying upon them the glory, the medium for whose manifestation, to be sure, is the body of the resurrection." He then adds, "Because the resurrection is a revelation of sonship . . . , it can be also called the 'adoption as sons.'"[60] Just as their vindication/justification will be open and made visible on that last day, so, too, the adoption will be public and on display. In this sense, adoption's forensic aspect remains fully intact in both the *already* and the *not yet*.

Yet while such a public display properly reflects a vital facet of consummative adoptive realization (Rom. 8:19) and the full disclosure/

---

58. Daniel J. Theron, "'Adoption' in the Pauline Corpus," *EvQ* 28, 1 (1956): 11. Cf. Robert Haldane, *Exposition of the Epistle to the Romans*, Geneva Series Commentary (Edinburgh: Banner of Truth, 1996), 376; Dunn, *Romans 1–8*, 491; Cranfield, *Romans I–VIII*, 419; Murray, *Romans*, 1:307–8; Hendriksen, *Romans*, 271; James Montgomery Boice, *The Reign of Grace—Romans 5:1–8:39* (Grand Rapids: Baker, 1992), 881.

59. Cranfield, *Romans I–VIII*, 419. Cf. William Sanday and Arthur C. Headlam, *A Critical and Exegetical Commentary on the Epistle to the Romans*, 5th ed., ICC (Edinburgh: T&T Clark, 1902), 209; F. F. Bruce, *The Letter of Paul to the Romans: An Introduction and Commentary*, rev. ed., TNTC (Leicester: Inter-Varsity Press, 1985), 164–65.

60. Vos, *Pauline Eschatology*, 198.

manifestation theme in Paul's theology,[61] to restrict the culminating eschatological reality of adoption to mere legal exhibition fails to do justice to the language in Romans 8:23. The final eschatological drama is not merely a display of what already was, but a display of what will be. As the sons share in the Son's resurrection, final eschatology is both transformative and revelatory. Manifestation occurs at glorification because manifestation requires glorification. Now *progressively* transformed by the Spirit of adoption, the revealed sons on the last day will be *fully* transformed sons. Final manifestation of the sons entails transformation into likeness of the Son par excellence, a vital consummative-eschatological and filial dynamic that Paul makes explicit.

In Romans 8:23, he writes, *ou monon de, alla kai autoi tēn aparchē tou pneumatos echontes, hēmeis kai autoi en heautois stenazomen huiothesian apekdechomenoi, tēn apolutrōsin tou sōmatos hēmōn* ("And not only the creation, but we ourselves, who have the firstfruits of the Spirit, groan inwardly as we wait eagerly for adoption as sons, the redemption of our bodies"). In other words, "what we have now is real, but it is not the whole (cf. 1 John 3:2), and our foretaste leads us to look forward with eager longing to the completion of what God has already begun in us (cf. v. 19)."[62] Several pregnant theological themes arise in this single and climactic verse, as Paul builds from creation's groaning (Rom. 8:20–22) to the sons' groaning. The sufferings and unrealized eschatological glory drive to a state of deep longing, personified in the creation's wails, and experienced in the souls of the yet-to-be-transformed sons. The resolution to the cosmic and existential crisis comes in the "redemption of our bodies," when the mortal becomes immortal and the corruptible becomes incorruptible (cf. 1 Cor. 15:35–57), as the sons of God become fully "conformed to the image of his Son" (Rom. 8:29). To do justice to Paul's language here, we must explore the seemingly odd juxtaposition of full adoptive acquisition with bodily redemption, which forces an interpretation beyond the limits of a public, judicial declaration.

61. Cf. Thomas Houston, *The Adoption of Sons, Its Nature, Spirit, Privileges and Effects: A Practical and Experimental Treatise* (Paisley, Scotland: Alex. Gardner, 1872), 193–95.
62. Morris, *Romans*, 324.

Was Huiothesia *Originally in Romans 8:23?*

Before determining the particular nature of this adoption/resurrection connection, it is imperative to assess the historicity of the term *huiothesia* in the Romans 8:23 autograph. Though a number of early manuscripts do not contain the term in this verse,[63] the acceptance of *huiothesia* actually makes for the more difficult reading. Initially, then, on the basis of the principle of *Lectio difficilior valet*, it remains most certain that the term is original.[64] Contrarily, Pierre Benoit contends that *huiothesia* was actually inserted here by a scribe who determined that hope for future redemption of the body lacked enticement. Hence, Benoit contends, a scribe likely inserted the word to stipulate greater cause for eschatological hope.[65]

Swetnam criticizes Benoit's view, citing the implausibility of a scribal insertion dominating the textual tradition if it was so antithetical to Paul's thought. Swetnam offers an alternative, suggesting that *huiothesia* is original, but that *apekdechomenoi* ("wait eagerly") in Romans 8:23 has suffered mistranslation. Instead, he insists that verse 23 supports rendering the participle *apekdechomenoi* (from *apekdechomai*) as "arrive by inference."[66] Though the semantic range of

63. The word *huiothesia* is found in many manuscripts, including a, A, B, C, K, P, and Ψ. Mainly, it is in some Western witnesses that the word is not found, including p[46vid], D, and G. *La Bible de Jérusalem* (1956) and the *Jerusalem Bible* (1966) omit the word. The UBS Greek New Testament (3rd ed.) gives the presence of *huiothesia* a *C* reading, indicating that *huiothesia* is most likely original, though certain manuscript evidence provides a measure of doubt. Notably, the rating in the UBS Greek New Testament (4th ed.) advances to an *A*, manifesting the high probability of its authenticity. Kent D. Clarke, *Textual Optimism: A Critique of the United Bible Societies' Greek New Testament*, Journal for the Study of the New Testament Supplement 138 (Sheffield: Sheffield Academic Press, 1997), finds the UBS ratings overly optimistic and methodologically inconsistent. Cf. Pierre Benoit, *Jesus and the Gospel*, trans. Benet Weatherhead (New York: Seabury, 1974), 40–41; John Ellington, "Adoption in Modern Translations," *Bible Translator* 36, 4 (1985): 438; Thomas R. Schreiner, *Romans*, BECNT 6 (Grand Rapids: Baker, 1998), 440–41.

64. Cf. James I. Cook, "The Conception of Adoption in the Theology of Paul," in *Saved by Hope: Essays in Honor of Richard C. Oudersluys*, ed. James I. Cook (Grand Rapids: Eerdmans, 1978), 139; Bruce Manning Metzger, *A Textual Commentary on the Greek New Testament* (London: United Bible Societies, 1971), 517.

65. Benoit, *Jesus and the Gospel*, 49–50. Cf. James Swetnam, "On Romans 8:23 and the 'Expectation of Sonship,'" *Biblica* 48 (1967): 103.

66. Swetnam, "On Romans 8:23," 107–8. Swetnam translates Romans 8:23 thus: "And not only creation, but we ourselves, who have the first-fruits of the Spirit, we also lament to ourselves, arriving by inference (*apekdechomenoi*) at sonship as the redemption of our

the verb allows for such a translation,[67] it hardly holds viability in view of the overall context of Romans 8:18–25. Paul employs *apekdechomai* two other times, in Romans 8:19 and 8:25, where the meaning "eagerly awaiting" is virtually unquestioned. It is highly doubtful that Paul would employ the same word with significantly differing meanings in the same immediate context.[68] Swetnam's lexical argument ends up as untenable as Benoit's text-critical one.

Defending the inclusion of *huiothesia* in the original text, Cranfield suggests that its absence in certain manuscripts "reflects the presence of bewilderment in the face of the apparent inconsistency between the present tenses of vv. 14 and 15 and the future sense of *apekdechomenoi*."[69] This seeming temporal and theological inconsistency is in part what leads Fitzmyer to omit *huiothesia* (as noted above): since "Christians are *already* adopted children of God (8:15)," how could they possibly become *more* adopted, as if a climactic legal/relational declaration could come by degrees?[70] The forensic restrictions imposed on *huiothesia* put Fitzmyer in a theological straitjacket. Yet in his argument for the omission of *huiothesia*, Fitzmyer concedes that it is difficult to figure how this word consistently appears in certain reliable manuscripts. In light of the evidence, the textual clues favor the acceptance of *huiothesia* in Romans 8:23 as original. Thankfully, however, even with the divergent manuscript evidence and unconvincing interpretations of the textual data, arguments for its inclusion or omission need not rely solely on external textual evidence. Some further theological and contextual factors (internal evidence) will assist in demonstrating the rightful place of *huiothesia* in Romans 8:23.

As mentioned above, some have mistakenly concluded that adoption is *all* future, entirely *unrealized*. To claim that adoption is

---

body." Ibid., 108.

67. See Gerhard Kittel and Gerhard Friedrich, eds., *Theological Dictionary of the New Testament*, trans. G. W. Bromiley, 10 vols. (Grand Rapids: Eerdmans, 1964–76), 2:50–59.

68. Cf. Dunn, *Romans 1–8*, 474; Schreiner, *Romans*, 439; Burke, "Adoption and the Spirit in Romans 8," 317n24.

69. Cranfield, *Romans I–VIII*, 419n1. Cf. Dunn, *Romans 1–8*, 466; Bruce Manning Metzger, *The Text of the New Testament: Its Transmission, Corruption, and Restoration*, 2nd ed. (New York: Oxford University Press, 1968), 201–3.

70. Fitzmyer, *Romans*, 510 (emphasis added). Cf. Dunn, *Romans 1–8*, 466.

altogether an unrealized reality betrays a misunderstanding of the present inaugurated eschatological state. Besides ignoring specific exegetical implications, which will soon be explored, such a view ignores the pervasive New Testament theme of an eschatological continuity between the *now* and *not yet*.[71] More specifically, this *now* but *not yet* structure unmistakably permeates Pauline theology, as Paul depicts the believer in an eschatological period between the defeat of the enemy and the ultimate surrender of the enemy, between "D-day" and "V-day."[72]

Every soteriological element, therefore, essentially bears both realized and unrealized, *now* and *not yet* realities. Justification has occurred definitively in the past (Rom. 5:1), but also entails a future reality (Gal. 5:5): "our justification has still to be made public or openly manifested. We have not yet been 'openly acquitted.'"[73] Sanctification entails a definitive past reality (Rom. 6:1–10), but looks ahead to a future realized completion (Phil. 1:6; 1 John 3:2).[74] Resurrection of the believer has in a vital sense already occurred (Rom. 6:1–4; Eph. 2:5–6), and yet the believer awaits a future bodily resurrection (Rom. 8:11; 1 Cor. 15:22, 42–49).[75] Since every aspect of redemption possesses inaugurated and future consummative eschatological realities, adoption could surely be no different. Paul speaks of the believer's present adoption confirmed by the Holy Spirit in the present cosufferings (*sumpaschomen*, Rom. 8:17) with Christ throughout the process of sanctification: *ou gar elabete pneuma douleias palin eis phobon alla*

71. Cf. Oscar Cullmann, *Salvation in History*, trans. Sidney G. Sowers (London: SCM, 1967), 166–85; Hoekema, *The Bible and the Future*, 68–75; Moo, 421; James D. G. Dunn, *Jesus and the Spirit*, 308–18.

72. Hoekema, *The Bible and the Future*, 21. Hoekema here develops Oscar Cullmann's familiar metaphor of *already* but *not yet* eschatological tension. Cf. Oscar Cullmann, *Christ and Time: The Primitive Christian Conception of Time and History*, trans. Floyd V. Filson, rev. ed. (Philadelphia: Westminster, 1964), 145; Cullmann, *Salvation in History*, 44.

73. Gaffin, *By Faith, Not by Sight*, 107. So "justification is an anticipation of God's verdict at the last judgement." C. K. Barrett, *From First Adam to Last: A Study in Pauline Theology* (London: Adam & Charles Black, 1962), 104. Cf. Dunn, *Jesus and the Spirit*, 309.

74. Murray, *Collected Writings*, 2:277–317.

75. Richard B. Gaffin Jr., *Resurrection and Redemption: A Study in Paul's Soteriology*, 2nd ed. (Phillipsburg, NJ: Presbyterian and Reformed, 1987), 46, 61–62, 133–34. Cf. Richard B. Gaffin Jr., "'Life-Giving Spirit': Probing the Center of Paul's Pneumatology," *JETS* 41, 4 (1998): 585; Ridderbos, *Paul*, 178–81.

elabete pneuma huiothesias en hō krazomen, Abba ho patēr ("For you did not receive the spirit of slavery to fall back into fear, but you have received the Spirit of adoption as sons, by whom we cry, 'Abba! Father!,'" v. 15). Yet Paul equally emphasizes the future realization of adoption: the coinheritance (*sugklēronomoi*, v. 17) with Christ, and the *bodily redemption* (v. 23) at the resurrection of the believer.[76]

With the adoptive sonship realized in Romans 8:12–17, it would seem only appropriate contextually for Paul to describe the unrealized realities of this doctrine in his description of eschatological consummation in Romans 8:18–23. He does not disappoint. Flowing from his organic eschatological outlook and having exposed adoption's *already* features, Paul unsurprisingly explicates its organic development in the *not yet*, and he does so in vivid terms of the glorious bodily redemption/resurrection. The realized and unrealized elements of adoption are not so much in tension as in organic continuity.

Currently suffering as sons, we "cry" (*krazomen*, Rom. 8:15), "Abba! Father!" Longing for our consummate adoptive glory as those who already "have the firstruits of the Spirit," we "groan inwardly" (*stenazomen*, v. 23). The cry of exultant identity *in* the Son coheres with the zealous longing for exalted and comprehensive transformation *like* the Son; the Christo-filial constitution infused at the moment of Spirit-wrought faith completes in the Christo-filial bodily resurrection at the last day. The theological contours of adoption realized correspond to the theological contours of adoption unrealized; the experience of adoption realized seamlessly interconnects with the experience of adoption unrealized.

Accordingly, in view of the prevailing Pauline eschatological outlook, the use of *huiothesia* in Romans 8:23 is almost certainly original because of its theological appropriateness in the flowing eschatological logic of Romans 8. Paul expresses the unrealized culmination of adoption in contextual and theological continuity with the realized blessing of adoption in Romans 8:15–17. In like

---

76. Note that even in this clearly eschatological context, Paul inexorably links the past and present dimensions of our salvation. In Romans 8:24–25, he speaks of salvation in the past ("we were saved"), and then points the believer to salvation in the future ("we wait for it with patience").

fashion, the pretemporal-to-eschatological orientation of Ephesians 1 and the explicit teleological purposes embraced by *huiothesia* warrant a comprehensive sweep of organic eschatological development. The adoption realized anticipates the adoption unrealized, all by virtue of union with Christ Jesus the Son of God. Corresponding to the organic treatment of *huiothesia* in Galatians 4:7, where Paul speaks of *present* sonship and a future inheritance connected with that sonship, Romans 8 weds eschatology inaugurated and consummated within the adoption motif. Paul's focus in Romans 8 differs from Galatians 4: in Galatians, the Christological accomplishment of adoption features more prominently. Old covenant sons were those under age; new covenant sons are mature sons because of the sonship of Jesus Christ. In Romans 8, in distinct yet compatible fashion, his intention is to build out the implications of the redemptive-historical in terms of the experience of adoption by the ministry of the Holy Spirit. Both texts share the redemptive-historical contours, but the prominent theological topography differs. Galatians 4 elevates redemption accomplished in the Son for the sons, and Romans 8 elevates redemption applied for the sons by the Son.

In returning to Romans 8:23, however, we must consider this pressing question: *In what sense is adoption related to bodily redemption/resurrection?*[77] Does one operate causally on the other? Are they detached realities that occur simultaneously? Do they present the same reality from different perspectives? Is one reality the subset of the other?

---

77. Though Paul constructs his soteriology around a conceptual mutuality of *redemption* and *adoption*, the concepts have scanty cultural/historical connection. Yet Theron, "Adoption," 10–11, suggests, "In man's own experience the Holy Spirit is the earnest and seal of redemption (Eph. 1:13f; 4:30, cf. 2 Cor. 3:17); and in the same way as redemption of a slave was a prerequisite for his sonship, so redemption is actually a step toward adoption." These conclusions lack strong historical defense. They lack even more theological plausibility. More accurately, James Scott writes, "For it has long been discussed whether Greek parallels of sacral manumission of slaves and paramone might provide the background to Paul's concept of redemption, and a connection between manumission and adoption might strengthen this hypothesis." Yet "judging by the meager extant sources, it would seem that manumission followed by adoption is a rather rare practice in the ancient world." *Adoption as Sons of God*, 86–87. With or without the first-century cultural relationship, in Pauline theology redemption and adoption function inseparably, and adoption situates the motive, goal, and familial contours of redemption in Christ Jesus the Son.

Adoption and Resurrection

Examining these questions necessitates a closer look at some syntactical matters. If *huiothesia* was not original to the Romans 8:23 text, the verse naturally places the phrase *tēn apolutrōsin tou sōmatos hēmōn* ("the redemption of our bodies") as the sole direct object of *apekdechomenoi* ("wait eagerly").[78] Without *huiothesia*, the future hope of the believer in this passage resides in an unstipulated future bodily redemption. Without the filial motif explicitly connected, we would have to ask: what actually *is* bodily redemption, and how is that redemption actually related to the "revealing of the sons of God" (Rom. 8:19)? If "the cross is perceived solely in terms of redemption the question arises what status was secured for those looking to it for redemption."[79] Assuming the originality of *huiothesia* in the autographs, then, we find a contextually clarifying and theologically fruitful explanation of the believer's hope. Syntactically, the accusative *tēn apolutrōsin* ("the redemption") resides in precise apposition to the accusative form of *huiothesia* ("adoption as sons"). This epexegetical relationship of the terms suggests that Paul is fusing these two future realities, and describing them—at least in some sense—as *one*. As Cranfield puts it:

> *Tēn apolustrōsin tou sōmatos hēmōn* interprets *huiothesian.* The full manifestation of our adoption is *identical* with the final resurrection of our bodies at the Parousia, our complete and final liberation from the *mataiotēs* and *phthorato*, to which we (like the sub-human creation) have been subjected.[80]

In the apostle Paul's syntactical and theological construction, then, realized bodily redemption *is* realized adoption; with this self-conscious conceptual conflation, he unambiguously tethers the filial and renovative features of the final resurrection.

78. Cf. Cranfield, *Romans I–VIII*, 419n1.

79. Tim J. R. Trumper, "The Metaphorical Import of Adoption: A Plea for Realisation II: The Adoption Metaphor in Theological Usage," *SBET* 15, 2 (1997): 110.

80. Cranfield, *Romans I–VIII*, 419 (emphasis added). Moo agrees: "This final element in our adoption is 'the redemption of our bodies.'" *Romans*, 521.

Interpretive Options and a Proposed Solution

Charles Hodge rejects any strict interpretation associated with the appositional relationship between *huiothesia* and *apolutrōsis* ("redemption") in Romans 8:23. Reacting to what he perceives to be a theological implausibility, he contends, "The adoption includes far more than the redemption of the body. But the latter event is to be coincident with the former, and is included in it, as one of its most prominent parts."[81] Possibly fearing the riches of adoption to be lost in Paul's syntax, Hodge downplays the coordination of the two thoughts. To him, the relationship between *huiothesia* and *apolutrōsis* is more of temporal coordination than of eschatological substance. Whatever substantial connection exists, however, places bodily redemption as an aspect of adoption.[82] In Hodge's favor, he seeks to maintain the difference between adoption and redemption. In the interpretive process, though, he errantly downplays the clear syntactical relationship between adoption and redemption in Romans 8:23, and thereby marginalizes the critical theological correlation.

With even more exacting theological analysis, Richard Gaffin insists that "adoption in Paul is a forensic reality" and is "judicially declarative."[83] He acknowledges both the past dimension of adoption— "Paul is emphatically clear that believers have already been adopted" —and the future dimension of adoption "at the time of the resurrection, given with or realized in bodily resurrection."[84] Here Gaffin initially leaves open the question whether future resurrection is coincidental with adoption or whether resurrection entails adoption. Affirming the judicial dimensions of the resurrection of Christ, he reinforces the "de facto forensic significance" with which the bodily resurrection "is invested."[85] Building on the strong revelational emphasis in Romans

81. Charles Hodge, *A Commentary on Romans* (Edinburgh: Banner of Truth, 1972), 276. Cf. Charles Hodge, *Commentary on the Epistle to the Ephesians* (Old Tappan, NJ: Fleming H. Revell, 1980), 41. Thomas Houston comes to an almost identical conclusion: "The saints' glorious resurrection is included in their adoption, and is one of its most prominent parts." *Adoption of Sons*, 198.

82. Cf. Stibbe, *From Orphans to Heirs*, 170–72.

83. Gaffin, *By Faith, Not by Sight*, 105.

84. Ibid., 106.

85. Ibid.

8:19 and 21, he concludes, "Believers await the open manifestation of their adoption in the resurrection of the body."[86]

As noted above, the forensic aspect of the resurrection and adoption abounds in Pauline argumentation. Yet more needs to be said concerning the relationship of adoption and this final display. As confirmed in the text, what the believer actually awaits is the very climax of redemption—adoption consummated, when by the Holy Spirit the redeemed is transformed in his resurrection as a *son*. This bodily redemption is not merely an aspect of adoption, but the very culmination of it, when by the final constitutive transformation and in direct continuity with the Spirit of adoption's sanctifying work the redeemed son receives the fullness of Christ's accomplished resurrection.[87]

A forensic emphasis is wholly commendable and surely consistent with the New Testament preoccupation with the full visibility of the previously invisible church (Col. 3:1–4) at the consummation. But does this forensic exclusivity, in both its past and future entailments, exhaust adoption? As we have seen to this point in our journey through the *huiothesian* texts, Pauline *huiothesia* embraces transformation. How adoption can embrace forensic and renovative categories without confusion or conflation in the application of salvation remains for subsequent consideration (chapters 8–10). But in view of the appositional relationship of the "redemption of our bodies" and "adoption" in Romans 8:23 and the comprehensive soteriological scope assumed by *huiothesia* in its other occurrences, it becomes necessary to "allow" the term to translate (forensic) and to transform (renovative). As Paul sees it, adoption reaches its *telos* with bodily redemption, because the privilege of eschatological, familial intimacy with the triune God can be realized only with thorough transformation of the fallen sons of Adam into glorified sons of God by the Christ-proffered adoption. Current adoptive sonship comes into full display *and* into fully transformed realization in the consummation.

86. Ibid.

87. Cf. J. Scott Lidgett, *The Fatherhood of God in Christian Truth and Life* (Edinburgh: T&T Clark, 1902), 417; Vellanickal, *Divine Sonship*, 85; Barrett, *Romans*, 167; Brendan Byrne, *Romans*, ed. Daniel J. Harrington, SP 6 (Collegeville, MN: Liturgical Press, 1996), 263.

Hence, the awaited glory shared with Christ (Rom. 8:17; cf. 1 Cor. 15:49–50) actually *is* this consummate transformation, moving the redeemed son into incorruptibility and immortality, that is, into full conformity to the resurrected Son of God. This complete Christo-filial conformity of the redeemed sons into the image of the Son of God is the goal of redemption: "For those whom he foreknew he also predestined to be conformed to the image of his Son, in order that he might be the firstborn among many brothers" (Rom. 8:29). Christ's own resurrection serves as means and model of the resurrection of his brothers.

In addition to the adoption theme that permeates Romans 8, a brief return to Ephesians further discloses the adoption/resurrection connection. As we have already seen in Ephesians 1:5, the goal of predestination (Paul uses the verb *proorizō*, "predestine") is adoption (*huiothesia*).[88] Notably, the goal of predestination (*proorizō*) in Romans 8:29 is conformity "to the image of his Son." Of course, it is plausible to assert *two* compatible, though not identical, ends for divine predestination. In view of the shared consummative eschatological contours of both passages, however, such a conclusion seems improbable. Both texts maintain an essential Christocentricity, making soteriological realization dependent on the value of Christ's redemptive work. In both places Paul shapes his Christological arguments around the eschatologically and soteriologically comprehensive *huiothesian* concept: what Paul has in view in both places is the singular divine purpose to bring redeemed sons into full conformity with the redeeming Son.

Ephesians 1 and Romans 8 describe divine predestination's goal in reciprocally interpretive fashion. The believer's adoption *is* conformity into the eschatological sonship of the resurrected Christ. Such fully realized conformity with Christ as the perfected Son (cf. Heb. 2:10; 5:7–10) exposes the profound redemptive efficacy of his filial obedience and sacrifice. After all, how could Paul find any hope for final eschatological adoptive privilege if the future promise did not ensure comprehensive transformation into the full likeness of the Son of God? By the God

---

88. For initial consideration of the relationship between Ephesians 1:4–5 and Romans 8, see chapter 5.

"who [in Christ] works all things according to the counsel of his will,"
"we have obtained an inheritance, having been predestined" according
to his purpose (Eph. 1:11). Or, put in Pauline shorthand, adoption is
the singular goal of redemptive history, an adoption that changes the
state of the sons, the hearts of the sons, and even the bodies of the sons.
At the consummation, the declaration of adoption fully coheres with
the transformation by adoption (cf. Phil. 3:20–21). The declarative
and the transformative conjoin in the filial.

Adoption therefore embraces all that the resurrection entails. It
encompasses the resurrection, transformation, and glorification of the
sons of God. Calvin remarks:

> For this reason, Paul terms "adoption" the revealing of adoption that
> will be made at the resurrection [cf. Rom. 8:18ff]; and afterwards
> he interprets it as the "redemption of our body" [Rom. 8:23]. But
> otherwise, just as estrangement from God is eternal death, so when
> man is received into grace by God to enjoy communion with him
> and be made one with him, he is transported from death to life—
> something done by the benefit of adoption alone.[89]

Adoption, as Calvin puts it here, translates and transforms. Adoption
transports one from death to life. The adoptive/resurrection translation from death to life facilitates actual union and communion.
Adoption comes not only as divine declaration, but also as divine work.
Adoption and resurrection are not only coterminous and coincidental,
but, even more importantly, mutually informing.

In similar fashion, entailed in his theology of filial grace, the
apostle John associates bodily transformation with eschatological
intimacy upon the return of the Son of God: "See what kind of love
the Father has given to us, that we should be called children of God;
and so we are. The reason why the world does not know us is that it
did not know him. Beloved, we are God's children now, and what we
will be has not yet appeared; but we know that when he appears we
shall be like him, because we shall see him as he is" (1 John 3:1–2).

---

89. Calvin, *Institutes*, 3.18.3.

New Testament soteriology, with its eschatological outlook, culminates in comprehensive change. Of course, we must avoid conflating Johannine and Pauline sonship motifs. They overlap and enrich each other, operating from distinct yet wholly compatible paradigms. John highlights the transformation by Spirit-wrought new birth; Paul highlights that transformation by resurrection/adoption flowing out of union with the Son of God. With the transformative focus of Johannine sonship (i.e., new birth, regeneration), the full dimensions of adoption provide a further point of contact between Pauline and Johannine sonship. Hence, any biblico-theological examination of the relationship between Pauline and Johannine sonship must reflect on this eschatological reality associated with both.[90]

Therefore, however a fusion of bodily redemption and adoption might appear to stretch biblical motifs or confuse distinct soteriological features, these doctrines of salvation applied openly conflate for Paul. The whole scope of the sons-in-the-Son gospel drives the apostle in his usage of the term *huiothesia*; contemporary cultural constraints of the selected term do not determine the message. The revelation of God in Christ motivates his selection of the term, and he stretches the term beyond its common conventions in order to underscore the exhaustive filial contours of the gospel of Christ Jesus. As Paul affirms in lockstep with the apostle John, at the resurrection the redeemed son will fully realize his redemption because his inheritance amounts to a glorious transformation, in which he is "supernaturally fitted for the final life of the Spirit, totally unhindered by any of [his] present weaknesses."[91] Pauline adoption and Johannine rebirth share in their central focus on solidarity with Jesus Christ as the *resurrected Son of God.*

Summarily, in view of adoption's thoroughgoing transformative cast in Romans 8:23, we must appreciate how *huiothesia* appropriates more than familial privilege by a judicial declaration. Declaration of sonship by the Father at the parousia is a pronouncement, but one contingent on the adopted sons' full transformation in Christ by his

---

90. See, e.g., Tim J. R. Trumper, "The Metaphorical Import of Adoption: A Plea for Realisation I: The Adoption Metaphor in Biblical Usage," *SBET* 14, 2 (1996): 129–45; Trumper, "Metaphorical Import II," 98–115.

91. Fee, *God's Empowering Presence*, 810.

Holy Spirit. Such transformation is essential to the integrity of salvation in its doxological and familial ends (cf. Eph. 1:4–5): only by this comprehensive moral, bodily, and filial transformation will believers "see God as He is—they are ever with Him; they are assimilated completely to His moral likeness, and are filled unto all His fullness."[92] By uniting the sons with the Son of God resurrected, the outpoured Spirit of adoption makes the filial declaration cohere with the consummative, filial transformation. In their final adoption-resurrection, the sons in the Son will be *like* the Son.

The Promise of the Spirit of Adoption: Adoption and Israel

Having established the vital resurrection/adoption connection in Romans 8:23, the apostle Paul draws Romans 8 to conclusion with the doxological and pastorally poignant question concerning the sons' security in the Son: "Who shall separate us from the love of Christ?" (Rom. 8:35a). According to his climactic eschatological, pneumatological, and filial argumentation, Paul knows his Christ-centered soteriology will raise pressing questions about God's past dealings with his people. Governed by Old Testament prophetic revelation and the eschatological revelation of God in Christ, the apostle looks back over his shoulder to the old covenant blessings of the former epoch, and aligns his comprehensive eschatological/soteriological argument with old covenant adoption. Paul moves from expressing the unfailing perseverance of God the Father in loving his adopted sons in and through his beloved Son (vv. 31–39) to the organic, covenantal continuity of God's unfailing love in the typological and redemptive-historical privileges of Israel, *his* son. In this rigorous defense of divine sovereignty and covenant faithfulness, adoption's extraordinary theological reaches continue to dominate Paul's thinking.

Appreciating the redemptive and historical plan involved in divine revelation, Bavinck reminds us how "all Old Testament concepts shed their external, national-Israelitish meanings and become manifest in

---

92. Houston, *Adoption of Sons*, 223.

their spiritual and eternal sense."[93] This is no less true of adoption in the thinking of the apostle Paul. In the history of redemption, God reveals his sovereign grace in selecting Israel as his son: Israel's election "was an expression of the grace, love, and fidelity of God."[94] This old covenant blessing protrudes conspicuously in Romans 9 because it stands first among the list of benefits enjoyed by those under the former covenantal administration. As Paul explains, Israel was adopted, and in fact experienced genuine (though juvenile) sonship privileges (cf. Ex. 4:22–23; Gal. 4:1–7).[95]

To be clear, the "national-Israelitish meanings" do not lack spiritual meanings; old covenant forms and promises are never nonredemptive. To the contrary, the old covenant forms deliver wholly spiritual truths—and, in fact, proleptically deliver the benefits of Christ. But precisely as intended in redemptive history, their typological roles are temporary and anticipatory. Once Christ comes, these forms give way to their promised substance. A vital redemptive and spiritual thread weaves throughout covenant history, but upon the arrival of the promised Christ Jesus, the cloak of the Righteous One replaces all prior and provisional garments.

As God's chosen nation, Israel was made God's son—a son by God's sovereign choice, not by genetic connection or some inherent

---

93. Herman Bavinck, *The Last Things: Hope for This World and the Next*, ed. John Bolt, trans. John Vriend (Grand Rapids: Baker, 1996), 97. Bavinck puts this spiritualizing principle insightfully: "The New Testament views itself—and there can certainly be no doubt about this—as the spiritual and therefore complete and authentic fulfillment of the Old Testament. The spiritualization of the Old Testament, rightly understood, is not an invention of Christian theology but has its beginning in the New Testament itself. The Old Testament in spiritualized form, that is the Old Testament stripped of its temporal and sensuous form, is the New Testament." Ibid., 96.

94. Willem A. VanGemeren, *The Progress of Redemption: The Story of Salvation from Creation to the New Jerusalem* (Grand Rapids: Baker, 1988), 79. Cf. John L. White, *The Apostle of God: Paul and the Promise of Abraham* (Peabody, MA: Hendrickson, 1999), 44; Allen Mawhinney, "*Yiothesia* in the Pauline Epistles: Its Background, Use, and Implications" (Ph.D. diss., Baylor University, Waco, TX, 1982), 74–77.

95. Burke, "Adoption and the Spirit," 314–15, points out how adoption was a Jewish eschatological hope (Hos. 1:10). This hope is attested by later rabbinical literature (*Jub.* 1:25; *T. Judah* 24:3–4). James Scott adds that in addition to the Old Testament typological corporate sonship, "there is a Hellenistic-Jewish topos of the prototypical proselyte who converts from polytheism by appealing to one true Creator-Father and thereupon becomes a son/daughter of God in a more particular and personal sense." *Adoption as Sons of God*, 96.

quality of Israel's Jewishness, might, or worth (cf. Deut. 7:7–8; 9:5–6; Isa. 63:8, 16; Jer. 31:9b; Hos. 11:1; Phil. 3:1–11). Redemptive grace procures the filial blessing. Consistent with its eschatologically realized form, redemptive sonship never owes to the intrinsic worth of the redeemed son, but to the grace and sovereign initiative of the Father. The divinely monergistic and gracious character of sonship in both Old and New Testaments remains constant. Accordingly, the antitypical (eschatological) adoption in its full Christological and soteric glory grows organically out of Israel's typological adoption.

In fact, Israel's typological adoption weds dynamic moral and redemptive themes in ways that lay the groundwork for the transformative, eschatological adoption of Romans. Such covenantal and spiritual-genetic connection of Israel's adoption with eschatological adoption stems from its shared scope of redemptive significance *and* its Christocentricity. The Spirit-given, actual yet anticipatory (subeschatological and typological) adoption for the old covenant people actually derives its theological significance in the Son of God, "the Christ who is God over all, blessed forever. Amen" (Rom. 9:5b). In the unfolding of covenant history, redemptive grace, moral transformation, and filial identity and privilege are fully embedded in old covenant *huiothesia*. Adoption's typological form and its antitype share a Christological core. Before further exploration of the covenantal and Christological significance of *huiothesia* in Romans 9, however, a text-critical matter surfaces and must be addressed.

Does Romans 9–11 Even Belong?

In commentaries on the book of Romans, chapters 9–11 have endured substantial critique[96] and have been cited as discontinuous with what precedes in Romans 8.[97] Moreover, it has been suggested that Romans 8 would transition nicely into Romans 12, with no break

96. Using his critical eye, Dodd matches this section with the *diatribé* or philosophical conversation like that of the Cynic and Stoic schools. See C. H. Dodd, *The Epistle of Paul to the Romans*, MNTC (New York: Harper, 1932), 148–49.

97. Some scholars insist that Romans 9–11 is an independent and post-Pauline imported section. See, e.g., Dodd, *Romans*, 148, 151; Sanday and Headlam, *Romans*, 225. Cf. Bruce, *Romans*, 171, 173; Barrett, *Romans*, 175; Ernst Käsemann, *Commentary on Romans*, trans. Geoffrey W. Bromiley (Grand Rapids: Eerdmans, 1980), 253.

of thought whatsoever. Since Romans 8:31–39 sufficiently draws to a close an extended theological exposition, "we might now expect Paul to solidify and apply his theology in a series of exhortations of the kind that often conclude his letters."[98] In fact, as John Murray admits, "If chapters 12 to 16 had immediately succeeded chapter 8 in this epistle the sequence would accord with a pattern easily understood and consonant with the order that we might expect."[99] Why, then, does Paul include Romans 9–11, or is this section a subsequent non-Pauline insertion?[100]

With closer examination, a strong case should be made that Paul could not properly move to the *oun* ("therefore") of Romans 12:1 without the exposition of Romans 9–11. Romans 1–8 introduces a perceptible dilemma concerning the relationship of God's sovereignty to the salvation of the sinner—both Jew and Gentile.[101] Motivated pastorally and theologically, the apostle Paul ventures into the depths of divine sovereignty and purpose, the coherence of a Christ-centered eschatological fulfillment of old covenant promises, and the integration of Jews and Gentiles in redemptive history. Paul's bold exposition of the lack of efficacy of circumcision *ex opere operato* (Rom. 2:25–29)[102] has already elevated the question of Israel's place in redemptive history. But his eschatological argumentation in Romans 8 was likely taken as a consummate anti-Semitic blow. Yet the heart of this Benjamite and Hebrew of Hebrews (Phil. 3:5) breaks over his fellow Jews' rejection

98. Moo, *Romans*, 547. It is true that the grammatical shift from 8:39 to 9:1 is abrupt, but the theological development is both natural and necessary. Grammar itself does not determine conceptual continuity. Cf. ibid., 555; William G. T. Shedd, *A Critical and Doctrinal Commentary on the Epistle of St. Paul to the Romans* (repr., Minneapolis: Klock & Klock, 1978), 271.

99. John Murray, *Romans*, 2:xi. Cf. Dodd, *Romans*, 148.

100. Nygren summarizes three common answers to this question: (1) Paul sets out the *locus classicus de praedestinatione*, (2) Paul presents his theodicy, or (3) Paul articulates his philosophy of history. See Anders Nygren, *Commentary on Romans*, trans. Carl C. Rasmussen (Philadelphia: Muhlenberg, 1949), 353–55. Though Paul surely accomplishes these tasks, none of these answers suffices to explain the *placement* of this section between Romans 8 and 12.

101. Murray adds, "It is, however, not merely the questions which emerge from this epistle that are answered in chapters 9 to 11. They are the questions which the biblico-theological perspective derived from the whole of Scripture necessarily provokes." *Romans*, 2:xii.

102. Cf. Barrett, *From First Adam to Last*, 34–45.

of Christ in view of Israel's stunning covenantal blessings, having come to them alone by God's grace (Rom. 9:1–3): "I am speaking the truth in Christ—I am not lying; my conscience bears me witness in the Holy Spirit—that I have great sorrow and unceasing anguish in my heart. For I could wish that I myself were accursed and cut off from Christ for the sake of my brothers, my kinsmen according to the flesh." (Cf. Rom. 10:1–4.)

Paul discerned ethnic, covenantal, and theological confusion blinding his fellow countrymen. The Israelites errantly perceived that God's character and his faithfulness to his covenant people conflicted with the Pauline Christ-centered message, and this perception raised a number of questions. Had the perpetual disobedience of the people of God finally led to God's reneging on his gracious promises of deliverance? Did Israel's unfaithfulness "not mean that God has revoked the promises He made to the fathers?"[103] How can Paul argue for God's faithfulness in the gospel when ostensibly God has turned his back on his covenant people? "Would it not be the most striking refutation of Paul's preaching, if its content were that, in the very moment that He is ready to fulfill His promises, God breaks them?"[104]

> Magnifying the problem is Paul's repeated insistence that what once apparently belonged to, or was promised to, Israel now belongs to believers in Jesus Christ, whether Jew or Gentile. Christians are Abraham's heirs (chap. 4), God's adopted children (8:14–17), possessors of the Spirit (chap. 8), and heirs of God's own glory (5:2; 8:18–30). If Jewish rejection of the gospel creates the problem Paul grapples with in Rom. 9–11, Gentile acceptance of that same gospel exacerbates it. It seems that Israel has not only been disinherited but replaced.[105]

---

103. Nygren, *Romans*, 357. Cf. Samuel G. Shepard, "The Pauline Doctrine of Sonship" (Ph.D. diss., Southern Baptist Theological Seminary, Louisville, KY, 1951), 20–27.

104. Nygren, *Romans*, 357.

105. Moo, *Romans*, 549. Judaistic and Christian tensions constituted this historical situation. "A decade of struggle to preserve the integrity and freedom of the gospel from a fatal mixture with the Jewish torah lies behind him; a critical encounter with Jews and Jewish Christians suspicious of him because of his outspoken stance in this very struggle lies immediately ahead (cf. Rom. 15:30–33). And the Roman Christians themselves are

It is with care for these critical concerns that Paul writes Romans 9–11. In response to the considerable consternation, he clings to the premise of the absolute faithfulness of God to his Word ("But it is not as though the word of God has failed," Rom. 9:6a). "One thing only cannot be; the promises have not failed; there has been no failure in the Promiser. What may seem such is rather man's misreading of the promise."[106] God remains truly faithful to his promises, for as the Almighty covenant-maker and covenant-keeper, he can do nothing less.

The Jews at large had misconstrued the blessings of God as nationalistic, and simultaneously sought respite in the form and shadow rather than the substance of divine grace. In so doing, they failed to accept how the old covenant subeschatological types and shadows anticipated none other than Jesus Christ himself (Rom. 9:6). Their historic covenants were in fact Christological, and to see them otherwise was to miss them altogether; it was to reject the consummate substance and purpose of the covenants, Jesus Christ the Lord. Yet "it is to the *true* Israel the promises are made and the purpose of God according to election stands fast (9:6–13); there is always a remnant according to the election of grace (11:5, 7). In this remnant the word of the promise is fulfilled."[107] This remnant will see Jesus Christ for who he really is—the long-awaited answer to the Jews' covenantal longings.

So why does Paul include Romans 9–11? It seems that he does so at least in part for missiological motives. The theological exposition serves evangelistic ends. For those blind to Christ Jesus as the Son who fulfilled divinely given prophetic promises, God's covenantal faithfulness (Hebrew, *hesed*) might well have looked like it was against

---

caught up in this issue, divided over the degree to which, as Christians, they are to retain the Jewish heritage of their faith." Ibid., 548. Cf. David N. Steele and Curtis C. Thomas, *Romans: An Interpretive Outline. A Study Manual of Romans, Including a Series of Interpretive Notes and Charts on the Major Doctrines of the Epistle* (Philadelphia: Presbyterian and Reformed, 1963), 74; Adolf Schlatter, *Romans: The Righteousness of God*, trans. Siegfried S. Schatzmann (Peabody, MA: Hendrickson, 1995), 199–203.

106. Handley C. G. Moule, *The Epistle to the Romans* (repr., Minneapolis: Klock & Klock, 1982), 249. Cf. Murray, *Romans*, 2:xiii.

107. Murray, *Romans*, 2:xiv (emphasis in original). Bavinck, *The Last Things*, 105, adds that "the promises of God have not failed because they concern the spiritual offspring of Abraham and will still consistently find their fulfillment in this spiritual offspring (11:1–10)."

the ropes, and Paul could not neglect this theological and spiritual misunderstanding. Jewish blindness to Christ as the comprehensive "Yes" and "Amen" (2 Cor. 1:20) to the promises of God necessitated the rigorous theological argumentation of Romans 9–11. Hence, these three chapters answer the perceived dilemmas by explaining God's sovereignty and faithfulness, precisely in the theologically organic nature of blessing from old covenant to new covenant. Compelled by the Son of God, constrained by the Spirit of the Son, and zealous for the redemption of his own people (Rom. 9:3), the apostle Paul turns his attention toward addressing the eschatologically sated grace of the gospel of Christ to *Jews* and the Gentiles.

Israel and Typological Adoption

Beginning this dramatic section, Paul explores the nature of the spiritual privileges granted to Israel in the pre-Christ epoch (cf. Rom. 3:1–2). It was to Israel that *huiothesia* was given; to Israel the "glory" (cf. Ex. 20, 33) and the "covenants" belong; to Israel the "law" was given; to Israel the "worship" and the litany of "promises" were given (Rom. 9:4–5). In view of his redemptive-historical construct in which the pre-Christ Spirit's presence would signify judgment, with doxological passion evoked and substantiations of divine redemption selected, Paul highlights the remarkable proleptic blessing graciously bestowed to corporate Israel in the former pre-Christ era.[108] Having already dismantled any concept of Jewish privilege on the basis of physical circumcision (Rom. 4:9–12; cf. Col. 2:8–15),[109] Paul assures his readers that the actual substance of spiritual, redemptive-historical, and typological privileges of his own people was simply breathtaking. In fact, in view of the extensive parameters of the Israelite blessing according to Romans 9:4–5, a dominant question surfaces: "What extraordinary advantage had God *not* given to this people?"[110]

108. Cf. Thomas F. Torrance, *The Christian Doctrine of God: One Being Three Persons* (Edinburgh: T&T Clark, 1996), 14, 67–68.

109. "Paul has argued that both Jews and Gentiles are under the power of sin, so that possession of the Torah and circumcision do not constitute a salvific advantage (1:18–3:20)." Schreiner, *Romans*, 469.

110. Nygren, *Romans*, 356 (emphasis added). Cf. Mawhinney, "*Yiothesia* in the Pauline Epistles," 138–39.

Putting into sharp focus the unqualified faithfulness of God, Paul underlines in a few short phrases (Rom. 9:4–5) the historico-theological heredity of the gospel in Christ. Explaining the place of Israel in this eschatological unfolding, he selectively outlines key strands of the redemptive-historical roots of new covenant blessing. In other words, the gospel that Paul preached (cf. Rom. 1:16–17) did not depart from the pre-Christ covenants (Gal. 3:8), but rather rendered the *fulfillment* of their shadows and types.[111] This vital organic connection of old and new covenants[112] grounds a proper understanding of God's historico-redemptive work.[113] Indeed, the apostle began his entire epistle with this transtestamental, Christocentric gospel continuity (Rom. 1:1–4), and by using the epithets in Romans 9:4–5, he unpacks the spiritual continuity between the Old and New Testaments.

With this redemptive-historical paradigm governing Paul's theology, Israel's corporate *huiothesia* could not be a categorically different *type* of adoption (that is, nonredemptive or merely nationalistic) from the adoption in Romans 8, Galatians 4, and Ephesians 1. Israel's adoption was typological and eschatologically anticipatory. By the gracious initiative of God, Israel was chosen as God's son (Ex. 4:22) and was redeemed from bondage as the *son* of God. This corporate adoption differs not in substance from its eschatological fulfillment but rather in *degree*. It typified the full realization of saving adoption into the family of God by the redemptive work of the covenant Mediator, Jesus Christ the Son of God. Though the last Adam alone was purposed

111. "As in the case of all God's institutions under the old covenant, a shadowy promise anticipated the reality of fulfillment.... As prophetic type of the anticipated reality, God's dealings with Israel as his elect people could only approximate the meaning of God's real purposes for those who were to be redeemed in Christ." O. Palmer Robertson, *The Christ of the Covenants* (Phillipsburg, NJ: Presbyterian and Reformed, 1980), 214.

112. How to understand this continuity requires exegetical and hermeneutical care. Some arguments for continuity maintain such a rigorous distinction between Israel and the New Testament church that the continuity suffers ambiguity at best, and incoherence at worst. For example, "*huiothesia* (referring to the church, 8:15, 23; referring to Israel, 9:4); *tekna theou* (church, 8:16, 17, 21; Israel, 9:8); *kalein* (church, 8:30; Israel, 9:7, 12); *doxazein/doxa* (church, 8:18, 21, 30; Israel, 9:4)." Jean-Noël Alletti, "L'argumentation paulinienne en Rm 9," *Biblica* 68, 1 (1987): 41–56, cited in Schreiner, *Romans*, 470n4.

113. Torrance, *Christian Doctrine of God*, 68–69. Dispensationalism errantly insists on an overstated covenantal discontinuity. See Meredith G. Kline, *Kingdom Prologue: Genesis Foundations for a Covenantal Worldview* (Overland Park, KS: Two Age, 2000), 340–50.

to deliver adoption in its fullness, by divine design Israel enjoyed adoption in incipient and anticipatory form.

In Pauline thought, Israel's historical redemption from bondage in Egypt conceptually and substantively prepares for the work of God in the new covenant, whereby he takes unbelievers enslaved to sin and frees them from the bondage of sin and death (Rom. 6:1–23; Gal. 4:1–6). Fulfilling the typology here, in the new covenant, God works graciously through Christ so that believers—whether Jew or Gentile (Rom. 11:23–25)—are engrafted into the tree of salvation. Thus, Paul in Romans 9:6b declares: *ou gar pantes hoi ex Israēl, houtoi Israēl* ("For not all who are descended from Israel belong to Israel"), and here builds a case for the faithfulness of God to his Word in a way that departs from many of his fellow Jews' assumptions. He exposes the redemptive significance of the old covenant promises as they come to fruition for peoples of all nations at the dawn of the eschatological age (cf. Gen. 12:3). In this theodicean defense, however, Paul unveils the underlying eschatological, redemptive-historical content of "Israel," identifying its referent as the genuine people of God in both Old and New Testaments (cf. Gal. 6:16).

In short, choice of the term *Israelites* here points to the redemptive-historical significance of the Abrahamic people (cf. Gal. 3:8), a significance that extends by promise and grace rather than genetics (Rom. 9:7–8). The spiritual-redemptive significance of the term *Israel* is no New Testament construction. Rather, as C. E. B. Cranfield attests, "The name 'Israel' was the regular self-designation of the Jews expressing their consciousness of being the people of God." He continues, "In the NT the names 'Israel' and 'Israelite' continue to have a salvation-historical significance (cf., for example, the occurrences in the Fourth Gospel: 1:31, 47, 49; 3:10; 12:13). So here Paul, by saying that his fellow-Jews are Israelites, is asserting that they are the chosen people of God."[114] Paul never minimizes the exalted place of the natural

---

114. C. E. B. Cranfield, *Introduction and Commentary on Romans IX–XVI: A Critical and Exegetical Commentary on the Epistle to the Romans* (Edinburgh: T&T Clark Limited, 1975), 460–61. Douglas Moo suggests that "in contrast to the colorless, politically and nationally oriented title 'Jew,' 'Israelite' connotes the special religious position of members of the Jewish people." He argues, "The appellation 'Israelites,' then, is no mere political or

descendants of Abraham in the redemptive plan of God. *Israel* includes physical descendants of Abraham who enjoyed the typological privilege of corporate redemption and corporate adoption. But *Israel* involves fuller spiritual and ecclesiological significance in both Testaments.

On the one hand, Romans 9:6b, *ou gar pantes ou ex Israēl outoi Israēl* ("For not all who are descended from Israel belong to Israel"), *narrows* the scope of *Israelites*, establishing the fact that not all who are Jewish by descent are Israel in their hearts; not all natural descendants of Abraham enjoy the saving grace of God. Biological connection does not circumcise the heart any more than physical circumcision itself does.[115] On the other hand, the statement *expands* the covenantal term, as Paul insists in his Jew/Gentile argumentation in Romans 9:19–33. Not only are physical descendants of Abraham not necessarily "children of God," but also those who are *not* physical descendants *become* "children of God" (9:8). Paul's appropriation of prophetic words is worth underscoring here:

> As indeed he says in Hosea,
>
> > "Those who were not my people I will call 'my people,'
> > and her who was not beloved I will call 'beloved.'"
> > "And in the very place where it was said to them, 'You are not my
> > people,'
> > there they will be called 'sons of the living God.'" (Rom.
> > 9:25–26)

Israel, in its realized redemptive-historical sense, consists of both Jew and Gentile who are children of promise by faith and by the mercy of God in Christ Jesus.[116]

---

nationalistic designation but a religiously significant and honorific title." *Romans*, 560–61.

115. Kline, *Kingdom Prologue*, 303.

116. Cf. Cullmann, *Salvation in History*, 86–87, 162; John Piper, *The Justification of God: An Exegetical and Theological Study of Romans 9:1–13*, 2nd ed. (Grand Rapids: Baker, 1993), 26; Benjamin B. Warfield, *Studies in Theology* (repr., Edinburgh: Banner of Truth Trust, 1988), 405; Robertson, *The Christ of the Covenants*, 39–40, 288–89. Contra F. F. Bruce, *The Epistle to the Galatians: A Commentary on the Greek Text*, NIGTC (Grand Rapids: Eerdmans, 1982), 274–75; William Dumbrell, "An Appreciation of the Theological Work

So, in the mission fields Paul sees Hosea's prophecy being fulfilled: the believing Gentiles are called to be God's sons and his people. This line of thought reflects both the OT/Jewish conception of Israel as the son (collectively) or sons of God and the Wisdom-tradition that especially designates the wise and righteous among the Jews as sons of God.[117]

Adopted sons are not necessarily the physical descendants of Abraham (Rom. 9:6–8; cf. John 1:12–13); "the children of the promise" (Rom. 9:8b) are the *true* Israel, the true sons (cf. Gal. 3:29).

Summarily, in Romans 9:6–8, *Israel* serves as a redemptive-historical term for the people of God, regardless of their ethnic descent (including old covenant proselytes, such as Ruth), and comprises "those who, in addition to being related to Abraham by natural descendency, also relate to him by faith, plus those Gentiles who are ingrafted by faith."[118] Such a conclusion does not defy or ignore the ethnicity of Israel, nor does it somehow obviate the commitment of God to the salvation of many Jewish people (Rom. 9:1–3; 10:1; 11:26).[119] Rather,

of Archbishop Donald Robinson," in *In the Fullness of Time: Biblical Studies in Honour of Archbishop Donald Robinson*, ed. David Peterson and John Pryor (Homebush West, Australia: Lancer, 1992), xxii.

117. Seyoon Kim, *The Origin of Paul's Gospel* (Tübingen: J. C. B. Mohr [Paul Siebeck], 1981), 317.

118. Robertson, *The Christ of the Covenants*, 40. Cf. Mark W. Karlberg, "Israel and the Eschaton," *WTJ* 52, 1 (1990): 131–41. Contra Homer A. Kent Jr., "The New Covenant and the Church," *Grace Theological Journal* 6, 2 (1985): 289–98.

119. There remains future redemption for those who are ethnically and culturally Jewish. In Romans 11, Paul does distinguish between ethnic Israel and the Gentiles, demonstrating God's continued mercy to his old covenant people, despite their historical hardening. Though the future of Israel nationally is a difficult and much-debated feature of this passage, I find Ridderbos and Bavinck most compelling in their insistence that "all Israel" in Romans 11:26 concerns the salvation of ethnic Israelites, but that this salvation consists of the full number of ethnic Israelite salvation over the course of history, rather than some climactic and comprehensive conversion at the end of history. See Bavinck, *The Last Things*, 106; Herman Ridderbos, "Israel in het Nieuwe Testament, in het bijzonder volgens Romans 9–11," in *Israel*, rev. informal trans. Richard B. Gaffin Jr., July 1999 (den Haag: Van Keulen, 1955), 57–64. With less convincing exegesis, Robertson, like Oscar Cullmann, *Salvation in History*, 162, insists that "all Israel" in Romans 11:26 refers to the eschatological salvation for the entirety of the elect—Jew and Gentile. See O. Palmer Robertson, *The Israel of God: Yesterday, Today, and Tomorrow* (Phillipsburg, NJ: P&R Publishing, 2000), 167–92. Cf. George R. Beasley-Murray, "Biblical Eschatology: The Interpretation of Prophecy,"

in Romans 9:6–33, Paul intends to identify the true nature of God's children of promise, those who are *spiritual* Israel. Furthermore, the "Israel" double entendre in Romans 9:6 conveys covenantal continuity between old covenant and new covenant, affirming the realized promises of the Abrahamic covenant in its extension to the nations (cf. Gen. 12:3), the Mosaic covenant with its redemptively contoured demands (cf. Ex. 20:1–2) for all "Israel," and the Davidic covenant with its filial/regal promises (cf. 2 Sam. 7:8b–14) for the people of God, the church under Christ Jesus.

With such redemptive continuity in mind, Paul in his use of *huiothesia* in Romans 9:4 intends to reveal the corporate and typological sonship of Israel—chosen by the grace of God as his son, in order to explicate the redemptive continuity of corporate Israelite *huiothesia* with the adoptive benefits in Christ of *true* Israelite *huiothesia* (whether Jew or Gentile). What corporate Israel experienced temporally and typologically, and for *true* Old Testament sons of Abraham *proleptically* by God's grace, true Israel realizes truly, personally, and eschatologically in the epoch of Christ's work. Adoption in Christ fills and fulfills ancient Israel's corporate adoption as son.

Hence, in the old covenant typological sense, *huiothesia* belonged to the Jews corporately, but it anticipated the new covenant in Christ, through whom *huiothesia* is realized for the children of *promise*— whether Jew or Gentile. The Old Testament gospel grace of adoption finds its New Testament realization in the person and work of Jesus Christ. In other words, the apostle here employs what Calvin describes as "degrees" of adoption in redemptive history, indicating that the efficacy and experience of sonship intensify in redemptive history, coming to full realization in New Testament adoption.[120]

EvQ 20, 3 (1948): 227; Howard Taylor, "The Continuity of the People of God in Old and New Testaments," *SBET* 3, 2 (1985): 13–26.

120. See Howard Griffith, "'The First Title of the Spirit': Adoption in Calvin's Soteriology," *EvQ* 73, 2 (2001): 142; John Calvin, *Commentaries on the First Book of Moses Called Genesis*, trans. John King, vol. 1 of *Calvin's Commentaries* (Edinburgh: Calvin Translation Society, n.d.; repr., Grand Rapids: Baker, 1989), 448. Cf. Peter A. Lillback, *The Binding of God: Calvin's Role in the Development of Covenant Theology*, ed. Richard A. Muller, Texts and Studies in Reformation and Post-Reformation Thought (Grand Rapids: Baker Academic, 2001), 214–17.

Contrary to any anti-Semitic allegation (which he directly counters in Romans 9:3), in his self-perception Paul "was never more truly a Jew than when he had become a Christian."[121] Or, to put it in Paul's filial language, his own *adoption* in Christ was the eschatological realization of the typological adoption of his forefathers. Though a Jew of Jews (Phil. 3:3–6), Paul was never more truly God's *son* than when he was by grace through faith united to the resurrected Son of God. Adoptive sonship in Christ makes one a true Israelite, a true son of Abraham (Gal. 3:29). Adoptive sonship comes through the one true and faithful Israelite, whose faithfulness as Son delivers in full the promises of his Father (Rom. 9:6; cf. Matt. 5:17). The litany of covenantal blessings belonging to Israel (Rom. 9:4–5) finds its eschatological substance, goal, and fulfillment in Jesus "Christ who is God over all, blessed forever. Amen" (9:5b). The explication of that continuity here serves the missiological purpose of Romans, which itself defines the very purpose of Paul's apostleship: "through whom we have received grace and apostleship to bring about the obedience of faith for the sake of his name among all the nations" (1:5; cf. 16:25–27).

Huiothesia in Romans 8 and 9

What, then, is the theological relationship between *huiothesia* in Romans 8:15, 23, and *huiothesia* in Romans 9:4? Two contrary arguments are posed here. Some argue that the meaning of Israel's *huiothesia* in Romans 9:4 is identical with that of believers in the New Testament (Rom. 8:15, 23), so that Paul's use of *huiothesia* in Romans 9:4 entails the full salvific meaning that it possesses in its prior references. When Paul writes of the adoption of the Israelites, he intends the *full* and *realized* spiritual adoption of ethnic Israel. By stark contrast, others contend either explicitly or implicitly that Israel's *huiothesia* in Romans 9:4 has no theological connection to the Spirit-wrought adoption in Romans 8:15 and 23. In Romans 8, Paul has in view the supernal filial blessings brought by the Spirit of

---

121. R. Alan Cole, *The Letter of Paul to the Galatians*, 2nd ed., TNTC (Leicester: Inter-Varsity Press, 1989), 148.

the risen Jesus Christ. In Romans 9, Paul has, in effect, a national or historico-theological conception formally related to New Testament *huiothesia*, but lacking any theological connection other than a broad manifestation of God's elective grace.

Illustrative of the first perspective is John Piper, who argues against a corporate, provisional, or typological *huiothesia* in Romans 9:4, concluding that the sonship of the Israelites in Romans 9:4b contains "the fullest [individual] saving significance of Rom 8:15, 23."[122] He insists that "there is no reason in Paul's milieu to cause us to construe the sonship of Israel in Rom 9:4b as a merely past or temporary blessing."[123] While Piper awkwardly attempts to maintain consistency with his futuristic interpretation of *huiothesia*, *doxa* ("glory"), and even *diathēkai* ("covenants"), his explanations of *nomothesia* ("giving of the law"), *latreia* ("worship"), and *epaggeliai* ("promises") weaken his case even further. It is difficult to see how Paul is not rehearsing God's covenantal faithfulness in the past as a defense of his covenantal faithfulness in the present/future.[124] The covenant-historical context of Romans 9:4–5 (along with the creation-to-consummation construct in Romans 8) moves from the typological-redemptive privileges of Israel in the old covenant to the antitypical fruition in the new covenant. Paul constructs his argument concerning the faithfulness of God to his promise in part on the *continuity* of the covenants. God's faithfulness is a *covenantal* faithfulness in the history of redemption.

Though Piper acknowledges the consummately singular eschatological people of God shown in the olive-tree analogy in Romans 11,[125] his failure to give covenantal continuity sufficient interpretive weight causes him to postulate two adoptions: a future one for ethnic Israel and a present/future one for the believing Gentiles, "adoptions" that are *theologically* and *substantively* the same.[126] Piper's expression of the free and gracious sovereignty of God is itself commendable, but

---

122. Piper, *Justification of God*, 32.

123. Ibid., 33. Citing Martin Rese, Heinrich Schlier, and Ulrich Luz as allies, Piper claims that *huiothesia* in all of Paul's citations possesses identical theological meaning. Ibid., 32–33.

124. See ibid., 31–40. Cf. Dumbrell, "An Appreciation," xxii–iv.

125. Piper, *Justification of God*, 26.

126. Ibid., 32.

inferring a static meaning for *huiothesia* in all five of its New Testament references fails to reckon amply with the progressive development of filial grace in redemptive history and Paul's theology.

Piper sees "the justification of God"[127] in individual salvation serving as the dominant question in Paul's mind, and shapes his exegesis around such *ordo salutis* concerns. In addition, he builds his case on a hermeneutically pivotal *future* for ethnic Israel (based on his exegesis of Romans 11)[128] and insists that the *huiothesia* of Israel in Romans 9:4 is not a reflection on its past privileges but its future salvific blessing. This interpretively decisive predisposition to Israel's national future shades his reading of this section in Romans, where, contrary to Piper's interpretation, Paul actually builds his argument on old-covenant-to-new-covenant *continuity* rather than on some ethnic or national discontinuity and futurist eschatology. Piper's attempt to interpret Romans 9:4–5 as an exclusively futuristic realization for ethnic Israel fails to persuade.

Charles Hodge views *huiothesia* in Romans 9:4 in a manner substantively unrelated to the soteric benefits of Romans 8:15, 23.[129] He essentially restricts the Israelite *huiothesia* to an external, theocratic sonship, and functionally severs any organic connection to realized New Testament *huiothesia*: the *huiothesia* in Romans 9:4 is "very different from that which [Paul] had spoken of in the previous chapter."[130] Israel's adoption becomes a historical phenomenon, conceptually sealed from embedded eschatological and pneumatological continuity with that realized in Christ Jesus. In a manner opposite to Piper, Hodge bifurcates old covenant and new covenant *huiothesia*. Such dichotomizing exegesis dismisses the contextual connection

127. Ibid., 217.

128. Cf. ibid., 25–30. Schreiner makes the same error in contending, "To see these privileges as passed on to the church badly misconstrues Paul's argument since his grief is due to the promises made to ethnic Israel." Schreiner, *Romans*, 485. A crass literalism governs Schreiner's method, leading him to misconstrue *Israel* as only an ethnic body. He fails to appreciate the redemptive-historical, spiritual, and covenantal significance of *Israel* as the whole spiritual people of God.

129. Hodge, *Romans*, 296–99; cf. Piper, *Justification of God*, 32. William G. T. Shedd, Charles Hodge, and A. A. Hodge take this external, theocratic view. See Shedd, *Romans*, 277; Archibald Alexander Hodge, *Outlines of Theology* (Grand Rapids: Eerdmans, 1949), 515.

130. Hodge, *Romans*, 298. Cf. Mawhinney, "*Yiothesia* in the Pauline Epistles," 253.

of Romans 8 and 9, and at a more fundamental level neglects the redemptive-historical continuity of blessing realized in the old covenant partially and enjoyed in the new covenant fully. To conclude that Paul intends mutually exclusive meanings to *huiothesia* in such close proximity (Rom. 8:23 and 9:4) is hardly hermeneutically satisfactory, because it gags the covenantal and filial continuation of Paul's thought between the chapters.

Hodge and Piper draw opposite conclusions about the meaning of adoption in Romans 9:4, but do so out of a shared method that flattens the redemptive-historical structure of the Pauline argument. Otherwise divergent perspectives, they share a hermeneutical method that fails to integrate the redemptive-historical and pneumatological concerns that drive the Pauline argumentation in Romans 8 and that raise the questions behind the apologetic argumentation in Romans 9–11. Both interpreters discount this epochal framework: Hodge disconnects typological and antitypical *huiothesia*, and Piper statically conflates redemptive-historical development in *huiothesia*, squelching its dynamic covenantal and Christological development.

Contrary to the Piper/Hodge approaches, it seems best to accentuate the epochal and Christo-pneumatic contours of Paul's theology. Paul uses *huiothesia* (as well as the other blessings listed in Romans 9:4–5) to underscore covenantal continuity as the interpretive framework for understanding God's faithfulness by Christ's redemptive work and its application to believers. Gazing into the past, he affirms God's covenant faithfulness. Looking toward Christ Jesus (v. 5), he affirms God's covenant faithfulness *historically* and *organically*. Israel was adopted as God's son *corporately*, and this corporate gracious election to sonship typified the glorious and gracious elective sonship in Christ (vv. 4–5) of true Israel—the true spiritual children of Abraham.[131] The covenantal gift of adoption in the Old Testament points to the Christological gift of adoption in the New Testament, when the Spirit who applied God's filial favor to Israel corporately in the former epoch is given in full measure in the resurrected Christ Jesus in the inaugurated eschatological epoch.

131. VanGemeren, *The Progress of Redemption*, 78–84.

What we find in the adoption of Israel delivers historical and conceptual freight into the eschatological sonship applied by the Spirit of adoption concerning the resurrected Son of God.[132] Thus, in view of Paul's argument in Romans 9:1–5 regarding the privileged status of Israel in the old covenant, and how that privileged status is consummated in the new covenant through Christ, we are constrained to recognize a thoroughgoing continuity between *huiothesia* in Romans 8 and *huiothesia* in Romans 9.[133] But such continuity does not necessitate or imply *stasis* or *identity*; in fact, redemptive-historical advance defies static, nonprogressive identity. Continuity intimates progression: a covenantal development from type to antitype, from shadow to substance, from corporate adoption in the Mosaic administration (Israel) to realized *Christological* adoption (true Israel) in the age of the Spirit. To say, then, that corporate Israel's sonship is theologically *identical* to new covenant sonship or *altogether other* than new covenant sonship neglects the underlying progressive and eschatological contours of Paul's paradigm.

Summarily, "Israel, considered collectively, is God's first-born, presumably as being His chosen people and as 'first-fruits' of all the peoples (Je. 31:9; 2:3),"[134] and this adoptive sonship, while differing from the eschatological fullness of new covenant *huiothesia* in Romans 8, is not *unqualifiedly* different. The people of God in the Old Testament— corporate Israel—provide the historical and theological grounding for the new covenant revelation of sonship. Thus, with Israel's adoption

132. If, as I affirm, Romans 9–11 is original and ought to be received as part of the Pauline letter and developing argument as a whole, the eschatological/epochal grid of Romans 8 is still in place here. The spiritual blessings under the old covenant anticipate the spiritual blessings in Christ by his Spirit in the new covenant. Put otherwise, Paul's emphasis on the Holy Spirit in Romans 8 ought to bear interpretive contours for our appreciation of the spiritual and typological blessings of the Old Testament people of God.

133. "Under the Old Covenant the Lord expected his people to display love and loyalty, provided for the atonement of their sins, and gave them the gifts of sonship, forgiveness, and life. Under the new covenant the grace of God is more evident in Jesus Christ, by whom the Father reconciles sinners to himself and gives them redemption in the Son. The superiority of the New Covenant is not that it provides forgiveness but that it offers a greater realization of the restoration and fulfillment of the promises." VanGemeren, *The Progress of Redemption*, 405.

134. R. Alan Cole, *Exodus: An Introduction and Commentary*, Tyndale Old Testament Commentaries 2 (London: Inter-Varsity Press, 1974), 78.

providing the theological ancestry for new covenant *huiothesia*, the transition into New Testament adoption springs forth in organic continuity. There are differences in old and new covenants—yet these are not differences in kind, but of development from eschatological anticipation to eschatological realization in redemptive-historical progression. The covenant of grace, in its Old and New Testament administrations, truly is for the apostle Paul a covenant of adoption— moving from its incipient and typological form into its eschatological filial grandeur in Christ Jesus, the Son par excellence.[135]

I return, then, to the ethnic Jew, a matter not lost on the apostle Paul in this very context. While he underscores the theological and redemptive-historical connection between Israel in the old covenant and Israel (Jew and Gentile) in the new covenant, he ministerially vindicates this point by his humble gratitude for his Jewish ethnicity. In fact, his love for his kinsmen is so deep that he presents a self-damning hypothetical scenario for their salvation, expressing his love for his fellow Jews, as the venue for expounding his theological concerns (Rom. 9:3).[136] For apologetic reasons, Paul is impassioned with expressing the theological continuity of the old covenant with the new covenant, longing that his brothers by ethnicity (v. 3) would embrace the Son of God and become his brothers by promise (v. 8). Those historically adopted by God corporately and typologically desperately needed the adoption by God in its full Christological and pneumatological substance. In fact, the failure to appreciate Christ as the answer to Israelitish adoption represented a failure to understand Israelitish adoption in the first place. Refusing to embrace the Christ of the new covenant represented a failure to embrace the promised Christ of the old. The type and antitype, the shadow and the substance are inseparable; though not historically identical, they share Christological and theological integrity, and maintain theological interdependence because of their shared Christological contours.

---

135. Calvin, *Institutes*, 2.7.2, 3.2.22.

136. "It is hypothetical to the effect that if it were possible and of avail for the salvation of his kinsmen he would be willing to be accursed on their behalf." Murray, *Romans*, 2:3. The hypothetical scenario established by Paul should be translated, "I could wish." Cf. Shedd, *Romans*, 273–77.

The apologetic strategy of Romans 9, then, is to express the gospel of grace to both Jew and Gentile, in order for them to recognize the vital connections between old covenant and new covenant, and to rest in the sovereignly gracious initiative of God in bringing peoples of all nations to salvation by faith (Rom. 9:30–10:15). It is not, *and never has been*, those who have physical connection to Abraham who enjoy the spiritual blessing. Instead, it is those who believe in Jesus who "have all the prerogatives of Israel in the OT: they are children of God, inheritors of promise, God's elect people, righteous in his sight, and assured of glorification."[137] What was typified by the corporate adoption of Israel, and proleptically experienced by the circumcised of heart in the old covenant, is eschatologically realized in the circumcised of heart in the new covenant.[138] Israel's sonship typified the sonship of Christ, proffering a foretaste of the realized sonship of the sons of Abraham in union with the Son of God by adoption.

Adoption, Christ, and Filial Transformation

One of the enlightening implications of the redemptive-historical continuity laid out in Romans 9:1–5 is the way in which the filial privileges interface with moral obligation. In keeping with the renovative aim exposed in Romans 8, which culminates in full *in Christ* filial conformity (Rom. 8:29), the Romans 9:4 typological adoption unsurprisingly draws moral concerns into focus. Illuminating this filial/moral interconnection is the literary parallelism used by the apostle Paul in his explication of Israel's old covenant benefits.[139] In view of the unusual choice of words in certain instances, and the symmetry of the couplets, it is only proper to conclude that Paul thereby intends to convey specific theological connections. Accordingly, Schreiner suggests that the pairing of *huiothesia* and *nomothesia* ("giving of the law") unveils the important connection of law and sonship; the pairing

137. Schreiner, *Romans*, 470.

138. Richard B. Gaffin Jr., *Perspectives on Pentecost: New Testament Teaching on the Gifts of the Holy Spirit* (Phillipsburg, NJ: Presbyterian and Reformed, 1979), 37–38.

139. See Scott, *Adoption as Sons of God*, 148; Piper, *Justification of God*, 21–23; Cranfield, *Romans IX–XVI*, 460; James D. G. Dunn, *Romans 9–16*, WBC 38B (Dallas: Word, 1988), 522.

of *doxa* ("glory") with *latreia* ("worship") refers to the cult "in which the glory of God was manifested in the tent and the temple"; and the pairing of *diathēkai* ("covenants") with *epaggeliai* ("promises") exposes the important connection between the historic covenants and revealed promises (cf. Eph. 2:12).[140]

Regardless of whether one takes *nomothesia* as the law given or the actual giving of the law, the syntactical connection between adoption and the law underscores the critical relationship between sonship and holiness. Correspondingly, the etymological relationship between *huiothesia* and *nomothesia* ought not to be dismissed as coincidental. Those placed as sons are those given the law; those given the law are those placed in divine grace and compelled to filial obedience. Divine adoption provides the gracious context for redeemed sons to walk in obedience, a matter that finds its full meaning in union with Christ by the Holy Spirit, whereby adopted sons walk in the obedient footsteps of their Elder Brother, the Son of God par excellence (Rom. 8:12–17). Filial obedience is the necessary fruit of filial grace.

The *locus classicus* for Old Testament redemptive sonship, Exodus 4:22–23, confirms this filial/moral connection and substantively informs the redemptive-historical backdrop for the theological concept of adoption. Rabbinic scholarship itself recognizes the centrality of this text; accordingly, Huonder writes, "We can consider this the classic text justifying Israel being called the Son of God."[141] The familial language of Exodus 4:22–23 affirms the redemptive and fatherly context, where the son's obligation to the Father infuses the familial relationship: God's expectations of his people are the expectations of a Father for his children.[142] "The first-born son in Israel was regarded as being naturally dedicated to God and in early times had certain cultic prerogatives and obligations. It is this that informs the concomitant demand of verse 23

---

140. Schreiner, *Romans*, 483–85.

141. V. Huonder, *Israel Sohn Gottes: zur Deutung eines alttestamentlichen Themas in der jüdischen Exegese des Mittelalters*, Oribs Biblicus et Orientalis 6 (Freiberg/Schweiz: Universitätsverlag, 1975), 54 [my translation of the following: "Wir können diesen Text die klassische Schriftstelle zur Begründung von Israels Gottessohnschaft nennen"]. Cf. Martin W. Schoenberg, "Huiothesia: The Adoptive Sonship of the Israelites," *American Ecclesiastical Review* 143 (1960): 269–71.

142. Cf. Mawhinney, "*Yiothesia* in the Pauline Epistles," 88–89, 94.

that Israel be allowed to worship in the wilderness."[143] Put otherwise, covenant obligation is not antithetical to sonship but constitutive of it.

Thus, saturating this central text regarding Israel's covenantal sonship is the *purpose* for that sonship. God's redemption of Israel was not merely for political freedom, nor even for freedom from the cruelty associated with Egyptian bondage. Instead, it was redemption *unto* the exercise of faithful worship of God (Ex. 20:1–17).[144] Called God's son by the Father himself, Israel received an explicit redemptive vocation: *filial obedience*—"I will make them walk by brooks of water, in a straight path in which they shall not stumble, for I am a father to Israel, and Ephraim is my firstborn" (Jer. 31:9b; cf. Jer. 31:31–34; 2 Cor. 6:14–18). The gracious redemptive provision of the Father grounded the mandate for obedience to the covenantal requirements (cf. Ex. 20:1–2). Summarily, in even its shadowy redemptive-historical unfolding, adoption inherently commends moral and ethical conformity, and in its adoption-unto-obedience construct actually anticipates the eschatological *enabling* presence of the Spirit of Christ Jesus to attain conformity to the Son—that is, conformity to him in his full obedience (Rom. 8:29; 2 Cor. 6).[145] Old and new covenant adoption situates worship and obedience within its filial grace.

This ethical thrust of covenantal sonship is forcefully expressed in numerous other Old Testament passages. In Deuteronomy 14:1–2, God calls his people "sons," and in so doing states clearly that such sonship mandates holiness (14:2). Later in Deuteronomy 32:5–6, Moses appeals to God's gracious redemption in filial terminology as

143. Nahum M. Sarna, *Exodus: The Traditional Hebrew Text with the New JPS Translation*, JPS Torah Commentary (Philadelphia: Jewish Publication Society, 1991), 24. Concerning Exodus 4:22, Brendan Byrne writes, "The first statement has the air of a solemn acknowledgement on God's part of Israel's status before him—an acknowledgement which implies . . . Israel's obligation to serve Yahweh as his people." Byrne, *"Sons of God"—"Seed of Abraham,"* 15.

144. "The whole revelation of covenant law is an unfolding of our duty to God, our duty to love and serve God. And that law of the covenant is the law of man's image-sonship." Kline, *Kingdom Prologue*, 65.

145. Mawhinney, *"Yiothesia* in the Pauline Epistles," 140, makes the astute observation that the concepts of *sonship* and *covenant* unite in Romans 9:4–5 with *glory*: "The chosen (adopted) son of God bears the glory/image of God, that glory which was displayed on Sinai at the forming of that covenant bond between God and Israel." This fact reiterates the *telos* of sonship as essentially doxological.

the basis for obedience. The Lord chastises the people, stating that they "are no longer his children" because of their perversity and rebellion. This use of poetic hyperbole does not confound the sonship of Israel, but points to the vile inconsistency of disobedience and rebellion with the gracious elective calling of God the Father (cf. Deut. 32:19).[146] Moses pointedly asks, "Do you thus repay the Lord, you foolish and senseless people? Is not he your father, who created you, who made you and established you?" (Deut. 32:6).

In Isaiah 43, God speaks of the gracious creation/redemption of his people, his "sons" and "daughters," whom he "formed" and who belong to him (43:1, 6). Who are these sons and daughters but those "who [are] called by my name" and "whom I created for my glory" (43:7)? The ultimate purpose of God's redeeming call of sons and daughters, his creation of a redeemed family, is for their glad obedience unto his glory. Divine possession of these blessed people comes by their gracious creation/redemption, and this ownership compels their filial fidelity. Jeremiah 3:14 and 22 further testify to the lavishness of God's grace, which beckons the repentant obedience of his sons and daughters (cf. Jer. 4:22). Divine glory is brilliantly revealed in his gracious forgiveness of the children's sins (Isa. 43:24–27; cf. Jer. 31:20), yet the driving call of God through the prophet Isaiah is that sonship privilege move them toward grateful obedience: "the people whom I formed for myself that they might declare my praise" (Isa. 43:21).

In Hosea 11:1, God called his covenantal "son" out of Egypt. Why the call? As established in the following verse, God's gracious elective sonship intended faithful obedience and worship. The adopted son is rescued from his place of bondage and placed under the jurisdiction of the adopting Father, under whose paternal leadership he must abide by the laws of the house (cf. Heb. 3:5–6). But as Romans 9:2–4 indicates, this ancient son (Israel) rejected the purpose of that adoptive call. Beckoned to obedient love, the chosen son failed to meet the covenantal obligations of filial love inherent in the sonship privilege. This covenant failure did not weaken the obligation to loyal love, but

---

146. Of course, in both Testaments, filial obedience attests to filial faith, and the absence of filial obedience raises ultimate spiritual questions (Prov. 3:11–12; Heb. 12:1–17).

rather manifests the necessity of a Son who would fulfill the Father's covenant and deliver the Father's promise. Despite Israel's covenantal failure, the expectations of familial obedience are no less intricately woven into the teleological fabric of adoptive grace and characterize the work of the faithful Son who accomplishes the Father's purposes. This consummately faithful Son, as Paul contends in Romans 9:1–5, is Jesus Christ.

Hence, when Paul puts *huiothesia* in parallel with *nomothesia* in Romans 9:4, he does so because he maintains the inviolable connection between sonship and worshipful, filial obedience. Therefore, the *telos* of Pauline *huiothesia*, consistent with its Old Testament type, is moral and spiritual purity, whereby the son dwells in peace with his Father, joyfully living as a loyal son compelled by the Father's love to conform to his Father's expectation. The consistent and perpetuated failure of Israel to achieve the calling of its covenantal obligations, however, draws history to a climactic and condemning tension. Israel's rebellion placed the nation under the wrath of God; simultaneously, the rebellion illuminated the need for the arrival of the Redeemer-Son, promised in Genesis 3:15, and typified through old covenant sonship and cultic provisions, listed in summary form in Romans 9:4–5. In every way, the typological adoption of Israel finds its end in Jesus Christ, the Son of God resurrected. The holy Son of God, from whom the Holy Spirit of adoption flows without measure, makes redeemed sons holy. Final adoption, secured by the Son of God and applied by the Spirit of the risen Son, ensures filial delight and secures filial covenantal success for all the redeemed, Jew and Gentile—the true sons of God.

Summary: Typological and Eschatological Adoption

The theological landscape in Romans 8 prominently elevates the ministry of the Holy Spirit. As the agent of union with Jesus Christ, the Holy Spirit applies the work of the resurrected Son of God to all the sons of God. As recipients of this outpoured eschatological Spirit of adoption, the redeemed sons live no longer in bondage unto fear. As adopted sons of God, they are led by the Spirit of Christ unto holiness. Declared sons in the Son of God by the Spirit of Christ, they are made Sonlike by this same Spirit of adoption. This consummate filial transformation occurs in the filially shaped resurrection, at which point the sons of God will enjoy full conformity into the image of the Son of God par excellence. Fully manifest as adopted sons, they experience their adoption as entailing their full transformation on the last day, when their sonship status declared will actually and wholly replicate their Elder Brother's holy disposition and resurrected body.

To some Jews in Paul's day, this gospel of adoption preached by the apostle Paul signaled God's unfaithfulness rather than his faithfulness to his covenant promises. In Romans 9, Paul takes great pains to demonstrate the faulty nature of such covenantally and Christologically blind misinterpretations. In fact, as he lists this filial blessing preeminently in a series of gospel-rich epithets, the Spirit of adoption had already rendered a typological and corporate adoption to the old covenant people of God (cf. Ex. 4:22–23). This adoption, while subeschatological and therefore incomplete, laid the historical/theological building blocks for the realization of that typological adoption's very goal: adoption in and by Jesus Christ, the Son of God. This old-covenant-to-new-covenant adoption sustains a rigorous covenantal continuity—highlighting both the forensic and the renovative dimensions of adoption, in all its redemptive-historical and soteriological contours. Under the former epoch of law and curse, the particular blessing enjoyed by the old covenant people of God is strikingly gracious. Even in that age of slavery and fear, Israel knew the filial blessing of God—typologically, but no less truly.

While the failure of Israel to keep its sonship obligations highlights the ultimate inefficacy of the old covenant provisions, the familial and covenantal expectations of worshipful, doxological obedience embedded in theological adoption anticipate another Son to come. Grounded in the holy *telos* of adoption predestined (Eph. 1:4–5) and consistent with Paul's development of old-to-new-covenant adoption (Rom. 9:4–5), the fulfillment of adoptive sonship comes in God's sending of his own Son (Gal. 4) in whom adoption of the sons of God by the Holy Spirit of adoption secures adoption's holy *telos* (Rom. 8:15, 23). The apostle Paul uniformly insists that the eschatological accomplishment of adoption comes in the resurrected Son of God alone (Rom. 1:3–4) and that its application comes to the sons of God by the Spirit of the Son of God, the Spirit of adoption. How exactly this eschatological adoption is secured for the sons in the Son requires further consideration of the progressive phases of sonship in the life of Jesus Christ himself. An examination of Christ's own multifaceted sonship, which culminates in his own resurrection/adoption, comes into focus in the following chapter.

PART 3

ADOPTION IN BIBLICAL AND SYSTEMATIC THEOLOGY

7

Jesus Christ, the
Son of God Adopted

The *Eternal* Son of God?

Nicene Orthodoxy

In keeping with the scriptural pattern of theological confession (e.g., 1 Cor. 15:1–3; 1 Tim. 3:16), the early church formulated creedal statements for succinctly articulating the core of apostolic doctrine. These creeds bore pedagogical significance, but they also served doxological and ecclesiological purposes, enabling the church gathered to share openly in her confession of Christ and the gospel, honoring the mandates of Hebrews 4:14 and 10:23. Creating the postapostolic creedal expressions came with great price, and their development offers a fascinating study in the church's solidifying self-consciousness concerning God, his Word, and the Christ of salvation. Space limitations prevent examining in any detail the creeds and the controversies that fueled their formulation, but a few brief words are in order.

The early creeds, in their summary statements concerning the Son of God, fully affirm his deity. The incarnate Christ, born of Mary, was the eternal Son of God made flesh. Before he was man, he was eternal God. The incarnation marked the assumption of a human nature and a human body by the second person of the Trinity, making him something that he never was before. But the eternally begotten Son of God has always been one with and equal to the Father. So, too, is the Holy Spirit, the third person of the Trinity, one in substance and equal with the Father and the Son. As expressed in the historical creeds of the church, the God of Scripture is triune, and the incarnate Son of God was and is *first* the eternal Son of God.

In its attempts to rebut heresy and to articulate an orthodox Christology with unambiguous precision, the church took nearly five hundred years to settle on suitable language concerning the hypostatic union.[1] The Nicene Creed (A.D. 325) confronted the subordinationism[2] of Arian heresy with a rigorous affirmation of the Son's deity and assumption of human flesh:

> We believe . . . in one Lord Jesus Christ, the Son of God, begotten of the Father, only-begotten, that is, of the substance of the Father, God of God, light of light, true God of true God, begotten not made, of one substance with the Father, through whom all things were made, things in heaven and things on earth; who for us men and for our salvation came down and was made flesh, and became man, suffered, and rose again on the third day, ascended into the heavens, is coming to judge the living and the dead.[3]

As additional Christological heresies subsequently appeared (Apollinarianism, Nestorianism, and Eutychianism), this creedal affirmation laid the groundwork for the more expansive expression of the hypostatic union in the Chalcedonian Creed (A.D. 451) at the Fourth Ecumenical Council:

> We, then, following the holy Fathers, all with one consent, teach men to confess one and the same Son, our Lord Jesus Christ, the same perfect in Godhead and also perfect in manhood; truly God and truly man, of a reasonable [rational] soul and body; consubstantial [coessential] with the Father according to the Godhead, and

---

1. *Hypostatic union* refers to Christ's personal unity, as fully God and fully man.

2. Subordinationism affirms the threeness of God, but insists that the Father is greater than the Son and the Spirit, and in so doing denies divine equality among the three persons.

3. Recorded in Philip Schaff, ed., *The Creeds of Christendom with a History and Critical Notes*, rev. David S. Schaff, 6th ed., 3 vols. (Grand Rapids: Baker, 1998), 1:28–29. For the original Greek text of the Nicene Creed, see ibid., 2:60. This creed was slightly revised at Constantinople in 381, and it is that Nicene-Constantinopolitan Creed that has become known today in ecclesial shorthand as the *Nicene Creed*.

consubstantial with us according to the Manhood; in all things like unto us, without sin; begotten before all ages of the Father according to the Godhead, and in these latter days, for us and for our salvation, born of the Virgin Mary, the Mother of God, according to the Manhood; one and the same Christ, Son, Lord, Only-begotten, to be acknowledged in two natures, *inconfusedly, unchangeably, indivisibly, inseparably*; the distinction of natures being by no means taken away by the union, but rather the property of each nature being preserved, and concurring in one Person and one Subsistence, not parted or divided into two persons, but one and the same Son, and only begotten, God the Word, the Lord Jesus Christ, as the prophets from the beginning [have declared] concerning him, and the Lord Jesus Christ himself has taught us, and the Creed of the holy Fathers has handed down to us.[4]

This Nicene-Chalcedonian Christology, as efficiently summarized here in WCF 8.2, has preserved the church's adherence to biblical and theological fidelity concerning the person of Christ Jesus:

The Son of God, the second person of the Trinity, being very and eternal God, of one substance and equal with the Father, did, when the fullness of time was come, take upon him man's nature, with all the essential properties, and common infirmities thereof, yet without sin; being conceived by the power of the Holy Ghost, in the womb of the virgin Mary, of her substance. So that two whole, perfect, and distinct natures, the Godhead and the manhood, were inseparably joined together in one person, without conversion, composition, or confusion. Which person is very God, and very man, yet one Christ, the only Mediator between God and man.

In summary, during the early centuries of the Christian church, Trinitarianism and Christology dominated ecclesial attention. Out of knotty theological debates over the divine preexistence of Christ Jesus and over his full humanity as Mediator and Savior, this pithy

---

4. Recorded in ibid., 2:62–63 (emphasis in original).

Westminster statement digests many historical affirmations of biblical Christology, which repudiate Ebionism, Arianism, Sabellianism, Apollinarianism, Nestorianism, and Eutychianism. The Son of God is "very and eternal God" who took "upon him man's nature." Christ's divinity lies antecedent to his humanity; "the essential or ontological forms the backdrop for and interprets the covenantal or contingent or historical, *and not vice versa*."[5] The Logos *asarkos* precedes and qualifies the Logos *ensarkos*.[6]

Contemporary Challenges to Orthodox Christology

Centuries of the church have upheld the Nicene-Chalcedonian-Westminsterian ontological, chronological, and theological precedence of the deity of Christ, and "not until the modern period would any serious heresy arise to challenge this orthodox Christology."[7] With exponential increase in biblical studies, and increased epistemological and methodological reliance on second-temple Judaistic discoveries and Greco-Roman historical analysis, formerly settled questions about Christology have once again become unsettled. Fresh (or, perhaps more precisely, renewed) critical challenges have erupted within the theological academy, causing modern scholarship to divide over divine Christology in ways reminiscent of the first five hundred years of the church.

Historical, biblical, and theological questions converge on matters vital to orthodoxy. Did the early church believe Jesus Christ of Nazareth to be the eternal Son of God incarnate? Does the New Testament uniformly attest to the divine ontological preexistence of Jesus? Or does the core of the New Testament present him as something less than divine, a man to be sure, but not the God-man as defined in the historical creeds and confessions of the church (e.g., Nicene Creed)?[8]

---

5. K. Scott Oliphint, *God with Us: Divine Condescension and the Attributes of God* (Wheaton, IL: Crossway, 2012), 199 (emphasis in original).

6. Logos *asarkos* ("without flesh; preincarnate") offers a succinct formulation to affirm the eternality of the Son of God. Before he became the Logos *ensarkos* ("incarnate"), he was the Logos *asarkos*. See, e.g., James J. Cassidy, "Election and Trinity," *WTJ* 71, 1 (2009): 53–81.

7. Gregg R. Allison, *Historical Theology: An Introduction to Christian Doctrine: A Companion to Wayne Grudem's Systematic Theology* (Grand Rapids: Zondervan, 2011), 377.

8. See Simon J. Gathercole, *The Preexistent Son: Recovering the Christologies of Matthew, Mark, and Luke* (Grand Rapids: Eerdmans, 2006), 1–2. Gathercole points out that even

Did he assume divine sonship at some point in his earthly life in history (at his baptism or resurrection), or was he the eternal Son of God *sent* from heaven? By harboring Nicene-Chalcedonian-Westminsterian formulations, has the church succumbed to philosophical and metaphysical speculation, and drawn conclusions about the person of Christ that depart both from the text of Scripture and from first-century understanding? Are the incarnation and hypostatic union philosophical innovations or a biblical teaching? Is divine preexistence of the Son of God read *into* the biblical text or read *out* of it? Answers to these and other related questions are neither simple nor trivial. The conclusions bear directly on Christian faith and practice, and biblical and doxological scrupulousness is in order.

Christology *from Above* vs. Christology *from Below*

Despite various efforts to affirm compatibility between disparate Christologies in their interpreted developments,[9] two mutually exclusive schools of scholarship have emerged: those that affirm the divinity of Christ as expressed in the historical creeds (a Christology *from above*—e.g., Richard J. Bauckham, Gordon Fee, Simon Gathercole)[10] and those that deny it (a Christology *from below*—e.g., Hendrikus Berkhof, James D. G. Dunn, J. Murphy-O'Connor, James F. McGrath).[11] Though some might accuse this dual taxonomy of lacking sufficient nuance,[12] and though there exist varying degrees of these so-called *high* (from above) and *low* (from below) Christologies, one either does or does not

---

in early Jewish texts, the concept of a preexistent Messiah exists.

9. See, e.g., James F. McGrath, "Change in Christology: New Testament Models and the Contemporary Task," *Irish Theological Quarterly* 63, 1 (1998): 39–50.

10. Recently, Chris Tilling has proposed a "Christ-relation" Christology, in which divine transcendence and the extraordinary grace of divine immanence come together in the God-man, that is, in Paul's divine Christology. See Chris Tilling, *Paul's Divine Christology*, Wissenschaftliche Untersuchungen zum Neuen Testament 2 Reihe 323 (Tübingen: Mohr Siebeck, 2012).

11. See Gathercole, *The Preexistent Son*, 1–20. Beginning with the precritical period and then into the twenty-first century, Gathercole provides a useful survey and taxonomy of the study of Christology.

12. Cf. Nicholas Lash, "Up and Down Christology," in *New Studies in Theology 1*, ed. Stephen Sykes and Derek Holmes (London: Duckworth, 1979), 31–46.

uphold the eternal and preexistent divinity of the Son of God. These positions remain forever binary.

As Colin Gunton has put it, "Christology from below aims to ground what it has to say primarily in the anthropological or, more generally, in that which has to do with time rather than eternity."[13] Though we must avoid philosophical dualism in all Christological formulations, in terms of a theological and epistemological starting point, the options remain mutually exclusive; and the historically orthodox view grounded in Christ's eternal, ontological, divine preexistence remains the only *high* Christology.[14] The debates have given particular attention to Pauline theology, as many deny that Paul views Christ as divine, at least in the historical, creedal, ontological sense of the word. The goal of this book is not to prove historic orthodoxy concerning the deity and eternality of the Son of God. Others with a Christology from above have done so cogently and persuasively.[15] In this volume, these fundamental truths concerning the Trinity and the Son of God are assumed, even celebrated. And despite intense pressure since the late nineteenth century until now to defy such ontologically framed, confessional, preexistent divine Christology, this Christology from above draws from the Scripture itself and, contrary to some stubborn scholarly opinion, indeed from the Pauline corpus.

God sent his Son (Rom. 8:3; Gal. 4:4), and this sending *does not create sonship, but presupposes it.*[16] "The divine glory of Christ, even already in his pre-existence with the Father prior to his redemptive

13. Colin E. Gunton, *Yesterday & Today: Studies of Continuities in Christology*, 2nd ed. (London: SPCK, 1997), 10–11.

14. Many scholars, including James Dunn, whose work we will consider at greater length here, insist on a *developing* Christology in the New Testament. That is to say, early Christian writings do not possess a divine Christology, though later (Johannine) writings do. Whatever may be said about biblical authorial distinctions and historical development per se, one must not claim that two New Testament authors possess incompatible views of Christ's identity and maintain a high view of revelation. If the Holy Spirit is the author of Scripture, then there can be no opposing biblical Christologies, only one Christology with fully complementary dimensions.

15. See, e.g., Gordon D. Fee, *Pauline Christology: An Exegetical-Theological Study* (Grand Rapids: Baker, 2007).

16. Herman N. Ridderbos, *Paul: An Outline of His Theology*, trans. John Richard DeWitt (Grand Rapids: Eerdmans, 1975), 69.

revelation, determines and underlies the Pauline Christology."[17] That Christ is eternal Son does not mean, however, that there is therefore no progressive, functional dimension to his sonship. His appropriation of a human nature opened new categories for his sonship, which entailed not only the hypostatic union but also his filial progression and maturity. To gain a fuller understanding into these ontological/functional dimensions of Christ's sonship, we will first survey some salient features of modern Christological debate.

The Revival of a Heresy

In the third century A.D., monarchian theories (e.g., Paul of Samosota)[18] waged war with orthodox Trinitarianism. Varying conceptions of subordinationism supplemented these monarchian heresies, as a means of affirming a single God and situating the Son and the Spirit as emanations or modes of the one God. In the eighth century, to these errors concerning the Trinity was added the claim that only the Logos is eternal Son of God, but that the man Jesus is adopted. So-called adoptionism, a heresy that appeared in various forms during the first thousand years of the church, claimed that Jesus was merely man and that only the Father was the eternal God. Jesus attained a particular favor with God, was adopted, and bore the title *Son of God*.[19] This adoptionist Christology has found revived adherence, and in its modern forms commonly insists that Jesus was not Son of God until his resurrection.

One of the more influential of the contemporary scholars averse to divine Christology is James D. G. Dunn. While less than orthodox, his work is formidable and cannot, with any academic integrity, be ignored. In short, Dunn and those sharing his theological commitments have revived an adoptionist (functional, rather than ontological) Christology. Dunn insists that *"primitive Christian preaching seems to have regarded Jesus' resurrection as the day of his*

17. Ibid., 70.

18. Sabellianism, modalism, and monarchianism were early heresies concerning the Trinity. Each of them eclipsed God's threeness for the sake of affirming his oneness.

19. Douglas F. Kelly, *Systematic Theology: Grounded in Holy Scripture and Understood in the Light of the Church*, vol. 1 (Fearn, Ross-shire, UK: Christian Focus, 2008), 552.

appointment to divine sonship, as the event by which he became God's son."[20] Though he does concede a divine Christology in Johannine literature,[21] Dunn finds it irresponsible to draw conclusions about the "earliest Jesus-tradition" on the basis of later Christological development in John, a development that is "at best tangential to the earlier tradition."[22] Just as he does concerning the Synoptics, Dunn denies Christ's *personal* preexistence in the Pauline corpus, and in his treatment of Colossians 1 and 1 Corinthians 8:6, for example, asserts instead the preexistence of God and of wisdom. The nonpreexistent Christ, on the other hand, in his death and resurrection, appropriates the wisdom of God: "Paul's Wisdom christology is wholly consistent with the continued confession of God's oneness (1 Cor. 8:6) and . . . for Paul the mystery of divine wisdom has been revealed as never before in Christ and his cross (1 Cor. 1:24)."[23]

In other words, the Pauline Christ is not divine, but is the greatest manifestation of divine wisdom—a wisdom put on full display in his death and resurrection. Dunn attempts to navigate the preexistence language of certain Pauline passages by distinguishing Jesus' person from the eternal wisdom of the one true God: "Wisdom's preexistence allowed amazing language to be used of Christ. The mistake would be to collapse the metaphor into a straightforward statement of historical fact."[24] Thus, to Dunn, Paul's Christ is "unambiguously *subordinated* to God,"[25] and his approach to Wisdom Christology and Adamic Christology drives him away from divine preexistence in Paul.[26] With no disregard to his formidable scholarship, perhaps more "amazing" is Dunn's predisposition to bend clear texts of Scripture to suit this theological program.

---

20. James D. G. Dunn, *Christology in the Making: A New Testament Inquiry into the Origins of the Doctrine of the Incarnation*, 2nd ed. (Grand Rapids: Eerdmans, 1996), 36 (emphasis in original).

21. "There is an overwhelming *scholarly* consensus that . . . Johannine sayings . . . imply preexistence." Gathercole, *The Preexistent Son*, 83 (emphasis in original).

22. Dunn, *Christology in the Making*, 31.

23. James D. G. Dunn, *The Theology of Paul the Apostle* (Grand Rapids: Eerdmans, 1998), 275.

24. Ibid., 288.

25. Tilling, *Paul's Divine Christology*, 2 (emphasis in original).

26. See Dunn, *Christology in the Making*, 266–93.

Though Dunn's thesis of incongruent New Testament Christologies—a less-than-divine, adoptionist Christ in Paul (and the Synoptics) with an inchoate preexistent divine Christ in John—finds ongoing advocacy, it also "has been widely criticized and rejected."[27] For example, responding to Dunn, N. T. Wright expresses appreciation for the Adamic backdrop to Philippians 2:5–11, and along *with Dunn* distinguishes the question of divine preexistence of Christ from the Adamic Christology behind Philippians 2. But Wright confronts Dunn's bifurcation of eternal wisdom from the personhood of Christ by appealing to the "language drawn directly and obviously from Isaiah 45:23," and based on the explicit monotheism of Isaiah 45, he concludes, "In Philippians 2:10f. Paul credits Jesus with a rank and honour which is not only in one sense appropriate for the true Man, the Lord of the world, but is also the rank and honour explicitly reserved, according to scripture, for Israel's God and him alone."[28]

Jesus Christ, the last Adam, is the preexistent Son of God made the incarnate Son. Christ's preexistence cannot be reduced to a strained concatenation of eternal "Lady Wisdom" intrinsic to God and the personifying display of that poetically qualified wisdom in the child born to Mary.[29] It should be added that much wisdom Christology suffers from impersonalizing wisdom even in its "Lady Wisdom" motif, and in so doing unavoidably introduces a theoretical conception of wisdom. Lady Wisdom is metaphorical and more abstract; divine wisdom is exhaustively vital and personal. In fact, if eternal wisdom is not personal, it cannot be divine. Accordingly, the *personhood* of Jesus (the Logos) antedates his incarnation, and he does not merely appropriate and manifest divine wisdom; he *is* the eternal, personal

27. Gerald O'Collins, *Christology: A Biblical, Historical, and Systematic Study of Jesus*, 2nd ed. (Oxford: Oxford University Press, 2009), 250.

28. N. T. Wright, *The Climax of the Covenant: Christ and the Law in Pauline Theology* (Minneapolis: Fortress, 1993), 93–94. As John 1 also affirms, "The earthly life of Jesus has . . . disclosed the full mystery of what Jewish speculation had arrived at in its poetic personification of the Wisdom of God. Wisdom is now disclosed to be a personal entity within the Godhead existing in personal relationship with the Father." Reginald H. Fuller, "Pre-existence Christology: Can We Dispense with It?," *Word and World* 2, 1 (1982): 33.

29. For a useful critique of wisdom Christology, see Gathercole, *The Preexistent Son*, 193–209.

Wisdom of God.[30] He is eternal God, the second member of the Trinity; thus, stating that Christ is the personification of wisdom is a tautology, but worse than that, by imposing *from below* theological categories, such a position evades the biblically consistent appreciation for and assumption of the Logos *asarkos*, the preincarnate and eternal Word. Christ is all-wise because he was and is forever the Son of God, just as the early-church creedal statements affirm.

Christology as Composite: A High Christology and Christ's Humanity

Dunn's insights, however, ought not to be entirely cast off. Despite his insistence on denying Christ's *personal* preexistence and on absorbing pneumatology and Christology into an abstract wisdom Christology, Dunn's Adam Christology provides some important biblico-theological and *filial* insights. Dunn is quite right to insist that "the prehistorical existence of Adam [serves] as a template on which a vivid Adam christology begins to be drawn."[31] It would be ill advised to retrench into Nicene categories in a manner that wholly obscures some of the functional Christological perspectives that Dunn and others highlight. To do so would be to throw out the indispensable filial baby with the contaminated filial bathwater.

Admitting that top-down and bottom-up Christologies operate with opposing epistemological orientations does not negate a functional Christology *that presupposes* and *depends on* preexistence. In fact, a faithful functional Christology relies on Trinitarian orthodoxy, and biblical soteriology relies on both. Despite some overreaction and scholarly resistance, reception of certain features of Adamic and wisdom functional Christological categories does not militate against ontological ones, and requiring a choice *between* ontological and *functional* categories in Christology fails to appreciate the reciprocally clarifying *biblical* relationship between the ontological and the covenantal/redemptive-historical.[32]

---

30. Richard Bauckham, *Jesus and the God of Israel: God Crucified and Other Studies on the New Testament's Christology of Divine Identity* (Grand Rapids: Eerdmans, 2008), 16–17.
31. Dunn, *The Theology of Paul the Apostle*, 292.
32. This statement offers no sympathy for the retroactively conditioned ontology of Wolfhart Pannenberg. To be sure, the ontological remains ultimate and provides the *raison*

The biblical record largely focuses on what might be labeled a *functional* Christology precisely because of the *redemptive* purpose of divine revelation. In this focus on redemption-securing incarnation lies the need for a functional Christology, in which the Son born to Mary and born under (the curse of) the law might progress through sufferings, comprehensively succeed in combatting temptation, die as the qualified covenant-keeping Son, and then fittingly enter into a new state of sonship, at which point he would receive the final (eschatological) approval of the Father. In short, eternal Christology expressly grounds Scripture's exposition of the Mediator-Son; and to be fair to the text of Scripture, we must acknowledge how functional Christology emphatically dominates the biblical exposition of this Mediator-Son. Again, *no* functional filial Christology exists without a preexistent one, but neither does any biblical soteriology materialize without preexistent *and* functional Christology.[33] The preincarnate Son became the incarnate Son, and then at his resurrection *was adopted as* Son of God in power, all so that we might become the sons of God by grace through him. This, contrary to contemporary bottom-up adoptionists *and* to many who seek to uphold historic orthodoxy, is the Pauline gospel.

Nicene-Chalcedonian Orthodoxy or Functional Christology

Yet not all who express orthodox Christology find room for a functional, progressive sonship in Jesus Christ, let alone an adoption. Donald Macleod, for example, commendably resists historical adoptionist formulations, which insist that Christ *became* Son of God and was not Son of God before punctiliar action in history. But in his otherwise compelling defense of orthodox Christology in *The Person of Christ*, Macleod denies Christ's personal filial change at his

---

d'être for the redemptive-historical. It is also true, however, that Scripture focuses Christology and soteriology in the historical, and that the revelation of Christ in the flesh aids in understanding his preexistent ontology. See footnote 48.

33. For a most insightful analysis of the theologically essential interface between the divine and human in Christ Jesus, see volume 3, chapter 3, of Geerhardus Vos, *Reformed Dogmatics*, ed. Richard B. Gaffin Jr. and Richard de Witt, trans. Annemie Godbehere, Roelof van Ijken, Kim Batteau, Daan van der Kraan, and Harry Boonstra, vols. 1–3 (Bellingham, WA: Lexham Press, 2013).

resurrection. Christological orthodoxy for Macleod retains its integrity only by an essentially static sonship, and he disavows any sense of Christ's adoption in his rejection of adoptionist heresy. Macleod cites several reasons why the eternal ontological sonship of Jesus Christ proscribes any such attained sonship, but can such a position stand the test of Scripture?

Contending that the strongest case for any Pauline adoptionist thought resides in Romans 1:4, Macleod openly rejects *any* functional sonship in this text and in Pauline theology as a whole. To do so, he appeals to the verb *exapesteilen* ("sent") in Galatians 4:4, and insists that the eschatological kingdom inaugurates at Christ's coming, not his resurrection. He maintains that the title *Son of God* "appears without the slightest hint of his becoming Son only at the resurrection,"[34] and concludes that introducing an adoptionist Christology in Romans 1:4, in a book written twenty years after Galatians, would seem "strange." Macleod traces the usage of "Son of God" in Romans itself, and contends that nowhere does the epistle attach Christ's sonship to the resurrection. Then, following Martin Hengel, Macleod sees no historical basis for aligning resurrection and exaltation, because "the exaltation of a martyr was not by any means taken as an indication of unique status."[35] Finally, Macleod argues, the perceived scandal of the cross was so overwhelming, no resurrection could stay its stigma; rather, the resurrection idea itself was equally mocked, and it simply could not have rendered an apologetic for an exalted Christ. "The resurrection itself was a stumbling-block; part of the problem rather than part of the solution."[36]

Notwithstanding the debate on whether the verb *exapesteilen* ("sent") in Galatians 4:4 intends preexistence,[37] by contending that the New Testament does not align sonship with resurrection in any place

---

34. Donald Macleod, *The Person of Christ*, Contours of Christian Theology (Downers Grove, IL: InterVarsity Press, 1998), 90.
35. Ibid., 91.
36. Ibid.
37. I concur with Macleod in affirming that it does. For further discussion of *exapesteilen*, see Trevor J. Burke, *Adopted into God's Family: Exploring a Pauline Metaphor*, NSBT 22 (Downers Grove, IL: InterVarsity Press, 2006), 107–9, 116–19.

other than Romans 1:4, Macleod fails to appreciate the synecdochal[38] character of *death* and *resurrection* references in Paul. "What is worth recalling at this point, because it is particularly applicable to Paul, is the observation made at least as early as Calvin that in Scripture references to the death alone or the resurrection alone are synecdochic."[39] In addition, a *dynamic* filial focus permeates New Testament theology, as seen at the baptism of Christ, the transfiguration, and the glory of the resurrection (cf. Luke 9:28–45). Paul aligns sonship and resurrection in Romans 1 precisely because of the historico-theological indivisibility of sonship from Christ's personal and covenantal development (Luke 2:52) and his ministerial/mediatorial qualifications and actions, all with their cosmic, eschatological implications. As attested at various points by the Father and the Spirit, no moment of his human existence obtains apart from his growing sonly identity and covenantal function, which culminate in his own filially conditioned resurrection.

Countering Calvin, Hodge, and other earlier interpreters, Macleod joins more recent Reformed scholarship's rejection of *pneuma* ("Spirit") and *sarx* ("flesh") in Romans 1:3–4 as reference to Christ's hypostatic union.[40] Instead, he rightly sees the contrast as redemptive-historical. He then emphatically rejects the translation of *horisthentos* as "declared," and opts instead for "appointed," suggesting that "the resurrection marks not his adoption but his investiture."[41] Christ did

38. Synecdoche is a literary tool in which a word meaning a part of something refers to a whole. An oft-repeated illustration is helpful: in the context of marriage, a woman's "hand" is a synecdoche for *all* of her—a man intends to marry an entire woman, not merely her hand. Paul will often employ the term *death* or *resurrection* and mean by it "death *and* resurrection," the whole of Jesus's work.

39. Richard B. Gaffin Jr., *By Faith, Not by Sight: Paul and the Order of Salvation*, 2nd ed. (Phillipsburg, NJ: P&R Publishing, 2013), 25–26. "Inseparability, however, is not indistinguishability. . . . The resurrection is not an aspect or component part of the death." Richard B. Gaffin Jr., *Resurrection and Redemption: A Study in Paul's Soteriology*, 2nd ed. (Phillipsburg, NJ: Presbyterian and Reformed, 1987), 115.

40. Calvin and Hodge represent older scholarship in seeing the hypostatic union in Romans 1:3–4. Herman Ridderbos, Geerhardus Vos, and John Murray represent Reformed scholarship's decisive trend toward the redemptive-historical interpretation. See David B. Garner, "The First and Last Son: Christology and Sonship in Pauline Soteriology," in *Resurrection and Eschatology: Theology in Service of the Church: Essays in Honor of Richard B. Gaffin, Jr.*, ed. Lane G. Tipton and Jeffrey C. Waddington (Phillipsburg, NJ: P&R Publishing, 2008), 256–57.

41. Macleod, *The Person of Christ*, 92.

not become Son at his resurrection; instead, he openly received what was rightfully his own as Son already. As the resurrected Son of God, "he is transfigured, regnant and pre-eminent."[42]

By way of response to Macleod, Richard Gaffin's careful consideration of *horisthentos* and Romans 1:3–4 deserves note. Observing the surprising choice of *horisthentos* as the verb put in parallel with *genomenou* ("descended"), Gaffin "suggests that [*horisthentos*] functions to bring out a noteworthy aspect of the resurrection not otherwise apparent."[43] Though the majority of older commentators translated *horisthentos* with "declared" rather than "appointed," they did so assuming that Paul had in view the hypostatic union in Romans 1:3–4, making appointment incoherent for an expression of ontology. Like Macleod, Gaffin finds the redemptive-historical understanding of the Romans prologue preferable, and has, like Macleod, opted for "appointed" as the meaning of *horisthentos*, but with an essential amplification. Though Gaffin acknowledges the dominant usage of the verb on the side of "appoint," he is equally quick to affirm the verb's declarative force in the Romans prologue and in other places. He draws to a pointed conclusion this way:

> Consequently, while the thought of effectual appointment is prominent, a declarative nuance is also present, so that in its effective, transforming character the resurrection has a declaratory significance. The resurrection is here viewed as a declaration which is constitutive in nature. Moreover, this verb has an unmistakable juridical tone. This suggests that the resurrection is a judicially constitutive declaration of sonship. In other words, *horisthentos* underscores what is already intimated in recognizing that "Son of God" is a messianic designation: the resurrection of Jesus is his *adoption* (as the second Adam).[44]

Gaffin, in other words, views the divine appointment as possessing declarative force because something happens in the resurrection itself.

42. Ibid.
43. Gaffin, *Resurrection and Redemption*, 117.
44. Ibid., 118 (emphasis in original).

A change occurs in Jesus at his resurrection, and the appointment as "Son of God in power according to the Spirit of holiness" (Rom. 1:4) declares this eschatologically consummative (epochal) and redemptively pivotal change (cf. 1 Cor. 15:45). Geerhardus Vos puts it this way: "From resurrection-beginnings, from an eschatological genesis dates the pneumatic state of Christ's glory which is described as a sonship of God ἐν δυνάμει [*en dunamei*, 'in power']."[45] Resonant with the Vosian thrust concerning the change brought *to Christ himself* in the resurrection, Gaffin's nuanced interpretation of *horisthentos* warrants serious attention.[46]

While rightly waging war against historical adoptionism, Macleod has failed to appreciate the exegetical propriety and theological necessity of Christ's unprecedented sonship attainment. Commendably fighting heresy, Macleod overreacts by obscuring the *filial* attainment in Christ Jesus that actually secured the reversal of the cosmic curse and secured blessing for those in him. As we will see, the resurrection and his newfound filial status are, in fact, critical to biblical Christology and biblical soteriology. Asserting that Christ became Son in a new way does not presume or demand that he became Son for the first time or that he became divine; instead, it secures his redemptive efficacy as the Son *confirmed* in covenant righteousness. To qualify as Redeemer, he had to *become* the Son par excellence. Christ's sonship did not commence at the resurrection; it changed forever, a change that secured the efficacy of his covenantal and mediatorial mission.

The soteriological implications leap from this filial fact. As Dunn rightly detects in the New Testament, there is a strand of shared *sonship* between Christ and his disciples, a sonship that renders intimacy with God in the purest of filial grandeur. The scope and meaning of this Christological solidarity with his followers may well be the Bible's most stunning manifestation of divine grace. "There is sufficiently

45. Geerhardus Vos, "The Eschatological Aspect of the Pauline Conception of the Spirit," in *Redemptive History and Biblical Interpretation: The Shorter Writings of Geerhardus Vos*, ed. Richard B. Gaffin Jr. (Phillipsburg, NJ: Presbyterian and Reformed, 1980), 105.

46. "The resurrection is to Paul the beginning of a new status of sonship: hence, as Jesus derived his sonship κατὰ σάρκα [*kata sarka*, 'according to the flesh'] from the seed of David, he can be said to have derived his divine-sonship-in-power *from the resurrection*." Ibid., 104 (emphasis added).

good testimony that Jesus taught his disciples to regard themselves as God's sons . . . [and] that he thought of their sonship as somehow derivative of his. Added to this is the probability that he saw his sonship in part at least as an *eschatological* commissioning."[47] Though Dunn wrongly rejects the concept of a preexistent sonship in Paul (and the Synoptic Gospels), and though this exegetical and methodological conclusion compromises his overall analysis of Pauline Christology (and soteriology!), he rightly perceives how the functional and eschatological dimension of sonship and the solidaric relationship of the eschatological Son of God with the redeemed sons of God function vitally in New Testament Christology and soteriology, including those categories in Paul. "Paul . . . sensed no opposition between the preexistence of the Son and his public installation into the function of sonship through resurrection (Rom. 1:4)."[48] Neither should we.

Macleod's final critique against Dunn's adoptionist Christology requires less detailed response. In the face of the perceived implausibility of crucifixion as divine victory over sin and evil, and even the resurrection, which as indicated earlier "itself was a stumbling-block,"[49] Macleod contends that Paul faced an uphill battle over such a foolish line of argument. Accordingly, he must warm hearers to the idea that the crucified and resurrected Christ was exalted. Macleod's argument gains traction only if the adoption/resurrection of Christ intends to issue raw persuasive proof, to provide a rationally credible case for trusting in him. Such a bottom-up epistemology serves us no better than a bottom-up Christology. As Paul himself knew theologically and

47. Dunn, *Christology in the Making*, 32 (emphasis in original).

48. Wolfhart Pannenberg, *Jesus—God and Man*, trans. Lewis L. Wilkins and Duane A. Priebe (Philadelphia: Westminster, 1974), 143. Pannenberg's theological program, including his Christology, contains pervasive problems. Positive appreciation of this specific Christological point does not indicate approval of his broader Christology, Trinitarian theology, or dialectical theological method. Pannenberg claims that Christ would not be Son if it were not for his resurrection; by contrast, I contend that Christ would not be the *adopted* Son if it were not for his resurrection. Pannenberg says that the resurrection historically creates and validates the ontology; I insist, by contrast, that the ontology (eternal sonship) ensures the functional sonship of Christ Jesus in all its facets. See Carlton Wynne, "History and Trinity Reconsidered: A Reformed Evaluation of Wolfhart Pannenberg's Retroactive Eschatology" (Ph.D. diss., Westminster Theological Seminary, Philadelphia, 2015), 133–95.

49. Macleod, *The Person of Christ*, 91.

experientially, apart from the work of the Spirit, preaching Christ's death and resurrection gained no hearing to spiritually deaf ears! Any warming to the gospel would not come *kath huperochēn logou ē sophias* ("with lofty speech or wisdom," 1 Cor. 2:1). The stumbling block of the cross and the foolishness of the gospel require the Spirit's illumining ministry, a need that framed Paul's entire *kerygma* ("preaching"), and explicitly the entire first letter to the church in Corinth. Such illumining work by the Spirit to the cosmic and personal significance of the redemptive work of Christ is "regeneration on its noetic side."[50]

Paul's arguments in 1 Corinthians 1–2 and 1 Corinthians 15 affirm how humanly preposterous the entire message of the gospel is, including the resurrection. He also affirms the resurrection as the sine qua non of gospel hope. Paul trusts in the power of the Spirit to illumine hearers to the Word of God, and to persuade them of the gospel's truthfulness and of the resurrection's soteric and eschatological significance. Uphill battles, including the rending of blinders from the heart's eyes, are no obstacle for the Spirit of the risen Christ. He draws sinners and persuades them of the splendor of Christ's cross and resurrection, by confirming in their hearts the veracity of God's Word. E. J. Young puts this spiritual character of gospel understanding judiciously:

> It is then from God Himself that we learn the true character of the Scriptures. In the very nature of the case, it must be so. Only God can identify what He Himself has spoken. If man, unaided, could identify God's Word, man would have powers, which are God's alone. And if man really has these powers, God, whatever else He might be, would not be the One of whom the Bible speaks. We are in reality face to face with the question of theism. Unless we first think rightly of God, we shall be in error upon everything else. Unless we first think rightly of God, we shall indeed be in error when we come to consider His Word. We Christians need not be ashamed to proclaim boldly that our final persuasion of the

50. John Murray, "The Attestation of Scripture," in *The Infallible Word: A Symposium by the Members of the Faculty of Westminster Theological Seminary*, ed. N. B. Stonehouse and Paul Woolley, 2nd ed. (Phillipsburg, NJ: P&R Publishing, 2002), 51.

Divinity of the Bible is from God Himself. God, in His gentle grace, has identified His Word for us; *He has told us that the Bible is from Himself. Those who know Him not may depreciate this doctrine of the internal testimony of the Spirit; those who are His know that God has truly brought them out of darkness into light.*[51]

Nicene-Chalcedonian Orthodoxy *for Functional Christology*

In his modern adoptionist proposal, Dunn makes prominent the diversity he perceives in New Testament Christologies. Having sized up what he believes to be the chronology of the New Testament books, having concluded various authorial and contextual emphases within the New Testament canon, and having asserted canonical discontinuities in Christology, he defends his method as one historically informed, rather than dogmatically imposed. Critiquing what he sees as an undue Nicene-Chalcedonian Christological influence in historical biblical and theological studies, Dunn operates with a methodological (and dogmatic!) assumption of his own, one that obfuscates the ontologically and hermeneutically determinative antecedent identity of the second person of the Trinity. Dunn's method also effectively rejects the role of the divine Holy Spirit in the giving of Scripture. His Christology from below presupposes a Bible and a hermeneutic from below. These theological commitments compromise Dunn's overall program, but not all his insights.

What makes theological errors compelling is not their flagrancy, but their proximity to biblical truth and their captivatingly fresh redefinitions. Often errors accentuate one truth in a way that winsomely clouds or recasts other truths in subtle but mistaken ways; doctrines get retooled in ways ostensibly close to biblical teaching, yet with departing nuances that dash biblical fidelity. In other cases, theological errors surface in reaction to opposite errors. Antinomianism, for example, advances because legalism is wrong. But legalism's errors do not justify antinomianism's rival pendulum swing. On the other hand, legalism gains favor when the appreciable beauty of grace has created

---

51. E. J. Young, *Thy Word Is Truth* (Edinburgh: Banner of Truth, 1963), 35 (emphasis added).

a disconcerting flippancy about biblical imperatives (cf. Rom. 6:1–4).[52] Lackadaisical treatment of grace is sinful, but so, too, is Pharisaism.

Response to error, therefore, must stem from the whole counsel of God. We must take action against theological aberration, but never in a way that counters imbalance with an opposite imbalance. This warning applies to orthodox Christology. Maintaining orthodoxy concerning Christ's deity remains of paramount importance, but doing so in *any way* that obscures Scripture's theological development of Christ's humanity and filial identity does not serve the church well because it does not honor Scripture well. Maintaining orthodoxy concerning Christ's divinity does not warrant the obscuring of his humanity. To do so is *unorthodox*, and any even subtle form of Docetism should receive the sharpest ecclesial and theological rebuke.

Not unlike other heresies, adoptionism contains an important, albeit misconstrued, emphasis. Adoptionism appreciates the humanity of Christ. It insists that the baptism and resurrection of Christ entail critical *filial* development in the life of Jesus Christ. The life of Jesus, as fully man, indeed undergoes various stages. Events in his life produce status changes, and his baptism and resurrection mark significant transitional moments in his filial identity that serve redemptive, cosmic purposes. To be sure, Paul of Samosata's adoptionist proposal grossly erred in its denial of the divinity of Christ; his Unitarian bias forced him to deny the critical theological reality of the coequality and personhood of the Father, Son, and Spirit. Dunn's proposal is equally problematic, laden as it is with imposed historico-critical misconceptions. But to cast away the adoption of Christ altogether fails to give credence to the way in which the New Testament celebrates the transitional events in the life of Jesus Christ, the Son of God.

Critiquing Hendrikus Berkhof's Christology from below, in which Berkhof denies Chalcedonian orthodoxy,[53] J. Faber makes an

---

52. For an examination of grace and holiness in the believers' lives, see volume 6 of John Owen, *The Works of John Owen*, ed. William H. Goold, 16 vols. (n.p.: Johnstone & Hunter, 1850–53; repr., Edinburgh: Banner of Truth, 1988); Mark Jones, *Antinomianism: Reformed Theology's Unwelcome Guest?* (Phillipsburg, NJ: P&R Publishing, 2013).

53. Hendrikus Berkhof presents a fourfold approach to Christology: (1) from behind— a redemptive-historical approach with Jesus arising out of the Old Testament; (2) from above—an approach that starts with God as Creator and his redemptive speech that became

important hermeneutical and theological point, which advocates of both high and low Christologies often miscarry. Having shown that Berkhof's functional Christology essentially revives ancient adoptionism and Arianism, Faber takes issue with Berkhof's hermetically sealed argumentation, which affirms Jesus's sonship as "entirely unique,"[54] but then insists that it is properly understood only as "a redemptive-historical concept."[55] Berkhof insists on "Jesus' unicity . . . situated within His humanness; we may not derive it from a kind of dual nature, human and divine. There was no pre-existence in Jesus; He did not exist before His birth."[56] Finding the early church guilty of turning covenant into abstract ontology, like Dunn, Berkhof makes a "contrast between the so-called Biblical thought of covenant and encounter, on the one hand, and Greek ontological thought, on the other hand. This sharp contrast is unacceptable."[57] In addition to Berkhof's unfortunate Barthian sympathies for revelation as encounter[58] and Scripture as fallible human witness (among other historico-critical commitments he sustains),[59] his theological method requires one to take *either* the ontological conclusion *or* the covenantal one concerning Christ.

Despite his claims to unite features of a Christology from above and below, and to accept "substance" and "functional" Christologies, Berkhof's attempted synthesis is wholly conditioned by his higher-critical commitments. In essence, those commitments mandate a *from below*

---

enfleshed; (3) from below—a historical and critical approach that weighs the evidence from extant sources; and (4) from before—a concern for the work of Christ through the centuries in human hearts. Hendrikus Berkhof, *Christian Faith: An Introduction to the Study of the Faith*, trans. Sierd Woudstra, rev. ed. (Grand Rapids: Eerdmans, 1986), 271. Berkhof's sympathies are self-consciously for a method *from below*, and this historico-critical orientation shapes his interpretation of all the biblical data. His "Jesus is [a] man, the perfected covenant man, *the* new man, the eschatological man." Ibid., 291. Openly rejecting Chalcedonian formulations, Berkhof contends that Christ is *not* the God-man. Ibid., 291–98.

54. Ibid., 287. Berkhof even notes that Christ's unique sonship establishes a filial duality, in which Jesus alone is the "firstfruits," and we are "but 'adopted sons,' destined as 'fellow heirs with Christ' 'to be conformed to the image of the Son.'" Ibid., 288–89.

55. Ibid., 286.

56. J. Faber, *Essays in Reformed Doctrine* (Neerlandia, AB: Inheritance Publications, 1990), 58.

57. Ibid., 61.

58. Berkhof, *Christian Faith*, 54.

59. Ibid. "Revelation takes place within the limits of . . . provisional existence and is thus determined and limited by that context." Ibid.

Christology only, which rejects the Son of God's essential preexistence. Faber (rightly) rejects Berkhof's Christological conclusions and his inbuilt polarization, and argues that Scripture concerns itself both with pretemporal ontology in Christ *and* God's covenantal revelation in history. Contrary to Berkhof, Faber embraces the redemptive-historical/ functional dimensions of Christ's sonship through the lenses of the preexistence of Christ, rather than eclipsing the essential features of Christology from above by sporting higher-critical hermeneutical lenses. Berkhof's approach is therefore illumining for us. Maintaining an orthodox *functional* Christology requires a theological commitment to the Scripture's (and therefore Nicene) affirmation of the preexistent eternal sonship of Christ. One cannot cherry-pick aspects of a high Christology while operating with a paradigm in which the Son of God is *only* human. In whatever sense Jesus *becomes* Son of God, he does so *as the preexistent* Son of the eternal God of heaven.

More needs to be said. Affirming a functional sonship does not militate against the divine, preexistent sonship of Christ, but rather *depends* on it covenantally, redemptive-historically, and incarnationally. Where Berkhof errs concerning a Christology from below, Macleod errs in parallel fashion by his version of a Christology from above. Put otherwise, Macleod's affirmation of an eternal sonship wrongly precludes acceptance of historically conditioned sonship in the experience of Jesus Christ. Michael Peppard captures well the reactionary spirit of postliberal conceptions of Christ's sonship: "Since Adolph von Harnack's *History of Dogma* popularized the term, 'adoptionism' has become one of heresiology's black holes, a center of gravity which collects into itself multifarious constellations of 'low' Christology, obscuring any nuanced perspective on them."[60]

In other words, because of his bottom-up approach, Berkhof squanders his opportunity to conjoin essential and functional sonship in Christ. In preferable fashion, but still with (lesser) theological problems, Macleod commits to Chalcedonian-Nicene orthodoxy in a way that prevents an appreciation of the *necessary* human and filial

---

60. Michael Peppard, *The Son of God in the Roman World: Divine Sonship in Its Social and Political Context* (Oxford: Oxford University Press, 2011), 94.

development of Christ. Faber, on the other hand, rightly appreciates the functional in light of the ontological. Starting with the divine preserves the divine; starting with the divine should, as with Faber, also preserve the human. The opposite, however, is never true. Bottom-up presuppositions hermetically seal theological reflection from the divine Christ. Starting with the human will never properly lead to orthodox Christology. Chalcedonian-Nicene orthodoxy grounds a proper understanding of Christ's divine and *human* sonship.

The stakes are not merely conceptual or philosophical. Christ attains no functional, eschatological sonship unless he *came from heaven* as first the eternal Son, precisely as expressed in historic Christology. In Christ's filial identity lies a constellation of features, divine and human, none of which may be wholly extracted from the others. The final eschatological affirmation of the Father concerning the Son (cf. Heb. 5:10) harks back to his eternal sonship as Creator, who holds all things together by the word of his power (Heb. 1:1–4; Col. 1:15–17). Surely the Father's pleasure in the Son is eternal, and such intra-Trinitarian mutuality and delight render the ontological substructure of all theology and history. But static eternal sonship does not produce redemptive sonship, and the Father's *revealed* pleasure lies not so much in Christ's eternal sonship as in his redemptive accomplishment as Son of God incarnate. Divine pleasure in the covenant of redemption (*pactum salutis*) attains in the covenant of grace. Ontology neither secures soteriology nor statically delivers eschatological purpose. For divine covenant purpose to be attained on earth, the eternal Son had to become the resurrected and adopted Son. And Christ brings *no* privilege of eschatological sonship (adoption) to believers if *he himself* has not attained to eschatological sonship (adoption) himself. As we will see in the remainder of this volume, failing to appreciate Christ's historical adoption undermines biblical soteriology, for out of eschatological sonship glory *attained* by Christ in his own life experience flows full-orbed filial grace in redemption. "It is not what Christ *is* but what He, as κοινωνός [*koinōnós*, 'sharer'] of both natures, *does* that saves us. Our salvation is a salvation by *deeds*, not by modes of existence."[61]

---

61. Vos, *Reformed Dogmatics*, 3:63 (emphasis in original).

Jesus is the Son of God, but not *only* by ontological stasis. Sonship is ontological, eternal, and archetypal; it is also functional, regal, ectypal, temporal, and eschatological. It is no *less* than divine and eternal, but in Christ's mediatorial capacity, sonship is also no less than *humanly* developmental. The stages of Christ's incarnate life, including the culminating stage of his filial designation and identity, are vital to biblical theology, Christology, and soteriology. To put it simply, without the human biography of Christ Jesus, capped by his own *adoption as the Son of God*, there is no salvation. In what sense, then, does Jesus become the adopted Son of God?

The Adoption of Christ: The Consummation of Sonship

The Son Made Excellent: Pure Sonship Perfected

All orthodox believers affirm Christ's full humanity, but his humanity often fails to get fully "fleshed" out, and even more particularly its *filial* contours suffer furtive, obfuscating treatment. Too frequently Christ's sonship gets squeezed into a static mold, driving theological reflection in ontological, or sometimes even Docetic, directions rather than redemptive-historical ones. Yet thrusting Christ's filial development into the shadows obscures his humanity, and the resulting ambiguity delivers deleterious soteriological consequences. A failure to understand the Father's adoption of the Redeemer will render misunderstanding of the Father's adoption of the redeemed. Such a consequence is simply unavoidable.

As argued earlier in the chapter, Paul's declaration of Christ's sonship in Romans 1:3–4 is an epochal designation of historically attained sonship rather than an ontological one concerning the hypostatic union. I repeat Gaffin's terse conclusion: "The resurrection is here viewed as a declaration which is constitutive in nature."[62] Affirmed by the Father in heaven, according to the comprehensive analysis of his full righteousness through weakness and temptations, the Son of David *kata sarka* ("according to the flesh") *becomes* the Son of

---

62. Gaffin, *Resurrection and Redemption*, 118. Cf. Geerhardus Vos, *The Pauline Eschatology* (Princeton, NJ: Princeton University Press, 1930), 152–53; Vos, "Eschatological Aspect," 104.

God *kata pneuma* ("according to the Spirit"). The Son of God enters a personally, historically, cosmically, and therefore soteriologically different stage of sonship. In short, Christ's resurrection *is* his adoption[63] as the resurrected Son—or, to put it slightly differently, Christ's resurrection entails adoption. His adoption as Son of God occurs *at* and *because of* his resurrection. Just as in Philippians 2, embedded in this Romans 1:3–4 declaration of adopting sonship is the redemptive-historical progress from humiliation to exaltation that qualified Jesus Christ as messianic Son. His resurrection, which marks his supreme transformation, qualifies him for this unrivaled sonship status and signifies his unprecedented glorified human constitution.[64]

The cosmically decisive moment of Christ's newfound adoption constitutes the eschatological culmination of his redemptive work *as Son of God*. "Verse 4 [of Romans 1] teaches that at the resurrection Christ began a new and unprecedented phase of divine sonship. The eternal Son of God, who was born, lived, and died *katà sárka* ['according to the flesh'], has been raised *katà pneûma* ['according to the Spirit'] and so has become what he was not before: the Son of God in power."[65] At his resurrection, Jesus stands as Son in a cosmically fresh way. The beloved Son is attested, affirmed, and therefore rightfully selected as the effectual redeeming Son. According to the all-wise plan of the Father, this eternal and incarnate Son has become the mature, tested, perfected, glorious Son. He attains fullest maturity and fullest glory. He is raised because he is Son; he becomes the Son in power because he is raised. *The Son of God has become the Son of God in an eschatologically, covenantally, and redemptively requisite way.* He remains forever now the *adopted* Son of God.

Christ's resurrection therefore delivered for him a personal change as the means of securing the cosmic, eschatological, and redemptive-historical changes. In the adoption-conferring resurrection, he *became* the Son of God in power, marking the point in redemptive history when promise gives way to realization. Filial anticipation has given way to

---

63. Gaffin, *Resurrection and Redemption*, 117–19.
64. Cf. Richard B. Gaffin Jr., "'Life-Giving Spirit': Probing the Center of Paul's Pneumatology," *JETS* 41, 4 (1998): 581–82.
65. Gaffin, *Resurrection and Redemption*, 111.

filial fulfillment. Redemption is accomplished, and the power of the Son freely flows to the sons in him (cf. 1 Cor. 2:1–16). Soteric power surges from his *attained* consummate filial excellence. Yet before Jesus was qualified to be the adopted Son, he had to learn, grow, develop in covenant faithfulness. Antecedent work had to be done *in him*[66] for filial grace and redemptive efficacy to flow from him. He had to grow "in wisdom and in stature and in favor with God and man" (Luke 2:52). Scripture profiles the improvement and covenantal attainment in the life experience of the Son of God with striking clarity.

To recapitulate and expand here, eternal sonship, true and necessary, does not in itself possess redemptive characteristics. Redemption required incarnation. Born of woman (Gal. 4:4), Jesus joins human genealogy, in his connection not only to Mary (Matt. 1:16–21) and to David (Rom. 1:3), but also to Adam (Luke 3:38).[67] This genetic solidarity with mankind establishes the historical and ontological grounds for his soteric efficacy. Redemptive efficacy requires this solidarity with the sons of Adam (cf. Rom. 8:3; Phil. 2:5–11; Heb. 2:10–18), but though his incarnation serves redemption, in a static sense it remains insufficient. The hypostatic union, as essential as it is to the gospel, does not save sinners. If it were indeed so, Christ's suffering would be incidental, superfluous, even cruel. It is not enough that the Son of God became man, but work and growth were required: what he *did* and what he *accomplished* as man served the soteriological ends. The inexperienced, immature, and untested Son was not yet ready to provide redemption. Heavenly affirmation of his filial readiness awaited tested, tried, and triumphant Spirit-wrought maturity.

Whether expressly or implicitly, the necessity of practiced obedience (righteousness) by the Son dominates the Pauline and indeed the New Testament's presentations of redeeming grace. Effectual grace and effectual redemption lie exclusively in the success of this particular divinely approved Son, who by his obedience even unto death would save his people from their sins (Matt. 1). In his learning

66. See David B. Garner, "God's Work in Jesus," *Sine Qua Non* (May 1, 2014), http://www.placefortruth.org/placefortruth/column/sine-qua-non/gods-work-in-jesus (accessed February 6, 2016).

67. His physical birth to Mary also ties him to Eve (Gen. 3:15; cf. 4:1; 1 Tim. 2:15).

and maturing, he became the Son par excellence. Each of his filial stages of genuine suffering and learned obedience (Heb. 2:10–18; 5:7–10; cf. Rom. 1:1–7; 8:1–3) was neither perfunctory nor artificial, but served as a measure of his adjudication, and in his fulfillment of the covenant demands made him the Father's exclusively suitable choice for adopted Son. Thus, the eternal Son became the incarnate Son. The incarnate but unqualified (inexperienced) holy Son in time *became* the qualified (mature and vindicated) holy, messianic Son. He grew personally, in his public ministry, and unto filial maturity for his consummate covenantal victory.

In the maturation of Jesus Christ by perfect faithfulness, he qualified himself as the Messiah-Son, as the One to be appointed the Son of God, the just Son who becomes the justifying Son (Rom. 3:21–26). The righteousness of the Son came by the progress of his excellent life, which itself gets summarized by its internal and external consistency as one comprehensive act of righteousness (Rom. 5:19; cf. 2 Cor. 5:21).[68] "The obedience of Christ accomplished more than Abraham's could ever have done; by his passion and triumph he has won the right and power to beat back the hostile cosmic forces—to 'retrieve the cosmic situation', as C. K. Barrett puts it—and ensure for his people participation in his victory."[69]

The Gospels explicitly and implicitly affirm the same progression unto attainment. The young son of Mary and Joseph had to grow "in wisdom and in stature and in favor with God and man" (Luke 2:52); and as Son he had to enter the wilderness to grow in obedience (Matt. 4; Luke 4; cf. Heb. 5:8). His wilderness temptations served not first to model the keys to victory, but more immediately to prepare and qualify him to *become* effective in his public ministry and ultimately the victorious Son. The Spirit's integral role at all points in Christ's human existence should not be passed over: "In his miraculous conception, his human nature was formed by the Holy Spirit, with initial grace in its

---

68. "The term covers His whole life, not just His passion and death." C. E. B. Cranfield, *A Critical and Exegetical Commentary on the Epistle to the Romans*, ICC 1 (London and New York: T&T Clark International, 2004), 291.

69. F. F. Bruce, *The Letter of Paul to the Romans: An Introduction and Commentary*, rev. ed., TNTC (Leicester: Inter-Varsity Press, 1985), 136.

highest degree of perfection; and when about to enter upon his public ministry in our nature, to seal his commission, and to qualify him in that nature of his work, the Spirit descended upon him in a bodily shape (Luke 3:21, 22)."[70] In the power and presence of the Spirit, Jesus Christ underwent growth and attained greater (and ultimately perfect!) favor with God in his covenantal obedience (Luke 2:52; cf. Isa. 61).

In each stage of his development, Jesus remains the Son of God, but at his ministry-inaugurating baptism and redemptive-culminating resurrection, the descent of the Holy Spirit and the approving voice of God concerning his Son affirm more than ontological or filial status quo. The paternal words of declaration entail more than redundant affirmations of Christ's sonship; they serve as markers of his filial and covenantal progress. At his circumcision, he is distinguished as not only a Son of the covenant, but *the* Son of the covenant given the heavenly name that prescribes his soteric function: "And at the end of eight days, when he was circumcised, he was called Jesus, the name given by the angel before he was conceived in the womb" (Luke 2:21). At his baptism, the Spirit descends and the Father speaks of him as the "beloved Son" (Matt. 3:16–17). He enters his public ministry with the presence of the Spirit and, affirmed by his Father, is set apart unto obedience for the sake of redemption.

That this identity as Son occupies prominence in the unfolding plot of redemption is attested not only by the declaration of the Father, but also by the explicit temptation by Satan to doubt his filial calling: "If you are the Son of God," the tempter dares Christ to doubt (Matt. 4:3, 6). Satan threatens Jesus at the very core of his identity, his covenant function for the Father and his elect people, and his filial purpose in the incarnation. To lure Jesus away from his Father's will would have compromised his filio-soteric duty, violated his covenantal obligations as Son, disqualified him from his future adoption, and irretrievably doomed all the sons of Adam to perdition. Essential, then, to Jesus's growth is filial obedience in order to attain his future redemption-securing adoption. Satan sought to inflict doubt

---

70. Robert Shaw, *An Exposition of the Westminster Confession of Faith* (Fearn, Ross-shire, UK: Christian Focus, 2008), 146.

on Jesus's identity, and tempted him to elude the suffering required for his covenantal and filial function. At every stage of his life, obedience remains comprehensively and covenantally tethered to *Christ's* filial fidelity (function), not primarily to the self-consciousness of his eternal sonship or the hypostatic union (ontology), though he assuredly (and mysteriously) possessed such self-consciousness as well.

A dominant motif in Hebrews as well is Jesus's filial advance, whereby his purposeful race through the wilderness and into the heavenly place (6:13–20) secures full and intimate access to God for the sons of God. Jesus Christ, the excellent and incomparable Son (1:1–2:9), is the filial forerunner (*prodromos*, Heb. 6:10). He is the pioneer (*archēgos*) Son who leads many sons to glory (Heb. 2:10) and the faithful filial captain (*archēgos*) on whom the sons are to fix their faith-filled focus (12:1–2). The believers/sons of God continue to race with confidence in victory, because of the Son who has run successfully before them, has "passed through the heavens" (4:14), and has "been made perfect forever" (7:28). Consistent with Paul, the author of Hebrews insists that the redemptively qualifying sonship of Jesus is *made*, not given. He becomes the qualified Son in glory in order to lead the sons to glory.

In Hebrews, Jesus's human identity takes an explicitly redemptive orientation in its connection with Abraham and the Abrahamic covenant, as his matured humanity qualifies him to help the "offspring of Abraham" (*spermatos Abraam*, Heb. 2:16).[71] Such particularized Abrahamic genetic identity (in distinction from the broader Adamic identity) serves the central purpose of exposing his peculiar covenantal solidarity with those he came to save; it is in view of this redemptive specificity that he brings *pollous huious eis doxan* ("many sons to glory," Heb. 2:10).

Similarly in Paul, the Abrahamic filial connection drives the redemptive narrative in an explicitly realized fashion, wherein those justified by faith are Abraham's seed (*ara tou Abraam sperma este*, "then you are Abraham's offspring," Gal. 3:29). The realization of redemptive filial grace depends on the gracious provision of the particular Son

---

71. Hebrews' reference to Christ's helping the "offspring of Abraham" weds genetic solidarity with the particularity of his redemptive purpose: the saving of the elect of God according to his covenant of grace.

genomenon ek gunaikos, genomenon hupo nomon ("born of woman, born under the law," Gal. 4:4). "It is . . . significant that the birth of Jesus (and not just his death and resurrection) has theological importance for Paul,"[72] but the years of subsequent life out of this birth form the stage on which he becomes the qualified Son, who learned obedience through the things he suffered (Heb. 5:7–10). Absolute faithfulness in those years of suffering unto death qualified him to be the chosen, adopted Son of God.

So why did the Son of God partake in the sore and sick realities of the harsh world and its pain? If Jesus was ready to be the Savior at the moment of his birth, why endure thirty-plus years of life and suffering? Why all the bumps, bruises, and batterings? Why all the criticisms, cursings, and cruelties? Why all the trials, testings, and temptations? Why not face a sudden childhood death rather than an excruciating adult one? Precisely because he must; he needed to traverse through these trials and temptations because the salvation of his people necessitated it. His identification with us did not come statically as though biological solidarity in itself rendered soteric efficacy. Yes, the Son of God took on human flesh and blood, but in so doing he took on covenantal life and did so in the sin-cursed world. Full identification with us required a process and came progressively: human birth, human life, human suffering, and human maturity. Saving identity required saving sympathy. Saving sympathy required immersion in and covenantal success in the world of sin and its cruel bondage.

As Hebrews puts it starkly, the Savior's life experiences did not merely function as an inconvenience or a cruel irony; his suffering came as a personal necessity for his redemptive efficacy: "In the days of his flesh, Jesus offered up prayers and supplications, with loud cries and tears, to him who was able to save him from death, and he was heard because of his reverence. Although he was a son, he learned obedience through what he suffered. And being made perfect, he became the source of eternal salvation to all who obey him" (Heb. 5:7–9). In this anguishing work of obedience, he *became* the perfect Friend of

---

72. David Wenham, *Paul: Follower of Jesus or Founder of Christianity?* (Grand Rapids: Eerdmans, 1995), 339.

sinners—the saving, helping, and redeeming Friend. Full qualification as the redeeming Son was attained even by denied prayer request (5:7). His heavenly Father refused his prayer for passing the cup of his death. It was a cup that he had to drink. And herein lies a critical feature of the pure gospel, one that weds the cradle, the crucible of Jesus's life, and the cross. In the constellation of sufferings that engulfed his life, he came to know the sons of Adam. He knows weakness, pain, and suffering. "For we do not have a high priest who is unable to sympathize with our weaknesses, but one who in every respect has been tempted as we are, yet without sin" (4:15). Here in Jesus's life came real temptation, inexplicable suffering, and thereby actual identification with sinners. The argument of Hebrews is striking. Reaching the qualifications to become our Savior required mature sympathy, a charity learned and earned by his filial chastity. He obeyed the Father to the end. His learned obedience, his "being made perfect," is the means by which he became the satisfactory sacrifice, the source of filial sympathy and of adoption/salvation.[73] At the resurrection, he became the qualified Son for adoption. At no point can his *mediatorial* identity be rightly severed from his filial development, purpose, and resurrection-secured attainment (adoption).

Was Christ Really Adopted?

In his treatment of Christ's sonship and the believers' adoption, Trevor Burke denies that Christ was ever adopted: "Jesus is already in possession of a unique status of sonship that cannot be bettered or improved upon."[74] Though the reasons for this conclusion are surely multiple, perhaps Burke most fears losing firm theological grip on the ontological sonship of Christ by insisting on filial change in Jesus Christ. Burke contends that Paul chooses not to use *huiothesia* in Romans 1:3–4 precisely because of Christ's superior sonship, and that *huiothesia* is a soteriological concept rather than a Christological one. Burke here commits a word/concept fallacy, insisting that the

---

73. These prior three paragraphs are a revision of David B. Garner, "Sympathy Made Perfect," *Sine Qua Non* (May 15, 2014), http://www.placefortruth.org/placefortruth/column /sine-qua-non/sympathy-made-perfect (accessed December 23, 2015).

74. Burke, *Adopted into God's Family*, 106.

absence of the term suggests the absence of the concept. He also makes a category error in his theological reflections, in which his admirable commitment to orthodox views of eternal sonship get applied in ways that improperly impinge on Christ's human sonship.

These interpretive decisions are not without severe consequences. Burke's rejection of the filial progress of the Son jeopardizes the very Christological point embedded in New Testament theology: Jesus's newly attained sonship marks the satisfaction of the Father, the securing of the eschatological kingdom, and the securing of the people of God as the sons of God according to divine predestined purpose (Rom. 8; Eph. 1). In Pauline theological construction, the messianic Son became the resurrected/adopted Son, and this culminating filial attainment marks the comprehensive, kingdom-inaugurating success of Jesus—cosmically, redemptively, and eschatologically. Not embracing this necessary filial development in Christ undermines the integrity of this boots-on-the-ground Pauline soteriology. Without the improvement of the Son unto eschatological-adoptive sonship, his life lacks soteric efficacy!

Also problematic is Burke's failure to maintain the dependence of the believers' adoption on Christ's personal life. Such a breach between Christ and those in union with him creates a strained, even artificial doctrine of salvation. To insist that *huiothesia* is soteriological and not Christological predicates that the believer receives a benefit from Christ not attained by him.[75] Yet if the gift in redemption is Christ himself, he cannot give what he does not possess; he does not yield what he does not attain. For redemption—in all its specific features—to be applied, redemption had to be accomplished—in those same specific ways. There is then *no* soteriology apart from Christology; there is no benefit gained than that benefit acquired by the Redeemer. To insist otherwise is to divorce soteriology from Christology.

For Burke, soteriology rides on ontology instead. He abstrusely ties the believers' adoption to Christ's eternal and incarnate sonship:

75. "This separation of the benefits of the gospel from Christ, who is the gospel, is also the mother of the many varieties of 'multiple stage' Christianity in which a person can enjoy some, but not necessarily all, of the discrete blessings." Sinclair B. Ferguson, *The Whole Christ: Legalism, Antinomianism, and Gospel Assurance—Why the Marrow Controversy Still Matters* (Wheaton, IL: Crossway, 2016), 52–53.

"Jesus as the eternal Son of God is uniquely equipped to exercise a salvific role as the only one through whom people can become God's children by adoption (Gal. 4:4–5)."[76] He then adds, "Our *huiothesia* is inextricably linked with and *dependent* upon Jesus' unique relationship to God as Son."[77] But these vague affirmations raise critical questions. How is it that the believers' adoption depends on Christ's divine sonship? What does Christ confer to believers by virtue of this unique relationship? The formulation here infers a participationist theology that inescapably clouds the Creator/creature distinction, and obscures the relationship between the Redeemer and the redeemed, the Son and the sons.

In Burke's direct ontology-to-soteriology formulation, not only is the relationship between Christology and soteriology obfuscated, but also the significance of Christ's transition from humiliation to exaltation gets equally obscured. If the filial status of the Son with the Father is not vitally changed by the resurrection in history, of what real significance is the resurrection for the adoption of the redeemed? Burke effectively constructs filial change for the redeemed sons on an unchanged sonship of Christ Jesus. This artificial conception fails to embrace the rugged human and covenantal contours of Pauline soteriology and the concomitant features of union with this Christ, which will get fuller attention in the final chapters.

Burke counters anticipated critiques with a textual argument: "*sonship* is Pauline-speak to describe Christ; *adoption* is Pauline-speak to describe Christians."[78] Burke draws his conclusion from the explicit usage of *huiothesia* in Paul, and concludes that believers get adopted and Jesus does not. For Burke, *huiothesia* distinguishes the redeemed from the Redeemer. While it is true that Paul explicitly employs *huiothesia* for believers and speaks of Christ as Son (*huios*) of God, he also frequently uses *huios* for believers, a fact that directly counters such categorical distinction. Furthermore, that Paul uses *huios* for Christ and *huios* and *huiothesia* for the redeemed intends to accentuate solidarity and shared filial identity (cf. Rom. 8:15–17) rather than dissimilarity.

---

76. Burke, *Adopted into God's Family*, 106–7.
77. Ibid., 107 (emphasis in original).
78. Ibid.

To be sure, Christ's sonship is unique. Believers do not redeem themselves, and no theology of union should conflate the Redeemer with the redeemed in a fashion that makes the redeemed any way causal of their own salvation or metaphysical participants in the divinity of Christ. But by insisting that believers attain their adoption *in* Christ that is not an adoption attained *by* Christ, Burke clouds union with Christ and creates a soteric filial fiction. Filial identity is for Christ Jesus contingent on filial fidelity; only at the successful end of his tenure is he declared Son of God in power. Adoption for Christ and for those in Christ rides on *his* covenantal obedience, which secures the cosmically, redemptively, and epochally significant change in Christ himself.

The resurrection of Jesus Christ delivers this critical change, a *filial* change; as Dunn puts it, it is *"a sonship which begins from the resurrection."*[79] But by his damaging denials of eternal ontology, Dunn (and other Christology-from-below advocates) distorts the cosmic and mediatorial value of this decisive filial change. By stark contrast, Christology-from-above advocate Robert Letham writes, "When [Christ] arose it was with new power as man, freed from the corruption and weakness that had hitherto attended him. He was 'appointed Son of God with power,' . . . raised in the power of the Spirit, incorruptible, immortal, glorious (1 Cor. 15:35ff.)."[80] Hence, in keeping with the declaration of his sonship prophesied in Psalm 2:7 (cf. Acts 13:33),[81] Jesus attained unprecedented sonship status through his covenantal faithfulness and obedience unto death, so that at his resurrection he overturned the cosmic, divine curse in his new glorified body (Rom. 8:18–21). Having been made excellent, he now attained glory irreversibly for himself and for all united to him by Spirit-wrought faith. His resurrection/adoption secured his glorious filial/redemptive efficacy for those united to him.

After Jesus's baptismal affirmation, the Father's declaration at the Mount of Transfiguration anticipates, even confirms, the forthcoming

---

79. Dunn, *Christology in the Making*, 35 (emphasis in original).

80. Robert Letham, *The Work of Christ*, Contours of Christian Theology (Downers Grove, IL: InterVarsity Press, 1993), 85.

81. Cf. Allen Mawhinney, *"Yiothesia* in the Pauline Epistles: Its Background, Use, and Implications" (Ph.D. diss., Baylor University, Waco, TX, 1982), 70–71, 80–83, 151–53.

resurrection declaration. As Luke offers this account just before the travelogue (Luke 9:51–19:27), during which time Jesus takes his final steps toward Jerusalem to complete his messianic mission, the redemptive, consummative, and cosmic concerns come positively into focus. The Son of God has neared the destiny of his sonly and covenantal responsibilities, and this mountaintop attestation by the Father combined with the display of divine filial glory profiles the eschatological import of his coming death and resurrection. In this Son's imminent death and subsequent resurrection of his "indestructible life" (Heb. 7:16), the heights of heaven will meet the bowels of earth, and the kingdom of the justifying and sanctifying Son will gain its final redemptive footing.

Manifesting the eschatological fruition of the Law and Prophets by the epochally significant presence of great Moses and great Elijah, and with a foretaste of the Son's transforming glory, the Father openly affirmed the Son, calling the hearers to "listen to him!" (Luke 9:35b). What the Father proleptically affirmed on the mountain informs the adoption/resurrection language employed in Romans 1:4. When Paul writes in Romans, this adoption is no longer a matter of anticipation; the Son of God has now died and been raised. At this resurrection, Jesus *became* Son of God in power by the Holy Spirit,[82] he *became* "a life-giving spirit" (1 Cor. 15:45); and in this cosmic and eschatologically consummate fashion, he enters a transformed filial glory for the sake of the redeemed sons (Rom. 8:18–30).[83] As resurrected-adopted Son, he becomes the life-giving Spirit of adoption.

Thus, by virtue of Jesus in the power of the Holy Spirit satisfying the covenantal demands on him, he was openly vindicated and

---

82. The precise language in Romans 1:4 is *pneuma hagiōsunēs* ("Spirit of holiness"), an admittedly unusual expression for the Holy Spirit, but it is likely a Hebraism. The choice of such a Hebraism should not offer a surprise because of Paul's explicit redemptive-historical outlook and, in particular, his immediate focus on the transtestamental character of the gospel (Rom. 1:1–4). See Gaffin, *Resurrection and Redemption*, 103–4.

83. Robert A. Peterson, *Adopted by God: From Wayward Sinners to Cherished Children* (Phillipsburg, NJ: P&R Publishing, 2001), 59–63, distinguishes four historical declarations of Jesus' adoption: (1) his baptism (Matt. 3:17), (2) his transfiguration (Matt. 17:1–13), (3) his resurrection (Acts 13:27–30), and (4) his ascension (Heb. 1:3–5). Cf. Robert A. Peterson, "Toward a Systematic Theology of Adoption," *Presbyterion* 27, 2 (2001): 122.

consecrated as the righteous Son in whom the Father is well pleased. The resurrection declaration in Romans 1:4 occasions no mere paternal restatement any more than Christ's resurrection renders yet just another miracle. The affirmation at the resurrection coincides with and confirms the cosmic significance of the Son's new resurrection-conditioned state. The Father's affirmation sounds the bell of his full pleasure in the Son, affirming the surpassing efficacy of his mediatorial life, death, and new life. Raised from the dead, he becomes King of kings and Lord of lords, the Son of God *in regal and soteric power*. Covenant purposes and kingdom inauguration converge in this Son-King, whose attained excellence elicits the divine acknowledgment. The Father's declaration marks the completion of redemption accomplished, a completion attained by the faithful and rightfully chosen Heir—the transformed, adopted Son.

The Excellence of the Huiothesian Metaphor

At least two forces oppose accepting Christ's resurrection as his own adoption. First, acknowledging filial development in the Son of God seems on the surface to compromise orthodox Christology, especially the sonship of Jesus Christ. That faulty conclusion has been corrected in the preceding argument, as functional filio-Christology has been shown to presuppose and rely on eternal filio-Christology. The second error stems from a distorted understanding of the key points of the first-century imperial practice of adoption, upon which the apostle Paul creates his rich analogies. These points of ancient Roman practice deliver sufficient value to occupy attention here.

Roman Catholic scholar Michael Peppard critiques the anachronistic manner in which biblical scholarship has conceived of Jesus as the Son of God and believers as sons and daughters of God. He faults those who, as he sees it, impose post-Nicene categories on pre-Nicene thinking. Historical concerns drive him, in a fashion not unlike Dunn. More narrowly than Dunn, however, Peppard in his self-described "historical-critical" method focuses on first-century *filial* conceptions, and he approaches the question of biblical sonship out of the pervasive influence of social practices of sonship in ancient Roman culture. He writes, "Concepts, especially metaphors, are almost always rooted in practices. Human beings do not think in isolation from their cultural practices: the metaphor of *divine* father-son relations only *means* in the context of *actual* father-son relations."[84] With this orientation, he challenges the notion that an adoptionist Christology as allegedly presented in the Gospel of Mark involves a *lowering* of Christ's sonship, because the Roman adoption concept involved the highest of privileges and honors. Adopted sons in the Roman context, "far from being second-class family members, . . . were pivotal and often favored."[85]

Presupposing a mutually informing conversation between early Christian theology and Roman culture and seeing the need to correct "old school" analysis of the Roman gods,[86] Peppard affirms inextricable ties of "son of God" and "adoption" ideology with the Roman world, where the emperor was known as son of God. His thesis is that Christian ideas of divine sonship (both of Jesus Christ and of redemptive sonship of believers by grace) truly grew *out* of this first-century context and were largely informed by it. Such theologizing, he contends, is unavoidable because of the milieu in which the Christian gospel came. As he concludes from contemporary literature, because of the allegedly blinding and permeating effects of Nicene Christology, "the aspects of imperial divine sonship that are most provocative for the study of early Christianity have only begun to be addressed—if noticed at all."[87] Calling for a radical revisiting of Roman culture and theology, Peppard seeks a fresh, first-century-informed analysis of the New Testament concept of divine sonship.

Despite numerous epistemological, hermeneutical, and theological problems, including a pervasive bottom-up orientation, Peppard's analysis of Roman imperialist adoption in the first century draws out notable themes, which surely commend Paul's choice of *huiothesia* for believers and the adoptive declaration concerning Jesus at his resurrection. As argued in chapter 3, Pauline sonship and *huiothesia* grow primarily out of the revealed message of the gospel,

84. Peppard, *Son of God*, 3 (emphasis in original). He repeats this sentence on p. 29.
85. Ibid., 4. He repeats this statement on p. 30.
86. Ibid., 31–49.
87. Ibid., 45.

but Paul's *selection* of *huiothesia* and the related filial themes draws on the particular common usage of the term in the first century. The question is not whether Paul chose the term because of its common usage, but rather what points of analogy he employs in order to express the grand filial facts of redemption as revealed from above. As attested by the prior exegetical-theological survey of the Pauline texts, *huiothesia* embraces the comprehensive contours of the gospel. But what does the particular first-century usage of *huiothesia* tell us about the adoptive sonship of Jesus Christ, and therefore what does it tell us about our redeemed sonship in and by him? What does first-century *huiothesia* divulge concerning the rich sons-in-the-Son motif in Pauline thought?

First-century Roman imperial adoption, rather than evidencing action for an orphaned child, offers a far different framework for adoptive practice, an elevated and functional expression of filial identity. Peppard's quote of Hadrian is worth reproducing:

> Now there is a distinction between natural and adopted sons: for a begotten son (*to gennōmenon*) becomes whatever kind of person seems appropriate to the heavenly powers, but a man takes an adopted son (*to poioumenon*, a "made" son) to himself through a deliberate selection. The result is that, through natural process, a man is often given a deformed and incompetent son, but through a process of judgment, one of sound body and mind is certain to be chosen.[88]

Peppard profiles several important features concerning the Roman emperor's adoption of a qualified son, one of "sound body and mind":

1. *The Good of the Father and the Dynasty.* Roman imperial adoption was not intended for the benefit of the one *adopted.* Rather, the adopted son served the good of the father/king and the family. While certain benefits may have accrued to the adopted son, the primary purpose of adoption was not for *him* but for the king and his kingdom.

88. Ibid., 73.

2. *The Preservation of the Family.* The adopted son entered the family as one who would serve the family's interests, ensuring the continuance of the family name and inheritance. He was selected to prevent familial obsolescence, to secure dynastic perpetuity.

3. *A Selection from within the Family.* The adoption generally stayed within the family bloodlines, in order to "keep the power in the same dynasty."[89] Though the emperor could choose anyone, he more commonly chose someone closer to him, particularly one of consanguinity.

4. *The Worthiness of the Adopted Son.* The choice of the adopted son came by virtue of his manifest qualifications. He was not adopted to become excellent; he was adopted because he had already become excellent. Selection of the son depended on his proven track record. Since "biological sons were not necessarily reliable, . . . an emperor might prefer to select his successor based on his proven merits."[90] Accordingly, Seneca quips, "Adoption is the remedy for chance."[91] A prospective son was not adopted unless he had proved himself worthy to carry the adopter's family name, reputation, and inheritance into the future. Such adoption necessarily applies to a mature and tested adult, not an immature, untested child.

5. *A Sovereign and Knowledgeable Selection by the Father.* Selection for adoption occurred by "unhampered judgment" of the emperor.[92] He witnessed excellence and then made his decision about adopting the adult son based on his analysis. The objective observation and informed selection of the adopted

89. Ibid.
90. Ibid. "An ideology of adopting successors did not cleanly supersede the dynastic ideology that pervaded Roman culture. A pure meritocratic system of imperial succession never won the day." Ibid., 74. This qualification, however, does not mitigate the evident motivation and occurrence of such imperial adoption. The son was chosen as successor because of his recognized qualifications.
91. Recorded in ibid., 82.
92. Ibid., 82. Peppard refers here to Tacitus's Galba. Ibid., 80–83.

son intended to counter the limiting factor of family genetics and the underperformance of any biological sons.

6. *The Father's Prominence and Its Correspondence to the Adopted Son.* The importance of adoption was tethered to the power and prominence of the father adopting. "The more powerful a father is—even all-powerful, as a god—the more relevant adoption becomes to understand that father's relationship to his son."[93] The greater the potentate, the more potent the adoption.

With these various first-century features of Roman adoption in view, Paul's selection of *huiothesia* ought to come with little surprise and should produce great profit for understanding this filial grace in Christ. In fact, its analogies beg for recapitulating Pauline adoption with an eye to the redemptive work of the adopted, glorified, and resurrected Son of God. Paul took *huiothesia* in possession (*possessio*),[94] and capitalized on many ripe theological correlations it projects.

The Good of the Father and the Dynasty

At some point, all metaphors deteriorate; they are not intended to deliver principles with airtight precision. Accordingly, that adoption is intended for the "good" of the Father in heaven requires a bit of clarification. God, of course, has need of nothing. Yet the pressing analogy resides in the Father's will to accomplish his good pleasure (Eph. 1:3–14) and to bless his redeemed family (Gen. 12:1–3). In view of the covenant of redemption (*pactum salutis*) that obtains in the adoption of his family through Jesus Christ, and by the unfailing commitment of the last Adam to obey the covenantal demands, to endure the covenantal curse, and to accomplish redemption, the resurrected Son of God secures the Father's good pleasure by establishing his kingdom on earth as it is in heaven (Matt. 6:10). He came to do the Father's will (Heb. 10:7–9; cf. Ps. 40:8), and obeyed even unto death on a cross (Phil. 2:1–11).

---

93. Ibid., 85.
94. See chapter 3.

In contrast to the first Adam/son who disobeyed, the last Adam/
Son obeyed (Rom. 5:12–21), and his obedience secured the kingdom.
He is the one Mediator between God and man (1 Tim. 2:5). He is
the One who took on the sins of his people and bequeathed his own
righteousness and reward (2 Cor. 5:21; Eph. 1:15–23; 2 Tim. 4:1–8).
His selflessness secured the redemption of God's people and the divine
telos (goal) of all history (Eph. 1:3–14).

What, then, does his adoption indicate? The good purpose of the
Father is met; the kingdom is established/preserved; the family of God
receives the full bounty of blessing he has secured. God's kingdom in
Christ endures forever (2 Sam. 7:16; Ps. 89:36; Dan. 2:44). Christ's
adoption secures the blessings of fellowship and perfection, promised in
the covenant that God made with Adam, Abraham, Moses, and King
David. As the excellent Son, the One born in the line of David, Jesus
ushered in the kingdom of God. In this Son, the Father's perpetual
kingdom purposes are met.

The Preservation of the Family

Similarly, in view of the curse on the earth (Rom. 8:19) and on all
mankind (Rom. 5:12), the destruction of the sons of Adam remained
certain. The two-Adam covenantal construction that Paul envisions
(1 Cor. 15; Rom. 5), the condemnation that looms on the horizon for
all who refuse to believe (Rom. 2:12–13; 9:19–22; cf. John 3:18–20),
and the message of grace in the face of wrath (Rom. 1:18; Eph. 2:1–10)
make it abundantly clear that human destiny apart from divine mercy
is destruction. Without an excellent Son, there is no preservation of
the people of God. Without the Son of God, there are no sons of God.

The adopted Son, according to Pauline theology, is the One who
proffers the good news to the remnant (Rom. 11:5) and by his own
attained excellence accomplishes the salvation and preservation of
God's family. Only the resurrected-adopted Son (Rom. 1:4) is capable
to save, and by his faithful life, death, and resurrection, he preserves
the people of God. The family will endure forever (Eph. 2:18–22;
3:14–21). The Father's appointment of Jesus as the adopted Son secured
his redeemed family for eternity, just as he purposed to do from before
the foundation of the world (Eph. 1:3–6).

A Selection from within the Family

Paul makes solidarity of Jesus with the sons of Adam a sine qua non of his redemptive qualifications (Rom. 1:3; 8:3; cf. Heb. 2:10–18). Before we probe this human affinity further, note that the Pauline filial concern for solidarity possesses two equally important strands— the divine and the human. As argued already, the Son of God is the eternal God.[95] He is "God over all, blessed forever" (Rom. 9:5b). The Son of God eternal remains forever God; as the second person of the Trinity, he remains forever a member of the triune "family." This fact is absolutely necessary theologically. His pretemporal sonship not only precedes his mediatorial sonship but actually qualifies him for it. "It must be maintained that Christ's existence as [eternal] Son has significance for His mediatorship. That He was the Son is in part the basis for His appearance as Surety and Mediator of the covenant of grace."[96] The Son, selected as Mediator, is the Son of God; he remains forever the second person of the triune family. But his eternal, static sonship is not in itself sufficient for salvation of fallen men, and the Pauline metaphor draws equally on his affinity with the sons of Adam.

For redemption to take place for those created in God's image (Gen. 1:26–28), Jesus had to become one with humanity. God sent "his own Son in the likeness of sinful flesh and for sin" (Rom. 8:3); he "partook" in "flesh and blood" (Heb. 2:14) so that he and those whom he redeems are in genetic solidarity (cf. Heb. 2:11). Without such solidarity, Jesus could not become the adopted, mediating Son. But in his condescension (Phil. 2:5–11), Jesus assumes creation, and becoming fully human, he is classified as a legitimate prospect for the Father's selection. Though much more is necessary for his selection, the Father's choice of Jesus as his adopted Son (cf. Ps. 2:7; Heb. 1:5–2:4) would not occur apart from solidarity with the human race. Incarnation secured identification; identification enabled redemption; redemption occurred in and through Jesus Christ, the Son of God incarnate. His

95. It is important to note that the Roman concept of adoption does not deny that the adopted son was already a son. Antecedent sonship does not eliminate qualification for adopted sonship. Even at this point, the Roman analogy serves Christ's adoption without compromising in any way his prior sonship status.

96. Vos, *Reformed Dogmatics*, 3:15.

selection as the adopted Son required his full identity with the sons of Adam. Preserving the elect family of God required one like us, Jesus of Nazareth, to become the adopted Son.

The Worthiness of the Adopted Son

Perhaps no other component of the Roman concept of adoption strikes a theological analogy like this one. The entire thrust of biblical revelation concerns a coming Redeemer, One who is excellent in every way—tried, tested, and triumphant (Phil. 2:5–11; cf. Heb. 5:8). From the loins of Eve, One is promised who will "bruise" the head of the serpent (Gen. 3:15). This Son, in contrast to the first Adam and his entire progeny, would obey the word of his Father. He would set his heart humbly on obeying God's will, submitting even to a shameful, hideous death on a cursed tree (Gal. 3:13). This Son would do "all things well" (Mark 7:37); he would become the One in whose personal righteousness we obtain the "righteousness of God . . . manifested apart from the law" (Rom. 3:21).

Divine selection of this Son at his resurrection and according to his resurrected glory marks the full success of this beloved Son, in whom the Father is well pleased (Col. 1:13; Eph. 1:6; cf. Matt. 3:17; 17:5; 2 Peter 1:17). God chose *Jesus* as his adopted Son because he had obeyed exhaustively. The incarnate man Jesus was first the eternally excellent Son of God. But at his resurrection, Jesus enters a new phase and new dynamic of sonship (Rom. 1:3–4) as the covenantally proven and eschatologically excellent Son.

This particular feature of Roman imperial adoption brilliantly illumines the exalted Christ-centeredness of Paul's soteriology, in which Christ served faithfully, and was thereby chosen fittingly as the adopted Son, the glorified Son par excellence. His covenantally conditioned sonship is comprehensively eschatological and salvific. He reigns as the regal Son because he obeyed fully as the humiliated One. Adoption of the sons in Christ (*ordo salutis*) draws on the adoption of the worthy One, the Son par excellence (*historia salutis*).

A Sovereign and Knowledgeable Selection by the Father

The heavenly Father serves as the perfect, objective witness to the deeds of men. As he surveyed the landscape of history and the hearts and habits of men (cf. 2 Chron. 16:9; Prov. 15:3), he concluded, "None is righteous, no, not one; no one understands; no one seeks for God" (Rom. 3:10–11). Almighty God had shown "forbearance" as "he had passed over former sins" (Rom. 3:25), but in Jesus he exercised no forbearance and passed over no sins. He did not have to and, at this climactic point in human history, would not do so. As the eyes of the Father witnessed the life of the Son of Mary (Gal. 4:4), he found him to be righteous (1 John 2:1), a spotless Lamb (1 Peter 1:19), and the perfect, beloved Son in whom he was well pleased (Matt. 17:5; Mark 1:11; 9:7; Luke 3:22; 9:35; 2 Peter 1:17). *Perfectly righteous* was the verdict rendered by the Spirit of God (1 Tim. 3:16).

Why, then, was Jesus the chosen Son to be adopted by the Father? Precisely because, in the comprehensive assessment of the omniscient God, Christ by his covenant obedience had attained the maturity/glory designed for the sons of Adam. The last Adam's covenant fidelity led to the family-securing verdict. Accordingly, he "was declared to be the Son of God in power according to the Spirit of holiness by his resurrection from the dead" (Rom. 1:4). Resurrection marked his vindication, his consummate consecration, and his filial attainment. The Son of God incarnate had become the Son of God adopted, on the basis of his divinely assessed and confirmed righteousness. He rightly and permanently enters this new phase of sonship upon the comprehensive judgment of his Almighty Father. The Father has spoken: Jesus is indeed the perfect Son, the beloved One in whom he is well pleased. On the stage of human history, the final Son has *finally* appeared and fulfilled the covenant demands in full. The Father's pleasure in his adopted Son is uncompromising and uncompromised, as this perfected Son fulfills the family covenant and secures the family of God.

The Father's Prominence and Its Correspondence to the Adopted Son
The value of any assessment depends on the value of the assessor. In Jesus's case, his analysis comes by the almighty God of the universe. Imperial lines have come and gone, but the kingdom of Christ Jesus stands unendingly: "Then the seventh angel blew his trumpet, and there were loud voices in heaven, saying, 'The kingdom of the world has become the kingdom of our Lord and of his Christ, and he shall

reign forever and ever'" (Rev. 11:15; cf. Dan. 2:44; 7:14; Rev. 19:6). The point here concerns the prominence given to Jesus as the chosen royal Son because *almighty God* declares his regal sonship. That the God of heaven adopts Jesus establishes the inestimable value of his sonship—he is a Son like no other, based on his intrinsic worth as measured by the Sovereign Father who has chosen him.

It is no wonder that Pauline theology offers a continual interface of Father and Son, because the value of the Son depends on the supremacy of his Father. The assessment by this heavenly Father illumines the value and validity of the adoption. For this reason, Jesus's adoption as Son draws on the cosmic implications of this eschatological, kingly appointment. Desiring his readers to grasp the cosmic contours of Christ's unprecedented and permanent exaltation, Paul prays that the Ephesian church would perceive, with Spirit-illumined eyes, the Father of glory's final pronouncement concerning this comprehensively qualified Son:

> I do not cease to give thanks for you, remembering you in my prayers, that the God of our Lord Jesus Christ, the Father of glory, may give you a spirit of wisdom and of revelation in the knowledge of him, having the eyes of your hearts enlightened, that you may know what is the hope to which he has called you, what are the riches of his glorious inheritance in the saints, and what is the immeasurable greatness of his power toward us who believe, according to the working of his great might that he worked in Christ when he raised him from the dead and seated him at his right hand in the heavenly places, far above all rule and authority and power and dominion, and above every name that is named, not only in this age but also in the one to come. And he put all things under his feet and gave him as head over all things to the church, which is his body, the fullness of him who fills all in all. (Eph. 1:16–23)

The Adoption of Christ: Summary and Conclusion

Jesus either was the faithful Son in solidarity with the sons of Adam or was not an effectual Redeemer. It is not enough that he joined humanity; he had to grow, learn, and *attain* fullest maturity as the Son of the covenant. Human genetics were essential, but not sufficient. In order to become the *archēgos* ("founder") of salvation, Jesus had to "share in flesh and blood" (Heb. 2:14; cf. Rom. 8:3) and be made "perfect through suffering" (Heb. 2:10b; cf. 5:7–10; Rom. 1:3–4) to be appointed Son (Heb. 7:28b; cf. Rom. 1:4). And so, exclaims Warfield, "we need not fear . . . that we may emphasize too strongly the true, the complete humanity of Christ. It is gain and nothing but gain. . . . All that man as man is, that Christ is to eternity."[97] And all that Christ became, as the adopted Son, applies, by the work of his Spirit, to those adopted in and with him.

The term *huiothesia* offered Paul a nearly perfect analogy. Replete with features, it tied Christ's personal development with his qualification to become Mediator and King, while maintaining the essential filial contours required for faithful Christology and soteriology. Its rich filial and regal contours underscored the necessary progress in Christ's development as Son, his selection as Heir and King of the redeemed family, and his affirmation by the heavenly Father as the Son of choice, the One par excellence. Who Christ is and what occurred in his life, death, and resurrection drove Paul to the term.

As the author of Hebrews sees it (cf. Heb. 2:14–15), Jesus Christ, the Son of God, "shared in our humanity, became a human being like us, in order to defeat the Evil One and redeem us from bondage."[98] Paul correspondingly articulates Jesus's identification with fallen humanity, and the stunning humiliation associated with it (Rom. 8:3; Gal. 4:4; Phil. 2:1–11). In Philippians 2,[99] the process from humiliation to exaltation for the messianic Son protrudes, since he is the One "whose obedience to God and selflessness toward humanity caused God to appoint him the rule before whom every knee would bend, in heaven, on earth, and under the earth."[100] This final appointment by the Father

97. Benjamin B. Warfield, "The Human Development of Jesus," in *Selected Shorter Writings*, ed. John E. Meeter, 2 vols. (Nutley, NJ: Presbyterian and Reformed, 1973), 1:162.

98. Peterson, *Adopted by God*, 57. Cf. Peterson, "Toward a Systematic Theology," 122–23.

99. Like James Dunn, Mawhinney places this passage in the context of the first Adam/last Adam motif. See Mawhinney, "*Yiothesia* in the Pauline Epistles," 129–31. Cf. Dunn, *Christology in the Making*, 114–21. Contra Donald Macleod, *Jesus Is Lord: Christology Yesterday and Today* (Fearn, Ross-shire, UK: Christian Focus, 2000), 30–39.

100. John L. White, *The Apostle of God: Paul and the Promise of Abraham* (Peabody,

occurred at the culmination of Christ's work, when he transitioned from a state of humiliation to a state of exaltation at the resurrection. The soteric, eschatological, and *filial* impact of this transition could scarcely be overstated.

Some might argue that Christ's final vindication as the excellent Son, the adopted One, was a foregone conclusion. He was, after all, the eternal Son. He would not and could not fail in his obedience. But this line of argument misses the point and, like a denial of his filial development, slides dangerously toward a Docetic Christology and therefore a vacuous soteriology. The primary soteriological point is *that* Christ obeyed as the suffering Son, and that by his obedience in life and death, he *became* qualified in his resurrection as the ever-interceding Savior of sinners. The certainty of his success does not invalidate the necessity of it, any more than the certainty of it invalidates the *accomplishment* itself. And at the divinely orchestrated point in history, the affirmation of the Father concerning his Son—"This is my beloved Son, with whom I am well pleased" (Matt. 17:5)—comes by perfect and objective witness to his attained excellence. In like fashion, that he could not fail does not annul the redemptively crucial point *that* his Father noted and declared his success. His process of learning and suffering, culminating in his cosmically and redemptively significant vindication at his resurrection, when he was adopted as "Son of God in power" (Rom. 1:4), secures the pretemporal purpose of God to adopt sons for himself (Eph. 1:3–14) and marks the accomplishment of that filial purpose in redemptive history (Rom. 1:3–4; cf. Heb. 5:10). The perfected Son had become the perfect Son, the fully adequate Savior. The Father placed (appointed, declared) him as Son according to this Son's excellence; by grace, the Father places the redeemed as sons in the Son.

How the Son's excellence is conferred to sinners raises key soteriological questions. *How* do the fallen sons of Adam become redeemed, adopted sons in Christ? How is the accomplished redemption applied? How does the *historia salutis* shape the *ordo salutis*? How does Christ's sonship make us sons? How does *his* adoption become *our* adoption? These and related questions occupy the three remaining chapters.

MA: Hendrickson, 1999), 153.

8

THE ORDO SALUTIS: FACT OR FICTION?

The *Ordo Salutis* Questions

The few Puritans and post-Reformation systematicians who have given adoption serious consideration have found in it both delight and distress. Such writers have conspicuously celebrated in, and even at many points written superbly of, its pastoral implications. Yet as noted already, even among those biblical and theological scholars discerning the riches of *huiothesia*, most have struggled to discern where to place it in relation to the other soteric benefits, such as justification and sanctification. Is adoption forensic? Is it transformative? If adoption is forensic, how does it relate to justification and then, in turn, to sanctification? If it is transformative, how does it relate to sanctification and glorification, as well as to justification? What happens relationally in adoption that does not happen in the other benefits of redemption?

The dramatic growth of insights from biblical theology has refocused these questions, exposing more crisply how Pauline *huiothesia* does not fit into exclusively forensic, transformative, or relational categories. Behind these fresh inquiries are hermeneutical and methodological questions concerning the relationship between biblical and systematic theology,[1] and between the *historia salutis* and the *ordo salutis*. Harking back to chapter 2, where we surveyed the deafening theological silence characterizing *huiothesia* since the WCF, disregard for divine adoption has consisted not only in its relegation to the shadows, but also in its awkward treatment. The problems with

---

1. See, e.g., Richard B. Gaffin Jr., "Biblical Theology and the Westminster Standards," *WTJ* 65, 2 (2003): 165–79.

its handling, however, extend beyond *huiothesia* itself to the way in which the *ordo salutis* relates to the *historia salutis*. How does what God has accomplished in Christ apply to believers in Christ? How, then, in particular does the believer's adoption relate to Jesus's person and redemptive work? Addressing such important questions in the remaining chapters requires first a consideration of critiques about the *ordo salutis*, a brief survey of the inconsistent placement of adoption in the *ordo salutis*, and a further explanation concerning the relationship between the *historia* and the *ordo salutis*.

The *Ordo Salutis*: Chronological or Logical

Numerous writers have critiqued, directly or indirectly, substantial inconsistencies in the *ordo salutis*. Debates have focused on the proper *order* of soteric benefits. In what order should calling, regeneration, faith, justification, and sanctification situate? In some cases, the ordering perceptibly reflects the respective weight given to divine sovereignty and human ability. But the complexity of the debate exceeds a question of monergism versus synergism. Reformed theology renders no silver bullet; within Reformed scholarship itself, the ordering of benefits differs widely. As debates continue both within and without Reformed theological scholarship, and as biblical theology has elevated the prominence of the filial in soteriology, the impetus for a cogent solution has only intensified.

Historically, *ordo salutis* proposals have isolated particular redemptive benefits from one another, not only classifying them conceptually but also dividing their respective application(s) to the redeemed sinner. "Nothing distinguishes the traditional *ordo salutis* more than its insistence that justification, adoption, and sanctification . . . are separate acts."[2] Berkhof contends, "God does not impart the fulness of His salvation to the sinner in a single act."[3] This sort of insistence has elicited less-than-sympathetic responses. The Ritschlian school abandoned the *ordo salutis* model altogether, since Ritschl

---

2. Richard B. Gaffin Jr., *Resurrection and Redemption: A Study in Paul's Soteriology*, 2nd ed. (Phillipsburg, NJ: Presbyterian and Reformed, 1987), 138.

3. Louis Berkhof, *Systematic Theology*, 4th ed. Grand Rapids: Eerdmans, 1949), 416.

considered the very concept a "symptom of decadence."[4] Some have challenged the integrity of Reformed theology as a whole because any postulation of proper ordering (temporal or logical) of benefits creates an inescapable imbroglio.[5] Weber rejects the *ordo salutis* because he assesses inanity in its purported progression: "If we accept this approach, we would have to assume that the person in the phase of 'sanctification' would be beyond that of 'justification,' in terms of his experience. Justification would be a passive fact, already integrated into the totality of the so-called 'order of salvation,' but in the phase of 'sanctification' it would be only indirectly influential."[6]

Before the twentieth century, A. A. Hodge tackled the *ordo salutis* by first posing some of the knotty questions surrounding justification:

> What is the true order of causation? Is the righteousness of Christ imputed to us that we may believe, or is it imputed to us because we believe? Is justification an *analytic* judgment, to the effect that this man, though a sinner, yet being a believer, is justified? Or is it a *synthetic* judgment, to the effect that this sinner is justified for Christ's sake?[7]

Hodge can only conclude that regeneration and justification occur simultaneously, and that any sense of progression in the *ordo salutis* is logical rather than temporal. Moreover, Hodge's proposed solution

---

4. G. C. Berkouwer, *Faith and Justification*, trans. Lewis B. Smedes, vol. 3 of *Studies in Dogmatics* (Grand Rapids: Eerdmans, 1954), 26. Cf. Berkhof, *Systematic Theology*, 416.

5. With varying degrees of sympathy and critique, explicit considerations of the *ordo salutis* include the following works: Karl Barth, *The Doctrine of Reconciliation*, ed. G. W. Bromiley and T. F. Torrance, trans. G. W. Bromiley, vol. 4:2 of *Church Dogmatics* (Edinburgh: T&T Clark, 1958), 502–11; Charles A. Briggs, *Theological Symbolics*, ed. Charles A. Briggs and Stewart D. F. Salmond, International Theological Library (New York: Charles Scribner's Sons, 1914), 366–71; Otto Weber, *Foundations of Dogmatics*, trans. Darrell L. Guder, 2 vols. (Grand Rapids: Eerdmans, 1981–83), 2:336–41; Berkhof, *Systematic Theology*, 415–22; Berkouwer, *Faith and Justification*, 25–36; J. Macleod, *Scottish Theology* (Edinburgh: Banner of Truth, 1974), 124–33; Gaffin, *Resurrection and Redemption*, 136–43; Sinclair B. Ferguson, *The Holy Spirit*, Contours of Christian Theology (Downers Grove, IL: InterVarsity Press, 1996), 94–100.

6. Weber, *Foundations of Dogmatics*, 2:337.

7. Archibald Alexander Hodge, "The *Ordo Salutis*; or Relation in the Order of Nature of Holy Character and Divine Favor," *Princeton Review* 54 (1878): 314 (emphasis in original).

focuses on the particular redemption of Christ, in which by a redemptive-historical union only the elect are justified *in Christ*.[8] Hodge presents justification as the "beginning and fountain of all practical grace,"[9] and by emphasizing the solidarity of the elect in the justifying work of Christ, he seeks to preserve divine monergism *and* a forensic priority.

To effect this construction, however, he deduces that justification actually *precedes* faith, and that in view of the priority of Christ's work, "the satisfaction and merit of Christ are imputed to the elect man from his birth."[10] Essentially, in two stages, the work of Christ is first applied to the elect at his first breath,[11] and then by faith at a later period in his life, he comes to a subjective conscious awareness of what is *already true* by virtue of Christ's substitutionary atonement and divine initiative. Accordingly, Hodge writes, "Christ and his righteousness are not given to the believer because of faith. Faith is the conscious trusting and receiving of that which is already given."[12]

While Hodge's emphasis on particular redemption and the believer's participation by grace in the atoning work of Christ proves helpful in certain ways, his doxastic model obscures the actual transition of the believer from wrath to grace (cf. Eph. 2:1–10) and risks reducing the believer's faith to mere consciousness. To a certain degree, Hodge proposes the doctrine of *faith by justification*, rather than justification by faith.[13] Intended to clarify, such ordering of the *ordo salutis* produces soteric schizophrenia, and not surprisingly has disenfranchised some from the *ordo salutis* altogether.

---

8. Ibid., 316–17.

9. Ibid., 321.

10. Ibid., 317.

11. Ibid., 318.

12. Archibald Alexander Hodge, *Outlines of Theology* (Grand Rapids: Eerdmans, 1949), 518.

13. Other theologians (e.g., Abraham Kuyper and Herman Hoeksema) attempt to preserve God's sovereignty in the *ordo salutis* by postulating eternal justification. See R. E. L. Rodgers, *The Incarnation of the Antithesis: An Introduction to the Educational Thought and Practice of Abraham Kuyper* (Edinburgh: Pentland Ltd., 1992), 18; Herman Hoeksema, *Reformed Dogmatics* (Grand Rapids: Reformed Free Publishing Association, 1966), 499, 502. Cf. William G. T. Shedd, *A Critical and Doctrinal Commentary on the Epistle of St. Paul to the Romans* (repr., Minneapolis: Klock & Klock, 1978), 266. The doctrine of eternal justification weakens the necessity of Christ's *historical* work. If justification occurs eternally, then of what *true* need is Christ's work historically?

Despite the anomaly in this particular formulation, Hodge represents a common approach in historical theology, which insists that the *ordo salutis* entails not temporal but logical progression. As Ferguson puts it, "The motivation in the older classical discussions of the *ordo salutis* was to discover not a chronological arrangement, but a logical one; the order in view was not primarily one of temporal priority, but was focused on logical relationships, on an order of nature."[14] Yet the assumptions concerning the existence of an ordered *ordo salutis* and a "movement"[15] of its benefits to the beneficiary remain intact in most historical considerations. For those still convinced of its propriety, such an approach to the *ordo salutis* has been assumed as biblical, centering discussion of salvation's application on answering the question of the proper *ordo* in an *ordo salutis*.

Contemporary Theology and the *Ordo Salutis*

Heightened contemporary debate concerning the meaning of justification (Greek, *dikaiosunē*) has intensified the *ordo salutis* controversy. In particular focus is New Perspective(s) on Paul (NPP) and Federal Vision (FV) advocacy, along with forensically dominated soteriology. Core questions surface: What is justification by faith? What is the relationship of justification to sanctification? How do justification and sanctification relate to union with Christ? The list of questioners and questions is long and growing.[16] Unraveling the

14. Ferguson, *The Holy Spirit*, 97. Cf. John Murray, *Redemption Accomplished and Applied* (Grand Rapids: Eerdmans, 1955), 79–87. Cf. Heinrich Heppe, *Reformed Dogmatics Set Out and Illustrated from the Sources*, ed. Ernst Bizer, trans. G. T. Thomson, rev. ed. (Grand Rapids: Baker, 1978), 510, 565. Later, in the seventeenth century, a psychologizing of the *ordo salutis* became dominant, leading to great confusion and contradiction. See Barth, *Doctrine of Reconciliation*, 502.

15. Adolf Schlatter, *Romans: The Righteousness of God*, trans. Siegfried S. Schatzmann (Peabody, MA: Hendrickson, 1995), 194.

16. Recent inquiries include Mark A. Seifrid, *Christ, Our Righteousness: Paul's Theology of Justification*, NSBT 9 (Downers Grove, IL: Apollos/InterVarsity, 2000); Mark Husbands and Daniel J. Treier, eds., *Justification: What's at Stake in the Current Debates* (Downers Grove, IL: InterVarsity Press, 2004); Bruce L. McCormack, ed., *Justification in Perspective: Historical Developments and Contemporary Challenges* (Grand Rapids: Baker Academic; Edinburgh: Rutherford House, 2006); James K. Beilby and Paul R. Eddy, eds., *Justification: Five Views*, Spectrum Multiview Books (Downers Grove, IL: IVP Academic, 2011);

complex tapestry of debated issues exceeds the purpose here. Instead, a brief survey of competing views will set the stage for the analysis of adoption in the *ordo salutis*—how adoption relates to justification, sanctification, and union with Christ. Confusion over adoption's relationship to union, justification, and sanctification has laid the conceptual groundwork for a number of soteriological aberrations. To demonstrate these mistakes as well as to heighten the awareness of their consequences, I must survey some common positions on the *ordo salutis* landscape, beginning first with forensically fixated soteriologies.

Forensic Fixation

As reviewed briefly in chapter 2, Martin Luther stood boldly before the religious authorities, where he courageously defended justification as a gift of God *to* sinners instead of something worked *in* sinners. Justifying righteousness is alien or it is not justifying. But there is more to say. The indispensability of the rediscovered doctrine of justification by faith alone took on methodological significance for those following Luther, taking forensic convictions beyond commendable (and orthodox) affirmation of justification. To these Lutherans, justification by faith was not merely a facet of theology, but the essence of it. The forensic served paradigmatically for their interpretive method, and continues to do so today for much Lutheran scholarship. One Lutheran scholar puts it this way: "Not only is it *fide* which is *sola*—the doctrine of justification itself is *sola*."[17] As the supreme gospel benefit, justification serves as the hermeneutical key to soteriology; justification draws God's historic work of redemption and all soteric benefits around its forensic core.[18]

The sheer bulk of Article IV in the *Apology of the Augsburg Confession* lends itself to a nearly exclusively forensic salvation.[19] Eric W. Gritsch and Robert W. Jenson develop their entire understanding of Lutheran

---

R. Michael Allen, *Justification and the Gospel: Understanding the Contexts and Controversies* (Grand Rapids: Baker Academic, 2013).

17. Robin A. Leaver, *Luther on Justification* (St. Louis: Concordia, 1975), 20.

18. See David B. Garner, Review of *The Binding of God: Calvin's Role in the Development of Covenant Theology*, by Peter A. Lillback, *Trinity Journal* 23, 2 (2002): 291–94.

19. See Theodore G. Tappert, ed. and trans., *The Book of Concord: The Confessions of the Evangelical Lutheran Church* (Philadelphia: Fortress, 1959), 107–68.

theology and history around the doctrine of justification.[20] Though commonplace in Lutheran theology, such forensic fixation does not terminate there. Some recent Reformed scholarship has also articulated justification in a way that remains essentially indistinguishable from a Lutheran understanding of justification in the *ordo salutis*:

> I am suggesting that we view all the items in the Pauline *ordo* as constituting one train, running on the same track, with justification as the engine that pulls adoption, new birth, sanctification, and glorification in tow. "Those whom he justified he also glorified" (Ro 8:30). This means that we never leave the forensic domain even when we are discussing other topics in the *ordo* besides justification proper. Although there is more to the new birth, sanctification, and glorification than the forensic, all of it is forensically charged. . . . The New Testament repeatedly returns to the forensic domain even in treating the new birth and sanctification.[21]

The forensic mold has been cast. Justification by faith is thus not only essential, but also king and cause; it is both the substance of the gospel and the effectual *source* of all other redemptive reality.[22]

---

20. Eric W. Gritsch and Robert W. Jenson, *Lutheranism: The Theological Movement and Its Confessional Writings* (Philadelphia: Fortress, 1976): vii, 6. See also ibid., 101–9. "The doctrine of justification by faith in the crucified and risen Christ is the *entire* gospel." Francis Pieper, *Christian Dogmatics*, 4 vols. (St. Louis: Concordia, 1950–57), 2:372 (emphasis in original). Lane Tipton wryly labels this statement "a high point for Lutheran theological hyperbole." Lane G. Tipton, "Union with Christ and Justification," in *Justified in Christ*, ed. K. Scott Oliphint (Fearn, Ross-shire, UK: Christian Focus, 2007), 43–44.

21. Michael S. Horton, *The Christian Faith: A Systematic Theology for Pilgrims* (Grand Rapids: Zondervan, 2011), 708–9. See also ibid., 573, 575, 589, 591, 595, 597, 610, 645. (Thanks to Rob Edwards for culling these sections of Horton's systematic theology to illustrate the prominence of this paradigm.) In Beilby and Eddy, *Justification: Five Views*, noteworthy is the editors' comment in the preface about ostensibly excluding a Lutheran view of justification: "There is . . . an omission that needs some explaining. Readers might be surprised to see the Lutheran view missing from the list. Our response is that Horton's traditional Reformed view is *functionally identical in all the significant theological aspects to the traditional Lutheran view*." Ibid., 10 (emphasis added).

22. John V. Fesko interprets John Owen's conception of redemption in this fashion, and writes of Owen sympathetically, "The legal elements of redemption are ultimately foundational for the transformative." John V. Fesko, "John Owen on Union with Christ and Justification," *Themelios* 37, 1 (2012): 18.

In such a theological construction, then, soteriology essentially *is* justification by faith.

It is probably fair to say that notwithstanding the N. T. Wright revolution concerning Paul and justification, evangelicalism generally perceives the forensic grace of justification *as* the essence of the gospel, with other benefits, such as sanctification, getting secondary notice, and some, such as adoption, warranting little mention at all. Such soteriological disproportion generates numerous negative consequences, some of a very serious nature. Antinomian and legalism abound when the legal features of gospel grace eclipse the transformative and the dynamic,[23] yet the consequences do not end with faulty soteriology, licentiousness, or Pharisaism.

When the engine of justification tows sanctification and glorification, justification becomes both gift *and* giver.[24] Such paradigms suffer soteriological *and* Christological derailment. Turning the benefit of justification into the font of redemption drives the person of Christ from source and center, and ironically pushes the Redeemer away from the redemption he provides. Redemptive benefits derive from other benefits, rather than from the Benefactor, Jesus Christ. To be clear, in such a construction, controlling primacy and causality of justification do not completely deny other features of redemptive grace, but unavoidably (though surely unintentionally) subjugate and/ or mute them; supposedly subordinate features of redemption lose their soteriological clout and clarity.[25] In addition, forcing the forensic into

23. See Mark Jones, *Antinomianism: Reformed Theology's Unwelcome Guest?* (Phillipsburg, NJ: P&R Publishing, 2013).

24. See, e.g., Fesko, "John Owen on Union," 7–19; John V. Fesko, *Beyond Calvin: Union with Christ and Justification in Early Modern Reformed Theology (1517–1700)*, Reformed Historical Theology 20 (Göttingen and Bristol, CT: Vandenhoeck & Ruprecht, 2012); John V. Fesko, "Peter Martyr Vermigli on Union with Christ and Justification," *Reformed Theological Review* 70, 1 (2011): 37–57; John V. Fesko, "William Perkins on Union with Christ and Justification," *Mid-America Journal of Theology* (2010): 21–34; Michael S. Horton, "Which Covenant Theology?," in *Covenant, Justification, and Pastoral Ministry: Essays by the Faculty of Westminster Seminary California*, ed. R. Scott Clark (Phillipsburg, NJ: P&R Publishing, 2007), 197–227.

25. Concerning justification as causal of sanctification, Paul Helm tries to dismiss this intramural debate in Reformed theology. He appeals to the various kinds of causation (vis-à-vis Aristotle) and makes a philosophical claim about the ways in which justification is and is not causative of sanctification. Notwithstanding the truthfulness of varying types

nonforensic categories evacuates forensic integrity. The irony here is patent. Forensically fixated theology weakens the very legal category it seeks to preserve, and moves in a direction that risks unwittingly and ironically conceding turf to NPP/FV formulations, and even to Rome.

Furthermore, and to our immediate concern, to think of justification (or even sanctification) apart from a proper understanding of adoption produces an abstract salvation applied and rips redemptive grace from its filial and Christological fiber. If antinomianism and legalism stem from justification's overdominance, fear, sterility, spiritual impotence, and Christological obscurantism gush from adoption's relegation to the theological sidelines. In all these distortions, the filial Christology of the New Testament gets buried beneath a forensically fixated soteriology. Forensic fixation risks eclipsing even the *Son of God*.

The NPP and FV

The point here is not, of course, to disparage the stunning grace of justification, but rather to situate it appropriately. Rich in biblical content and theological freight, forensic justification and imputation have met historical and contemporary opposition. In addition to the sustained pushback of post-Tridentine (after the Council of Trent) scholarship, which has accused the Reformers of *legal fiction* (declaring those righteous who are really not so[26]), some current scholarship has reworked Pauline theology in ways that flatly deny imputation and a forensic justification. The deconstruction and reconstruction of Pauline soteriology by N. T. Wright, James Dunn, and other Pauline revisionists are stained by this version of theological and methodological innovation.[27] Leaving no post-Reformation tradition untouched, these very innovations have come to roost in self-identifying evangelical and

---

of causation, the disagreement cannot be reduced to theological miscommunication over differing types of causation. Helm fails to persuade. See Paul Helm, "Does Justification Cause Sanctification?," *Helm's Deep* (blog), June 1, 2011, http://paulhelmsdeep.blogspot.com/2011/06/does-justiification-cause.html (accessed February 6, 2016).

26. See, e.g., Allen, *Justification and the Gospel*, 127–28.

27. See, e.g., N. T. Wright, *What Saint Paul Really Said: Was Paul of Tarsus the Real Founder of Christianity?* (Grand Rapids: Eerdmans, 1997). See especially ibid., 151ff.

Reformed scholarship.[28] All such aberration must receive articulate, orthodox, and steadfast rebuttal.

These NPP[29] and FV theologies conflate the legal and the renovative (justification and sanctification) in a manner distinct from, yet discernibly complicit with, Rome. "2 Corinthians 5:14–21 suggests that inherent within the very notion of reconciliation/justification are both participation and transformation,"[30] writes Michael Gorman. As explicitly as Gorman makes justification *transformational*, any paradigm that makes justification entail transformation is closer to Roman Catholic theology than readily admitted. Furthermore, dropping justification from a vertical concern (the relationship of God to man) and turning it into a horizontal one (relationship of believers with one another), "the New Perspective decenters justification in Paul, not by questioning that it has an important place in his teaching, but by denying that it is central in his *soteriology*, especially as the Reformation tradition understands it to be central."[31] In other words, the NPP not only stretches justification to include transformation, but also resituates justification as a subset of ecclesiology.

The interest generated in recent years over NPP and FV theories has generated faithful re-expression of justification by faith in its pure, biblical forensic identity. Thankfully, by highlighting the primacy of union with Christ, certain scholars have effectively confronted paradigms that require justification to tote the weight of nonforensic soteric benefits. These analyses offer helpful corrections

28. See, for example, the essays by Robert Gundry ("The Nonimputation of Christ's Righteousness," 17–45), Robert Kolb ("Contemporary Lutheran Understanding of the Doctrine of Justification: A Selective Glimpse," 153–76), and Paul Molnar ("The Theology of Justification in Dogmatic Context," 225–48) in Husbands and Treier, *Justification*; and the essays by Bruce L. McCormack ("*Justitia aliena*: Karl Barth in Conversation with the Evangelical Doctrine of Imputed Righteousness," 167–96), Simon Gathercole ("The Doctrine of Justification in Paul and Beyond," 219–41), and N. T. Wright ("New Perspectives on Paul," 243–64) in McCormack, *Justification in Perspective*.

29. Though N. T. Wright's influence is profound, his NPP is not the only NPP. The various NPPs advanced, however, share core features of Wright's thesis.

30. Michael J. Gorman, *Inhabiting the Cruciform God: Kenosis, Justification, and Theosis in Paul's Narrative Soteriology* (Grand Rapids: Eerdmans, 2009), 46–47.

31. Richard B. Gaffin Jr., *By Faith, Not by Sight: Paul and the Order of Salvation*, 2nd ed. (Phillipsburg, NJ: P&R Publishing, 2013), 3 (emphasis in original).

to the misalignment and mischaracterization of justification (by both forensic exclusivists and NPP advocates), and have properly argued for a thoroughly Christocentric and Christo-solidaric paradigm for saving grace. The tide of renewed Roman Catholic, NPP, and FV views of justification has been firmly countered, and in some cases with strong exegetical and theological arguments.[32]

Others have countered Rome and NPP/FV advocacy with a forensic-dominant soteriology. They "emphasize the irreducible legal dimension of union with Christ in justification in a way that may (however unintentionally) imply that the analogy of an external legal decree is sufficient in itself."[33] To whatever degree it has succeeded in countering NPP and FV category confusion about justification and sanctification, such forensically fixated soteriology introduces confusion of its own and has failed to reckon adequately with certain NPP and FV concerns. To be sure, defending imputation against the NPP and FV theses is critical to biblical orthodoxy, but if framed according to a forensic hegemony in which the legal causes or produces the transformative, argumentation will fail to persuade because it lacks a remedy to driving soteriological and *ordo salutis* questions. Though coupled to most post-Reformation dogmatic forensic emphases (justification) are transformative components (sanctification, glorification), forensic-heavy paradigms affirm them in ways less cogently and forcibly than they ought. In addition, often

32. See, e.g., Gaffin, *By Faith, Not by Sight*; Guy Prentiss Waters, *Justification and the New Perspectives on Paul: A Review and Response* (Phillipsburg, NJ: P&R Publishing, 2004); Guy Prentiss Waters, *The Federal Vision and Covenant Theology: A Comparative Analysis* (Phillipsburg, NJ: P&R Publishing, 2006); Richard B. Gaffin Jr., "Paul the Theologian," *WTJ* 62, 1 (2000), 121–41; Oliphint, *Justified in Christ*; Mark A. Garcia, *Life in Christ: Union with Christ and Twofold Grace in Calvin's Theology* (Cumbria, UK: Paternoster, 2008); William R. Edwards, "John Flavel on the Priority of Union with Christ: Further Historical Perspective on the Structure of Reformed Soteriology," *WTJ* 74, 1 (2012): 33–58.

33. J. Todd Billings, *Calvin, Participation, and the Gift: The Activity of Believers in Union with Christ* (Oxford: Oxford University Press, 2007), 22–23. Billings surveys (and later critiques) contemporary Calvin scholarship—the "Gift" theologians and the "Radical Orthodox" theologians—summarizing how many impose on Calvin a rigorous forensic logic that "ultimately results in the arbitrary opposition and separation of God and humanity." Ibid., 11. In surveying Calvin's theology of union and participation, Billings returns to his critiques of the "Gift" theologians. See ibid., 31–33, 68–69, 105, 114–16, 137–44, 157, 186–95.

squeezed from prominence in popular expressions of soteriology are the relational and ecclesiological features of the gospel and, indeed, the familial (adoption)—all key concerns for the NPP/FV program.

While FV and the NPP have improperly turned the epiphenomenon of the church into the gospel phenomenon, subjugating the soteriological to the ecclesiological, these movements' concerns for the communal and familial ought not to face outright dismissal.[34] Nor can the concern for the dynamic eschatological/transformational be properly eclipsed. Union with Jesus Christ renders a comprehensive complex of redemptive benefits—legal, moral, somatic (the resurrection of the body), and relational-*filial*. The forensic must be studied, proclaimed, and celebrated, but never in a way that obscures the full bounty of redemptive grace in Christ Jesus—including the dynamic morally and bodily transforming efficacy of Christ's work for the sons of God. Forensic fixation and its "legalized" *ordo salutis* rob the church of a fuller grasp of the comprehensive riches of union with Christ, including the filial, transformative grace proffered by the Son of God and his Spirit. A forensically acclimatized *ordo salutis* thus steers in the wrong direction, reducing key features of gospel grace to secondary or tertiary status. Adoption, too, finds itself cast into the casualty pile; though often even relegated to the sidelines, it has not escaped the *ordo salutis* quagmire.

34. David B. Garner, "A World of Riches," *Reformation 21* (April 2011), http://www.reformation21.org/articles/a-world-of-riches.php (accessed December 24, 2015). Cf. J. Todd Billings, *Union with Christ: Reframing Theology and Ministry for the Church* (Grand Rapids: Baker, 2011), 27n28. Kevin Vanhoozer views adoption as key to bridging the divide between the classic Reformed position on justification and the NPP: "By tying together justification, union with Christ, and adoption, I have tried to bridge the ugly ditch that divides." Kevin J. Vanhoozer, "Wrighting the Wrongs of the Reformation? The State of the Union with Christ in St. Paul and Protestant Soteriology," in *Jesus, Paul, and the People of God: A Theological Dialogue with N. T. Wright*, ed. Nicholas Perrin and Richard B. Hays (Downers Grove, IL: InterVarsity Press, 2011), 257. Vanhoozer rightly affirms the usefulness of adoption for bringing clarity to this controversy, but his framework still mistakenly presupposes the essential propriety of N. T. Wright's proposal *and* limits adoption to a "forensic act." Ibid., 256. In order for adoption to render correctives and bear the ecclesiological fruit that Vanhoozer desires, the historic Reformed (and, I insist, *biblical*) understanding of justification as *imputation* must remain, and grasping adoption in its fuller biblical contours must emerge. Cf. Grant Macaskill, *Union with Christ in the New Testament* (Oxford: Oxford University Press, 2013), 242–43.

Adoption in the *Ordo Salutis*

In some cases, no doubt in part from reading it through human legal practice, adoption's assumed forensic character has gotten it squeezed into justification. In other cases, it has found an odd home in Johannine material, getting awkwardly aligned with John's new-birth model of sonship. Post-Reformation systematics have generated a potpourri of disparate *ordo salutis* proposals—most of them shaped by the subsumption of adoption under justification and the conflation of Johannine and Pauline filial conceptions.

Filial Grace Subsumed: Adoption as the "Other Part of Justification"

One of the most influential Reformed theologies written in the sixteenth and seventeenth centuries was Francis Turretin's (1623–87) four-volume work *Institutio Theologiae Elencticae*.[35] It became the chosen text for Reformed training throughout Europe and in America in the eighteenth and nineteenth centuries, and its important role continues today in the West because of its welcomed English translation.[36] Turretin's work, written just shortly after the completion of the WCF, rather than emphasizing adoption as a distinct doctrine, under his major heading of justification, identifies it as "the other part of justification."[37] Though his work provides some useful though brief analogical insights into the doctrine from the contemporaneous Greco-Roman civil adoption, Turretin's inclusion of adoption under the heading of justification subtly drives away from apposite focus on union with the risen Son of God and simultaneously compromises adoption's own scope.

Though one might argue that Turretin did not intend a full system of theology in his *Institutio Theologiae Elencticae*, defending

---

35. This volume has been translated into English as Francis Turretin, *Institutes of Elenctic Theology*, ed. James T. Dennison Jr., trans. George Musgrave Giger, 3 vols. (Phillipsburg, NJ: P&R Publishing, 1992–94).

36. See Douglas F. Kelly, "Adoption: An Underdeveloped Heritage of the Westminster Standards," *Reformed Theological Review* 52, 3 (1993): 112; Robert Alexander Webb, *Christian Salvation: Its Doctrine and Experience* (Richmond, VA: Presbyterian Committee, 1921), 399.

37. Turretin, *Institutes*, 2:666. Cf. Heppe, *Reformed Dogmatics*, 552.

his treatment of adoption by appealing to apologetic or pedagogical intent is a futile attempt to dodge the problem.[38] It is rather his explicit subsumption of adoption that generates theological confusion by deprecating the doctrine: "Adoption is included in justification itself as a part which, with the remission of sins, constitutes the whole of this benefit."[39] As Turretin has it, justification swallows adoption.

This subsumption regrettably typifies the inattention that adoption has suffered since the Westminster Assembly, and no doubt has fueled the eighteenth- and nineteenth-century tendency to obscure the fatherly dimension of God beneath the prominence of unfiltered sovereign-grace decrees of the Almighty.[40] Following Turretin's lead, R. L. Dabney (1820–98), the Southern Presbyterian theologian from Union Theological Seminary in Virginia and Austin Theological Seminary in Texas, found little room for the discussion of adoption in his systematic theology. In fact, in an abbreviated paragraph,[41] Dabney also unflinchingly concatenates adoption and justification: "Adoption cannot be said to be a different act of grace from justification . . . . [Adoption] performs the same act for us, in Bible representations, which justification does: translates us from under God's curse into fatherly favor."[42] Following in lockstep with his predecessors, Louis Berkhof carried this dismissive propensity into the twentieth century.

38. The title *Institutio Theologiae Elencticae* indicates that Turretin was intending to refute extant false doctrine, not to pen a thorough systematic theology. In fact, he himself introduces this work by stating, "Let no one think that a full and accurate system of theology is delivered here. For this was not indeed the design proposed to me, but only to explain the importance of the principal controversies which lie between us and our adversaries (ancient and modern)." Turretin, *Institutes*, 1:15. Unfortunately, some have neglected this important caveat in Turretin's work, and these volumes have been used as the primary textbook for systematic theology in many theological institutions. That being said, the problems concerning adoption in Turretin cannot be reduced to its apologetic intent.

39. Ibid., 2:668.

40. Kelly, "Adoption," 111.

41. Ferguson notes that he writes only twenty-two lines on the topic. Sinclair B. Ferguson, "The Reformed Doctrine of Sonship," in *Pulpit and People: Essays in Honour of William Still on His 75th Birthday*, ed. Nigel M. de S. Cameron and Sinclair B. Ferguson (Edinburgh: Rutherford House, 1986), 83.

42. R. L. Dabney, *Syllabus and Notes of the Course of Systematic and Polemic Theology*, 2nd ed. (St. Louis: Presbyterian Publishing, 1878; repr., Edinburgh: Banner of Truth, 1996), 627.

He gives only slight mention to adoption in his *ordo salutis*, relegating it to a subset of justification.[43]

Assuming a single forensic theological category, these men fuse justification and adoption, making them little more than two sides of the same *ordo salutis* coin. Merging justification and adoption into one benefit, as Turretin, Dabney, and Berkhof do, surely compromises adoption, but it further obscures the nuances of *both* features of biblical soteriology.[44] If their theological synthesis accurately reflects Scripture, the Westminster divines were sadly mistaken in distinguishing adoption from other soteric benefits, and Calvin's extensive redemptive-historical elucidation of this familial motif appears misguided. On the contrary, "to view adoption merely as the positive side of justification is inadequate"[45]—inadequate for the doctrine of adoption, but also inadequate for an appropriate understanding of the triune God, who has most perspicuously revealed himself as *Father* to those redeemed fallen sons of Adam whom he graciously unites to his own adopted Son.

Beyond the soteriological confusion, the placement of adoption under justification seeks to induce from this latter forensic benefit more than it can deliver. Justification does not house adoption any more than it spawns the renewing grace of sanctification. How possibly could a strictly legal benefit inherently entail a filial blessing? Vindication

43. Berkhof, *Systematic Theology*, 281. Cf. Robert A. Peterson, "Toward a Systematic Theology of Adoption," *Presbyterion* 27, 2 (2001): 120–21; Henry C. Sheldon, *System of Christian Doctrine* (Cincinnati: Jennings and Pye, 1903), 452.

44. Turretin, Dabney, and Berkhof typify Reformed dogmatics in this regard. For example, in his extended treatment of soteriology, Shedd does not even find a place for adoption. William G. T. Shedd, *Dogmatic Theology*, classic repr. ed. (Grand Rapids: Zondervan, 1950), 353–587. Buswell restricts adoption to an entirely future eschatological reality, and thereby dismisses it as a relevant concept in present soteriological reality. James Oliver Buswell, *A Systematic Theology of the Christian Religion*, 2 vols. (Grand Rapids: Zondervan, 1963), 2:212–13. John V. Fesko's recent study of the Westminster Standards offers no chapter on adoption, and gives it only brief historical and theological consideration in relation to justification. Fesko's work is admittedly selective in its detail, but the selectivity in this case simply perpetuates the forensic heaviness of many Reformed soteriologies. John V. Fesko, *The Theology of the Westminster Standards: Historical Context and Theological Insights* (Wheaton, IL: Crossway, 2014), 234–37.

45. Robert Lee Riffe, "A Study of the Figure of Adoption in the Pauline Epistles" (ThM thesis, Dallas Theological Seminary, 1981), 44.

by a sovereign Judge does not render the acquitted a *son*. The state of vindication may evoke gratitude and even motivate love, but vindication alone could never produce the Spirit-wrought love and filial obedience. Mark Jones astutely observes:

> The fact that the [judicial] sentence has been passed provides a great motivation for our sanctification and great assurance of our salvation (Rom. 5:1). The existential experience of the believer does not always match up with the order of salvation. Union with Christ is the ground of both justification and sanctification, so justification does not cause sanctification, and Christ is the meritorious cause of both. . . . Sanctification would be utterly impossible, apart from having been justified. But that does not mean that justification, as an applied benefit, can cause another applied benefit.[46]

Adoption surely shares critical soteric features with justification, but a strained concatenation of these redemptive benefits obfuscates rather than illumines.

Filial Concepts Conflated: Adoption and New Birth

Appreciating the familial milieu of the gospel and attempting to establish systematic theological unity and consistency, many have imagined adoption in the writings of the apostle John. Evidence of this presumption abounds. Though Pauline literature stands alone in its employment of the word *huiothesia*, systematic theologies call upon Johannine material (John 1:12; 1 John 3:1–3) for adoption proof texts. In fact, these passages from John typically receive first mention in systematic theologies, betraying the force of theological inference over textual/exegetical dependence.[47]

---

46. Jones, *Antinomianism*, 101. This quotation requires a bit of clarification. Union with Christ is not truly the "ground" of justification; Christ's righteousness is. But Jones's larger point is the focus: however we might find the forensic motivational, justification in itself does not *cause* sanctification.

47. See, e.g., William Ames, *The Marrow of Theology*, ed. and trans. John D. Eusden, 3rd ed. (Durham, NC: Labyrinth, 1968), 164; John Dick, *Lectures on Theology*, 2 vols. (New York: M. W. Dodd, 1850), 2:227; Dabney, *Syllabus and Notes of . . . Theology*, 623, 627; A. H. Strong, *Systematic Theology: A Compendium* (Valley Forge, PA: Judson Press, 1907), 857.

Martin Luther's translation of *huiothesia* in its five New Testament occurrences fairly represents this propensity to conflate these Johannine and Pauline concepts. Understanding *huiothesia* as sonship rather than adoption, Luther uses *Kindschaft* ("childhood" or "childship") in every *huiothesian* passage except Romans 8:15, which he translates *kindlichen Geist* ("childlike spirit"). The word *kindlichen* shares the same stem with *Kindschaft*.[48] While surely affirming the solidarity of familial themes between Paul and John, such translation conceals Paul's proprietary use of *huiothesia* and his particular intentions for *huios* ("son") and *huioi* ("sons"), and by contrast John's preference for *tekna* ("children") and the safeguarding of *huios* for Jesus.[49]

Tracing Luther's footsteps, most Reformed treatments of adoption, in addition to subsuming adoption under justification, have simultaneously fused the Pauline and Johannine sonship models. Mingling distinct perspectives on familial grace robs Paul and John of their unique representations of soteric privileges. John and Paul operate with unsullied theological compatibility: adoption and new birth share core theological concerns—Christological solidarity, redemption, resurrection, eschatology, and ecclesiology. But the important nuances of the respective authors should not get steamrolled by indiscriminate systemic theological confluence.[50]

The seeming incompatibility of new birth and adoption has rendered more radical conclusions. Finding no place for adoption at all, W. A. Jarrel contended that *huiothesia* became "adoption" by a mistranslation in the Vulgate, which renders *huiothesia* as *adoptio filiorum*.[51] Though he formally critiques an alleged translation error,

---

48. See *Die Bibel, oder die ganze Heilige Schrift des Alten und Neuen Testaments nach der Übersetzung Martin Luthers* (Württembergische: Bibelanstalt Stuttgart, 1967). Cf. Tim J. R. Trumper, "The Metaphorical Import of Adoption: A Plea for Realisation I: The Adoption Metaphor in Biblical Usage," *SBET* 14, 2 (1996): 132–33. Cf. Mark Stibbe, *From Orphans to Heirs: Celebrating Our Spiritual Adoption* (Oxford: Bible Reading Fellowship, 1999), 15–16.

49. See Trumper, "Metaphorical Import I," 129–45; Tim J. R. Trumper, "The Metaphorical Import of Adoption: A Plea for Realisation II: The Adoption Metaphor in Theological Usage," *SBET* 15, 2 (1997): 98–115.

50. Seeking an appreciable degree of biblical care, some speak of "Johannine adoption" in contrast to "Pauline adoption." Sympathetic with this notable improvement, I still find it less than optimal to impose the Pauline term on the Johannine model of sonship.

51. W. A. Jarrel, "Adoption Not in the Bible Salvation," *RExp* 15 (1918): 467.

his argument is more theological than etymological: "By birth, sons, being already introduced into the family as sons with all their rights and privileges, no infinite number of adoptions can render them more so."[52] For Jarrel, adoption does not even exist in Scripture by word or concept. Subsequent etymological research wholly negates Jarrel's conclusions, but Jarrel's decision to eclipse adoption by new birth ignites the questions about the proper way to understand Paul and John. Confusion over the compatibility of Johannine and Pauline models of sonship has led to Jarrel's unfounded conclusion, further exposing the problematic concatenation of new birth (John) and adoption (Paul) in commentaries and systematic theologies. As Jarrel's stark though errant conclusions make bare, discerning the relationship between the two filial models requires great exegetical and theological care, so that the distinctively robust priorities of the respective apostles concerning the familial cast of the gospel gain full traction in soteriological expression.

The instability of historical conflation and subsumption, along with the growing recognition that Paul's use of *huiothesia* pushes back against conventional forensically fixated constructions, has left many unanswered questions, and in fact simply exacerbates the suspicion concerning the viability of common *ordo salutis* models, especially as constructed in post-Reformation dogmatics. When adoption and its familial implications get lost beneath any form of forensic hegemony or the inappropriate conflation of familial conceptions, resulting *ordo salutis* constructions fail to present redemption applied in a theologically faithful manner. The meandering and anemic treatments of adoption in theological history simply intensify the need for a comprehensive reassessment of the *ordo salutis*, including how adoption relates to the other redemptive benefits in union with Jesus Christ, the Son of God. By the cosmic, eschatological, and soteriological significance of Christ's own resurrection/adoption, Paul's theology of adoption actually provides considerable guidance in addressing the interrelationship between Christology and soteriology, how the *historia salutis* and *ordo salutis* mutually inform.

52. Ibid., 461.

A Fresh Look: The *Ordo Salutis,* Pauline Theology, and Filial Fact

In Romans 8:29–30, the apostle Paul writes, "For those whom he foreknew he also predestined to be conformed to the image of his Son, in order that he might be the firstborn among many brothers. And those whom he predestined he also called, and those whom he called he also justified, and those whom he justified he also glorified." If not a logical or chronological ordering, what does Paul intend in this benefit-rich text? As argued in the prior treatment of Romans 8, the apostle understands salvation in cosmic terms, affirming a dynamic creation-to-consummation construct, with the goal of creation realized in the divine work of redemption. The Pauline outlook centers on the accomplishment of redemption in fulfillment of the purposes and promises of God. Arriving at Romans' culminating redemptive-historical argument, he speaks about the completed work of Christ Jesus and the eschatological outpouring of his Holy Spirit (Rom. 8:23, 26, 27). From these events in redemptive history, he moves fluidly to the attendant filial hope for the sons in the Son (vv. 24–25) to the fatherly love of God for his sons (v. 35) and to the Father's sovereign oversight of all things for the good of his sons—those who in the Son par excellence love him (v. 28). What required a process on the stage of human history *and* in the life experience of Christ Jesus comes instantaneously and wholly in the saving life given to the redeemed sons by the Spirit of Christ Jesus.[53] Throughout these expressions in Romans 8, the filial contours—the Son of God and his brothers, the sons of God—saturate and situate the argument.

In addition, the apostle Paul indeed affirms temporal concerns, but the chronology in view is redemptive-historical, not existential. In the Pauline framework, history's chronology culminates in the last Adam, the beloved Son of God, whose death and resurrection mark the full attainment of promised redemptive reality. There is also logic to redemption for the apostle Paul: redemption accomplished *logically* precedes redemption applied.[54] Redemption has culminated in the work

---

53. This point does not negate *progressive* sanctification; rather, it establishes the basis for it. See footnote 56 below.

54. Believers of all ages depend on Christ's person and work—those who lived pre-Christ

of the Son, and his outpoured Spirit unites those of faith to him as the eschatological Son par excellence. Paul envisages the application of redemption as conditioned by its accomplishment (the acts of God in Christ Jesus), but he conceives no temporal or logical precedence among the benefits themselves. Rather, his soteriological argumentation relies on the cosmic and redemptive significance of the resurrection/adoption *event* in the experience of Christ Jesus (Rom. 1:3–4), and the resultant and attendant outpouring of the eschatological Spirit who, in one gracious act, gives the redeemed the whole Christ.

This singular appropriation of the whole Son by the sons gains even clearer traction when looking at another Pauline text concerning the application of redemption. Demands for sequential (temporal or logical) ordering of benefits in Romans 8:29–30 create conflict with 1 Corinthians 6:11, where the apostle Paul lists sanctification *before* justification: "And such were some of you. But you were washed, you were sanctified, you were justified in the name of the Lord Jesus Christ and by the Spirit of our God."[55] His point to the church in Corinth is not that their experience of salvation operates with sanctification before justification, while the Romans' operates in reverse. Rather, in both passages, he expresses the benefits in diverse fashion because he envisions *no* logical or chronological priority. Salvation entails a vital and solidaric union with the resurrected Son of God (1 Cor. 6:12–20), whom every believer receives once for all by faith. Believers do not receive justification *or* sanctification in sequence—logically or chronologically—any more than they receive Jesus himself incrementally; they receive all redemptive graces simultaneously, because at the moment of Spirit-wrought faith union, they receive the Son of God resurrected.[56]

Contrary to Hodge and others who insist on a series of *ordo salutis* acts in the life of a believer, the application of redemption is punctiliar

---

depend proleptically, and those post-Christ depend retrospectively.

55. See Berkouwer, *Faith and Justification*, 31–32. Cf. Weber, *Foundations of Dogmatics*, 2:336.

56. This in no way denies the *progress* of sanctification. In fact, it is due to the punctiliar nature of the gift of definitive sanctification in the risen Christ that the sons of God progress in this transformative grace. The full provision daily for life and godliness (cf. 2 Peter 1:3) draws on the full possession of the Son of God.

with durative force. Union with Christ, the resurrected Son of God, delivers Christ directly to those tethered to him by Spirit-wrought faith. For Paul and the other New Testament writers, the sons of God enjoy union with the Son of God by the Spirit of the Son. Union with Christ is union with the Son of God *as* the resurrected Son of God. *Christology procures soteriology through pneumatology.*

Accordingly, since this "present union with Christ—sharing with him in all he has accomplished and now is, by virtue of his death and resurrection—is . . . at the center of Paul's soteriology,"[57] this factor must govern the expression of the *ordo salutis.* Given the primacy of union with Christ and its biblically given theological associations, Christ-centeredness in the accomplishment of salvation occupies functional primacy in its application. Such nonspeculative theologizing requires upholding the biblical nexus between the work of Christ and the ministry of his Spirit. Discussion of any relationship between the particular benefits of union can, with discernible profit, come *subsequently.* But such benefit connections must yield to the functional preeminence of union with Christ, rather than assuming or imposing paradigms toward interpretation of this union. In other words, to maintain biblical fidelity, discussion of the relationship between faith, justification, sanctification, adoption, and glorification flows properly out of the biblical preeminence of the work of God in Christ and the gift of the Spirit. The beneficiary/Benefactor relationship precedes the beneficiary/benefits consideration. To interpret links in a "golden chain" in passages such as Romans 8:29 apart from the theologically prior conception of vital union with the risen Christ will produce unending speculation.[58] It already has.

The Westminster Standards and the Ordo Salutis

As seen in the prior theological exposition of Romans 8,[59] faithful Christ-centeredness also requires attendant Spirit-centeredness. In short, the *ordo salutis* actualizes in the lives of Christ's church precisely because the Holy Spirit applies his work to his people, the people of God. The

---

57. Gaffin, *By Faith, Not by Sight*, 45.
58. See Ferguson, *The Holy Spirit*, 98–99.
59. See chapter 6.

work of salvation becomes the application of salvation because the One who worked salvation bestows his Spirit on those for whom he worked it. "Union with Christ is not one aspect of the process of salvation but is the overall context in which all aspects are to be seen."[60]

Because of the enduringly pressing errors in the *ordo salutis*, it is "perpetually necessary for the church to reflect on the *ordo salutis*, or, as we think better to say on the *way of salvation*. The purpose of her reflection is not to refine and praise the logical systematization. It is to cut off every way in which Christ is not confessed exclusively as *the Way*."[61] Such urgency is not novel to the contemporary church. In fact, scrupulous Christ-centered expression of soteriology, in the wake of John Calvin, finds abundant expression in the early generations of the Reformation. The Westminster Assembly itself treasured this Christ-centered theological stipulation, and adroitly defined the respective soteriological *benefits* without defusing the functional primacy of union with the Benefactor. In this regard, the Westminster Standards provide striking balance, one worthy of careful attention.

Though they do not answer all the questions, including some vital ones concerning adoption, in many ways the Westminster documents offer a helpful model of addressing union with Christ and the distinctions in the redemptive gifts. With this interface in view, Letham writes:

> The [Larger] Catechism considers the whole of the application of salvation to us by the Holy Spirit—the *ordo salutis*, as it is called—to be an aspect of union with Christ. Whereas in the [Westminster] Confession justification is the first of the blessings of salvation, followed by adoption, sanctification, perseverance, and assurance, the Catechism treats them all as aspects of our union and communion with Christ in grace and glory (65–90). Obviously, the members of the Assembly saw no discrepancy in

---

60. Robert Letham, *Union with Christ in Scripture, History, and Theology* (Phillipsburg, NJ: P&R Publishing, 2011), 89.

61. Berkouwer, *Faith and Justification*, 36 (emphasis in original). For implications at a pastoral level by giving inordinate prominence to *ordo salutis* categorization, see Sinclair B. Ferguson, *Children of the Living God* (Colorado Springs: NavPress, 1987), 19.

these two perspectives. They understood them as complementary, not competitive.[62]

Letham discerningly distinguishes the WLC from the WCF, while affirming their conceptual compatibility. Several important points surface here.

First, special prominence is given to justification in the Westminster Standards.[63] The Roman Catholic theological interlocutor forced special attention on forensic justification, but beyond such apologetic necessity, justification's distinctive character remains a sine qua non of the biblical gospel and thereby mandates unrelenting attention. Second, the divines chose to place justification first each time they delineated redemptive benefits.[64] Though the maintenance of this ordering simply keeps the Westminster documents internally consistent, it also affirms a theological prominence for justification among these seventeenth-century churchmen. Third, the Westminster Standards have no theological latitude for a partial application of redemption: all who are united to Christ receive all of Christ and his benefits.[65] Justification is by faith alone; but union with the justifying Christ never proffers justification in isolation. The vigorous treatment of sanctification, the law, and good works for the believer delivers an elevated emphasis for the divines. Though there is no salvation apart from declared righteousness, there is also no salvation apart from actual righteousness. Both imputation and infusion find a home in the Westminster Standards. Fourth, the Standards directly associate justification with adoption, but only in a fashion that affirms that the recipients of one grace are necessarily the recipients of the other. All who are justified are adopted; none of the adopted are not also justified; and none justified and adopted are not also sanctified.[66] In all their expressions, the Westminster Standards never infer a causal relationship between benefits—temporal, logical, or existential. The constellation

---

62. Letham, *Union with Christ*, 76–77. Cf. ibid., 88–91.
63. See WCF 3.6; 19.5; WSC 32; WLC 52, 69, 74.
64. WCF 3.6; 8.1.
65. WCF 11.2.
66. WCF 12; WLC 74.

of redemptive benefits manifests union, and the soteric engine is Christ from whom all the blessings flow. The benefits of redemption reside in him. Christ is the engine who pulls the redeemed, and the Spirit clasps the redeemed sons to the Redeemer-Son. The sons go wherever the Son of God takes them and nowhere else; they enjoy all he has given, and nothing else. Salvation is truly *in*, *for*, and *through* Jesus Christ.

As in New Testament theology, the application of salvation in the Westminster Standards is wholly Christological and pneumatological. The Spirit ties the redeemed to Christ so that everything he is and has attained as Mediator is given by virtue of union with him. More than this, union with Christ in salvation provides the reason for Christ's incarnate work at all. Salvation's application is not an afterthought or a passive residual effect of Christ's efficacious work. In the application of redemption lies the purpose of its accomplishment, and just as Christ and his Spirit were active in its accomplishment, they never work passively in its application. "In heaven, Christ continues his prophetic, priestly, and royal activity. The application of salvation is *his* work. He is the active agent. By an irresistible and inamissable [incapable of being lost] grace, he imparts himself and his benefits to his own."[67] He does so by the ministry of his Spirit whom he sovereignly, graciously, and efficaciously dispenses. The bond of believers with Christ, the sons-in-the-Son solidarity, is wholly spiritual, purposeful, dynamic, and efficacious.

Unavoidably pressing against NPP, FV, *and* any forensically fixated paradigms, probing adoption through this vital bond of believers with the Son of God in his life, death, and resurrection will surely challenge a variety of soteriological distortions. Because the goal here is primarily positive construction—to show how adoption's meaning derives only from Jesus Christ, the Son of the living God adopted, and to recover the categorical and comprehensive implications of Spirit-wrought union with the adopted Son Jesus Christ—polemics must function only secondarily. Systematic theological expression of the believers' adoption in Christ begs for renewed analysis by attention to Christ's own *developed* and *consummated* filial identity. Since its

---

67. Herman Bavinck, *Reformed Dogmatics*, ed. John Bolt, trans. John Vriend, 4 vols. (Grand Rapids: Baker, 2006), 3:524 (emphasis in original).

meaning for Christ predicates its meaning for those *in* him, how does his own adoption, his final glorified state of sonship (Rom. 1:3–4), define the believers' adoption in him?

This critical question shifts the focus in the *ordo salutis* from benefit-shuffling to rigorous examination of the life, death, and resurrection of the Benefactor. The primary error beneath common approaches to the *ordo salutis* is not soteriological, but in fact is Christological and pneumatological: viewing benefits given the redeemed apart from benefits acquired by the Redeemer and obscuring the work of the Spirit in his exact application of Christ's work. "The benefits of the gospel are *in Christ. They do not exist apart from him.* They are *ours* only *in him.*"[68] Seeking solutions to the *ordo salutis* confusion merely by reorganizing the redemptive benefits perpetuates the problem. Instead, we must consider the implications of the believer's union to the resurrected Son of God, and grapple seriously with the actual accomplishment of redemption. Any other approach will invariably venture into speculation and create fictions of many sorts: legal, filial, or otherwise.

Legal Fiction and Renovative Fiction?

As detailed in historical theology, Roman Catholic theologians repudiated the Protestant doctrine of justification by faith alone, claiming that it fabricated justification by declaring people righteous who are not. To Rome, the Reformers' doctrine of justification advanced a legal fiction. But the justification/vindication of Christ is anything but fictional! In fact, the declaration of righteousness concerning Christ at his resurrection is a divine assessment of fact. Christ obeyed completely, and his obedience, learned through suffering as Son of God, qualified him for the full vindication. The declaration of sonship confirms the divine, comprehensive assessment. The Father looks squarely at the heart and conduct of this particular Son, and assesses his performance as perfect, complete, and unblemished. Christ's justification is a matter of historical performance, rendering his personal verdict a matter of *divine analysis*.

68. Sinclair B. Ferguson, *The Whole Christ: Legalism, Antinomianism, and Gospel Assurance—Why the Marrow Controversy Still Matters* (Wheaton, IL: Crossway, 2016), 44 (emphasis in original).

What proves true for Christ is then counted to those who become the children of God by Spirit-wrought faith. Justification is *analytic* concerning Christ, and *synthetic* concerning the redeemed.[69] Justification concerns Christ's historic faithfulness; the believer's imputed justification comes by the believer's full participation in Christ's performance by the uniting ministry of the Spirit of Christ. Justification is, as a matter of *fact*, truly, demonstrably, and divinely assessed *in Christ*.[70] To be sure, "justification concerns our status, or relative position, before God's tribunal. It refers to God's act of acquittal of those who are worthy of condemnation,"[71] but this acquittal is operative on the basis of the representational function of the Son and the force of his obedience. This divine acquittal is wholly true. Therefore:

> Once union with Christ is brought to bear . . . , it is no longer a case of God's punishing the innocent and letting the guilty off scot-free. Because of the union established between Christ and his elect people, the wrongs done by the guilty parties have become Christ's as well. In turn, the righteousness of the One who bears the punishment actually belongs to the other, since both are regarded as one.[72]

In this biblical perspective, there is neither fictional guilt nor fictional righteousness; there is *no* legal fiction. Instead, the truly righteous Son of God represents the actual people of God with their actual sin, and is *actually* condemned in their place. In turn, the people of God receive the actual verdict of the actual righteousness of the Son of God. By the inviolable solidarity of the people of God with their covenant Representative, their actual sin and their Representative's actual punishment warrant their "not guilty" verdict. J. Todd Billings puts it well: "The first grace of imputation takes place not through the distance of believers from Christ, but through their becoming one with

---

69. Gaffin, *Resurrection and Redemption*, 132.
70. See Oliphint, *Justified in Christ*.
71. Cornelis Venema, *Accepted and Renewed in Christ: The Twofold Grace of God and the Interpretation of Calvin's Theology* (Göttingen: Vandenhoeck & Ruprecht, 2007), 100.
72. Letham, *Union with Christ*, 64.

Christ by faith; imputation takes place together with the engrafting on to the vine of Christ and adoption as children of a gracious Father."[73] Application of vindication comes by union with the vindicated Son. Solidaric union repudiates legal fiction.

One irony of forensically charged confrontations of the NPP/ FV is the introduction of a revived and refaced theological fiction. In asserting the efficacy of justification as a benefit to produce other benefits, scholars introduce a transformative power into this forensic benefit. Speech-act theory[74] has provided a novel tool for turning forensic declaration into the transformative sphere, in which the forensic locution allegedly bears transformative illocutionary force. For example, Bruce McCormack defends the transformative efficacy of justification in this fashion:

> My own answer would be that justification and regeneration are conceptually distinguishable "moments" in a single act of God. The term "justification" has its home in the judicial sphere. In justification, God pronounces a judicial verdict upon the sinner. But God's verdict and the divine word pronounced in it are not at all that of a human judge. The human judge can only *describe* what he hopes to be the real state of affairs. The human judge's judgment is in no sense effective; it does not create the reality it depicts. It seeks only to conform to an already given reality. God's verdict differs in that it creates the reality it declares. God's declaration, in other words, is itself constitutive of that which is declared. God's word is always effective. When it goes forth, it never returns to Him void. So a judicial act for God is never merely judicial; it is itself transformative.[75]

73. Billings, *Calvin, Participation, and the Gift*, 107. Billings continues, "The second part of this double grace also relates to the oneness with Christ that comes with the engrafting and adoption of believers. The second grace is regeneration and sanctification." Ibid.

74. See Michael S. Horton, *Covenant and Eschatology: The Divine Drama* (Louisville, KY: Westminster John Knox, 2002), 126–31, 145–46.

75. Bruce L. McCormack, "What's at Stake in Current Debates over Justification? The Crisis of Protestantism in the West," in *Justification: What's at Stake in the Current Debates*, ed. Mark Husbands and Daniel J. Treier (Downers Grove, IL: InterVarsity Press, 2004), 107 (emphasis in original).

McCormack's functional appropriation of speech-act theory to "justify" the transformative effect of justification fails to persuade. Like others with such forensic fixation, he locates transformation within justification. McCormack asks of justification more than it possesses capacity to deliver, forcing it to issue a fictional outcome. This is not to say that the divine word is impotent: God issues a cosmic judicial pronouncement *in fact* for his people. Justification radically and cosmically changes man's status and his relationships, but it does not renew his heart. To be sure, the "not guilty" verdict in Christ is a most splendid and potent fact. But it is a *legal* fact, not an internally and morally transformative one. Justification attests to Christ's victory over the guilt of sin; in distinction from his justification, sanctification marks his victory over sin's corrupting power. It is only Christ's simultaneous victory over the *power* of sin that produces efficacy in the life of the believer for combatting indwelling sin. Justification justifies; sanctification sanctifies. Jesus supplies both.

How does this grace of sanctification come to us? Again, Christ occupies center stage, securing our purification by giving us his sanctifying Spirit:

> Christ was identified with sin when he died, and for that reason alone did he die upon the accursed tree. But, because it was *he* who died, he died to sin—he destroyed its power, executed judgment upon it, and rose triumphant as the Lord of righteousness and life. He established thus for men the realm of life. And since his people were in him when he wrought victory and executed judgment, they also must be conceived of, in some mysterious manner that betokens the marvel of divine conception, wisdom, reckoning, and grace yet really in terms of a divine constitution, as having died to sin also and as having been raised up to newness of life. It is this fact that is basic and central. The mysteriousness of it must not be allowed to impair or tone down the reality of it in God's reckoning and in the actual constitution established by him in the union of his people with Christ. It is basic and central because only by virtue of what did happen in the past and finished historical[ly] does it come to pass in the sphere of the practical and existential that we

actually come into possession of our identification with Christ when *he* died to sin and lived unto God.[76]

John Murray here underscores how sanctification relies on Christ's work precisely as justification does. Sanctification is no fruit of justification, in the sense of cause and effect; rather, sanctification and its efficacy in the life of the believer stem from the power of Christ's victory over sin and death. No derivative grace or secondary gift, sanctification draws on Christ's resurrection life. The legal vindication associated with his death and resurrection occupies only part of the gospel story. The victory secured in Christ's work overwhelms the guilt of sin for our justification and the power of sin for our consecration/sanctification and glorification. In his resurrection, Christ is himself consecrated/sanctified, and his resurrection power issues consummate victory over the spiritual forces of sin and Satan himself (Eph. 1:15–23; 6:10–20; cf. Heb. 2:10–18). For the redeemed, his life-giving resurrection secures their legal standing before God *and* their holy transformation for dwelling in his presence.

To be clear, no one ought to deny that justification *does* something, nor do we need overworked speech-act theory to demonstrate its unsullied efficacy.[77] The question is not whether justification accomplishes something, but *what* in particular it accomplishes. The heavenly verdict of righteousness is efficacious, but not in the sense of what McCormack and others claim, that it *cleanses* or at least provides the theological capacity for purification.[78] Justification loses its legal integrity here; sanctification forfeits its authentic power. By drawing attention to one benefit and deflecting attention from the one

---

76. John Murray, "Definitive Sanctification," *CTJ* 2, 1 (1967): 20 (emphasis in original).

77. Michael Horton explicitly employs speech-act theory as a key to arguing for the transformative force of justification. Horton, *The Christian Faith*, 117–22, 555, 569–71.

78. Without mentioning speech-act theory, but implementing its tools, Simon Gathercole calls on Romans 4–5 to build a case similar to McCormack's. He does so more cautiously, but more ambiguously. Having stated that "justification is a divine declaration of status, a declaration that does not include any infusion of moral righteousness," he insists that the declaration is also ontological. Gathercole, "The Doctrine of Justification," 226. "God's act of justification is not one of *recognition*, but is, rather closer to *creation*. It is God's *determination* of our new identity rather than a recognition of it." Ibid., 229 (emphasis in original).

Benefactor, one who gives the forensic such efficacy in the soteriological domain effectively fictionalizes the legal and the transformative.

Salvation: Vindication and Transformation of the Sons

By sharp contrast, Reformed soteriology affirms the doctrines of *imputation* and *infusion*. Believers are not merely counted righteous; they are made truly righteous. The former is justification (Rom. 5:1), the latter sanctification—holiness, "without which no one will see the Lord" (Heb. 12:14). "Through the first grace of imputation the demands of the law are fulfilled ('ought'), and the second grace gradually enables the believer to obey the law ('can'). What holds these two graces together—in both the old and the new dispensations of the covenant—is participation in Christ."[79] These dual and parallel manifestations of union with Jesus come distinctly, inseparably, and simultaneously.[80] Not only does Spirit-wrought faith apply justification, but "the Spirit infuses grace within us, whereby he motivates and empowers the believer unto Christ-like faith and obedience. . . . Grace is astounding not just because God forgives our sin, but because he enables us to do good works which he ordained (Eph 2:10)."[81] Efficacy for both justification and sanctification reside in the Spirit of the risen Christ poured out on the people of God.

The Westminster Standards helpfully distinguish justification as an "act" of God on the believer's behalf (WSC 33) and sanctification as a "work" of God in the believer (WSC 35). Both accomplish the purposes for which they are sovereignly dispensed—nothing more, nothing less. Justification accomplishes a radical judicial *change*; it produces a change of state and relations. Once condemned and guilty, the believer stands before the Judge vindicated. His once-guilty status reverses, and by

---

79. Billings, *Calvin, Participation, and the Gift*, 150.

80. Tipton, "Union with Christ," 39–42. Concerning Christ Jesus himself, Tipton writes, "Jesus Christ, as crucified and resurrected, contains within Himself—distinctly, inseparably, simultaneously and eschatologically—every soteriological benefit given to the church." Ibid., 32.

81. David B. Garner, "You Just Might Be an Antinomian," review of *Antinomianism: Reformed Theology's Unwelcome Guest?*, by Mark Jones, *Reformation 21* (February 2014), http://www.reformation21.org/shelf-life/antinomianism-reformed-theologys-unwelcome -guest.php (accessed February 6, 2016).

the forgiveness granted, he lives at peace with God, fully reconciled. Justification inverts his guilty verdict and changes his relationship with the Creator/Judge. To be sure, such cancellation of debt and release of guilt provide extraordinary motivation for grateful obedience.[82] But apart from heart change by the Spirit of God, motivation lacks any genuine traction. Forgiveness may change a relationship and a perspective, but in itself it does not produce a new heart.

Sanctification, a necessary component of the gospel delivered by the resurrected Son of God, changes the believer's nature and character. The sinner not only is forgiven, but also receives a new, changed heart. The power of the Spirit indwelling him overwhelms indwelling affections for rebellion and breaks the bondage of sin's power. Sanctification brings heart and life change, having freed the sinner from the mastery of sin and released him to the freedom of obedience to his heavenly Father (Rom. 6:1–14). The power of Christ's resurrection life ensures the moral transformation of the redeemed. Renovation is no more fictional than is corruption, and Christ's redeeming work efficaciously attacks indwelling sin. Solidaric union repudiates renovative fiction.

More specifically, the imputation of righteousness and the infusion of grace for empowered obedience come exclusively in the *Son of God*. Redemptive grace—in all its contours, forensic and transformative—is thoroughly *filio-Christological*: it comes to us only in Jesus, the resurrected Son of God. According to the Father's good purpose and by means of the work of his Son par excellence, the redeemed are actually sons of the living God! Justification and sanctification of the sons of God come *in* and *by* the Son of God. When the justification engine drives the soteriological train, the adoption and sanctification cars inevitably derail. So, too, does the justification engine itself. With risks such as these, situating these redemptive benefits properly is a serious matter. For justification and sanctification to maintain integrity and to benefit believers in their biblical and theological force, adoption, too, must reside in its apposite, *factual* place.

---

82. See John Calvin, *Institutes of the Christian Religion*, ed. John T. McNeill, trans. Ford Lewis Battles, 2 vols. (Philadelphia: Westminster, 1960), 3.16.4.

In Christ Filial Fact

Adoption, properly understood, is not a gift of Christ to believers yet unattained by him. Just as it proffers no legal or renovative fiction, the gospel proffers no *filial fiction*. To avoid the accusation, adoption must not lie buried obscurely and artificially beneath some other saving benefit or conflated with another expression of gospel grace. Exegetical and biblico-theological scrupulousness, with an eye to the biblical prominence of union with Christ, will advance the veracity of adoption: the redeemed are sons and daughters of God precisely because Jesus Christ the Son incarnate became the resurrected-*adopted* Son. A properly retooled systematic articulation of adoption will understand redemptive adoption as historically and explicitly secured in Christ's own experience.

John Murray proclaims that "nothing is more central or basic than union and communion with Christ."[83] To Murray, because union involves mystery and in relation to its archetypes functions analogously rather than identically, union along with its concomitant communion seemed best described apophatically:

> [It] is not the kind of union that we have in the Godhead—three persons in one God. It is not the kind of union we have in the person of Christ—two natures in one person. It is not the kind of union we have in man—body and soul constituting a human being. It is not simply the union of feeling, affection, understanding, mind, heart, will, and purpose. Here we have a union which we are unable to define specifically. But it is union of an intensely spiritual character consonant with the nature and work of the Holy Spirit so that in a real way surpassing our power of analysis Christ dwells in his people and his people dwell in him.[84]

83. Murray, *Redemption Accomplished and Applied*, 161. Union is also described analogously with other metaphors: union within the Godhead (John 14:23; 17:21–23), stones and the Chief Cornerstone (Eph. 2:19–22; 1 Peter 2:4–5), the Head and the body (Eph. 4:15–16), and the Vine and the branches (John 15). See Murray, *Redemption Accomplished and Applied*, 167–68. The scope of these metaphors reveals that the full nature of this union is beyond the capacity of our finite minds.

84. Murray, *Redemption Accomplished and Applied*, 166. Murray does give union positive articulation, but sees here "mysticism on the highest plane. It is not mysticism of vague

Richard Gaffin helpfully frames union with Christ according to three distinct, yet inseparable biblical features: predestinarian, redemptive-historical, and present/existential. Distancing himself from an *ordo salutis* progression and from any disparity in the accomplishment and application of redemption, Gaffin affirms that "these distinctions . . . point not to different unions, but to different aspects or dimensions of a single union."[85] He positively draws several verdant features of union: representative and legal (Rom. 5:12–19; 1 Cor. 15:21–22, 45, 47), mystical (Rom. 8:34; Eph. 5:32), spiritual (1 Cor. 15:45; 2 Cor. 3:17), reciprocal (Col. 1:27), and indissoluble (Rom. 8:17; 1 Cor. 15:20, 23; Eph. 1:14).[86] He then concludes, "No matter how close justification is to the heart of Paul's gospel, in our salvation there is an antecedent consideration, a reality that is deeper, more fundamental, more decisive, more crucial: Christ and our union with him, the crucified and resurrected, the exalted."[87] In addition to Gaffin's apt and biblical descriptions of union, one underlying principle needs to become more explicit. Union with Christ comprehensively draws on the *filial*. Redemptive union is irreducibly a filially qualified union, in which believers are spiritually and vitally tethered to the Son of God raised in glory.

As a comprehensive qualifier, adoption helps us grasp the meaning of this personal, Holy Spirit-ual union more concretely. The union of the sons in the Son grants believers full personal appropriation of the person and work of Christ, their Elder Brother. This exhaustively filial union takes on the deepest implications of solidarity and gracious brotherhood. No greater cohesion exists than the bond created by the Spirit of the Son with the sons. The filial solidarity (sons in the Son) by the Spirit makes Christ's journey of faith and faithfulness personally and efficaciously instrumental in the lives of believers, who along their own pathway through suffering unto final adoptive glory

---

unintelligible feeling or rapture. It is mysticism of communion with the one true and living God." Ibid., 172.

85. Gaffin, *By Faith, Not by Sight*, 42. Gaffin eloquently illustrates their inseparability and distinctions. Ibid., 42–43. Cf. Robert A. Peterson, *Salvation Applied by the Spirit: Union with Christ* (Wheaton, IL: Crossway, 2015), 275–94.

86. Gaffin, *By Faith, Not by Sight*, 40–45.

87. Ibid., 49.

(Rom. 8:15–17) await the firstborn's return, when full conformity into his image comes to glorious fruition (Rom. 8:18–30; Col. 1:1–4; cf. 1 John 3:1–3).

To be clear, union with Christ creates no absorption into or ontological participation in the hypostatic union; union involves no appropriation of divine attributes by the redeemed. "We deny that Christ's essence is mixed with our own."[88] The Son of God remains distinct from us; the church does not somehow meld into Jesus Christ, making each indistinguishable from the other. Union is, rather, the full, personal participation in the Son and his well-lived life, efficacious death, and filially determinative resurrection. Adopted as Son, he proffers adoption to those in union with him. The redeemed sons are really in and with the Son, intimately and permanently. As Calvin has put it, "the promise, by which God adopts us to himself as his sons, holds the first place among . . . [all the promises]. Now the cause and root of adoption is Christ."[89] Biblical union is union with the adopted Son: the sons in the Son, as a matter of fact, not fiction. The sons of Adam become the adopted sons of God, and do so by a Spirit-wrought, faith-enabled solidarity with the resurrected Son. Tethered by the Spirit to the Son par excellence, adopted sons in the Son enjoy by grace the full filial glory attained by the perfected and perfect Son. The redeemed are *in fact* adopted sons of God. Their sonship is as real as is that of their Elder Brother, because their sonship is shared with and in his adopted sonship. Solidaric union repudiates filial fiction.

Though many have properly and helpfully recalibrated the *ordo salutis* according to the *historia salutis*, preserving the force of union with Christ and unpacking the implications of that vital union for understanding the forensic and renovative benefits, adoption has

---

88. Calvin, *Institutes*, 3.11.5. This union "does not involve Christ 'transfusing his substance into us' (*non quia suam in nos substantiam trasnfundat*), but involves rather a 'spiritual' communication to us." Venema, *Twofold Grace*, 88–89.

89. John Calvin, *Commentaries on the First Book of Moses Called Genesis*, trans. John King, vol. 1 of *Calvin's Commentaries* (Edinburgh: Calvin Translation Society, n.d.; repr., Grand Rapids: Baker, 1989), 138. Cf. John Owen, *The Works of John Owen*, ed. William H. Goold, 16 vols. (n.p.: Johnstone & Hunter, 1850–53; repr., Edinburgh: Banner of Truth, 1988), 2:207; Tim J. R. Trumper, "An Historical Study of Adoption in the Calvinistic Tradition" (Ph.D. diss., University of Edinburgh, 2001), 18.

continued to struggle for a clear place in the explication of redemption. Indeed, the filial cast of the gospel has enjoyed implicit affirmation in many ways, but the explicit function of adoption in redemption has not yet found its proper and stable place in soteriology.

Maintaining the functional priority of union with this "cause and root" Son in the application of redemption preserves the filio-Christological character of redemption and prevents the speculation associated with chronological or logical ordering of redemptive benefits. With such Christological focus, adoption understood as *filial* fact ensures the biblical integrity and mutually informing character of Christology, soteriology, and pneumatology. Understanding the permeating function of adoption in the accomplishment and application of redemption properly also situates justification and sanctification properly. In short, with adoption gaining rightful theological traction and position in systematic theology, the *ordo salutis* imbroglio can be put to rest. Before settling on its placement in the *ordo salutis*, how more specifically Christ's adoption and the believers' adoption by Christ's Spirit interface beckons fuller deliberation. To that topic we turn in chapter 9.

9

The Sons in the Son:
Adoption and Union with Christ

Having surveyed the *huiothesian* texts, charted the filial progress and mature attainment in the life of Christ, and expressed the punctiliar and durative qualities of the *ordo salutis* in its full dependence on Christ Jesus's own experience (*historia salutis*), we move now to explore how Paul's theology capitalizes on the vigorous sons-in-the-Son motif that *huiothesia* carries and affirms. The realities entailed by *huiothesia* tie many features of Pauline theology together, facilitating a filial framework for his Christology, pneumatology, and soteriology.

As the preceding chapters indicate, adoption possesses a vast biblico-theological scope, one that originates in pretemporal intra-Trinitarian decree (Eph. 1) and consummates in the eschatological realization of glorified sonship at the resurrection (Rom. 8). Expressed by the heavenly Father's unrelenting determination to create a family for himself, this filial motif qualifies the redemptive acts of God and makes adoption a defining feature of God's grace from creation to consummation. Before moving to an explicit argument for how to place adoption in the *ordo salutis*, fuller attention is due concerning the depth, breadth, and scope of adoption in Paul's thought. It is vital to grasp how his rigorous covenantal theology, two-Adam paradigm, and overarching Christ-centeredness with its concomitant eschatological and pneumatological emphases rely on this filial framework for his conception of history and union with Christ. If Calvin's soteriology is rightly called "the gospel of adoption,"[1] it is only so because he follows Pauline thought with exegetical care and theological discernment.

Adoption: The First Adam, Israel, and the Last Adam

The unfolding covenants telescopically unify Paul's concept of preredemptive and redemptive history.[2] In addition to the covenantal argumentation in places such as Romans 1:1–4, Romans 9:1–5, 2 Corinthians 3, and Galatians 3–4, the paradigmatic function of covenant becomes virtually unquestionable in his development of the parallelism between first Adam and last Adam (Rom. 5:12–21; 1 Cor. 15:20–49). As sons of God themselves, these respective Adams bear covenantal roles (representation, federal headship) for those made in God's image, the created sons of God (Rom. 5:12–21; 1 Cor. 15:20–49).[3]

The first Adam was created within an eschatological environment, whereby through his obedience to the covenant of works he would attain the divine *goal* of creation for himself and for those whom he represented. The very nature of the covenantal obligations bestowed on him conveys a probationary period for obedience, at the end of which he would attain his intended glorification, moving him and his progeny into the fullness of covenant blessing. At the heart of Adamic probation, then, was its eschatological and covenantal anticipation, whereby in Adam's obedience to the covenant of works he would achieve "a higher or different kind of body,"[4] a glorified body that "is

---

1. Brian A. Gerrish, *Grace and Gratitude: The Eucharistic Theology of John Calvin* (Edinburgh: T&T Clark, 1993), 89.

2. See Steven L. McKenzie, *Covenant* (St. Louis: Chalice, 2000), 97–109; O. Palmer Robertson, *The Christ of the Covenants* (Phillipsburg, NJ: Presbyterian and Reformed, 1980), 17–199. While Paul selects the word *diathēkē* ("covenant") only eight times (Rom. 9:4; 11:27; 2 Cor. 3:6, 14; Gal. 3:15, 17; 4:24; Eph. 2:12), the infrequency of the term, much like *huiothesia*, does not diminish its architectonic function. For example, Paul's entire argument in Romans 4 appropriates the continuity of the covenant promise with Abraham in the new covenant in Christ, and yet without mention of the word *covenant* (*diathēkē*).

3. "Just as Adam, in his sin and death, represents old mankind, Christ likewise represents, in His death and resurrection, new mankind." Herman N. Ridderbos, *When the Time Had Fully Come: Studies in New Testament Theology* (Grand Rapids: Eerdmans, 1957), 55.

4. Richard B. Gaffin Jr., *Resurrection and Redemption: A Study in Paul's Soteriology*, 2nd ed. (Phillipsburg, NJ: Presbyterian and Reformed, 1987), 82. Cf. Geerhardus Vos, "The Eschatological Aspect of the Pauline Conception of the Spirit," in *Redemptive History*

distinguished even from the body . . . possessed before the fall; it is immortal, imperishable, spiritualized, and glorified (1 Cor. 15:42f.; Phil. 3:21)."[5] Adam enters the world in immaturity, with a view to a permanent state of glorified existence yet to be attained.

Therefore, for Paul, the longing of creation (Rom. 8:19, 22) exists not first because of the effects of sin, which derailed eschatological consummation through the first Adam, but because of the divinely instilled eschatological thrust of creation itself, in the constitution of man and in the covenant of works. Before the fall, "blessing sanction promising a consummation of man's original glory as image of God was . . . built into man's very nature as image [son] of God. This eschatological prospect was in-created. It was an aspiration implanted in man's heart with his existence as image of God."[6] Therefore, the eschatological anticipation of the sons' revelation and glorification (Rom. 8:19, 23) is not initiated by redemption; rather, the suffering, anguish, and futility introduced in postlapsarian creation serve to intensify this divinely appointed covenantal longing for eschatological consummation. Because of sin, eschatological anticipation turns into eschatological angst, but the goal of final glory precedes sin and persists in spite of it.

For Paul, this eschatological and covenantal anticipation occurs in a thoroughly filial framework. As created son, the first Adam actually anticipated the mature and confirmed state of sonship to come through his obedience. A son of God created, he is not yet a son of God glorified; a son of God in covenant conditionality, he does not yet enjoy final covenant inheritance. His future inheritance depends on his filial obedience, so that for him to enter the state of eschatological sonship required his fulfillment of the demands of the covenant. In this covenantal structure, as attested by the first Adam/last Adam parallel drawn by the apostle Paul (Rom. 5:12–21), the declaration of the last Adam's consummate sonship in Romans 1:3–4 would have

---

and Biblical Interpretation: The Shorter Writings of Geerhardus Vos, ed. Richard B. Gaffin Jr. (Phillipsburg, NJ: Presbyterian and Reformed, 1980), 105–6; M. M. B. Turner, "The Significance of Spirit Endowment for Paul," VE 9 (1975): 57.

5. Herman Bavinck, The Last Things: Hope for This World and the Next, ed. John Bolt, trans. John Vriend (Grand Rapids: Baker, 1996), 137.

6. Meredith G. Kline, Kingdom Prologue: Genesis Foundations for a Covenantal Worldview (Overland Park, KS: Two Age, 2000), 92.

been received by the first Adam if he had remained sinless. In other words, the covenant of works for the first Adam was actually the means toward his consummative sonship—a sonship commensurate and coterminous with the historic, eschatological translation into the glorified state of full blessing and inheritance.

What Paul means by *adoption* in redemptive history, then, Adam anticipated in the promises associated with the first covenant made with him. In other words, *huiothesia* delivers the eschatological reward and transformation promised to the first Adam, but attained by the last. In the covenant of works, mature and confirmed sonship—adoption—lay in Adam's sights. Because of his failure as covenant representative, that glorious inheritance, confirmed righteousness, and perfect fellowship with the Creator/Father were lost to him and his progeny. *But* in the grace of the gospel, the adoption of Christ delivers the filial life that Adam anticipated. In the postfall age, adoptive glory comes by Christ's securing covenantal obedience *and* enduring covenantal curse.

Notably, the callings of the first and last Adams were covenantally parallel (Rom. 5:12–21), but their demands were wholly unequal. Adam was called to trust and obey in a context of a "very good" world (Gen. 1:31). The pathway to confirmed righteousness and filial glory was smooth. By contrast, as last Adam, Christ Jesus had to trust and obey in the context of a corrupt and perverse world (see Rom. 8:18–23), under the curse of the law (Gal. 4:1–4), and in human weakness (Rom. 8:3). Christ had to overcome temptation, curse, sin, and death (vv. 18–23) to secure the filial destiny. The continuity from Adam to Adam lies, however, in the securing of the originally anticipated eschatological glory. Rather than by the first son (Adam), this filial glory has come by the last Son (Christ).[7] The attained and attested sonship of the last Adam triumphs in two ways: it conquers the first Adamic curse and corruption while it successfully delivers the first Adamic filial purpose. Adoption in Christ *delivers* the adoption

---

7. David B. Garner, "The First and Last Son: Christology and Sonship in Pauline Soteriology," in *Resurrection and Eschatology: Theology in Service of the Church: Essays in Honor of Richard B. Gaffin, Jr.*, ed. Lane G. Tipton and Jeffrey C. Waddington (Phillipsburg, NJ: P&R Publishing, 2008), 276–79.

anticipated by Adam. The adoption secured by Christ Jesus obtains creation's goal.[8]

After the covenant failure of Adam, the covenant God still pursued a holy son. Among other ways on the stage of redemptive history, with reference to the call of Abram (Gen. 12) and the covenant of grace made with him (Gen. 15, 17), God demonstrated his gracious commitment to a redemptive realization of blessed filial destiny. This goal attains a new level of clarity when God delivered on his promises to Abraham by sovereignly adopting Israel as his own son, an act that "is from the nature of the case unmeritorious."[9] As surveyed earlier, Romans 9:4 expresses this corporate and typological sonship of Israel. Israel's sonship emerges explicitly in the national deliverance from Egypt (Ex. 4:22–23),[10] and cohering with creation's embedded and anticipated eschatological glory, this corporate adoption typified eschatologically realized adoptive sonship through the messianic (antitypical) Son.

Israel's adoption further draws out epochal distinctions. As rich as they were, old covenant provisions were impotent for securing final filial obedience: "The commandments could teach a person how to live, but they could not impart life to a sinner dead in his trespasses and sins."[11] Typological sonship served its historical-redemptive function but was not itself eschatological sonship; so while the corporate filial obligations prevailed and were clarified under Mosaic law, this greater

8. Cf. Oscar Cullmann, *Salvation in History*, trans. Sidney G. Sowers (London: SCM, 1967), 146.

9. Geerhardus Vos, *Biblical Theology: Old and New Testaments* (Grand Rapids: Eerdmans, 1948; repr., Edinburgh: Banner of Truth, 1996), 114. He continues, "The source of Israel's privilege lies exclusively in free divine grace, not in any good qualities possessed by the people from themselves (Deut. 7:7; 9:4–6)." Ibid. Cf. John Calvin, *Institutes of the Christian Religion*, ed. John T. McNeill, trans. Ford Lewis Battles, 2 vols. (Philadelphia: Westminster, 1960), 1.10.1.

10. Vos contends, "The exodus from Egypt *is* the Old Testament redemption." Vos, *Biblical Theology*, 109 (emphasis in original). He continues, "The term 'redemption' enters into religious use here. Its specific meaning (different from such general terms as 'to rescue', 'to deliver') lies precisely in this, that it describes the loving reacquisition of something formerly possessed." Ibid., 114. Cf. Daniel J. Theron, "'Adoption' in the Pauline Corpus," *EvQ* 28, 1 (1956): 10–11.

11. Norman Shepherd, *The Call of Grace: How the Covenant Illumines Salvation and Evangelism* (Phillipsburg, NJ: P&R Publishing, 2000), 54. Though quoting Shepherd on this particular point, let me make clear that I reject the neonomian paradigm that he espouses.

perspicuity was not joined by filial ability. Israel never succeeded in its holiness, for which it was freed from bondage. Yet this typological sonship under the old covenant functions no less as a historical link between the failed sonship of Adam and the prophesied redemptive sonship anticipated by Adam and Eve (Gen. 3:15; 4:1; cf. Gal. 3–4).[12]

Israel's corporate sonship failure is a macrocosm of Adam's individual sonship failure, but it is also a microcosm of the covenantal failure of *all* the sons of Adam—whether Jew or Gentile. Hence, as Paul sees it, Israel's covenantal rebellion affirms the *cosmic* necessity of the work of the messianic Son (cf. Rom. 8:19–23; Col. 1:20) to bring filial glory. In order to demonstrate this sonship continuity from Adam through Israel[13] to Christ, after laying the theological foundation of creation to consummation in Romans 8, in Romans 9:5 Paul articulates the consummation of old covenant adoption arriving in Christ himself, the Son par excellence, the Messiah.[14] In Paul's theological perspective, Israel's corporate sonship anticipated Christ's cosmically significant sonship, wherein the global scope of Adamic sonship failure is overturned by the exhaustively satisfactory redemptive work of the last Adam, the Son par excellence. The adoption of Israel was the seed form of eschatological adoption, and God's purposes for a family of faithful sons would not go thwarted by either the first son's or the typological son's disobedience.

12. Eve's expression in Genesis 4:1 likely does not indicate that she anticipated her firstborn son to be the Redeemer, but instead experienced in his arrival the historical potentiality of the Genesis 3:15 promise. H. C. Leupold, *Exposition of Genesis* (Grand Rapids: Baker, 1965), 189–90. Cf. Claus Westermann, *Genesis 1–11: A Commentary*, trans. John J. Scullion (Minneapolis: Augsburg, 1984), 288–91. Contra Robert S. Candlish, *Studies in Genesis* (repr., Grand Rapids: Kregel, 1979), 91–92.

13. Demonstrating the further connection between creation and redemption, Israel's corporate sonship is actually called a "creation" of God redemptively (Isa. 43:14–15; Mal. 2:10a).

14. "By describing Jesus' oneness with God, not disturbed by any restraint, by means of this forceful formulation, Paul . . . shed light on the depth of the contrast that separated Judaism from him. To the Jewish ears his statement [of Jesus' deity] was an abomination. With indignant protest Judaism was enraged over the notion that Jesus was to be attributed God's sonship in the totality that transferred the name of 'God' to him. In this manner he expressed forcefully the greatness of grace given to Israel, as well as the burning enigma of Israel's fall." Adolf Schlatter, *Romans: The Righteousness of God*, trans. Siegfried S. Schatzmann (Peabody, MA: Hendrickson, 1995), 202–3. Cf. William G. T. Shedd, *A Critical and Doctrinal Commentary on the Epistle of St. Paul to the Romans* (repr., Minneapolis: Klock & Klock, 1978), 278–79.

Thus, the divinely ordained consummation of sonship in adoption, anticipated by Adamic sonship and typified by Israel's corporate adoption, is realized only in the resurrection of this eschatological Son of God, the true Israel. The filial strands are tightly woven throughout the covenantal dealings of God with his people. United in redemptive-historical continuity under the archetypal sonship of the eternal Son are the created/ectypal sons, the corporate/typological son, the adopted/eschatological sons, and the messianic/antitypical Son. In short, what the Godhead ordained eternally, Adam anticipated covenantally, Israel's sonship typifies redemptively, and the last Adam consummated adoptively.

Adoption: The Adams and the Cosmos

In keeping with divine purpose, Christ's resurrection marked the culmination, solidification, and comprehension of all *his* covenantal work on behalf of the sons—his justification, sanctification, and glorification (Rom. 8:29–30; 1 Cor. 1:30; 1 Tim. 3:16);[15] it marked the end of his humiliation and the securing of his perpetual exaltation. Now dwelling in his glorified body by his resurrection from the dead, Jesus Christ qualified to bear the title *Son* in a new and crowning sense. This unprecedented personal transition for Christ marks the attainment of the goal of Adamic sonship, the victory over sin's power and guilt, the historical realization of the perfect image of God (cf. Rom. 8:29), and the acquisition of the spiritual, eschatological body (1 Cor. 15:44–45). As Vos puts it tersely concerning the resurrection body in 1 Corinthians 15:42–50, "the world of creation and the world of eschatology are thus related, the one points forward to the other; on the principle of typology the first Adam prefigures the second Adam, the psychical body, the pneumatic body (cf. Rom. 5:14)."[16] This prefigured new body is nothing less than the transformed one given in the adoption/resurrection.

---

15. See Gaffin, *Resurrection and Redemption*, 114–27; James M. Scott, *Adoption as Sons of God: An Exegetical Investigation into the Background of* YIOTHESIA *in the Pauline Corpus*, Wissenschaftliche Untersuchungen Zum Neuen Testament 48 (Tübingen: J. C. B. Mohr [Paul Siebeck], 1992), 244.

16. Vos, "Eschatological Aspect," 106n26.

As Vos affirms, Christ's personal filial attainment and transformed body bear directly on the "world of creation," the cosmos itself. In the theological background of the resurrection/consummation themes in Romans 8 (cf. Col. 1–2) lies the mandate in Genesis 1:26–28, when Adam and Eve were entrusted with the stewardship of all creation. Their sin made them guilty and corrupt, and it further compromised their ability to steward creation as required. Failed filial obedience invoked judgment, and also invoked a curse on the earth. "Because of sin, the whole order of creation [was] subverted."[17] Adam's sin repositioned him as the federal head of *fallen* men, whereby his guilt as the created son of God was imputed to his entire posterity (Rom. 5:12–21)[18] and, by the declaration of God himself, brought corruption to the entire cosmos (8:20–21). He failed in his coregency over the earth, making his sin bear not only personal consequences, but also cosmic ones.

Jesus Christ, the last Adam, the Son par excellence, fulfilled the covenantal obligations and bore the covenantal curse, so as to bring the sons of Adam into eschatological sonship and to free the earth from its cursed condition. Christ's filial success bears cosmic significance because, as the divine Representative, he flawlessly exercised his covenant stewardship responsibilities on earth. His resurrection and exaltation at God's "right hand in the heavenly places" (Eph. 1:20) includes his coronation as King over "all things" (Eph. 1:22) so that he might exercise the comprehensive dominion designed for those made in God's image (cf. Ps. 8). The revelation of the adopted sons at the consummation then conjoins Christ's filial success with his gracious bestowal of filial success to the sons in solidarity with him so that, in turn, creation enjoys release from its futility. For this reason, Paul describes the consummation of adoption as benefiting not merely the sons but the entire cursed creation (Rom. 8:20–22).[19] In view of the geocentricity and anthropocentricity of biblical redemption, it is Christ's work as *messianic* Son that remains

17. Bruce K. Waltke, *An Old Testament Theology: An Exegetical, Canonical, and Thematic Approach* (Grand Rapids: Zondervan, 2007), 267.

18. John Murray, *The Imputation of Adam's Sin* (Philadelphia: Presbyterian and Reformed, 1959), 64–70.

19. Vern S. Poythress, *The Shadow of Christ in the Law of Moses* (Phillipsburg, NJ: Presbyterian and Reformed, 1991), 243.

the focal point in the *historia salutis*, when he accomplishes the full redemption of the created sons and, in his bodily transforming adoption, secures creation's divinely purposed end.[20] The reach of adoption in Christ attains regal, global, and cosmic proportions.

The adoption of Christ, then, synonymous with his resurrection/transformation, fulfills in every way the cosmic goal of Adam's sonship. By way of summary, the chart below demonstrates this redemptive-historical and covenantal flow of adoptive sonship, under the eternal, archetypal sonship of Christ (A). Attested by the architectonic structure of covenant in Paul, *huiothesia* engages cosmic, covenantal, redemptive, and eschatological consummation. Adoptive sonship *anticipated* by the ectypal first Adam (B), and *typified* by Israelite corporate adoption, corresponds to adoptive sonship *realized* in the last Adam, the eschatological Son (C). Covenant history is filial history.

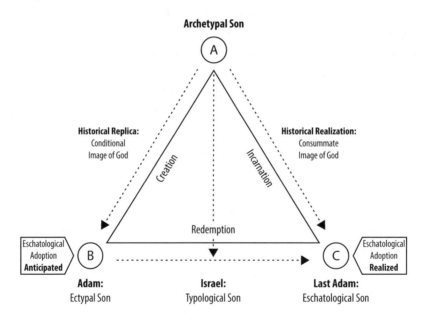

Fig. 9.1. Adoption in Its Covenantal and Redemptive-Historical Relationships[21]

20. W. David Stacey, "Paul's Certainties: God's Purpose in Creation—Romans 8:22–23," *Expository Times* 69 (1958): 180.
21. Note that this figure does not show the personal development of Christ whereby he *became* the consummate image of God at his resurrection/adoption. It intends instead to show the covenant-historical function of adoption in Pauline soteriology.

Summarily, this age of the Spirit is the eschatological age anticipated by Adam in Eden, but ushered in by the last Adam, the Son of God (cf. 1 Cor. 15:21–49), in his adoption. The goal of the covenant of works is met in the messianic Son and applied to the sons of Adam through the covenant of grace. It is with this covenantal and redemptive-historical perspective alone that we can understand Pauline soteriology, since in view of its preredemptive and redemptive scope eschatology ultimately informs the character of soteriology. Therefore, because the humiliation and exaltation of Christ mark the transition into the last days (cf. 1 Cor. 10:11; Heb. 1:2–4; 1 Peter 1:20), realized and unrealized soteriological privilege is nothing less than fully eschatological. Contrary to many *ordo salutis* approaches, eschatology does not await glorification, but rather characterizes the entire scope of soteriology. Indeed, "soteriology *is* eschatology,"[22] and therefore, in view of the two-Adam paradigm, Israel's typological adoption, and the cosmic purview of Paul's filial motif, *adoption* is eschatology.[23] As such, the adoption of the sons in the Son necessarily bears the cosmic, covenantal, and eschatological significance of Christ's adoption/resurrection.

Soteriology and Christology

The Sons in the Son: Christ and Huiothesia[24]

Well recognized in Paul's letters is his Christ-centeredness; a biblico-theological examination of *huiothesia* in its own right crystallizes and clarifies Pauline Christology as filio-Christology. While it would be redundant to traverse each of the *huiothesian* texts at length here, in order to display the far-reaching theological scope of *huiothesia* and related filial/familial themes, we summarize here Pauline filio-Christology on which rides the believers' *huiothesia*. James Cook helpfully summarizes four of the *huiothesian* texts:

22. Gaffin, *Resurrection and Redemption*, 138 (emphasis in original).
23. Herman N. Ridderbos, *Paul: An Outline of His Theology*, trans. John Richard DeWitt (Grand Rapids: Eerdmans, 1975), 198.
24. This section of the chapter draws, in amended form, from Garner, "First and Last Son," 276–78.

The four texts (and their contexts) which deal with Christian adoption manifest Paul's customary emphasis on the essential role of Christ and the Spirit. Romans 8 makes plain that adoption (v. 15) means that Christians are both children and heirs of God (v. 16); and that to be heirs of God . . . is at the same time to be fellow-heirs . . . with Christ (v. 17). This christological connection is carried through to the end of the paragraph by the verbs *sympaschomen* and *syndoxasthomen*. As was noted above, v. 23 of the same chapter links adoption with "the redemption of our bodies." Once again the christological connection is made, albeit more subtly. For apart from the resurrection of Christ there would, of course, be no Christian expectation of the redemption of the body. In Gal. 4:4f. the place of the work of Christ in the adoption of his people is made perfectly clear. The purpose for which God sent forth his Son, the goal of the incarnation itself, is "that we might receive adoption as sons." And in Eph. 1:5 it is emphasized that just as all the blessings described in that doxology are received in Christ, so also God predestined Christians for adoption "through Jesus Christ." The cumulative testimony of these passages asserts forcefully that Christians do not receive adoption apart from Jesus Christ.[25]

Though Cook does not list it here, Romans 9:4 further accentuates the Christological focus in *huiothesia*. When Paul explains the covenantal blessings enjoyed by those under the old covenant in Romans 9:1–5, he lists several features that illustrate the riches of blessing under the old covenant. In his explication of these divine blessings, Paul crowns his argument with the antitype of them all: Christ "according to the flesh" (9:5).[26] Biology does not qualify one as a descendant of Abraham in the truest sense (9:8), and Paul proclaims that any perceived failure of God to fulfill his promises to Israel (11:1) represents

25. James I. Cook, "The Conception of Adoption in the Theology of Paul," in *Saved by Hope: Essays in Honor of Richard C. Oudersluys*, ed. James I. Cook (Grand Rapids: Eerdmans, 1978), 141–42.

26. John Murray, *The Epistle to the Romans: The English Text with Introduction, Exposition and Notes*, 2 vols. combined (repr., Grand Rapids: Eerdmans, 1997), 2:6; Joseph A. Fitzmyer, *Romans: A New Translation with Introduction and Commentary*, Anchor Bible 33 (New York: Doubleday, 1993), 547.

not a failure on God's part, but a failure of the Jews to understand the international heart of the covenant of grace (11:28–32)—now come unto its fruition in Jesus Christ. The substantive link between old covenant and new covenant, according to Paul, is the incarnate Christ;[27] the Christological culmination of the expanding covenants serves as the explicit basis for the continuity of blessing between the dispensations. Old covenant provisions, the means of God's blessing under the Mosaic administration, were temporary provisions with a forward look, anticipating divine fulfillment, exclusively *in Christ*.[28]

More particularly, it was Jesus Christ according to the flesh (Rom. 1:3) who brought the promised covenantal blessings to fruition when he became the resurrected Son (1:4). The adopted Son (1:4) served as the antitype for Israel's corporate *adoption* (9:3). From a redemptive-historical perspective, then, the contrasts between old covenant *huiothesia* and new covenant *huiothesia* unite in the true Israel—Christ himself, who alone fulfills old covenant type and shadow. Christ, the Son par excellence, the prophesied Prophet, Priest, and King, efficiently accomplishes redemptive sonship for those old covenant and new covenant spiritual sons of Abraham. Exclusively as the adopted Son of God he accomplishes redemption: typological adoption and eschatological adoption unite in the person of Christ, the Son of God par excellence. Romans 9 offers no exception to *huiothesia*'s pervasive Christology.

These five *huiothesian* texts fit securely in theological and historical juxtaposition: the eternal Son of God participated in the pretemporal decree for adoptive sonship (Eph. 1:5) and answered to the divine counsel as the *incarnate, then adopted* Son on history's stage; born of woman and born under the law (Gal. 4:4–5), this Son fulfilled the covenantal and typological purposes of Israelite corporate sonship (Rom. 9:4–5); as Son par excellence, in his humiliation unto exaltation, he

27. Geerhardus Vos, *The Self-Disclosure of Jesus: The Modern Debate about the Messianic Consciousness*, ed. Johannes G. Vos (Grand Rapids: Eerdmans, 1954), 149.

28. Cf. Robertson, *The Christ of the Covenants*, 296–97. Because of the perfect coalescence of the eschatological Son and the eschatological Spirit (2 Cor. 3:17), "the community of the Spirit" operates in continuity with old covenant blessing (Rom. 9:4–5) and further attests to the Christological coordination of old covenant and new covenant. Willem A. VanGemeren, "The Spirit of Restoration," *WTJ* 50, 1 (1988): 92.

inaugurated the eschatological and pneumatic age (age of the Spirit) of adoptive sonship in all its relational, judicial, and transformational efficacy (Rom. 8:15; Gal. 4:4–5); and finally, his resurrection as the first Son of God in power secured and commenced the resurrection/adoption harvest of his elect family (Rom. 8:23; Eph. 1:4–6; cf. Rom. 1:3–4).

The Sons in the Son: Union with Christ

As affirmed in chapter 8, grounded in the *historia salutis*, union with Christ serves as Paul's nuclear soteriological concept: it is "really the central truth of the whole doctrine of salvation not only in its application but also in its once-for-all accomplishment in the finished work of Christ."[29] His repeated usage of forms such as "*in* Christ" and "*with* Christ" (cf. Eph. 2:6; Col. 2:20; 3:1) highlights the supreme importance of this conception.[30] Put negatively, apart from union, the benefits from Christ would remain entirely out of reach. Thus, to detach the believer's sonship redemptive-historically from Christ's adoptive sonship is to introduce a foreign element into biblical soteriology, and thereby enter into speculative reconstruction at worst and theological abstraction at best. In this regard, "the bond between the believer and Christ is so close that, from Paul's point of view, a detachment of the Christian's interest not only, but even a severance from his *actual life* from the celestial Christ-centered sphere is unthinkable."[31] Believers are adopted sons in and through Christ Jesus or they are not adopted sons at all. Any other soteriological schema is unthinkable.

Focusing, then, on the *historia salutis*, union with Christ places the believer *historically* with Christ in his humiliation and exaltation, his death and his resurrection—indeed, his adoption (Rom. 1:3–4).[32]

29. John Murray, *Redemption Accomplished and Applied* (Grand Rapids: Eerdmans, 1955), 161.

30. See Constantine R. Campbell, *Paul and Union with Christ: An Exegetical and Theological Study* (Grand Rapids: Zondervan, 2012); John Murray, *The Collected Writings of John Murray*, 4 vols. (Edinburgh: Banner of Truth, 1976–82), 2:291–92; Samuel J. Baird, *The Elohim Revealed in the Creation and Redemption of Man* (Philadelphia: Parry & McMillan, 1860), 643.

31. Geerhardus Vos, *The Pauline Eschatology* (Princeton, NJ: Princeton University Press, 1930), 37 (emphasis added).

32. Cf. Robert Letham, *The Work of Christ*, Contours of Christian Theology (Downers Grove, IL: InterVarsity Press, 1993), 84–85; Sinclair B. Ferguson, *The Holy Spirit*, Contours of Christian Theology (Downers Grove, IL: InterVarsity Press, 1996), 105.

Several points of interest surface here. First, Christ's adoption from a redemptive-historical perspective marks the ushering in of the eschatological age, so that all those adopted in Christ participate in his cosmically significant adoption in *all* its ramifications. Adoption in Christ involves participation in the historical transition from the former epoch to the eschatological epoch, a cosmic transition from wrath to grace.[33] Integral to this transition is the ministry of the Holy Spirit, whose outpouring (Joel 2:28–32; Acts 2) marks the inauguration of the new age. To uphold the thrust of adoption, this Spirit-eschatological character must govern any theological explication of the adoption/resurrection.

Second, since the declaration at Jesus's resurrection involves his full vindication (cf. 1 Tim. 3:16), the judicial and declaratory dimension of adoption remains critical to its understanding. Adoption possesses a distinct forensic dimension, a feature noted already with some degree of consistency whenever adoption has received theological consideration. Accordingly, the righteousness in Christ vindicates the believer, and the sonship attained by him belongs to those with him. The justified Son justifies the sons. No longer guilty under the law or bound by man-made religious trappings (Gal. 4:3), the adopted son finds himself forgiven of his sins by his Father (Eph. 1:7), granted full inheritance (Gal. 4:1–6; Eph. 1:11–14), graciously transferred from one kingdom to another (Col. 1:13), and translated from one mode of sonship to another (Rom. 8:2–4). Those who were not sons of God are now, by grace, the family of God. Having entered the kingdom of the beloved Son, the former sons of darkness become sons of light. Sons in the fallen first Adam become sons in the resurrected last Adam.

Third, and perhaps more surprising to common theological instincts, inasmuch as Christ's adoption indicates his full consecration and renovation as the Son par excellence, his resurrection confirms him as Victor over sin, corruption, and death. The Son's empty tomb renders full filial power to combat corruption. By the power of Christ's resurrection life in the Spirit, adoption for the redeemed entails moral and, on the last day, bodily renovation. By virtue of the consummative filial glory of Christ, the believers' adoption changes both their state

---

33. Gaffin, *Resurrection and Redemption*, 116.

and nature. It is striking in this regard that the adoption texts seem to capitalize prominently on the Spirit-produced transformative features of eschatological, filial grace.

The Sons in the Son: Christ as the Eschatological Spirit of Adoption

In both Old and New Testaments, the Holy Spirit's role is creation and re-creation.[34] Instrumental in the creation account (Gen. 1:1–2; cf. 2:7), the Holy Spirit serves an even more prominent role in carrying out God's redemption plan: "the principle of *tota Scriptura* (OT and NT) sustains the correlation of the Spirit in the totality of restoration."[35] Accordingly, as part of the eschatologically focused work of the Spirit, a central privilege promised and granted in the new covenant is the renewing power[36] of the Spirit of God for obedience (Isa. 11:1–10; Jer. 31:31–34; Ezek. 36:26–27; Rom. 8:4). The responsibility to obey the covenant God persists within the conscience of created humanity (Rom. 1:32; 2:14ff.), because men are created sons in the likeness of God: "this ultimate standard continues as the constant canon of human conduct."[37] The Spirit's presence does not create this need for obedience, but, in the gospel of grace, renews adopted sons unto it: "The Spirit not only commands but also renders man capable of doing what is required."[38]

A dominant feature of new covenant faith is this enablement, grounded in the success of the Son of God in his perfect covenantal obedience. Jesus' filial obedience, in fact, makes the new covenant *new,*

34. VanGemeren, "The Spirit of Restoration," 81–102; Vos, "Eschatological Aspect," 91–125; Gordon D. Fee, *God's Empowering Presence: The Holy Spirit in the Letters of Paul* (Peabody, MA: Hendrickson, 1994), 319–20, 332, 590, 602, 779–83, 857–60; Gordon D. Fee, *Paul, the Spirit, and the People of God* (Peabody, MA: Hendrickson, 1997), 9–23; Ridderbos, *When the Time Had Fully Come,* 51–52, 71. Cf. Thomas F. Torrance, *The Christian Doctrine of God: One Being Three Persons* (Edinburgh: T&T Clark, 1996), 217–18; Ridderbos, *Paul,* 215.

35. VanGemeren, "Spirit of Restoration," 99.

36. Donald William Mills, "The Concept of Sinlessness in 1 John in Relation to Johannine Eschatology" (Ph.D. diss., Westminster Theological Seminary, Philadelphia, 1998), 286–90.

37. Kline, *Kingdom Prologue,* 62.

38. Ridderbos, *When the Time Had Fully Come,* 71. For a fuller treatment of the distinguishing features of the Spirit's ministry to believers in the Old and New Testaments, see Richard B. Gaffin Jr., "The Holy Spirit," *WTJ* 43, 1 (1980): 58–78.

in that "the new covenant . . . boasts a unique feature in its power to transform its participants from within their hearts. This uniqueness sets the new covenant apart from the previous covenantal dealings of God with his people."[39] This primary demarcation of new covenant inauguration concerns the outpouring of this eschatological Spirit (cf. Joel 2; Acts 2; 8:14–25; 10:44–48; 11:15–18; 19:1–7), who, in his ministry of union with Christ, effectively applies the work of this eschatological Son. "Having the Spirit is the equivalent, indeed the very mode, of having the incarnate, obedient, crucified, resurrected and exalted Christ indwelling us so that we are united to him as he is united to the Father."[40]

To be clear, the gospel under the old covenant also entailed heart change, but during the pre-Christ, Old Testament age, by the Spirit believers enjoyed the work of Christ proleptically. A perspicuous meticulousness is in order here so as to avoid understating the presence and role of the Holy Spirit in the Old Testament, on the one hand, and to avoid diminishing the radical significance of the eschatological outpouring of the Spirit in the New Testament, on the other. However we insist on soteriological continuity between the Testaments, it is proper to affirm that proleptic (Old Testament) benefit lacks equal efficacy with the eschatological (New Testament).[41] In the age of the Spirit, the application of soteriological benefits teems with "more fullness, evidence and spiritual efficacy" (WCF 7.6). The Pentecost event, tied to the resurrection of the Son of God, emerges prominently in a biblical doctrine of the Spirit—redemptive-historically

---

39. Ferguson, *The Holy Spirit*, 71.

40. Robertson, *The Christ of the Covenants*, 276. Cf. Calvin, *Institutes*, 1.9.3; Peter A. Lillback, *The Binding of God: Calvin's Role in the Development of Covenant Theology*, ed. Richard A. Muller, Texts and Studies in Reformation and Post-Reformation Thought (Grand Rapids: Baker Academic, 2001), 274; Trevor J. Burke, "Adoption and the Spirit in Romans 8," *EvQ* 70, 4 (1998): 313–14.

41. Richard Gaffin scrupulously engages the distinctions between the experience of the Spirit in the pre-Christ and post-Christ epochs. He shifts attention away from any emotional and psychological experience, and directs attention to the ecclesiological, international, and moral implications of Christ as life-giving Spirit in this new age. See Gaffin, "The Holy Spirit," 70–78. See also WCF 7.6 and 8.6; Wilhelmus à Brakel, *The Christian's Reasonable Service*, ed. Joel R. Beeke, trans. Bartel Elshout, vol. 2 (Grand Rapids: Reformation Heritage Books, 1993), 16.

and, derivatively, in the life of the believer. "We may not say only that at Pentecost Christ pours out on the church the gift of the Spirit, but also that Pentecost is the coming to the church of Christ himself as the life-giving Spirit. The Spirit of Pentecost is the resurrection life of Jesus, the life of the exalted Christ, effective in the church."[42]

With an eye to the adoption motif as seen in Paul, we find that the consummate purpose of God in redemption is the thorough renovation of the redeemed *sons* of Adam—holy sons in the holy Son; true freedom *from* slavery is full freedom *for* filial obedience in Christ.[43] For this reason Paul regularly weaves Spirit-guided ethical responsibility in his explication of the familial relationship (cf. Eph. 5:1–14; Phil. 2:14–16; 1 Thess. 5:2–10).[44] "The dynamic of Pauline ethics is in the fact that the same Spirit who is the energizing force of the new creation [resurrection] in Christ and of the final transformation of the son of God into the image of the Son, is also the power of the present new life in Christ."[45] In broader biblical scope, the Holy Spirit's ministry in adoptive sonship, empowering the redeemed for spiritual life, recapitulates his presence in the creative sonship of man, when by the *breath* of God he gave man life. Such renewed life-giving is far from coincidental, as attested by the covenantal and creation context that buttresses Romans 8:18–23. Just as the Spirit of God breathed life into lifeless Adam in the garden (Gen. 2:7),[46] so also he breathes life into the spiritually dead man, giving him *spiritual* life (cf. Ezek.

42. Gaffin, "The Holy Spirit," 69.

43. See John R. W. Stott, *The Cross of Christ* (Downers Grove, IL: InterVarsity Press, 1986), 182; Robert A. Peterson, *Adopted by God: From Wayward Sinners to Cherished Children* (Phillipsburg, NJ: P&R Publishing, 2001), 79.

44. Cf. Samuel G. Shepard, "The Pauline Doctrine of Sonship" (Ph.D. diss., Southern Baptist Theological Seminary, Louisville, KY, 1951), 132–46. Missing this focal reality of the resurrection in understanding adoption leads Thomas Boston to state mistakenly, "Adoption is not a real change in the sinner's nature; but, as justification a relative change of his state." *The Complete Works of the Late Rev. Thomas Boston*, ed. Samuel M'Millan, 12 vols. (London: William Tegg & Co., 1853; repr., Wheaton, IL: Richard Owen Roberts, 1980), 1:615.

45. Allen Mawhinney, "*Yiothesia* in the Pauline Epistles: Its Background, Use, and Implications" (Ph.D. diss., Baylor University, Waco, TX, 1982), 235.

46. Linda Belleville, "'Born of Water and Spirit': John 3:5," *Trinity Journal* 1, 2 (1980): 138. Cf. M. M. B. Turner, "The Concept of Receiving the Spirit in John's Gospel," *VE* 10 (1977): 33; Vos, "Eschatological Aspect," 108.

37:1–14), resurrecting the adopted sons (cf. Rom. 8:9–11; Eph. 2:1–10) for eschatologically charged transformation.[47]

Genesis 2:7 graphically portrays how God the Spirit himself initiated life, taking Adam from a lifeless state to a living one, by breathing life into his nostrils. Yet the New Testament concept of the Holy Spirit's indwelling indicates a manifestation of power that exceeds the physical life that he issued the first Adam. While the breath of the Spirit blown into the dust quickened the lifeless matter in Genesis 2, the breath of the Spirit in Romans 8 *resurrects* the dead (cf. Rom. 8:11). The first breath in the first son of God inaugurates the former age—creation; the eschatological breath from the last Son of God inaugurates the final age—re-creation and glorification. The Holy Spirit gives spiritual life, transitioning the redeemed from the epoch of flesh to the epoch of the Spirit, taking sons of Adam from spiritual deadness in sin to spiritual life in Christ (Eph. 2:1–10). The dual role of the Holy Spirit in creation and eschatological life-giving implicitly demonstrates the correlation between created and redeemed sons.[48] It is the Holy Spirit's eschatological renewal/resurrection of the adopted sons that, in coalescence with the work of the eschatological Son, secures the very purpose of created sonship. Created sons of Adam become the adopted sons of God by the ministry of the "Spirit of adoption" (Rom. 8:15).[49]

While one might suggest that the title "Spirit of adoption" conveys assurance, this conclusion, while derivatively accurate, misses the epochal (eschatological) environment in which such assurance occurs. The Spirit's affirming ministry happens within the context of Christ's filial consecration, in which his victorious resurrection and new filial identity terminates the age of fear and the dominion of sin. Because of the cosmic and epochal change, the renewing, resurrecting Spirit of adoption leads the sons unto holiness in the new age of spiritual

47. Cf. Daniel Block, "The Prophet of the Spirit: The Use of *RWH* in the Book of Ezekiel," *JETS* 32, 1 (1989): 35.

48. See Turner, "Significance of Spirit Endowment for Paul," 57.

49. Calvin calls this title of the Spirit his *first* title, "because he is the witness to us of the free benevolence of God with which God has embraced us in his only-begotten Son to become a Father to us." Calvin, *Institutes*, 3.1.3. Cf. Howard Griffith, "'The First Title of the Spirit': Adoption in Calvin's Soteriology," *EvQ* 73, 2 (2001): 135.

freedom, of realized adoptive sonship. In this age, he draws the adopted sons to participate in the refining sufferings[50] of the Son par excellence in a shared pathway of obedience (Rom. 8:16–17). "Where the Spirit functions to bring life and freedom in Christ, there the content of the law and obedience to it make up the very substance of that freedom."[51] That in the context of sanctification the Holy Spirit is entitled the "Spirit of adoption" itself divulges the inexorable tie between progressive sanctification (conformity into the image of the perfect Son) and adoptive sonship. It is the sons of God whom he leads into holiness: "For all who are led by the Spirit of God are sons of God" (Rom. 8:14).

On the basis of the cosmic scope of Christ's resurrection and the concomitant outpouring of the Spirit on the redeemed sons of God, assurance surely follows. The assurance, understood properly, bears directly on the cosmic, redemptive-historical events. That is, the sons' existential affirmation consists of reassuring participation in the epochal transition accomplished in the work of the eschatological Son. In Spirit-enabled filial obedience, the adopted sons verbalize the eschatological privilege (cf. Gal. 4:6), which they share with the resurrected Son. The Spirit of the *historia salutis* confirms the completion of redemption in the hearts of the redeemed, so that the exclamation on the lips of the adopted children (*ordo salutis*) echoes their Elder Brother's own words at the greatest crisis point of his suffering (Mark 14:36; cf. Heb. 5:7–10). Because of union with Christ, the cry of the adopted sons' spirits (Rom. 8:15–16) reverberates with the cry of the Spirit of adoption within them (Gal. 4:6). The Son cries; the Spirit cries; the sons in the Son cry: "Abba! Father!" The *ordo salutis* and the *historia salutis* manifestly converge in this Spirit-generated outburst. The personal/experiential exclamation of the soul confirms the eschatological reality; the soteriological echoes the Christological by means of the pneumatological.

These cries serve ends beyond verbal mimicking or existential identification. Instead, they affirm the sanctification of the sons of God through suffering *and* the previous victory of the Son in suffering and

---

50. Cf. Col. 1:24. On this text, see Richard B. Gaffin Jr., "The Usefulness of the Cross," *WTJ* 41, 1 (1979): 228–46.

51. Gaffin, "The Holy Spirit," 77.

death. In the crucible of the sons' suffering, the walk of filial obedience elicits the imitative cry, precisely because the adopted sons live in the power of the Son's Spirit as they walk in his footsteps. Whereas for Christ sanctification through suffering accomplished redemption (served the *historia salutis*), for those adopted in him, sanctification through suffering, as Paul argues in Philippians 3:8–21, secures redemption (serves the *ordo salutis*). While surely a divine act, union with Christ is no static concept; it "*is a soteric replication in the structure of the believer's life-experience of what happened antecedently in the life-experience of Christ, namely, death and resurrection.*"[52] Its dynamic efficacy is enjoyed in the emulation of the obedience of Christ, but done in the power of the Spirit of the resurrected Christ. Christ's filial obedience *created* redemptive efficacy; the adopted sons' obedience *evidences* redemptive efficacy. The obedience of both the Son and the sons is necessary; in fact, the covenantal solidarity of the sons in the Son makes the shared suffering and obedience of the sons essential to the eschatological realization of the shared resurrection glory (Rom. 8:15–17).

To be clear, the obedience of the sons in the Son is redemptively *consequential*, while the obedience of their Elder Brother is redemptively *causal*. Neither obedience, however, is optional; both occur as an essential means to the consummation. Both in fact belong together in a theologically vital fashion:

> Not only can the sufferings of believers be viewed as Christ's and as being conformed to his death, but also the personal, past-historical sufferings of Christ and the present afflictions of the church are seen together as constituting one whole. Again, certainly not in the sense that the sufferings of the church have some additive atoning, reconciling value. But there are aspects other than soteriological

---

52. Lane G. Tipton, "Union with Christ and Justification," in *Justified in Christ: God's Plan for Us in Justification*, ed. K. Scott Oliphint (Fearn, Ross-shire, UK: Christian Focus, 2007), 25 (emphasis in original). Tipton clarifies: "Two qualifications seem necessary. First, the replication in view occurs in the life-experience of the sinner, which means that an analogical relationship exists between the death and resurrection of Christ, on the one hand, and the death and resurrection of the believer in Christ, on the other hand. Second, both the structure and redemptive reality of what is replicated in the believer's life-experience are nothing less than the resurrection life of Christ, given to believers in the act of union with Christ." Ibid., 25–26n6.

from which the church's sufferings can be bracketed with the suffering of Christ himself. These aspects we may designate apostolic or missiological, having to do with the gospel-mission in the world of the church together with its Head.[53]

The growth in holiness by the sons in the Son necessarily follows because of Christ's fully excellent sonship, in which they participate. The eschatological Spirit breathes life into the nostrils of the sons of God; he is the life-giving power for filial faith and faithfulness. The freeing power of the Spirit of holiness marks the age of new covenant faith, in which the adopted sons exercise filial grace, as they eagerly and perseveringly replicate the gait of their Elder Brother.

To frame this point against forensic fixation, it remains difficult to see how justification is *ultimately* more important than sanctification/glorification. To be sure, the forgiveness of sins and the imputed righteousness of Christ are a sine qua non of the gospel. Without unrelenting insistence on the pure *grace* of forgiveness, the gospel loses its uniqueness, authority, and biblical fidelity. Without justification, the gospel is no longer the gospel. Truly the door of biblical soteriology swings on the hinge of justification.

But that soteriological door requires a second hinge, which bears the weight of an equally critical feature of gospel grace—that is, the efficacy of Christ's life, death, and resurrection to *make* sinners righteous. This transforming power of Christ's work is also a sine qua non of the gospel. The sons of God declared are the sons of God changed. The Spirit of Christ leads the true sons in holiness (Rom. 8:9–11). To wit, the grand finale of the gospel entails more than a declaration of justification or of legal sonship; it is a manifestation of the sons *transformed* into the image of their Elder Brother. The final filial announcement (v. 23) coincides with glorious filial attainment, conformity into the image of the first Son.

Biblical soteriology offers purity and holiness not as an afterthought of Christ's work, but as its final filial goal (Eph. 1:3–6).[54] To insist

---

53. Gaffin, "Usefulness of the Cross," 242.
54. See chapter 4.

that justification is more important than sanctification is to insist that Christ's work to forgive sin is more important than his power over its mastery; such a conclusion emasculates the consummate covenantal victory of the Son of God and distorts biblical soteriology as a whole! That God does not count sin against the sinner but against his Son's life, death, and resurrection is the efficacious *pronouncement* of gospel grace; that God takes sinners and makes them pure by the power of his Son's life, death, and resurrection is the efficacious *provision* of gospel grace. Therefore, the forgiveness of sin, in its full biblical sense, requires a parallel and equally prominent gospel feature: the purification of the sinner. The latter *will not* occur without the former, but neither does the former cause the latter. The parallel benefits (Calvin's *duplex gratia*) of gospel grace flow directly from the Son of God and are poured out by his Spirit. The gospel of the adopted Son takes sinners and *makes* them saints; the Redeemer/Son takes the hideously corrupted sons of Adam and makes them truly excellent sons of God. The Spirit of Christ, that is, the Spirit of adoption, proffers this filial purification of heart, mind, and body (Rom. 8:1–30). Without this sanctification, the gospel is no longer the gospel.

Drawing on 2 Samuel 7:14, James Scott connects adoption with the renovating Spirit in the Davidic covenant: "the *huiothesia* of believers recalls the 2 Sam. 7:14 tradition, which looks forward to the outpouring of the Spirit on the eschatological people of God who are adopted sons of God with the Messiah."[55] This connection of the eschatological outpouring is "further substantiated by the fact that . . . the Spirit is seen as the fulfillment of Ezek. 36:26–28 in connection with divine adoption."[56] As Ezekiel 36 puts it, the eschatological people of God would possess the Spirit in their hearts, which in turn would cause them to obey the commandments of God. Scott notes that this

---

55. Scott, *Adoption as Sons of God*, 263. Scott asserts that "the national expectation of divine adoption, converging as it does with the messianic expectation, leads to an appropriation of 2 Sam. 7:14a to the eschatological people of God as a whole, a sort of national identification with the sonship of the *Heilbringer*." Ibid., 117; cf. ibid., 96–117, 174–86. Others also develop this connection of adoption with 2 Samuel 7. Cf. Peterson, *Adopted by God*, 20–23; Russell Radoicich, "'Adoption' in the Pauline Epistles" (unpublished paper, St. Vladimir's Orthodox Theological Seminary, Crestwood, NY, 1999), 23–24.

56. Scott, *Adoption as Sons of God*, 263.

same Spirit who quickens the hearts of those under the new covenant is the *"pneuma huiothesias* [Spirit of adoption] (v. 15) by which the sons of God are 'led' to live in accordance to the will of God (v. 14).["](57)" Hence, with the replete exodus typology included in Romans 8, Scott insightfully argues that freedom from bondage is actually "because they have the Spirit of *huiothesia*."[58] In keeping with the Spirit of adoption outpoured in the new covenant, the sons in the new epoch enjoy the efficacy of their Elder Brother's faithfulness for their own obedience.

Calvin has helpfully put this sanctification in its Christological/ pneumatological *and* adoptive context: "whomever . . . God receives into grace, on them he at the same time bestows the Spirit of adoption, *by whose power he remakes them to his own image.*"[59] This comprehensive remake is as essential to the gospel as is the declaration of forensic righteousness in the vindicated Son. Only those who are *led* by this eschatological, renewing Spirit are truly the adopted sons of God, because "the Spirit of adoption is also the Spirit of mortification."[60] In the process of obedience, the adopted son's cry (Rom. 8:15) coalesces with the Spirit's enabling and affirming presence, confirming the genuine reality of union with Christ in his own eschatological adoption (vv. 14, 16).

As detailed in chapter 7, important in Pauline argument is the ministry of the Spirit in the life of Jesus. At Christ's resurrection, the outpouring of the promised Spirit occurs because of the Spirit-wrought change in the incarnate Son. Concerning Christ himself, Vos writes, "The resurrection . . . is . . . according to Paul the entering upon a new phase of sonship characterized by the *possession and exercise of unique supernatural power.*"[61] The "possession and exercise" of this newfound power shoulder colossal weight in Pauline soteriology. The redemptive significance of the resurrection of the Son of God comes by the Spirit-wrought change *in* him, so that the saving power of his resurrection/ adoption flows *from* him. His resurrection power exists not finally for

57. Ibid., 264.
58. Ibid. Cf. Brendan Byrne, *Romans*, ed. Daniel J. Harrington, SP 6 (Collegeville, MN: Liturgical Press, 1996), 252n15.
59. Calvin, *Institutes*, 3.11.6 (emphasis added).
60. Sinclair B. Ferguson, *Children of the Living God* (Colorado Springs: NavPress, 1987), 104.
61. Vos, *Pauline Eschatology*, 156n10 (emphasis added).

his personal benefit, but for the benefit of the church—those united to him. The resurrection of the Son occurs *for* the resurrection of the sons. Christ's filial resurrection power propels from him, and by the sheer force of his attainment as resurrected Son, Christ's filial grace radiates to those in his light.

Paul builds this case vigorously in 1 Corinthians 15. "The incarnate Christ ('the last Adam') has been so transformed by the Spirit and is now in such complete possession of the Spirit that he has 'become life-giving Spirit,' with the result that now 'the Lord [= the exalted Christ] is the Spirit' (1 Cor. 15:45; 2 Cor. 3:17)."[62] Now as life-giving Spirit (1 Cor. 15:45), the resurrected Son of God in his new spiritual body is characterized by an unprecedented dynamic, a Spirit-realized, life-giving, salvific resourcing for those united to him. Resurrected by the Spirit, the Son of God is the firstfruits of a single harvest of resurrection (1 Cor. 15:20, 23). Because of Christ's having attained consummate glory in his adoption (cf. Eph. 1:15–23), his filial power and glory surge to those in union with him. As resurrected/adopted Son, he comprehensively equips the blessed sons in the Son with full armor to wage war effectively with the spiritual forces of darkness (Eph. 6:10–20) and to ensure their own final resurrection-adoption at the end of the age (Rom. 8:23).

Thus, the Son's resurrection acquires significance not primarily for him, but, more importantly and purposefully, for all who are *in solidarity* with him: "adoption fulfills itself in the somatic transformation of the resurrection, so that in view of the (Adamic) unity of the resurrection of Christ and believers, what is true of the latter holds for the former."[63] The Christological transformation serves the soteriological and eschatological purpose. The risen Son then becomes the life-giving Spirit of adoption. As such, he freely gives himself to those in union with him, securing their filial declaration and transformation.

62. Richard B. Gaffin Jr., *By Faith, Not by Sight: Paul and the Order of Salvation*, 2nd ed. (Phillipsburg, NJ: P&R Publishing, 2013), 44.

63. Gaffin, *Resurrection and Redemption*, 119. Letham, *The Work of Christ*, 221, adds, "Therefore, the relation between the resurrection of Christ in AD 30, and ours, is so unbreakable that if one part were not true the other would also be false."

Adoption of the sons, therefore, necessarily draws on the resurrection power of the Son of God, and consists of renovative progression/sanctification (cf. Rom. 8:14–15) until consummate filial realization at the resurrection of the body (v. 23). Transforming resurrection power, realized now through the eschatological Spirit of adoption, draws and energizes the adopted son for filial obedience. "Paul emphasizes repeatedly that the Spirit who works life in believers is the identical Spirit who wrought and still is life for the exalted Lord (Rom. 8:9, 11; 2 Cor. 13:4)."[64] The *historia salutis* attains its purposed vitality in this intersection of the life of Christ and the lives of his people. This dynamic juncture of the sons with the Son wholly situates Pauline filio-Christology and filio-soteriology, a relationship of theological reciprocity that deserves a bit of further analysis here.

Theological Reciprocity: Filio-Christology and Filio-Soteriology

Christology, in its functional, covenantal contours, exists in service of soteriology. In fact, in most poignant fashion, the solidarity of the sons with the Son *gives meaning* to Christ's resurrection/adoption event itself. Richard Gaffin writes:

> The resurrection of Christ is the resurrection of the firstfruits, the firstborn, the second Adam. It has *no meaning apart from the solidarity between Christ and believers, apart from what he has in common with them*. With reference to Christ's person, for Paul the resurrection concerns his human nature, not his divine nature. Moreover, as such, its significance is not purely noetic. For as 1 Cor. 15:45 and 2 Cor. 3:17 make clear, the resurrection produces a real transformation in the person of Christ, a change which is analogous to that experienced by believers (cf. esp. 1 Cor. 15:51 with vv. 45ff.).[65]

64. Vos, "Eschatological Aspect," 113–14. Vos further underscores the *ethical* implications of this: "to Paul the Spirit is preeminently the Spirit of Christ and therefore as thoroughly equable and ethical in His activity as the mind of Jesus Himself." Ibid., 122.
65. Gaffin, *Resurrection and Redemption*, 104–5 (emphasis added). Cf. Mawhinney,

In other words, without the *ordo salutis*, the *historia salutis* tumbles into a theological abyss. So intricately tied to the work of Christ is its redemptive purpose that his own resurrection lacks value without it. Such indissoluble integration of Christology and soteriology surfaces regularly throughout the Pauline corpus. Paul overtly employs this paradigmatic interface in 1 Corinthians 15:12–19, where he tethers Christ's resurrection/adoption with that of the redeemed in a counterintuitive fashion: "But if there is no resurrection of the dead, then not even Christ has been raised" and "For if the dead are not raised, not even Christ has been raised" (1 Cor. 15:13, 16). Here the apostle argues in reverse order from what one might expect. Rather than arguing *from* the resurrection of Christ *to* the resurrection of those united to him, he begins with the consequent resurrection and then moves to its antecedent. In other words, he argues from the redeemed to the Redeemer, from the resurrection of the sons to the resurrection of the Son. For Paul, the historicity and significance of Christ's resurrection rely on the pneumatic bond between the sons and the Son.

To put it otherwise, Paul makes the Christological act of resurrection/adoption retrospectively *contingent* on the solidarity of the sons with him. That is, if the sons of God will not be raised in history, neither was the firstborn Son of God raised in history. The preaching of Christ's resurrection concerns a single resurrection, of which he is the "firstfruits" (1 Cor. 15:20). This preaching of Christ's death/resurrection not only is a matter of its historicity, but concerns its theological value "for our sins" (v. 3). If believers are not raised from the dead, neither did Christ die and rise from the dead for their sins. Accordingly, if the sons of Adam do not become the resurrected-adopted sons, neither did Christ become the resurrected-adopted Son. The resurrection of the sons on the *last day* drives the necessity and attainment of the resurrection of the Son at the inauguration of the *last days*. The certain spiritual solidarity of the sons in the Son requires such historical and theological reasoning.

"*Yiothesia* in the Pauline Epistles," 152; William D. Dennison, *Paul's Two-Age Construction and Apologetics* (Lanham, MD: University Press of America, 1985), 42–43.

The very language of Romans 1:4 also lends itself to the solidaric concerns of the gospel, in which the sons of God are placed in the Son of God. "The collective implication [sic] of Jesus' resurrection are hinted at in Paul's phrase *ex anastaseos nekron*, literally 'from the resurrection of the dead ones' (1:4). There is a link from here to the 'firstfruits' image in 1 Cor. 15:20."[66] Expressly in this theologically rich prologue to Romans, soteriological solidarity drives the Christological point. The force of Christ's resurrection/adoption is not internal, but external; his resurrection power is not self-serving, but family/sons/church-serving. Biblical Christology functions for soteriology, and this soteriology establishes ecclesiology. In all ways it is filial—adopted sons together in the adopted Son. The Christo-filial is ever ecclesio-familial.[67]

Because of this sons-in-the-Son solidarity, the eschatological value of Christ's own resurrection-adoption defines the *now* as well as the *not yet* for the church. Through union with Christ, resurrection is already complete in the inner man,[68] quickening and enabling the redeemed sons to covenant faithfulness by the leading of the eschatological Spirit of adoption (Rom. 8:14–15). By the life-giving Spirit of adoption (Rom. 8:15; 1 Cor. 15:45), these sons are progressively perfected (Phil. 1:6) until and *unto* their complete renovation at the parousia (Rom. 8:23). "In other words, by the Spirit we are already becoming the man who we are to be through the resurrection."[69] What takes place at the last day completes our spiritual renovation, when our conforming into the image of the first adopted Son reaches its eschatological, transforming culmination (Rom. 8:18–23), completing that which God has already begun (Phil. 1:6). Already defining the believers' current inner-man resurrection state, adoption in its

---

66. N. T. Wright, *The Resurrection of the Son of God*, Christian Origins and the Question of God 3 (Minneapolis: Fortress, 1992), 243n77.

67. "It is precisely now God's intention that there should be many other sons beside the 'first-born,' whose image . . . remains normative for the 'many brethren' [Rom. 8:29] who share his identity and his glory." Paul G. Bretscher, "Exodus 4:22–23 and the Voice from Heaven," *JBL* 87, 3 (1968): 310.

68. "'Our outer man' and 'our inner man' do not belong to a psychological dualism (e.g., as our body and soul respectively) but to the fundamental eschatological dualism of the man that is seen now and the man that will be revealed on the final day." Turner, "Significance," 58. Cf. Vos, "Eschatological Aspect," 115–16.

69. Turner, "Significance of Spirit Endowment for Paul," 58.

dénouement *requires* the resurrection of the redeemed (Rom. 8:23), precisely as it did for the redeeming Son (1:4).

Replicating the final adoption of the resurrected Son, "sonship will be unassailable and complete only in the *apolutrōsis tou sōmatos* [redemption of the body]."[70] But because our adoptive sonship depends exhaustively on his, and because of the Spirit-wrought solidarity enjoyed with him, the future bodily redemption—our resurrection and adoption as sons—attains absolute certainty. The revelation of the sons is not a matter of *if*; it is a matter of *when*. Christ is the firstborn Son only because his resurrection power secures the resurrection of his "many brothers" (Rom. 8:29); Christ can serve as firstfruits of the resurrection harvest only because as life-giving Spirit he infallibly delivers the resurrection of the sons (1 Cor. 15:23; cf. Rom. 8:23).

In this fashion and with no exceptions, throughout the Pauline corpus the *historia salutis* and *ordo salutis* mutually inform. The Christological acts serve the soteriological purpose; the soteriological purpose defines the Christological acts. The *historia salutis* informs and situates the *ordo salutis*. The *ordo salutis* informs and regulates the *historia salutis*. Without an ounce of distinction, that which is *accomplished* is applied, and whatever is *applied* has been accomplished. That is, in order to maintain biblical integrity in soteriology, we must not import foreign conceptions as redemptive benefits; we have no theological (or historical!) basis for asserting benefits of union with Christ that do not draw directly from his own historical experience. For soteriology to maintain its fidelity, the Redeemer must have acquired every benefit enjoyed by the redeemed. What the believer receives explains what the Son has done; what the Son has done determines what the sons receive.

To the point, there is no adoption of believers *in* Christ Jesus without the adoption *of* Christ Jesus. To insist otherwise forces a

---

70. Ernst Käsemann, *Commentary on Romans*, trans. Geoffrey W. Bromiley (Grand Rapids: Eerdmans, 1980), 237. Scott concurs: "The sons enter into the inheritance with the Son at the Parousia, when they undergo physical transformation (conformity to the image of the Son) by the resurrection, since 'flesh and blood cannot inherit the kingdom of God' (1 Cor. 15:50)." He continues to argue that the purpose for the constitutive transformation of the *sons* is "that the Son might be the Firstborn among many brothers." Scott, *Adoption as Sons of God*, 254–55.

soteriological abstraction in which believers would acquire salvation in some way other than by the Son. That Paul does not use the term *adoption* for the resurrection of Christ simply cannot then lead to the simplistic and errant conclusion that Christ was never adopted. To the contrary, Paul's method of theological reciprocity between Christology and soteriology mandates the adoption of the Lord Jesus. Since the believers' resurrection is adoption (Rom. 8:23), so, too, Christ's resurrection was his adoption (1:4).

Of course, the critical distinctions that exist between the One who accomplishes and the ones to whom the benefits apply should not be overlooked. Christ is intrinsically holy; his justification depends on his actual holiness. What is for Christ a matter of analysis is for those united to him a matter of synthesis. Christ attains victory over sin and death's grip according to his untarnished excellence and attained resurrection power. His sanctification/consecration prevails because he personally and permanently conquered sin and death. The holy, resurrected power of Jesus, as covenant Head of his people, extends to those united to him. Believers are infused with holy power by grace because he *by right* possesses and distributes it. Christ attains glorified status as resurrected Son in power; his filial privilege depended on his filial excellence. To those sons united to him, this filial excellence comes by divine grace. In it all, genuine soteric solidarity of the sons in the Son stands inviolably by virtue of the covenant of grace.

In his treatment of Romans 8, James Scott insightfully ties adoption to the Davidic covenant and covenant representation:

> Since the purpose for which the elect will be conformed to the image of the Son at the resurrection is that the Son might be the Firstborn among many brothers (v. 29c), the adoption of the sons (v. 23) is directly related to the adoption of the Firstborn. In fact, it can be said that the sons who share in the messianic inheritance and reign with the Son (vv. 17b, 32b) are adopted on the basis of the same Davidic promise as the Son, because they participate in the sonship of the Son.[71]

71. Scott, *Adoption as Sons of God*, 255.

This important historical and theological connection underscores the essential nature of Christ's personal, redemptive work—that is, his fulfillment of historic, covenantal duties for the acquisition of the historic, covenantal promises. But it also places adoption in a context of prominent covenantal and relational identity, so that those united to Christ enter fully into Spirit-applied covenant blessing and covenant responsibility. According to the terms of covenant, Jesus worked salvation as the Son of God, and by his faithfulness attained adoption in his resurrection. As the adopted Son, he applies his newfound filial identity as covenant Son to those united to him. So writes Calvin:

> He benefits only those whose "Head" he is [Eph. 4:15], for whom he is "the first-born among brethren" [Rom. 8:29], and who, finally, "have put on him" [Gal. 3:27]. This union alone ensures that, as far as we are concerned he has not unprofitably come with the name of Savior. The same purpose is served by that sacred wedlock through which we are made flesh of his flesh and bone of his bone [Eph. 5:30], and thus one with him. But he unites himself to us by the Spirit alone. By the grace and power of the same Spirit we are made his members, to keep us under himself and in turn to possess him.[72]

The seamless solidarity is such that, as the ancient hymn writer put it so simply, "I am his and he is mine."[73] With the scope of such grace, to grasp such sacred mutuality—the Son in the sons, and the sons in the Son—engages "a collage of mutually illuminating images"[74] in biblical revelation. For Paul, the *huiothesian* concept means that the adoptive sonship attained by Christ is the adoptive sonship attained by those who belong to him. While the Redeemer is the source and

72. Calvin, *Institutes*, 3.1.3.
73. George Wade Robinson, "Loved with Everlasting Love" (1890), public domain.
74. J. Todd Billings, *Calvin, Participation, and the Gift: The Activity of Believers in Union with Christ* (Oxford: Oxford University Press, 2007), 51. In Pauline theology, these concepts include the varying forms of "in Christ," fellowship, and engrafting. Billings sees this interface of Pauline participation concepts in Calvin: "Working from Romans 8:12–17, 26–27, Calvin emphasizes that believers are adopted as children of God, given access to the Father through the Spirit, who prays through believers. In Romans 11:17–19, Calvin finds his well-loved image of the engrafting of believers by faith." Ibid., 51.

cause of adoption, the redeemed enjoy the fullness of the adoption attained. Jesus attains the adoption; the believers receive the adopted Jesus. With its source in God the Son *adopted*, the salvation of the redeemed sons involves the full possession of their Savior, all he is and has accomplished as exalted Son. And by divine grace, in terms of the rich essence and exalted benefits of adoption itself, there exists *no* difference between the Son and the sons.

Conclusion

Ever the eternal Son, Christ as man introduced a redemptive-historical character of sonship for him. "The Messianic sonship is simply the eternal sonship carried into a definite historical situation."[75] Though Christ's antecedent, archetypal sonship resides in the pretemporal, ontological substructure of redemptive history, his derivative, incarnate sonship serves as the means of accomplishing redemption. Accordingly, Scripture makes explicit the necessity and assumption of human flesh for him to identify with created and fallen man. As the author of Hebrews sees it (cf. Heb. 2:14–15), Jesus Christ, the Son of God, "shared in our humanity, became a human being like us, in order to defeat the Evil One and redeem us from bondage."[76] Nimbly avoiding any hint of Christ's personal participation in sin, Paul similarly identifies Jesus with fallen humanity (Rom. 8:3; Gal. 4:4; Phil. 2:1–11) as an essential component of his soteric efficacy.

Created for the covenant of works in the garden of Eden, man was formed as the son of God (Gen. 1:26–28; cf. 5:1–4), reflecting the archetypal sonship of the eternal Son of God, and anticipating

75. Vos, *Self-Disclosure*, 190. Cf. Vos, *Pauline Eschatology*, 155n10; George Eldon Ladd, *A Theology of the New Testament*, ed. Donald A. Hagner, rev. ed. (Grand Rapids: Eerdmans, 1993), 458–59, 531–32; C. K. Barrett, *From First Adam to Last: A Study in Pauline Theology* (London: Adam & Charles Black, 1962), 70–71; Sinclair B. Ferguson, "The Reformed Doctrine of Sonship," in *Pulpit and People: Essays in Honour of William Still on His 75th Birthday*, ed. Nigel M. de S. Cameron and Sinclair B. Ferguson (Edinburgh: Rutherford House, 1986), 87; Letham, *The Work of Christ*, 85; John L. White, *The Apostle of God: Paul and the Promise of Abraham* (Peabody, MA: Hendrickson, 1999), xxviii. Contra Shepard, "Pauline Sonship," 102–3.

76. Peterson, *Adopted by God*, 57. Cf. Robert A. Peterson, "Toward a Systematic Theology of Adoption," *Presbyterion* 27, 2 (2001): 122–23.

an adopted, glorified state through his covenantal obedience. Upon his failure to comply with the covenantal demands, Adam forfeited the privileges and intimacy of confirmed familial relationship with his Creator/Father. Through federal participation in Adam's first sin, his progeny entered guilt, took on corruption, and faced humanly irretrievable separation from the Father. The created sons became alienated sons.[77] Adam relinquished Edenic bliss *and* future filial glory. Into this cosmic rebellion and chaos entered divine grace, thoroughly steeped in filial and familial promise: one day a representing Son would come to redeem, restore, and secure eschatological sonship for his elect. Such covenant representation of a son for the sons entirely shapes the Bible's theological structure, as the first and last Adams frame revelatory history.

By the eternally determined plan of the triune God, the last Adam—the eschatological Son of God—represented his people for salvation. More specifically, Christ's *adoption* served as the means to retrieve, restore, and glorify the elect sons of Adam, the *fallen* sons of God. This sovereignly orchestrated plan was accomplished in the messianic Son, Jesus Christ, whose perfect covenantal obedience and comprehensive reception of the Father's unfurled judgment did not merely restore Edenic sonship, but in his death and resurrection attained the covenantal goal of Adamic sonship anticipated in Eden. Countering the failure of the first son, the last Son delivered the divinely appointed filial goal of history, the adoption of the elect from among the sons of Adam. The first words of the opening doxology in Ephesians bear repeating:

> Blessed be the God and Father of our Lord Jesus Christ, who has blessed us in Christ with every spiritual blessing in the heavenly places, even as he chose us in him before the foundation of the world, that we should be holy and blameless before him. In love he predestined us for adoption as sons through Jesus Christ, according to the purpose of his will, to the praise of his glorious grace, with which he has blessed us in the Beloved. (Eph. 1:3–6)

77. See Theron, "Adoption," 10.

According to Paul, saving adoption is "through Jesus Christ" and "in the Beloved." That is, for the elect, the adoption *in* Christ is participation in the historical adoption *of* Christ. While Christ's uniqueness as both eternal Son and *messianic* Son remains inveterately inimitable, in view of his covenant role as last Adam, his adoption *is* the believer's adoption. In the beloved Son in whom the Father is well pleased the redeemed become the sons in whom the Father is well pleased. Such is the potency of divine grace, as it flows interminably from the Redeemer to the redeemed.

The vast scope of adoption's significance in covenant and redemptive history, its Christological solidarity, and its eschatological dynamic require a thorough reconsideration of adoption's place in systematic theology and the *ordo salutis* in particular. In all its filio-Christological and spiritual grandeur, adoption cannot simply be limited to a forensic category, forced into Johannine theology, or stymied by staging it in an imposed *ordo salutis* progression. Instead, it must entail the full scope of Christological/soteriological import invested in it by the apostle Paul, whose gospel truly is the *gospel of adoption*. How exactly to express this gospel of adoption requires full attention to adoption's role in biblical revelation and to the unobstructed interface between adoption accomplished and applied. These matters of biblical and systematic theology for the *ordo salutis* converge in the next and final chapter.

10

THE SONS IN THE SON:
ADOPTION, SYSTEMATIC THEOLOGY,
AND THE *ORDO SALUTIS*

Adoption has suffered too long as a nomad. Though in many circles adoption is still exiled by the perpetuation of subsumption and conflation and by the stubborn edifice of forensic fixation, adoption's cry for a permanent home in the *ordo salutis* has not fallen on deaf ears. "The truth is that . . . much work has yet to be undertaken to ascertain correctly how [adoption] functions in Paul's application of salvation."[1] Building on the exegetical and biblico-theological study just traversed, in this closing chapter I undertake that very question. How does adoption function in the application of salvation? To land finally on a proposed *ordo salutis* warrants a brief survey of Calvin's arguably unrivaled appreciation for adoption, followed by a glance at the terse though illumining formulation of A. A. Hodge. Their constructions demonstrate a historical trajectory with which this *ordo salutis* formulation aligns cleanly.

John Calvin, A. A. Hodge, and Adoption

In contrast to various chronological/logical speculations associated with much historical *ordo salutis* argumentation, John Calvin avoided

1. Tim J. R. Trumper, *When History Teaches Us Nothing: The Recent Reformed Sonship Debate in Context* (Eugene, OR: Wipf and Stock, 2008), 62.

confusion by affirming the *simultaneity* of redemptive appropriation in the gift of the outpoured Spirit of Christ Jesus. "Pre-eminently *the theologian of the Holy Spirit*," as Warfield famously dubbed him in a 1909 lecture,[2] Calvin pairs two distinct but inseparable classes of redemptive benefits in Christ. In his oft-referenced *duplex gratia* ("double grace") formulation, he insists on the centrality of union with Christ by the Holy Spirit.[3] Accomplished by Christ himself, redemption as applied depends on the ministry of his Spirit.

First, in answer to the question of how redemption accomplished gets applied to those whom God has elected, Calvin begins with the Mediator who is the source of redemption: "Christ himself, through the operation and office of his Spirit, claims us for himself by applying to us and making effective in us what he has accomplished on our behalf in his life, death, and resurrection."[4] For Calvin, "the Holy Spirit is the bond by which Christ effectively unites us to himself."[5] Central to Calvin's conception is the procuring, uniting, and indwelling ministry of the Spirit of Christ Jesus with his people. To put it negatively, without the ministry of the Spirit, the work of Christ evaporates into nothingness. In book 3 of his *Institutes*, Calvin lays to rest any notion of the uselessness of the work of Christ by celebrating the concomitant, coalescing, and wholly efficacious work of the Spirit.

2. Benjamin B. Warfield, "Calvin as Theologian" (1909), http://www.the-highway.com /caltheo_Warfield.html (accessed December 14, 2015) (emphasis in original).

3. Debates continue concerning the relationship of union and justification in Calvin. See, on the one hand, Mark A. Garcia, *Life in Christ: Union with Christ and Twofold Grace in Calvin's Theology* (Cumbria, UK: Paternoster: 2008), and, on the other hand, John V. Fesko, *Beyond Calvin: Union with Christ and Justification in Early Modern Reformed Theology (1517–1700)*, Reformed Historical Theology 20 (Göttingen and Bristol, CT: Vandenhoeck & Ruprecht, 2012). It is my strong contention that Garcia faithfully represents Calvin and the historic Reformed approach to insisting on the priority of union with Christ for justification, rather than any alternative. See Garcia's thoughtful and detailed analysis of Fesko's arguments, beginning at http://www.winceandsing.com/blog/2013/12/03/union-with -christ-the-reformed-tradition-and-research-reading-fesko-1/ (accessed December 14, 2015).

4. Cornelis Venema, *Accepted and Renewed in Christ: The Twofold Grace of God and the Interpretation of Calvin's Theology* (Göttingen: Vandenhoeck & Ruprecht, 2007), 84. See John Calvin, *Institutes of the Christian Religion*, ed. John T. McNeill, trans. Ford Lewis Battles, 2 vols. (Philadelphia: Westminster, 1960), 3.1.1–3.

5. Calvin, *Institutes*, 3.1.1.

Second, the union that believers enjoy is not with Christ as the pretemporal, eternal Son, but rather concerns his "human nature."[6] Solidaric union is not of the creature with the Creator, but of the creature with the Creator who became Creature. This is not to say, however, that the redeemed somehow embrace Christ's humanity rather than his divinity (forcing a move from orthodox Christology into Nestorianism). Christ is not the amalgamation of two persons, of which believers are aligned to only one. The Christ whom the redeemed embrace is the eternal Son *made* incarnate; he is one person, who upon taking human flesh became the God-man. Though the hypostasis in itself does not redeem, union with him is made possible by his incarnate identification with the sons of Adam (Rom. 8:3). Union relies on his condescension and accommodation, not the believer's elevation or deification. In short, redemptive union can occur because of his humiliation, his identity with the sons of Adam (and Abraham), his having been made one with mankind in his flesh and blood (Heb. 2:10–18; Rom. 8:3).

Third, believers do not possess redemptive benefits without possessing Christ. Christ "offers himself with all of his benefits to us, and we receive him by faith."[7] We do not receive abstracted benefits or a selected portion of benefits that Christ decides to bestow; in gospel grace, *we receive Christ Jesus himself and all that belongs to him.* That is, by faith, believers receive Christ Jesus the *Mediator* and everything that he has realized, acquired, and attained in his own life and death. Salvation applied comes in this particular Savior who has accomplished the covenantal demands, has borne the covenantal curse, and has secured the covenantal promises. It is the historical Christ and his work that count toward us, and we properly count relation with him *as our own* because of a Spirit-wrought faith union. Put otherwise, believers receive all that Christ has attained and none of what he has not. There is no soteric benefit enjoyed that he did not himself *attain* and does not himself *possess.*[8] The Redeemer claims the redeemed;

---

6. Ibid., 3.11.12.

7. Ibid., 4.17.5.

8. Calvin writes, "With what confidence would anyone address God as 'Father'? Who would break forth into such rashness as to claim for himself the honor of a son of God

the redeemed claim their Redeemer. Soteriology vitally and actually depends on the work of Christ.

Calvin and the Duplex Gratia

The gifts that Christ gives are so tied to his person that attempts to isolate the gifts forces one to divide the Giver in pieces. "Christ cannot be torn into parts, so these two which we perceive in him together and conjointly are inseparable—namely, righteousness and sanctification."[9] Just as Christ does not isolate certain blessings for disposal, we do not pick and choose which benefits we prefer, nor do we rightly esteem one benefit as more honorable than another. To eclipse the legal by exclusively accentuating the transformative fails the Christological weight given to canceling guilt. To eclipse the transformative by exclusively celebrating the forensic eclipses the corresponding Christological weight given to the divine work of renovating hearts. Sinners are objectively guilty; they are also corrupt and impure. Without confusion and without compromise, the gospel of Christ Jesus comprehensively addresses both facets of human sin; the Spirit of Christ meets the sinner with forgiveness *and* purification.

In the *Institutes*, Calvin admits having chosen to address sanctification (regeneration)[10] first, because of the exigencies of his day, in which the Reformation doctrine of justification led to frequent accusations of disregard for personal holiness.[11] In addressing

---

unless we had been adopted as children of grace in Christ? He, while he is the true Son, has of himself given us a brother that what he has of his own by nature may become ours by benefit of adoption . . . ." Ibid., 3.20.36. See also ibid., 3.20.1, 37–40. Unlike the argument in this volume, Calvin distinguishes the redeemed from the Redeemer by adoption. Christ is Son by nature, the believers by adoption. Calvin fails to apply his theology of union consistently here, because of his commendable desire to preserve the filial uniqueness of Christ Jesus. While I, too, affirm the unique filial identity of Christ as eternal and incarnate Son, believers share with Christ in his covenantal and eschatological sonship—adoption.

9. Ibid., 3.11.6.

10. Calvin uses the term *regeneration* essentially as a synonym for *sanctification*, or, as he often prefers to put it, *repentance*. Later dogmatic usage aligns regeneration to the quickening of the dead heart, and more closely with effectual calling. In either usage, *regeneration* concerns the work of the Spirit in the human heart.

11. See Richard B. Gaffin Jr., "Justification and Union with Christ," in *Theological Guide to Calvin's Institutes*, ed. David W. Hall and Peter A. Lillback (Phillipsburg, NJ: P&R Publishing, 2008), 254.

sanctification first, he in no way diminishes the value of justification. In fact, he admits a peculiar importance to justification as the "main hinge on which religion turns,"[12] yet Calvin operated with full theological freedom to accentuate the transformative class of benefits first because both strands of redemptive grace manifest union with the risen Christ. Christ Jesus "has been given to us for sanctification in order that he may bring us, purged of uncleanness and defilement, into obedience to God's righteousness."[13]

Surely he could have begun with justification. The need for faithful articulation of justification stemmed from his contemporary scene as well; the forensic and imputative righteousness suffered great ridicule and resistance by the Roman Catholic Church, which would soon even declare the Reformation doctrine of justification anathema at the Council of Trent. Calvin actually viewed justification *first* in the twofold benefit: "justification or reconciliation is 'the main hinge on which religion turns' (*praecipuus esse sustinendae religionis cardo*)."[14] But that high view of justification did nothing to diminish the high value placed on sanctification and the third use of the law. In fact, in his *Institutes*, Calvin chose to delve into sanctification/regeneration first, deeming it exigent *and* biblically faithful to do so.

What distinguishes the Christian faith from other, impostor faiths is, in great part, its doctrine of pure divine grace in the forgiveness of sin. The doctrine of imputation, the glorious exchange—sinners' sin for Christ's righteousness—set Christianity apart in Calvin's day

12. Calvin, *Institutes*, 3.11.1.

13. Ibid., 3.3.14.

14. Venema, *Accepted and Renewed in Christ*, 96–97. Venema argues for a theological superiority to justification in Calvin, and that sanctification is intentionally and importantly the *second* aspect of the *duplex gratia*. Venema speaks here of free forgiveness as "the source of all God's blessings to us," and insists that the revelation of the God who forgives sin discloses the "true logic of piety." Ibid., 97. Calvin, Venema points out, details multiple causes of justification—efficient cause as the mercy of the Father, material cause as Christ Jesus himself, instrumental cause as faith, and final cause as God's glory and praise of his justice. See ibid., 104n50. See also ibid., 136n9, where Venema distances himself from Mark Garcia and Craig Carpenter, "who overstate the extent to which union with Christ 'coordinates' . . . justification and sanctification." It seems to me that Venema, in his otherwise valuable insight to Calvin's *duplex gratia*, errs in his assessment of the unequal priority of the benefits. Garcia's work on union far better captures the essence of Calvin's functional priority of union and the resultant balance of the forensic and renovative benefits.

and continues to do so in our own. But a high view of justification ought not to cloud our appreciation for the parallel strand in the *duplex gratia*. In fact, it is fair to say that similar to my reasoning in the previous chapter, Calvin argued for the equal theological necessity of both strands, not for contemporary contextual reasons, but for biblical ones—or, more precisely, Christological ones. Justification (the forgiveness of sins) only partially unveils the good news of the gospel, because without the indispensable concomitant of actual holiness, God's redeeming work is incomplete. Actual holiness is as important as declared holiness. In other words, Jesus Christ delivers complete forgiveness of sin *and* complete washing of the sinner; the gospel secures imputation of Christ's righteousness *and* infusion of his righteousness.[15]

Calvin's *duplex gratia* then extols the parallel benefits by extolling the singular Benefactor: "Why, then, are we justified by faith alone? Because by faith we grasp Christ's righteousness, by which alone we are reconciled to God. Yet you could not grasp this without at the same time grasping sanctification also."[16] Calvin brings his argument to a climax: "Although we may distinguish [justification] and [sanctification], Christ contains both of them inseparably in himself. Do you wish, then, to attain righteousness [justification] in Christ? You must first possess Christ; but you cannot possess him without being made partaker in his sanctification, because he cannot be divided into pieces [1 Cor. 1:13]."[17]

Calvin rightly preserves Christological integrity by ensuring comprehensive soteriological efficacy. He also preserves soteriological integrity by his theology of the Holy Spirit. His theological paradigm is bidirectional, moving fluidly between the redeemed and the Redeemer. In solidaric union, the Spirit brings Christology to soteriology. What we learn of Christ as Mediator wholly governs a proper grasp of salvation

---

15. "Repentance not only constantly follows faith, but is also born of faith." Calvin, *Institutes*, 3.3.1.

16. Ibid., 3.16.1. Having quoted 1 Corinthians 1:30, he continues, "Christ justifies no one whom he does not at the same time sanctify. These benefits are joined together by an everlasting and indissoluble bond, so that those whom he illumines by his wisdom, he redeems; those whom he redeems, he justifies; those whom he justifies, he sanctifies." Ibid.; cf. ibid., 3.11.6.

17. Ibid., 3.16.1.

itself, and a biblical grasp of salvation will lead one rightly to the work that Christ accomplished. Accordingly, because of the uniting ministry of the Holy Spirit, Calvin moves seamlessly between Christ's redemptive work accomplished and that redemptive work applied. The Spirit-given application informs and confirms the Christological reality; the Christological acts predicate the Spirit-wrought soteriological application. There is no division in substance between redemption accomplished and redemption applied because there is no breakdown between the purpose and work of the Son and of his Spirit.

Calvin and the Scope of Adoption

By maintaining this theological solidarity between Spirit and Son, union with Christ avoids otherwise certain abstraction and soteric fiction. Yet at this point, we note a seemingly glaring absence in Calvin. In this consideration of the two classes of benefits—forensic and transformative—adoption as a manifestation of this union with Christ appears to lack a theological home. In fact, Calvin views the redemptive grace bestowed on believers as a *duplex gratia*, not a *triplex gratia*. There is no place in these formulations for a third parallel strand of filial grace. Why is this the case?

The answer is as stunning as it is simple. Adoption offers no third strand of redemptive benefit not because of its inferiority, but rather because of its permeating function.[18] For Calvin, the filial character of grace transcends and envelops the dual benefits as it binds these *ordo salutis* strands in a filial casing. In fact, he integrates adoption directly into his discussion of the *duplex gratia*. He links adoption to justification[19] and then, in his refutation of Osiander, affixes adoption to sanctification as well: "Whomever, therefore, God receives into grace, on them he at the same time bestows the spirit of adoption [Rom. 8:15], by whose power he remakes them into his own image."[20] Not surprisingly, then, he insists on the moral remit of adoptive grace:

18. For an excellent study of adoption in Calvin, see Howard Griffith, "'The First Title of the Spirit': Adoption in Calvin's Soteriology," *EvQ* 73, 2 (2001): 135–53.
    19. Calvin, *Institutes*, 3.11.4.
    20. Ibid., 3.11.6.

> For we have been adopted as sons by the Lord with this one
> condition: that our life express Christ, the bond of our adoption.[21]

> By partaking of him, we principally receive a double grace: namely,
> that being reconciled to God through Christ's blamelessness, we may
> have in heaven instead of a Judge a gracious Father; and secondly,
> that sanctified by Christ's spirit we may cultivate blamelessness
> and purity of life.[22]

As Calvin here captures, in Paul's mind, the forensic and the renovative
are distinct, but simultaneous and inseparable because they are tied
to the resurrected Christ to whom believers are bonded by the Spirit
of adoption. "Calvin uses the image of adoption as a way to describe
the double grace of justification *and* sanctification received in union
with Christ."[23]

Such a bond concerns both the *now* and the *not yet*, describing
the present relationship of believers to God, and the believer's
eschatological hope.

> Paul terms "adoption" the revealing of adoption that will be made
> at the resurrection [cf. Rom. 8:18ff.]; and afterwards he interprets
> it as the "redemption of our body" [Rom. 8:23]. But otherwise, just
> as estrangement from God is eternal death, so when man is received
> into grace by God to enjoy communion with him and be made one
> with him, he is transported from death to life—something done
> by the benefit of adoption alone.[24]

21. Ibid., 3.6.3.
22. Ibid., 3.11.1. Cf. Pierre Marcel, "The Relation between Justification and Sanctification in Calvin's Thought," *EvQ* 27, 3 (1955): 134; Ronald S. Wallace, *Calvin's Doctrine
of the Christian Life* (Tyler, TX: Geneva Divinity School, 1982), 25–26; Peter A. Lillback,
The Binding of God: Calvin's Role in the Development of Covenant Theology, ed. Richard A.
Muller, Texts and Studies in Reformation and Post-Reformation Thought (Grand Rapids:
Baker Academic, 2001), 139–41, 296.
23. J. Todd Billings, *Union with Christ: Reframing Theology and Ministry for the Church*
(Grand Rapids: Baker, 2011), 20–21.
24. Calvin, *Institutes*, 3.18.3. Griffith notes that Calvin misunderstands the *already* but
not yet of adoption, as evidenced by the Reformer's struggle with Romans 8:23. See Griffith,
"'The First Title of the Spirit,'" 146.

With the *ordo salutis* in view, Calvin insists on the eschatological continuity of adoption realized and adoption consummated, the filial grace *now* and the filial grace *not yet*. To do so, Calvin somewhat murkily, but no less directly, ties adoption with the glorious transformation in the resurrection. But Calvin's view of adoption is not restricted to these redemptive benefits.

Adoption embraces the covenant of grace, divine election, the *duplex gratia*, and the eschatological *now* and *not yet*. In his "gospel of adoption," Calvin coordinates adoption with divine election.[25] He further draws on adoption in the application of redemption by tying it to God's covenant grace.[26] For Calvin, the relationship with God— both for Old Testament Israel and for the New Testament church—is described in terms of *adoption*. In his reflection on Christ's fulfilling the law, Calvin describes the covenant of God with his people as the "covenant of *free adoption*."[27] This intimate connection—or, better, equipoise—of covenant with adoption discloses its overarching prominence for the Genevan Reformer.[28]

Calvin finds reason to employ adoption frequently in such a far-reaching manner. In fact, noting the necessity of Christ's resurrection for the future hope of the believer, he identifies the gospel itself with adoption: "Accordingly, [if Christ were not raised from the dead] the authority of the gospel would fall not merely in one part but in its entirety, *which is embraced in our adoption* and the effecting of our

25. Ibid., 138–39. See Calvin, *Institutes*, 3.22.4; 3.24.1.

26. See Calvin, *Institutes*, 3.11.6; 3.18.3.

27. Ibid., 2.7.2 (emphasis added). The freedom that adoption provides does not obliterate the need for the law; rather, it indicates a freedom from enslavement and fear: "we should not be borne down by an unending bondage, which would agonize our consciences with the fear of death." Ibid., 2.7.15. Hence, adoption depicts the filial realities enabled by God's covenant with his people—fearless access to God the Father and uncompromised acquisition of the righteousness of Christ. See also ibid., 3.18.2.

28. In his discussion of the relationship between old and new covenants, Calvin equates the covenant of grace with adoption again in ibid., 2.10.1: "Now we can clearly see from what has already been said that men adopted by God into the company of his people since the beginning of the world were covenanted to him by the same law and by the bond of the same doctrine as obtains among us." In 3.2.22, where he also uses the phrase "covenant of adoption," Calvin develops the relationship between adoption and the covenant in terms of the sovereignly dispensed grace of God on Jews and Gentiles. See also ibid., 3.21.5–7; 3.22.1, 4; 3.24.4.

salvation."[29] He similarly defines salvation in terms of God's loving paternity, so that the divine and human relationship is one of "fatherly favor, in which our salvation consists."[30]

More could be said, but this brief survey of adoption's height, breadth, and depth in Calvin evidences his appreciation for the pervasive importance of adoption. Lifting adoption to another stratum in his theological paradigm, Calvin situates both strands of the *duplex gratia* within adoptive grace. By virtue of the Holy Spirit of Christ and the union he secures, believers are justified and sanctified *sons*. As noted in chapter 2, far too few have taken Calvin seriously on this point. The exceptions to the rule refresh, and despite the earlier critique of his *ordo salutis*, A. A. Hodge's insights concerning the grace of adoption are worthy of brief mention before moving to my own explicit *ordo salutis* formulation.

A. A. Hodge: Adoption, the New Creature, the New Relations

Blazing the trail for a proper systematic conception of this familial doctrine, Hodge rebuffed the historical curtailing of adoption. No doubt influenced by Paul's expansive treatment of the term, Calvin's aligning every facet of redemption with adoption, and the Westminsterian affirmation of adoption's uniqueness, Hodge enlarged the scope of the term and sought to retrieve it from a Turretine eclipse.

> Adoption presents the new creature in his new relation; his new relations entered upon with a congenial heart, and his new life developing in a congenial home, and surrounded with those relations which foster its growth and crown it with blessedness. Justification is wholly forensic, and concerns only relations, immunities, and rights. Regeneration and sanctification are wholly spiritual and moral, and concern only inherent qualities and states. *Adoption comprehends the complex condition of the believer as at once the subject of both.*[31]

29. Ibid., 3.15.3 (emphasis added). See also ibid., 2.14.5; 3.1.3; 3.20.36; 3.21.1; 3.21.37–40; 3.22.7; 3.25.3; 4.1.7; 4.16.9.

30. Ibid., 2.2.18. Cf. ibid., 2.12.2; 2.14.6.

31. Archibald Alexander Hodge, *Outlines of Theology* (Grand Rapids: Eerdmans, 1949), 516 (emphasis in original). Expanding this point further, Hodge writes, "'Adoption' and

With lamentably little detail but a no less provocative paradigm, Hodge unites the forensic and the moral/regenerative in adoption. He carefully distinguishes justification from regeneration/sanctification, but then views adoption as a broader concept capable of carrying the legal and the renovative. In this way, he conceives of adoption as bearing the weight of legal change, relational change, and heart change. Hodge provides an insightful development beyond, but compatible with, the Westminster Standards. He corrects Turretin's forensic fixation, and while he brings into focus adoption's resistance to exclusively forensic characterization, he rightly disallows its dismissal merely to the renovative sphere.

To the point concerning the *ordo salutis*, Hodge does not relegate adoption to the same class as justification and sanctification. He commendably pairs the forensic and renovative in the concept of adoption, by placing adoption in a mode that embraces the twofold grace of justification and sanctification. Since its filial reach extends beyond a single benefit, adoption aligns with the vast scope that union itself entails. In this way, he echoes Calvin's integrative and permeating approach to this filial grace. That is, forensic and transformative benefits flow from union with Christ, and adoption in some way ties these benefits to one another. In short, adoption delivers a complex matrix to characterize the full manifestation of union, in which the sons of God are *declared* righteous and *made* righteous. Adoption has a home that is evidently palatial.[32]

Adoption and the *Ordo Salutis*

Building on Calvin and Hodge and the biblico-theological analysis in this work, rectifying the historical conundrum of where and how to place adoption in the *ordo salutis* requires clear expression. Throughout this study, formative questions antecedent to *ordo salutis*

'Sonship' as used in Scripture, express more than a change of relation, and they are more adequately conceived of as expressing a complex view, including the change of nature together with the change of relation, and setting forth the new creature in his new relations." Ibid.

32. Describing adoption as a "metaphor," Billings has recently captured the scope of adoption in similar and commendable fashion: "Paul's overall usage of the adoption metaphor describes both the legal dimension of being transferred into God's family and the transformative dimension of growing in God's family." Billings, *Union with Christ*, 20.

questions have received detailed exploration. In advance of positing a revised *ordo salutis*, I will review some of these central themes in bullet-point fashion, expressing both what adoption is and what it is not.

1. *Adoption* is not simply another term, even if a warmer and gentler one, for the forensic. The concept of adoption is not reducible to the other side of justification, nor does it function merely as a familial appositive for it.

2. Adoption is not a feature of the gospel enjoyed by believers but somehow unattained by Christ Jesus himself. Adoption is a gift given to those united to Christ because of the filial status and glory gained by Christ himself. Adoption belongs to the redeemed because the Redeemer attained it truly and historically, vicariously and efficaciously. Adoption is a matter of fact, not fiction.

3. Adoption does not serve to distinguish the redeemed from the Redeemer, but serves rather to align the believing sons with the covenantally faithful, chosen, and exalted Son. What Christ in his own person attained by right, he distributes to his own family by grace. *Adoption* is a term denoting not inferior filial status, but consummate filial excellence. Importantly, then, adoption does not distinguish the redeemed from the Redeemer, but discloses the filial heights of redemptive grace enjoyed by the redeemed in the Redeemer.

4. The vortex of saving grace is the death/resurrection of Christ. Christ's own resurrection marks the moment of his adoption— when he was vindicated by the Spirit (1 Tim. 3:16) for our justification; became life-giving Spirit for our holiness (Rom. 8:9–11; 1 Cor. 15:45); and received approval, confirmation, and appointment by the Father (Rom. 1:3–4; Heb. 5:5–10; cf. Heb. 1:5–14; 2:5–18). The resurrection marks the cosmic and redemptive event of transition from wrath to grace, and this mark embodies filial grace. *As resurrected Son in his*

gloriously transformed body, Christ attained full glory and was
appointed as King.

5. A Pauline category of substantial importance, *huiothesia*
comprehensively relays God's covenant grace to sinners in
and through the Son of God. Adoption reveals, interprets,
qualifies, conditions, and situates the divine program of
salvation. The triune God—Father, Son, and Holy Spirit—
purposes, accomplishes, and applies gracious adoption to the
elect. The gospel is filial and familial because God is Father and
Jesus Christ is his perfect and perfected Son. The eternal Son
becomes the Son of Mary (Gal. 4:4) so that he might become
the adopted Son of God (Rom. 1:3–4) and the firstfruits of
the adopted sons (Rom. 8–9).

6. Adoption is pretemporal (Eph. 1). The divine intention for
adoption resides in the *pactum salutis*. Adoption commences
in eternity past; it attains in history because it was purposed
before the foundation of the world. Adoption resides in the
center of the divine counsel and divine purpose.

7. Adoption is redemptive-historical (Rom. 9; Gal. 4). Adoption
locates soteriology in the life experience of Christ Jesus.
Adoption attains because Christ Jesus, the beloved Son in
whom the Father is well pleased, becomes the Son of God
in power according to the Spirit of holiness. Holy adoption
comes by and through the covenant fidelity and resurrection
power of Christ Jesus alone. The consummate sonly success
of Jesus Christ grounds the consummate sonly success of the
redeemed in him.

8. Adoption is existential, applicational (Rom. 8). Adoption
turns fallen and condemned sinners to certain hope in their
resurrection from the dead in and through the Son of God. So
vital is the union of the sons in the Son that Pauline theology
operates with a vital bidirectional concept of adoption: the sons

in the Son and the Son for the sons. The adoption/resurrection of the sons gives meaning to the adoption/resurrection of the Son, who is the firstfruits and firstborn from the dead. Adoption of the Son par excellence grounds and qualifies the fact and character of the sons' adoption. Similarly, the meaning of Christ's adoption finds illumination by the manner in which the apostle Paul speaks of the adoption of the redeemed sons.

9. Adoption engages Christology, pneumatology, eschatology, soteriology, and ecclesiology in mutually informing ways. Christ the adopted Son pours out his Spirit in these last days that he inaugurated, redeeming sinners so that they become God's family of sons. Thus, adoption situates the broad theological contours of the gospel in familial categories. The filio-Christology of the New Testament and its concomitant filio-pneumatology establishes its filio-soteriology and filio-ecclesiology. Gospel grace is adoptive grace because God is Father, and Jesus is the adopted Son, who pours out himself by his Spirit of adoption. The bride of Christ is made up of the sons of God.

10. The *ordo salutis* is *salus filiorum* ("salvation of/for the sons") because the *historia salutis* is *salus Filio* ("salvation in/by the Son"). Accordingly, Pauline adoption extends theologically and redemptive-historically, situating and shaping both facets of the *duplex gratia*. Justification and sanctification come in and by the resurrected, adopted Son of God.

As evidenced by post-Reformation dogmatics, most, if not all, of these features concerning adoption have strayed from their biblical home. At times, adoption has been absent altogether. Other times, when looking for a place to plant roots in the *ordo salutis*, adoption has wandered as a hapless nomad. As a means of prescribing a distinctive way forward for adoption in the *ordo salutis*, I offer a brief survey of adoption's transient *ordo salutis* life in the last several hundred years. The proposed *ordo salutis* intends to correct the errors of these formulations, and seeks to honor adoption's full-orbed biblical profile.

The Ordo Salutis: *Forensic Fixation*

The forensically fixated versions of the *ordo salutis* typically situate benefits linearly, launching from justification as the source of the other benefits.[33] Whether or not the models assign chronology or logical primacy (or both) to justification, its precedence and essence wholly govern the *ordo salutis*. Making no place for adoption except perhaps derivatively, the *ordo salutis* in figure 10.1[34] places justification before union with Christ, establishing that union is not the conduit for redemptive blessings but that all blessing, including union, results from justification. Accordingly, as portrayed in this *ordo salutis* model, those committed to the hegemony of justification argue for a salvation that is comprehensively shaped by the forensic (e.g., Pieper, Horton, McCormack).[35] As Michael Horton puts it, "If union with Christ in the covenant of grace is the matrix for Paul's *ordo*, justification remains its basis, even for adoption. We do not move from the topic of justification to other (more interesting) ones."[36]

Fig. 10.1. Forensically Fixated *Ordo Salutis*

The problems with such forensic fixation have received sufficient critique earlier in this volume.

33. This discussion of the *ordo salutis* is necessarily selective. Other features of the *ordo salutis*—regeneration, faith, and glorification, among others—are beyond the scope of explicit concern here. It is not uncommon to generalize other features of the *ordo salutis*, just as expressed in WLC 69's "and whatever else."

34. Figure 10.1 stands for *Ordo Salutis* Diagram 1. The *ordo salutis* diagrams that follow are numbered consecutively for reference purposes.

35. See chapter 8. By contrast, in this volume we have argued for salvation as irreducibly filial.

36. Michael S. Horton, *The Christian Faith: A Systematic Theology for Pilgrims* (Grand Rapids: Zondervan, 2011), 645.

The Ordo Salutis: *Adoption as Justification*

As expressed in Turretin and those in his theological wake (e.g., Dabney, Berkhof), adoption functions as a familial appositive for justification. As such, adoption operates exclusively in the forensic sphere, and merely warms courtroom speech with familial features and relational benefits. Adoption, in this structure, serves as the affable face of the forensic. An improvement on an *ordo salutis* bereft of the familial grace of adoption, the following two diagrams represent similar *ordo salutis* positions: figure 10.2 is more closely aligned with the Lutheran theological tradition and therefore nearly identical to figure 10.1, and figure 10.3 is more greatly influenced by the Reformed primacy of union with Christ. Still maintaining the forensic priority, figure 10.2 coordinates adoption with justification. The logical construction stays in place. Subsumption of adoption under justification allots little space for this familial grace in the *ordo salutis*. Figure 10.3, more closely in line with Calvin (though still short of his concept of adoption itself), still leaves adoption wholly coordinated with, or more commonly subsumed under, justification.

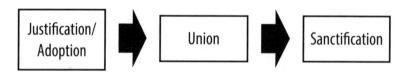

Fig. 10.2. Forensically Fixated *Ordo Salutis* with Adoption as Justification

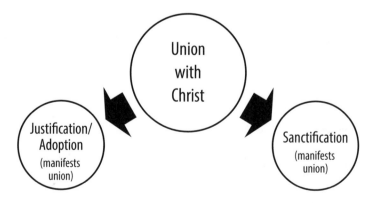

Fig. 10.3. Union with Christ Sourced *Ordo Salutis* with Adoption as Justification

The Ordo Salutis: *Union with Christ, Adoption as Distinctive*

Reformed versions of the *ordo salutis*, such as that of the WCF, often situate adoption after justification in the ordering of the benefits, but because of the functional commitment to union with Christ, this priority of justification does not require or imply causality to justification for adoption or the other benefits. Rather, each of the benefits manifests union with Christ distinctly though indivisibly from the other benefits. At this point, figure 10.4 is conceptually identical to figure 10.3. What distinguishes figure 10.4 from any of the prior models is how it handles adoption. As the answer to WLC 69 reads, "The communion in grace which the members of the invisible church have with Christ, is their partaking of the virtue of his mediation, in their justification, adoption, sanctification, and whatever else, in this life, manifests their union with him." In keeping with this Westminsterian language and the elevation of adoption as a separate locus in the WCF (chapter 12), adoption in figure 10.4 earns distinctive placement, and draws on union with Christ in like fashion to justification and sanctification.[37] By those in this Puritan tradition, adoption finds highest praise in terms of its intimacy and pastoral value. For this reason, in figure 10.4, adoption stands atop the graphic as the crowning benefit of union with Christ.

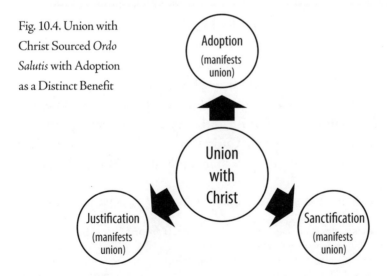

Fig. 10.4. Union with Christ Sourced *Ordo Salutis* with Adoption as a Distinct Benefit

Adoption (manifests union)

Union with Christ

Justification (manifests union)

Sanctification (manifests union)

37. In the WCF, justification (chapter 11) precedes adoption (chapter 12), which in turn precedes sanctification (chapter 13).

This model of the *ordo salutis* properly centers redemption in Christ and its application in Spirit-wrought union. As spokes extending from Christ at the center, redemptive benefits relate to one another by virtue of their shared pneumato-Christological cog, not by some interdependent logic or progression among the benefits themselves. Furthermore, the model's distinguishing of adoption from justification evidences the influence of Calvin and the Westminster Standards. On the other hand, though an improvement on the prior models, its directly parallel placement of adoption aside justification and sanctification (not something, I believe, that reflects Paul or Calvin) still misaligns this filial grace. Adoption indeed manifests union with Christ, yet it functions more comprehensively than this formulation permits. Adoption does not manifest union in the same narrow fashion as justification and sanctification. It operates in a different sphere from the components of the *duplex gratia*.

A Corrected Ordo Salutis: *Adoption in Its Proper Orbit*

John Murray contends, "Union with Christ reaches its zenith in adoption and adoption has its orbit in union with Christ."[38] With comparable fervor, J. I. Packer affirms the elevated place of the doctrine: "adoption is . . . *the highest privilege that the gospel offers*: higher even than justification."[39] For Murray and Packer, the heights of union reside in theological adoption.[40] However true this may be, to grasp the splendor of adoption, one must consider its Christological elevation to truly appreciate its soteriological vistas. Adoption's heights in the *ordo salutis* grow out of its heavenly reaches in the *historia salutis*, and precisely how adoption "has its orbit in union with Christ" is the present and final concern.

There is nothing given us in Christ that is not tied to his resurrection/ adoption event and the Father's cosmic approval in it. Sinclair Ferguson

---

38. John Murray, *Redemption Accomplished and Applied* (Grand Rapids: Eerdmans, 1955), 170.

39. J. I. Packer, *Knowing God*, 20th anniversary ed. (Downers Grove, IL: InterVarsity Press, 1993), 206 (emphasis in original).

40. Murray's theological intuition concerning adoption seems to track in some ways with the Pauline *huiothesian* paradigm, but he departs from Calvin's integrative approach, restricting adoption to the forensic and its relational implications. See John Murray, *The Collected Writings of John Murray*, 4 vols. (Edinburgh: Banner of Truth, 1976–82), 2:223–34.

rightly observes the concatenation of all the soteric features in Christ at his resurrection: "In Christ the forensic and the transformative are one (Rom. 6:7). More, justification, sanctification and glorification are one; declaratory, transformatory and consummatory coalesce in this resurrection."[41] The blessedness of this coalescence secures the comprehensive, once-for-all efficacy of Christ's forensic and transforming work. Since Paul treats adoption and resurrection as not only coterminous but also mutually explanatory and interdependent (Rom. 1:3–4; 8:15, 23), and since he envisions adoption as the ultimate purpose of Christ's work (Gal. 4:5; Eph. 1:5), no dimension of redemption accomplished comes to fruition without Christ's own adoption. Adoption marks the culminating event in the work of Jesus Christ, and therefore it entails the whole of Jesus's soteriological usefulness. If the "declaratory, transformatory and consummatory coalesce in this resurrection," by virtue of the mutuality of resurrection and adoption, these same features necessarily coalesce in his adoption. Christ's adoption marks the full success of the Son in his covenant obligations and situates the comprehensive soteric value that surges from him as the resurrected Son.

Implications for the *ordo salutis* are pervasive. Solidarity with the Son is solidarity with him resurrected, adopted. Just as Christ's resurrection is vindication, consecration, transformation, and glorification, so, too, the believer's union with the Son of God in all his eschatological glory necessarily entails the whole range of redemptive graces. What is true for the Son is true for the sons. What is "one" for Christ is *once for all* for the sons united to him. By the Spirit of adoption, believers enjoy vindication/justification. By the Spirit of adoption, believers enjoy consecration/sanctification unto full conformity with the Son of God in their own bodily resurrection (Rom. 8:23, 29), of which Jesus is firstfruits. The eschatological *now* coheres with the eschatological *not yet*, so that the believer currently enjoys the full measure of the resurrected Son in his inner man, and anticipates the complete realization of the Son's benefits upon bodily resurrection (Rom. 8:23; Phil. 3:20–21). In fact, at the consummation, what coalesced for Christ at his resurrection

41. Sinclair B. Ferguson, *The Holy Spirit*, Contours of Christian Theology (Downers Grove, IL: InterVarsity Press, 1996), 250.

will coalesce in the believers' experience as well. What is declared for the sons (justification) will be fully realized for the sons in their fully sanctifying glorious transformation. The open verdict of justification will align with the actual transformed condition of the sons; they will be holy as their heavenly Father and Elder Brother are holy. Declared righteousness and actual righteousness will finally cohere on the last day.

To put it slightly differently, Paul qualifies his entire soteriological paradigm by the filial because he qualifies Christology by the filial. When Christ rises from the dead, he becomes the Son of God in power. In that resurrection, when the Son of God becomes life-giving Spirit (1 Cor. 15:45), he becomes the Spirit of adoption. The Spirit of adoption gives and sustains[42] resurrection life in all its filial glory for the redeemed; the Son in his own resurrection-adoption secures the forensic (now invisible; on the last day, open and public justification) and the renovative (now definitive and progressive sanctification; on the last day, comprehensive bodily transformation/glorification). By the *huiothesian* concept, Paul tethers Christology, pneumatology, and eschatology for his soteriology. Christ the adopted Son becomes Christ the life-giving Spirit of adoption so that the redeemed might become the justified sons, sanctified sons, and glorified sons. The gospel is filiocentric; the gospel *is* adoption.

Accordingly, with a view to *ordo salutis* construction, adoption elucidates the nature of union with Christ because such union is *with the Son of God who himself qualified as Redeemer when he was resurrected and adopted*. Such defining and framing eminence for adoption fields the balance and interface of justification and sanctification, even as it preserves their distinctiveness yet inseparability. When adoption functions according to its given theological scope, it militates against the polarizing errors of forensic fixation on the one hand and Roman Catholic and FV/NPP benefit conflation on the other. Justification maintains its forensic purity, and sanctification retains its unique transformative force. Neither drives or eclipses the other; neither distorts

---

42. "The Spirit is not only the one who teaches us to stand in this childlike relationship to God and to pronounce steadfastly the name Father in spite of all that still raises itself against this relationship; he is also the one who *maintains this living communion*." Herman N. Ridderbos, *Paul: An Outline of His Theology*, trans. John Richard DeWitt (Grand Rapids: Eerdmans, 1975), 202.

the other by infringing on its distinctive nature. Justification remains forensic; sanctification retains its renovative efficacy; both attain by the eschatologically appointed Son. Thus, by seeing the *duplex gratia* as an expression of the adoption of the Son, we observe that these dual graces of justification and sanctification turn from abstract concepts to vital, filial realities. This in-Son orientation circumvents competing theological emphases that give undue priority to justification or sanctification, and instead centers redemptive grace where it belongs—on personal union with the Son of God whose victory over sin's guilt and victory over sin's power bear equal weight as the result of his filial, covenantal success. Unsullied justification and pure sanctification maintain only when the personal, filial, and covenantal force of adoption frames the redemptive benefits. Justification does not produce or overshadow sanctification, and sanctification does not produce or overshadow justification. Christ, as adopted Son of God, tenders both.

Accordingly, in the *ordo salutis* adoption embraces the whole of what union with Christ manifests. Adoption clarifies and qualifies all the other benefits, tying them to Christ's newly attained sonship at his resurrection, and framing all union according to its eschatological and filial character. In addition, justification and sanctification, while irreversibly tethered to each other, manifest distinct aspects of the filio-Christology and filio-pneumatology that govern Pauline filio-soteriology. Adoption, as a more comprehensive concept, manifests the covenant-filial character of all soteriology. Adoption is *the* benefit of union with Christ; justification and sanctification are core subsets of that benefit. Soteric benefits are not logically or chronologically sequential; rather, they are eschatologically vital—the already-justified and progressively sanctified sons will be the openly justified and wholly sanctified sons on the last day. The work that God began in the sons he will complete on the last day (Phil. 1:6) when he will fully conform the sons into the image of the Son par excellence (Rom. 8:29–30).[43]

43. In Burke's assessment of the relationship between *huiothesia* and *pneuma* in Romans 8:15, he concludes, "Adoption and the Spirit are mutually dependent and intertwined aspects of the Christian's experience of salvation rather than separate developments in the Christian's life." He summarizes, "Just as it is impossible to think of the Spirit divorced from the Sonship of Christ so it is equally inconceivable to think of the Spirit apart from

Thus, the corrected *ordo salutis* must reflect how union with the adopted Son makes all those united to this Son adopted. Solidaric union is sonly union. In the believers' adoption comes the *duplex gratia*—justification and sanctification—because the redeeming Son has secured these in his own person and faithfully delivers both dimensions of soteric grace.[44] That is, the manifestation of union ought not to suffer abstraction, extracting it from the filial/personal context from which it flows. Manifestation of union with Christ the Son of God is irreducibly filial because the resurrected Redeemer *is* the Son of God adopted. Thus, justification manifests union because the adopted sons manifest the cosmically vindicated and justified Son of God. Sanctification manifests union because the adopted sons manifest the cosmically consecrated and victorious Son of God. The believers' adoption manifests their Redeemer's adoption. Union secures justified

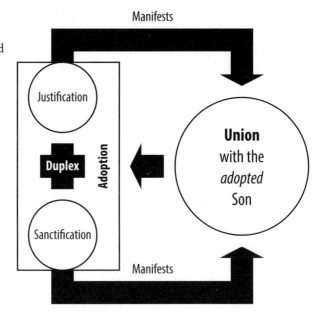

Fig. 10.5. Union with Christ Sourced *Ordo Salutis* with Adoption as the Inclusive Benefit

---

the Christian's adoption as son." Trevor J. Burke, "Adoption and the Spirit in Romans 8," *EvQ* 70, 4 (1998): 316–18. Cf. Allen Mawhinney, "*Yiothesia* in the Pauline Epistles: Its Background, Use, and Implications" (Ph.D. diss., Baylor University, Waco, TX, 1982), 158–61.

44. The Westminster Standards do not expressly require the figure 10.4 version of the *ordo salutis*, though many (most?) would assume this model. The figure 10.5 proposal also operates consistently with the Westminster Standards, since the placement of adoption in chapter 12 of the WCF does not limit the doctrine to a category *parallel* to justification and sanctification.

and sanctified sons who are, in the Son, justified and sanctified. From the first moment of faith unto its consummation on the last day, adoption of the sons manifests the adoption of the Son.

Rather than imposing extrabiblical (and ostensibly unbiblical) logical or chronological relationships for the redemptive benefits, we must rest in the Pauline *en Christō* ("in Christ") formulas[45] and locate union in the exalted Son. Contrary to common *ordo salutis* distortions that turn union with Christ into a series of events, the bounty of redemptive graces comes punctiliarly when, in the moment of saving faith, the redeemed receive the Son of God by the ministry of the Spirit of adoption. That faith union for the sons in the Son shapes the whole scope of soteriological graces, and rightly situates salvation in the Son of God's attained, adoptive sonship. The consistent stress in the New Testament is the once-for-allness of this resurrection event, and associated with it is the once-for-allness of the Spirit's work in bonding the redeemed to the resurrected and resurrecting Savior. Manifestation of this eschatologically pregnant and pastorally rich union appears in the lives of the sons *with* the sons, because of their shared new life in the Son par excellence.

A number of the Puritans and the Westminster divines appreciated the vast pastoral riches of adoption.[46] WCF 12 itself profiles several of these pastoral and existential benefits tersely yet richly. In moving to the conclusion of this work, it is worth restating this chapter in full:

> All those that are justified, God vouchsafeth, in and for his only Son Jesus Christ, to make partakers of the grace of adoption; by which they are taken into the number, and enjoy the liberties and privileges of the children of God; have his name put upon them, receive the spirit of adoption; have access to the throne of grace with boldness; are enabled to cry, Abba, Father; are pitied, protected,

---

45. This "idiomatic expression" in Paul represents a theological construction that extends beyond the formula itself to associated expressions. Constantine R. Campbell, *Paul and Union with Christ: An Exegetical and Theological Study* (Grand Rapids: Zondervan, 2012), 25–27. Cf. ibid., 369–72.

46. See Joel R. Beeke, *Heirs with Christ: The Puritans on Adoption* (Grand Rapids: Reformation Heritage Books, 2008).

provided for, and chastened by him as by a father; yet never cast off, but sealed to the day of redemption, and inherit the promises, as heirs of everlasting salvation.

The church worldwide would with great benefit soak in these pastoral treasures as catalogued in this confessional statement. What makes adoption the supreme benefit, however, is not first its filial assurances but its Christological substance. Such pastoral benefits are actually embraced only when adoption is vitally "in and for his only Son Jesus Christ."

An umbrella benefit, adoption locates the manifestation of union in its proper personal—Christ-centered—orbit; in this way, manifestation of union preserves its filial integrity. Justification, sanctification, and other redemptive benefits do not manifest union independently or abstractly (cf. WLC 69); rather, they do so by the practice of filial grace in the rich fellowship of spiritual familial life (2 Cor. 13:14). Such familial manifestations in the visible church are no more fictional than the historical Son-secured soteriological realities themselves. Adoption draws the soteriological into the ecclesiological; the visible church is where the manifestation of union lives and breathes. Legally sons of God by divine grace, the redeemed possess the Spirit of adoption who compels and enables their hearts to relish and pursue obedience (Rom. 8:9–11), to serve one another with spiritual gifts (1 Cor. 12), to forgive one another as forgiven sons (Eph. 4:32), and to love one another in the humility of their Elder Brother (Phil. 2:1–11). It is no wonder that the apostle Paul speaks so consistently of the body of Christ in familial language: the brothers are to love, serve, and bless one another. It is no wonder that Paul unrelentingly calls the church to gospel grace, truth, peace, love, forgiveness, joy, and obedience. Christ's adoptive grace beckons and enables the church to practice—to manifest!—adoptive graces. The in-Son union secures the sons-with-sons communion; the filial indicative warrants the familial imperatives. This rich filio-Christology and filio-soteriology supply unending pastoral treasures that the WCF mines tersely though ever so warmly.

With this Son-ward and eschatological Spirit orientation, adoption ceases its nomadic existence and finds its resting place in the *ordo salutis*. To summarize, adoption marks the culmination of Christ's covenantal obedience, his appointment as reigning Son, his unprecedented resurrection power, his cosmic victory over sin and death, and his entrance into the full blessing of the Father whose pleasure resides thoroughly (redemptively and eschatologically) on him. Christ's adoption entails his cancellation of the debt of sin and his conquering of the power of sin. He enters the glorified state of sonship in his resurrected body, a sine qua non of adoption itself. Each of these consummating, cosmic, and redemptively efficacious features sets him apart as last Adam, the Mediator of the covenant of grace, and the redeeming Son. In these comprehensive *Christological* ways, adoption attains its unique and exalted station for those in union with him. Returning to Packer's and Murray's pregnant statements, adoption surely is the highest privilege of redemption, but not merely because of its warm, familial tone. It marks the supreme benefit to the sons because it marks their comprehensive reception of the comprehensive attainment of their Elder Brother, who is *himself*, as adopted Son of God, the very "life" of the redeemed sons (Col. 3:4).

Conclusion: Adoption in Christ—the Sons in the Son

John Calvin, in his last will and testament, asserts, "I have no other defence or refuge for salvation than His gratuitous adoption, on which my salvation depends."[47] Surely there are many ways that Calvin could have expressed his deathbed gospel convictions. With summary reflection and filial warmth, he chooses to affirm that his salvation depends on God's *gratuitous adoption*. The gospel, acquired for him in the atoning "merits of [Christ's] death and passion,"[48] propelled Calvin toward confident expectation of his imminent welcome before *his* heavenly Father: "I trust to no other security for my salvation than this, and this only, viz. that as God is the Father of mercy, He will show Himself a Father to me, who acknowledge myself to be a miserable sinner."[49] The Son of God's

47. Recorded in Philip Schaff, *Modern Christianity: The Swiss Reformation*, History of the Christian Church 8 (Grand Rapids: Eerdmans, 1910), 829.

48. Ibid.

49. Ibid.

merciful work overwhelmed Calvin's desperate plight and enabled him to "stand at the judgment-seat."[50] For Calvin, the entire scope of the gospel derived its splendor and hope from adoptive grace bestowed on him in Christ Jesus, which granted him unfettered fellowship with the merciful Father. As we have seen, adoptive grace took such primacy for Calvin because it did so for the apostle Paul.

Pauline theological and hermeneutical logic operates with a dynamic convergence of Christology, pneumatology, and soteriology: the historico-theological character of scriptural revelation (*historia salutis*) structures the application of redemptive grace (*ordo salutis*); the biblico-theological—that is, Christ-centered—thrust of Scripture wholly serves gospel appropriation. Such biblico-theological orientation unveils the filio-Christology, the filio-pneumatology, and the filio-soteriology at work in divine grace. These mutually interpreting theological categories vividly profile adoption and its integrative role in the application of redemption. Biblical grace is filial grace.

Relying on the Pauline treatment of adoption as traversed in the previous pages and tapping in to Calvin's permeating treatment of this filial grace, we have found that placing adoption properly within the *ordo salutis* has required re-recalibration. This re-placement has involved precise tuning of the *ordo salutis* to the *historia salutis*, where Paul's sons-in-the-Son paradigm flourishes exclusively in and through the last Adam, the firstborn, the firstfruits of the Spirit, the adopted Son of God. By the outpouring of Christ's Spirit of adoption, the sons possess the Son *because*, by his efficacious work, the Son possesses the sons. The Son of God does not dispense selected benefits to the redeemed sequentially or atomistically, as if he could divide himself and his work in bits; he gives himself—adopted and resurrected—to them once for all. Correspondingly, the filial grace of adoption envelopes the redeemed precisely because this adopted Son—vindicated, consecrated, and glorified—embraces them in his unrelenting grace. When Christ is given in redemption, *he* comes to the sons instantaneously, completely, and permanently. Spirit-wrought faith tethers the sons to the Son irreversibly. The golden chain of

50. Ibid.

salvation then comes to the redeemed not as consecutive links, but at once as a gloriously completed crown of divine filial grace. The Father crowns the redeemed sons with adoption because he has crowned his own redeeming, resurrected Son with adoption.

Though the theological inclination to preserve the uniqueness of Christ is commendable, the Melanchthonian-styled insistence (see Introduction) that adoption differentiates the redeemed from the Redeemer misses the very point of this filial grace.[51] In fact, adoption is not intended to distinguish us from the exalted Son of God, but to express the nature of our privileged solidarity with him. Preserving Christ's eternal, ontological sonship does not proscribe filial/covenantal progress in the Son of God, nor does it drive a filial wedge between the redeemed sons and the redeeming Son. To the contrary, grounded in Trinitarian ontology and covenantal decree (*pactum salutis*), redemptive grace depends on divine condescension in the incarnate Son and his concomitant filial development (humiliation) for securing covenant promises at his resurrection (exaltation). Believers are adopted sons of God precisely because Jesus Christ, the one Mediator between God and man, was first adopted himself. He is the firstborn among many brothers, the firstborn from the dead (1 Cor. 15:23; Col. 1:18; cf. Rev. 1:5a).

Moreover, Pauline theology repudiates any theological gymnastics that divorce Christology and soteriology or that illegitimately rend the blessings enjoyed by the sons of God from the realities procured by the Son of God. Paul unwaveringly weds redemptive benefits to the historical work, progress, and personal attainment of the Son of God par excellence. Not unlike other features of biblical salvation, adoption is not granted to the redeemed without its first being secured by the Redeemer. Such an assertion does not threaten orthodox Christology, but affirms and safeguards it, even as it preserves the vital theological interface between the Son of God, the Spirit of adoption, and the redeemed sons.

Much more can and should be said on other Pauline themes that adoption expansively informs. This book's analysis does not sufficiently

---

51. Philipp Melanchthon, *Commentary on Romans*, trans. Fred Kramer (St. Louis: Concordia, 1992), 174–75.

address adoption's relation to matters such as the *imago Dei* ("image of God"), eschatological glory, the kingdom of God and the reigning of the sons with the Son, sacramental theology (covenant baptism and the Lord's Table), ecclesiology (the rich filial implications of union for familial communion), and gospel ethics.[52] My goal here has been more focused and modest, but it is also more foundational. With a conscious dedication to a biblically grounded mutuality of biblical and systematic theology, this study addresses *huiothesia*, exploring its paradigmatic function in Paul and following his filial/redemptive contemplations on the basis of the filial/redemptive acts of God in the Lord Jesus Christ, the Son of God. Therefore, considering the vast theological notions embraced by *huiothesia*, I have sought to define the *soteriological* conclusions to which the apostle Paul guides us in his Christ-centered and eschatologically ripe conception of redemptive grace.

To summarize, the believer's redemptive benefits draw on the actual biography of Jesus Christ. The Spirit applies exactly what Jesus Christ accomplished, earned, and attained. Failure to preserve the vital connection between Christ's experience and the believers' redemptive benefits in him elicits theological abstraction, diluting Christ's work and fictionalizing redemption applied. Accordingly, there is justification for the sons only because of the Son's own vindication. There is sanctification of the sons only because of the Son's own victory over the stranglehold of sin. There is glorification of the sons only because of the Son's own resurrection. Appreciating these features of redemptive grace in their sweet and proper coalescence, we see that there is adoption of the sons only because of the Son of God's own adoption. The redeemed are sons—justified and sanctified, because we are, by the life-giving Spirit of adoption, gloriously and permanently adopted sons in the Son.

Soli Patri Gloria. Soli Filio Gloria. Soli Spiritui Gloria.

---

52. Todd Billings offers some very insightful and pastorally useful theological expositions about adoption, prayer, and sacraments. J. Todd Billings, *Calvin, Participation, and the Gift: The Activity of Believers in Union with Christ* (Oxford: Oxford University Press, 2007), 105–43.

BIBLIOGRAPHY

Allen, R. Michael. *Justification and the Gospel: Understanding the Contexts and Controversies*. Grand Rapids: Baker Academic, 2013.

Allison, Gregg R. *Historical Theology: An Introduction to Christian Doctrine: A Companion to Wayne Grudem's Systematic Theology*. Grand Rapids: Zondervan, 2011.

Ames, William. *The Marrow of Theology*. Edited and translated by John D. Eusden. 3rd ed. Durham, NC: Labyrinth, 1968.

Anselm. "Why God Became Man." In *A Scholastic Miscellany: Anselm to Ockham*, edited and translated by Eugene R. Fairweather, 100–183. Library of Christian Classics 10. Philadelphia: Westminster, 1956.

The Ante-Nicene Fathers. Edited by Alexander Roberts and James Donaldson. 10 vols. 1885–87. Reprint, Peabody, MA: Hendrickson, 1994.

Arnold, Clinton E. *Ephesians*. ZEC 10. Grand Rapids: Zondervan, 2010.

———. "Returning to the Domain of the Powers: Stoicheia as Evil Spirits in Galatians 4:3, 9." *Novum Testamentum* 38, 1 (1996): 55–76.

Bahnsen, Greg L. *Van Til's Apologetic: Readings and Analysis*. Phillipsburg, NJ: P&R Publishing, 1998.

Baird, Samuel J. *The Elohim Revealed in the Creation and Redemption of Man*. Philadelphia: Parry & McMillan, 1860.

Barker, William S. *Puritan Profiles: 54 Influential Puritans at the Time When the Westminster Confession of Faith Was Written*. Fearn, Ross-shire: Mentor, 1996.

Barr, James. "'Abba, Father' and the Familiarity of Jesus' Speech." *Theology* 91 (1988): 173–79.

———. *The Semantics of Biblical Language*. Oxford: Oxford University Press, 1961.

Barrett, C. K. *A Commentary on the Epistle to the Romans*. Edited by Henry Chadwick. Harper's New Testament Commentaries. New York: Harper & Row, 1957.

———. "The Eschatology of the Epistle to the Hebrews." In *The Background of the New Testament and Its Eschatology*, edited by W. D. Davies and David Daube, 363–93. Cambridge: Cambridge University Press, 1956.

———. *From First Adam to Last: A Study in Pauline Theology*. London: Adam & Charles Black, 1962.

Barth, Karl. *The Doctrine of Creation*. Edited by G. W. Bromiley and T. F. Torrance. Translated by J. W. Edwards, O. Bussey, and Harold Knight. Vol. 3:1 of *Church Dogmatics*. Edinburgh: T&T Clark, 1958.

———. *The Doctrine of Reconciliation*. Edited by G. W. Bromiley and T. F. Torrance. Translated by G. W. Bromiley. Vol. 4:2 of *Church Dogmatics*. Edinburgh: T&T Clark, 1958.

Bauckham, Richard. *Jesus and the God of Israel: God Crucified and Other Studies on the New Testament's Christology of Divine Identity*. Grand Rapids: Eerdmans, 2008.

Bauer, Walter, William F. Arndt, F. Wilbur Gingrich, and Frederick W. Danker. *Greek-English Lexicon of the New Testament and Other Early Christian Literature*. 2nd ed. Chicago: University of Chicago Press, 1979.

Bavinck, Herman. *In the Beginning: Foundations of Creation Theology*. Edited by John Bolt. Translated by John Vriend. Grand Rapids: Baker, 1999.

———. *The Last Things: Hope for This World and the Next*. Edited by John Bolt. Translated by John Vriend. Grand Rapids: Baker, 1996.

———. *Our Reasonable Faith: A Survey of Christian Doctrine*. Translated by Henry Zylstra. Grand Rapids: Eerdmans, 1956.

———. *Reformed Dogmatics: Sin and Salvation in Christ*. Edited by John Bolt. Translated by John Vriend. 4 vols. Grand Rapids: Baker, 2006.

Bavinck, J. H. *Introduction to the Science of Missions*. Translated by David H. Freeman. Philadelphia: Presbyterian and Reformed, 1960.

Baxter, Richard. *An End of Doctrinal Controversies Which Have Lately Troubled the Churches by Reconciling Explication, without Much Disputing*. London: Printed for John Salusbury at the Rising Sun, 1691.

Beach, J. Mark. "The Doctrine of the *Pactum Salutis* in the Covenant Theology of Herman Witsius." *Mid-America Journal of Theology* 13 (2002): 101–42.

Beale, G. K. *A New Testament Biblical Theology: The Unfolding of the Old Testament in the New*. Grand Rapids: Baker, 2011.

————. "The Use of Hosea 11:1 in Matthew 2:15: One More Time," *JETS* 55, 4 (2012): 697–716.

Beale, G. K., and D. A. Carson. *Commentary on the New Testament Use of the Old Testament*. Grand Rapids: Baker Academic, 2007.

Beardslee, John W., III. *Reformed Dogmatics*. Grand Rapids: Baker, 1977.

Beasley-Murray, George R. "Biblical Eschatology: Apocalyptic Literature and the Book of Revelation." *EvQ* 20, 4 (1948): 272–82.

————. "Biblical Eschatology: The Interpretation of Prophecy." *EvQ* 20, 3 (1948): 221–29.

————. "A Century of Eschatological Discussion." *Expository Times* 64 (1953): 312–16.

————. "The Eschatology of the Fourth Gospel." *EvQ* 18, 2 (1946): 97–108.

————. *John*. 2nd ed. WBC 36. Nashville, TN: Thomas Nelson, 1999.

————. "John 3:3, 5: Baptism, Spirit and the Kingdom." *Expository Times* 97 (1985–86): 167–70.

————. "New Testament Apocalyptic—A Christological Eschatology." *RExp* 72 (1975): 317–30.

Beeke, Joel R. *Heirs with Christ: The Puritans on Adoption*. Grand Rapids: Reformation Heritage Books, 2008.

————. "Transforming Power and Comfort: The Puritans on Adoption." In *The Faith Once Delivered: Essays in Honor of Dr. Wayne R. Spear*, edited by Anthony T. Selvaggio, 63–105. Phillipsburg, NJ: P&R Publishing, 2007.

Beeke, Joel R., and Mark Jones. *A Puritan Theology: Doctrine for Life*. Grand Rapids: Reformation Heritage Books, 2012.

Beilby, James K., and Paul R. Eddy, eds. *Justification: Five Views*. Spectrum Multiview Books. Downers Grove, IL: IVP Academic, 2011.

Belleville, Linda. "'Born of Water and Spirit': John 3:5." *Trinity Journal* 1, 2 (1980): 125–41.

Benoit, André. *Saint Irénée: Introduction à l'Étude de Sa Théologie*. Edited by R. Mehl. Études d'Histoire et de Philosophie Religieuses 52. Paris: Presses Universitaires de France, 1960.

Benoit, Pierre. *Jesus and the Gospel*. Translated by Benet Weatherhead. New York: Seabury, 1974.

Berkhof, Hendrikus. *Christian Faith: An Introduction to the Study of the Faith*. Translated by Sierd Woudstra. Rev. ed. Grand Rapids: Eerdmans, 1986.

Berkhof, Louis. *Systematic Theology*. 4th ed. Grand Rapids: Eerdmans, 1949.

Berkouwer, G. C. *Faith and Justification*. Translated by Lewis B. Smedes. Vol. 3 of *Studies in Dogmatics*. Grand Rapids: Eerdmans, 1954.

———. *Man: The Image of God*. Translated by Dirk W. Jellema. Vol. 8 of *Studies in Dogmatics*. Grand Rapids: Eerdmans, 1962.

Best, Ernest. *A Critical and Exegetical Commentary on Ephesians*. ICC. Edinburgh: T&T Clark, 1998.

Betz, Hans Dieter. *Galatians: A Commentary on Paul's Letter to the Churches in Galatia*. Hermeneia—A Critical and Historical Commentary on the Bible. Philadelphia: Fortress, 1979.

Billings, J. Todd. *Calvin, Participation, and the Gift: The Activity of Believers in Union with Christ*. Oxford: Oxford University Press, 2007.

———. *Union with Christ: Reframing Theology and Ministry for the Church*. Grand Rapids: Baker, 2011.

Blekkink, Evert J. *The Fatherhood of God Considered from Six Inter-Related Standpoints*. Grand Rapids: Eerdmans, 1942.

Blinzler, Josef. "Lexikalisches zu dem Terminus *Ta Stoicheia Tou Kosmou*." In *Studiorum Paulinorum Congressus Internationalis Catholicus 1961*, 429–43. Vol. 2 of Analecta Biblica 17–18. Rome: Pontifical Biblical Institute, 1963.

Block, Daniel. "The Prophet of the Spirit: The Use of *RWH* in the Book of Ezekiel." *JETS* 32, 1 (1989): 27–49.

Blum, Edwin A. "The Apostles' View of Scripture." In *Inerrancy*, edited by Norman L. Geisler, 37–53. Grand Rapids: Zondervan, 1980.

Boettner, Loraine. *Studies in Theology*. 8th ed. Philadelphia: Presbyterian and Reformed, 1967.

Boice, James Montgomery. *Foundations of the Christian Faith: A Comprehensive & Readable Theology*. Rev. ed. Downers Grove, IL: InterVarsity Press, 1986.

———. *The Reign of Grace—Romans 5:1–8:39*. Grand Rapids: Baker, 1992.

Boston, Thomas. *The Complete Works of the Late Rev. Thomas Boston*. Edited by Samuel M'Millan. 12 vols. London: William Tegg & Co., 1853. Reprint, Wheaton, IL: Richard Owen Roberts, 1980.

————. *Human Nature in Its Fourfold State of Primitive Integrity, Entire Depravity, Begun Recovery, and Consummate Happiness or Misery*. Edinburgh: Banner of Truth, 1964.

Brakel, Wilhelmus à. *The Christian's Reasonable Service*. Edited by Joel R. Beeke. Translated by Bartel Elshout. Vol. 2. Grand Rapids: Reformation Heritage Books, 1993.

Bretscher, Paul G. "Exodus 4:22–23 and the Voice from Heaven." *JBL* 87, 3 (1968): 301–11.

Briggs, Charles A. *Theological Symbolics*. Edited by Charles A. Briggs and Stewart D. F. Salmond. International Theological Library. New York: Charles Scribner's Sons, 1914.

Brown, Colin, ed. *New International Dictionary of New Testament Theology*. 4 vols. Grand Rapids: Zondervan, 1975–85.

Brown, Raymond E. *The Gospel according to John (i–xii)*. Anchor Bible 29. Garden City, NY: Doubleday, 1966.

Bruce, F. F. *The Book of the Acts*. Rev. ed. NICNT. Grand Rapids: Eerdmans, 1988.

————. *The Epistles to the Colossians, to Philemon, and to the Ephesians*. NICNT. Grand Rapids: Eerdmans, 1984.

————. *The Epistle to the Galatians: A Commentary on the Greek Text*. NIGTC. Grand Rapids: Eerdmans, 1982.

————. *The Epistle to the Hebrews*. NICNT. Grand Rapids: Eerdmans, 1964.

————. *The Letter of Paul to the Romans: An Introduction and Commentary*. Rev. ed. TNTC. Leicester: Inter-Varsity Press, 1985.

————. *Paul: Apostle of the Heart Set Free*. Grand Rapids: Eerdmans, 1977.

Brümmer, Vincent. "Metaphorical Thinking and Systematic Theology." *Nederlands Theologisch Tijdschrift* 43 (1989): 213–28.

Bruner, Fredrick Dale. *A Theology of the Holy Spirit*. Grand Rapids: Eerdmans, 1970.

Bultmann, Rudolf. *The Gospel of John: A Commentary*. Translated by G. R. Beasley-Murray, R. W. N. Hoare, and J. K. Riches. Philadelphia: Westminster, 1971.

————. *Theology of the New Testament*. Waco, TX: Baylor University Press, 2007.

Bundrick, David R. "*Ta Stoicheia Tou Kosmou* (Gal 4:3)." *JETS* 34, 3 (1991): 353–64.

Burge, G. M. *The Anointed Community: The Holy Spirit in the Johannine Tradition*. Grand Rapids: Eerdmans, 1987.

Burger, Hans. *Being in Christ: A Biblical and Systematic Investigation in a Reformed Perspective*. Eugene, OR: Wipf and Stock, 2008.

Burgess, Anthony. *Spiritual Refining or A Treatise of Grace and Assurance*. London: Printed by A. Miller for Thomas Underhill, 1652.

Burke, Trevor J. *Adopted into God's Family: Exploring a Pauline Metaphor*. NSBT 22. Downers Grove, IL: InterVarsity Press, 2006.

———. "Adoption and the Spirit in Romans 8." *EvQ* 70, 4 (1998): 311–24.

———. "The Characteristics of Paul's Adoptive-Sonship (Huiothesia) Motif." *IBS* 17, 2 (1995): 62–74.

———. *Family Matters: A Socio-Historical Study of Kinship Metaphors in 1 Thessalonians*. Journal of the Study of the New Testament Supplement Series 247. London: T&T Clark International, 2003.

———. "Pauline Adoption: A Sociological Approach." *EvQ* 73, 2 (2001): 119–34.

Burkhardt, Helmut. *The Biblical Doctrine of Regeneration*. Downers Grove, IL: InterVarsity Press, 1974.

Burris, Thomas S. "The Meaning of *HUIOTHESIA* in the New Testament." ThM thesis, Dallas Theological Seminary, 1970.

Burton, Ernest de Witt. *A Critical and Exegetical Commentary on the Epistle to the Galatians*. ICC. Edinburgh: T&T Clark, 1959.

Buswell, James Oliver. *A Systematic Theology of the Christian Religion*. 2 vols. Grand Rapids: Zondervan, 1963.

Byrne, Brendan. Review of *Adoption as Sons of God: An Exegetical Investigation into the Background of* YIOTHESIA *in the Pauline Corpus*, by J. Scott. *Journal of Theological Studies* 44 (1992): 288–94.

———. *Romans*. Edited by Daniel J. Harrington. SP 6. Collegeville, MN: Liturgical Press, 1996.

———. *"Sons of God"—"Seed of Abraham": A Study of the Idea of the Sonship of God of All Christians in Paul against the Jewish Background*. AnBib: Investigationes Scientificae in Res Biblicas 83. Rome: Biblical Institute, 1979.

Calvin, John. *Commentaries on the First Book of Moses Called Genesis*. Trans. John King. Vol. 1 of *Calvin's Commentaries*. Edinburgh: Calvin Translation Society, n.d. Reprint, Grand Rapids: Baker, 1989.

————. *The Epistles of Paul the Apostle to the Romans and to the Thessalonians.* Edited by David W. Torrance and Thomas F. Torrance. Translated by Ross MacKenzie. Vol. 8 of *Calvin Commentaries.* Edinburgh: Oliver & Boyd, 1960.

————. *Institutes of the Christian Religion.* Edited by John T. McNeill. Translated by Ford Lewis Battles. 2 vols. Philadelphia: Westminster, 1960.

Campbell, Constantine R. *Paul and Union with Christ: An Exegetical and Theological Study.* Grand Rapids: Zondervan, 2012.

Candlish, Robert S. *The Fatherhood of God: Being the First Course of the Cunningham Lectures Delivered before the New College, Edinburgh, in March 1864.* 5th ed. Edinburgh: Adam and Charles Black, 1869.

————. *Studies in Genesis.* Reprint, Grand Rapids: Kregel, 1979.

Carson, D. A. *Exegetical Fallacies.* 2nd ed. Grand Rapids: Baker, 1996.

————. "God Is Love." *Bibliotheca Sacra* 156 (1999): 131–42.

————. *The Gospel according to John.* Leicester: Inter-Varsity Press, 1991.

Cassidy, James J. "Election and Trinity." *WTJ* 71, 1 (2009): 53–81.

Chafer, Lewis Sperry. *Systematic Theology.* 8 vols. Dallas: Dallas Seminary Press, 1948.

Chryssides, George D. "Meaning, Metaphor, and Meta-Theology." *Scottish Journal of Theology* 38, 2 (1985): 145–53.

Clarke, Kent D. *Textual Optimism: A Critique of the United Bible Societies' Greek New Testament.* Journal for the Study of the New Testament Supplement 138. Sheffield: Sheffield Academic Press, 1997.

Cloete, G. Daan. "Christmas: Heirs of God, the Father, through Jesus, the Son, Incarnated (Galatians 4:4–7)." *Journal of Theology for Southern Africa* 85 (1993): 53–60.

Clowney, Edmund P. *The Unfolding Mystery: Discovering Christ in the Old Testament.* Phillipsburg, NJ: Presbyterian and Reformed, 1988.

Cole, R. Alan. *Exodus: An Introduction and Commentary.* Tyndale Old Testament Commentaries. London: Inter-Varsity Press, 1974.

————. *The Letter of Paul to the Galatians.* 2nd ed. TNTC. Leicester: Inter-Varsity Press, 1989.

The Confession of Faith. 3rd ed. Atlanta: Committee for Christian Education & Publications, 1990.

Cook, James I., ed. *Saved by Hope: Essays in Honor of Richard C. Oudersluys.* Grand Rapids: Eerdmans, 1978.

Cooper, John W. *Our Father in Heaven: Christian Faith and Inclusive Language*. Grand Rapids: Baker, 1998.

Cranfield, C. E. B. *A Critical and Exegetical Commentary on the Epistle to the Romans*. ICC 1. London and New York: T&T Clark International, 2004.

———. *Introduction and Commentary on Romans I–VIII: A Critical and Exegetical Commentary on the Epistle to the Romans*. Edinburgh: T&T Clark Limited, 1975.

———. *Introduction and Commentary on Romans IX–XVI: A Critical and Exegetical Commentary on the Epistle to the Romans*. Edinburgh: T&T Clark Limited, 1975.

———. "Some Observations on Romans 8.19–21." In *Reconciliation and Hope: New Testament Essays on Atonement and Eschatology*, edited by Robert Banks, 224–30. London: Paternoster, 1974.

Crawford, Thomas. *The Fatherhood of God Considered in Its General and Special Aspects and Particularly in Relation to the Atonement with a Review of Recent Speculations on the Subject*. Edinburgh: William Blackwood and Sons, 1867.

Cruver, Dan, ed. *Reclaiming Adoption: Missional Living through the Rediscovery of Abba Father*. Adelphi, MD: Cruciform, 2011.

Cullmann, Oscar. *Christ and Time: The Primitive Christian Conception of Time and History*. Translated by Floyd V. Filson. Rev. ed. Philadelphia: Westminster, 1964.

———. *Salvation in History*. Translated by Sidney G. Sowers. London: SCM, 1967.

Dabney, R. L. *Syllabus and Notes of the Course of Systematic and Polemic Theology*. 2nd ed. St. Louis: Presbyterian Publishing, 1878. Reprint, Edinburgh: Banner of Truth, 1996.

Davids, Peter H. *The Epistle of James: A Commentary on the Greek Text*. NIGTC. Grand Rapids: Eerdmans, 1982.

Davis, John Jefferson. *Worship and the Reality of God: An Evangelical Theology of Real Presence*. Downers Grove, IL: IVP Academic, 2014.

Denney, James. *St. Paul's Epistle to the Romans*. Expositor's Greek Testament 2. Grand Rapids: Eerdmans, 1974.

Dennison, William D. *Paul's Two-Age Construction and Apologetics*. Lanham, MD: University Press of America, 1985.

Dick, John. *Lectures on Theology*. 2 vols. New York: M. W. Dodd, 1850.

Die Bibel, oder die ganze Heilige Schrift des Alten und Neuen Testaments nach der Übersetzung Martin Luthers. Württembergische: Bibelanstalt Stuttgart, 1967.

Dockx, Stanislas. *Fils de Dieu par Grâce*. Paris: Desclée, de Brouwer, 1948.

Dodd, C. H. *The Epistle of Paul to the Romans*. MNTC. New York: Harper, 1932.

Donner, Herbert. "Adoption oder Legitimation? Erwägungen zur Adoption im Alten Testament auf dem Hintergrund der altorientalischen Rechte." *Oriens Antiquus* 8 (1969): 87–119.

Dorman, Robert C. "A Study of Paul's Use of *Hyiothesia*: Its Background, Development, and Importance concerning Spiritual Adoption." Unpublished master's thesis, Covenant Theological Seminary, St. Louis, 1997.

Dumbrell, William. "An Appreciation of the Theological Work of Archbishop Donald Robinson." In *In the Fullness of Time: Biblical Studies in Honour of Archbishop Donald Robinson*, edited by David Peterson and John Pryor, xvii–xxviii. Homebush West, Australia: Lancer, 1992.

Duncan, George S. *The Epistle of Paul to the Galatians*. MNTC. London: Hodder and Stoughton, 1934.

Dunn, James D. G. *Christology in the Making: A New Testament Inquiry into the Origins of the Doctrine of the Incarnation*. 2nd ed. Grand Rapids: Eerdmans, 1996.

———. *The Epistles to the Colossians and to Philemon: A Commentary on the Greek Text*. NIGTC. Grand Rapids: Eerdmans, 1996.

———. *The Epistle to the Galatians*. Black's New Testament Commentary. Peabody, MA: Hendrickson, 1993.

———. *Jesus and the Spirit: A Study of the Religious and Charismatic Experience of Jesus and the First Christians as Reflected in the New Testament*. Philadelphia: Westminster, 1975.

———. *Romans 1–8*. WBC 38A. Dallas: Word, 1988.

———. *Romans 9–16*. WBC 38B. Dallas: Word, 1988.

———. *The Theology of Paul the Apostle*. Grand Rapids: Eerdmans, 1998.

Durham, John I. *Exodus*. WBC 3. Waco, TX: Word, 1987.

Ebel, Frank J., Jr. "The Christian's Filial Relationship to God." ThM thesis, Dallas Theological Seminary, 1957.

Edwards, William R. "John Flavel on the Priority of Union with Christ: Further Historical Perspective on the Structure of Reformed Soteriology." *WTJ* 74, 1 (2012): 33–58.

Ellington, John. "Adoption in Modern Translations." *Bible Translator* 36, 4 (1985): 437–40.

Erickson, Millard J. *Christian Theology*. Unabr. one-vol. ed. Grand Rapids: Baker, 1985.

Faber, J. *Essays in Reformed Doctrine*. Neerlandia, AB: Inheritance Publications, 1990.

Falk, Z. W. *Hebrew Law in Biblical Times*. Jerusalem: Wahrmann, 1964.

Fantino, Jacques. *La Théologie d'Irénée: Lecture des Écritures en Réponse à l'Exégèse Gnostique, une Approche Trinitaire*. Paris: Les Éditions du Cerf, 1994.

Fee, Gordon D. "Baptism in the Holy Spirit: The Issue of Separability and Subsequence." *Pneuma* 7, 1 (1985): 87–99.

———. *1 and 2 Timothy, Titus*. International Biblical Commentary. Peabody, MA: Hendrickson, 1988.

———. *God's Empowering Presence: The Holy Spirit in the Letters of Paul*. Peabody, MA: Hendrickson, 1994.

———. *Pauline Christology: An Exegetical-Theological Study*. Grand Rapids: Baker, 2007.

———. *Paul, the Spirit, and the People of God*. Peabody, MA: Hendrickson, 1997.

Feigin, Samuel. "Some Cases of Adoption in Israel." *JBL* 50, 3 (1931): 186–200.

Feinberg, John S., ed. *Continuity and Discontinuity: Perspectives on the Relationship between the Old and New Testaments: Essays in Honor of S. Lewis Johnson, Jr.* Westchester, IL: Crossway, 1988.

Ferguson, Sinclair B. *Children of the Living God*. Colorado Springs: NavPress, 1987.

———. *The Christian Life: A Doctrinal Introduction*. Edinburgh: Banner of Truth, 1981.

———. *The Holy Spirit*. Contours of Christian Theology. Downers Grove, IL: InterVarsity Press, 1996.

———. "The Reformed Doctrine of Sonship." In *Pulpit and People: Essays in Honour of William Still*, edited by Nigel M. de S. Cameron and Sinclair B. Ferguson, 81–88. Edinburgh: Rutherford House, 1986.

————. *The Whole Christ: Legalism, Antinomianism, and Gospel Assurance—Why the Marrow Controversy Still Matters*. Wheaton, IL: Crossway, 2016.

Fesko, John V. *Beyond Calvin: Union with Christ and Justification in Early Modern Reformed Theology (1517–1700)*. Reformed Historical Theology 20. Göttingen and Bristol, CT: Vandenhoeck & Ruprecht, 2012.

————. "John Owen on Union with Christ and Justification." *Themelios* 37, 1 (2012): 7–19.

————. "Peter Martyr Vermigli on Union with Christ and Justification." *Reformed Theological Review* 70, 1 (2011): 37–57.

————. *The Theology of the Westminster Standards: Historical Context and Theological Insights*. Wheaton, IL: Crossway, 2014.

————. "William Perkins on Union with Christ and Justification." *Mid-America Journal of Theology* (2010): 21–34.

Fitzmyer, Joseph A. *Romans: A New Translation with Introduction and Commentary*. Anchor Bible 33. New York: Doubleday, 1993.

Fitzwater, P. B. *Christian Theology: A Systematic Presentation*. Grand Rapids: Eerdmans, 1948.

Foley, George Cadwalader. *Anselm's Theory of the Atonement*. London: Longmans, Green, and Co., 1909.

Foulkes, Francis. *The Letter of Paul to the Ephesians: An Introduction and Commentary*. 2nd ed. TNTC. Downers Grove, IL: InterVarsity Press, 1989.

France, R. T. *The Gospel according to Matthew: An Introduction and Commentary*. TNTC. Leicester: Inter-Varsity Press, 1985.

Franchino, T. Scott. "*Yios* and *Teknon* in the Doctrine of Adoption: Romans 8." Unpublished master's thesis, Grace Theological Seminary, Winona Lake, IN, 1984.

Freedman, David Noel. *The Anchor Bible Dictionary*. New York: Doubleday, 1992.

Fuller, Reginald H. "Pre-existence Christology: Can We Dispense with It?" *Word and World* 2, 1 (1982): 30–34.

Fung, Ronald Y. K. *The Epistle to the Galatians*. NICNT. Grand Rapids: Eerdmans, 1988.

Gaffin, Richard B., Jr. "Biblical Theology and the Westminster Standards." *WTJ* 65, 2 (2003): 165–79.

————. *By Faith, Not by Sight: Paul and the Order of Salvation*. 2nd ed. Phillipsburg, NJ: P&R Publishing, 2013.

———. "The Holy Spirit." *WTJ* 43, 1 (1980): 58–78.

———. *Introduction to Redemptive History and Biblical Interpretation: The Shorter Writings of Geerhardus Vos.* Edited by Richard B. Gaffin Jr. Phillipsburg, NJ: Presbyterian and Reformed, 1980.

———. "Justification and Union with Christ." In *Theological Guide to Calvin's Institutes,* edited by David W. Hall and Peter A. Lillback, 248–69. Phillipsburg, NJ: P&R Publishing, 2008.

———. "'Life-Giving Spirit': Probing the Center of Paul's Pneumatology." *JETS* 41, 4 (1998): 573–89.

———. "Paul the Theologian." *WTJ* 62, 1 (2000): 121–41.

———. "Pentecost: Before and After." *Kerux* 10, 2 (1995): 3–24.

———. *Perspectives on Pentecost: New Testament Teaching on the Gifts of the Holy Spirit.* Phillipsburg, NJ: Presbyterian and Reformed, 1979.

———. *Resurrection and Redemption: A Study in Paul's Soteriology.* 2nd ed. Phillipsburg, NJ: Presbyterian and Reformed, 1987.

———. "Systematic Theology and Biblical Theology." *WTJ* 38, 3 (1976): 281–99.

———. "Theology of Hebrews." NT 881 class notes presented at Westminster Theological Seminary, Philadelphia, 1999.

———. "Theology of Romans." ST 781 class notes presented at Westminster Theological Seminary, Philadelphia, 1998.

———. "The Usefulness of the Cross." *WTJ* 41, 1 (1979): 228–46.

Garcia, Mark A. *Life in Christ: Union with Christ and Twofold Grace in Calvin's Theology.* Cumbria, UK: Paternoster, 2008.

———. "Union with Christ, the Reformed Tradition, and Research: Reading Fesko." *Wince and Sing* (blog). December 3, 2013. http://www.winceandsing.com/blog/2013/12/03/union-with-christ-the-reformed-tradition-and-research-reading-fesko-1/.

Garner, David B. "Adoption in Christ." Ph.D. diss., Westminster Theological Seminary, Philadelphia, 2002.

———. "Beloved Sons in Whom He Is Well-Pleased." *Ordained Servant Online: A Journal for Church Officers* (March 2016): 4–10. http://www.opc.org/OS/2016/OS_Mar_2016.pdf.

———, ed. *Did God Really Say? Affirming the Truthfulness and Trustworthiness of Scripture.* Phillipsburg, NJ: P&R Publishing, 2012.

————. "The First and Last Son: Christology and Sonship in Pauline Soteriology." In *Resurrection and Eschatology: Theology in Service of the Church: Essays in Honor of Richard B. Gaffin, Jr.*, edited by Lane G. Tipton and Jeffrey C. Waddington, 255–82. Phillipsburg, NJ: P&R Publishing, 2008.

————. "God's Work in Jesus." *Sine Qua Non* (May 1, 2014). http://www.place fortruth.org/placefortruth/column/sine-qua-non/gods-work-in-jesus.

————. "Irenæus: Fountain Father of Adoption Theology." Unpublished paper, Westminster Theological Seminary, Philadelphia, 1999.

————. Review of *The Binding of God: Calvin's Role in the Development of Covenant Theology*, by Peter A. Lillback. *Trinity Journal* 23, 2 (2002): 291–94.

————. "Sympathy Made Perfect." *Sine Qua Non* (May 15, 2014). http://www.placefortruth.org/placefortruth/column/sine-qua-non /sympathy-made-perfect.

————. "A World of Riches." *Reformation 21* (April 2011). http://www .reformation21.org/articles/a-world-of-riches.php.

————. "You Just Might Be an Antinomian." Review of *Antinomianism: Reformed Theology's Unwelcome Guest?*, by Mark Jones. *Reformation 21* (February 2014). http://www.reformation21.org/shelf-life /antinomianism-reformed-theologys-unwelcome-guest.php.

Gataker, Thomas. *The Christian Man's Care: A Sermon*. London: J. Haviland, 1624.

Gathercole, Simon J. *The Preexistent Son: Recovering the Christologies of Matthew, Mark, and Luke*. Grand Rapids: Eerdmans, 2006.

Gerrish, Brian A. *Grace and Gratitude: The Eucharistic Theology of John Calvin*. Edinburgh: T&T Clark, 1993.

————. "John Calvin on Luther." In *Interpreters of Luther: Essays in Honor of Wilhelm Pauck*, edited by Jaroslav Pelikan, 67–96. Philadelphia: Fortress, 1968.

Gibbs, John G. *Creation and Redemption: A Study in Pauline Theology*. Supplements to Novum Testamentum 26. Leiden: E. J. Brill, 1971.

————. "The Relation between Creation and Redemption according to Phil. II.5–11." *Novum Testamentum* 12, 3 (1970): 270–83.

Gill, John. *A Complete Body of Doctrinal and Practical Divinity or a System of Evangelical Truths, Deduced from Sacred Scriptures*. New ed. Paris, AR: Baptist Standard Bearer, 1989.

Girardeau, John L. *Discussions of Theological Questions*. Edited by George A. Blackburn. Richmond, VA: Presbyterian Committee, 1905.

Goodwin, Thomas. *The Works of Thomas Goodwin*. Reprint, Eureka, CA: Tanski, 1996.

Gore, Ralph Jackson, Jr. "The Lutheran *Ordo Salutis* with Special Reference to Justification and Sanctification: A Reformed Analysis." STM thesis, Faith Theological Seminary, Baltimore, 1983.

Gorman, Michael J. *Inhabiting the Cruciform God: Kenosis, Justification, and Theosis in Paul's Narrative Soteriology*. Grand Rapids: Eerdmans, 2009.

Gouge, William. *A Guide to Goe to God*. London: Printed by G. M. for Edward Brewster, 1636.

Grams, Rollin G. Review of *Adoption as Sons of God: An Exegetical Investigation into the Background of* YIOTHESIA *in the Pauline Corpus*, by J. Scott. *JBL* 113, 3 (1994): 548–50.

Grenholm, Cristina, and Daniel Patte, eds. *Gender, Tradition and Romans: Shared Ground, Uncertain Borders*. New York: T&T Clark, 2005.

Griffith, Howard. "'The First Title of the Spirit': Adoption in Calvin's Soteriology." *EvQ* 73, 2 (2001): 135–53.

Gritsch, Eric W., and Robert W. Jenson. *Lutheranism: The Theological Movement and Its Confessional Writings*. Philadelphia: Fortress, 1976.

Grubbs, Judith Evans, and Tim Parkin, eds. *The Oxford Handbook of Childhood and Education in the Classical World*. Oxford: Oxford University Press, 2013.

Grudem, Wayne. *Systematic Theology*. Grand Rapids: Zondervan, 1994.

Gunton, Colin E. *Yesterday & Today: Studies of Continuities in Christology*. 2nd ed. London: SPCK, 1997.

Guthrie, Donald. *Galatians*. New Century Bible, n.s. Greenwood, SC: Attic Press, 1969.

———. *New Testament Introduction*. 4th ed. Downers Grove, IL: InterVarsity Press, 1990.

Haldane, Robert. *Exposition of the Epistle to the Romans*. Geneva Series Commentary. Edinburgh: Banner of Truth, 1996.

Harnack, Adolf von. *What Is Christianity?* Translated by Thomas Bailey Saunders. Philadelphia: Fortress, 1986.

Heard, J. B. *The Tripartite Nature of Man: Spirit, Soul, and Body*. Edinburgh: T&T Clark, 1875.

Helm, Paul. "Does Justification Cause Sanctification?" *Helm's Deep* (blog). June 1, 2011. http://paulhelmsdeep.blogspot.com/2011/06/does -justiification-cause.html.

———. *John Calvin's Ideas*. Oxford: Oxford University Press, 2004.

Hendriksen, William. *Exposition of Paul's Epistle to the Romans*. NTC. Grand Rapids: Baker, 1981.

———. *Exposition of the Gospel according to Matthew*. NTC. Grand Rapids: Baker, 1973.

———. *Galatians and Ephesians*. NTC. Reprint, Grand Rapids: Baker, 1979.

Heppe, Heinrich. *Reformed Dogmatics Set Out and Illustrated from the Sources*. Edited by Ernst Bizer. Translated by G. T. Thomson. Rev. ed. Grand Rapids: Baker, 1978.

Hodge, Archibald Alexander. *A Commentary on the Confession of Faith*. Philadelphia: Presbyterian Board of Publication, 1885.

———. *The Confession of Faith*. Reprint, Edinburgh: Banner of Truth, 1998.

———. "The *Ordo Salutis*; or Relation in the Order of Nature of Holy Character and Divine Favor." *Princeton Review* 54 (1878): 304–21.

———. *Outlines of Theology*. Grand Rapids: Eerdmans, 1949.

Hodge, Charles. *A Commentary on Romans*. Edinburgh: Banner of Truth, 1972.

———. *Commentary on the Epistle to the Ephesians*. Old Tappan, NJ: Fleming H. Revell, 1980.

———. *Systematic Theology*. 3 vols. Grand Rapids: Eerdmans, 1979.

Hodges, Zane C. "Water and Spirit—John 3:5." *Bibliotheca Sacra* 135 (1978): 206–20.

Hoehner, Harold W. *Ephesians: An Exegetical Commentary*. Grand Rapids: Baker Academic, 2002.

Hoekema, Anthony A. *The Bible and the Future*. Grand Rapids: Eerdmans, 1979.

———. *Created in God's Image*. Grand Rapids: Eerdmans, 1986.

Hoeksema, Herman. *Reformed Dogmatics*. Grand Rapids: Reformed Free Publishing Association, 1966.

Horton, Michael S. *The Christian Faith: A Systematic Theology for Pilgrims*. Grand Rapids: Zondervan, 2011.

———. *Covenant and Eschatology: The Divine Drama*. Louisville, KY: Westminster John Knox, 2002.

———. "Which Covenant Theology?" In *Covenant, Justification, and Pastoral Ministry: Essays by the Faculty of Westminster Seminary California*, edited by R. Scott Clark, 197–227. Phillipsburg, NJ: P&R Publishing, 2007.

Houston, Thomas. *The Adoption of Sons, Its Nature, Spirit, Privileges and Effects: A Practical and Experimental Treatise.* Paisley, Scotland: Alex. Gardner, 1872.

Howard, George. *Paul: Crisis in Galatia.* Edited by G. N. Stanton. 2nd ed. Society for New Testament Studies Monograph Series 35. Cambridge: Cambridge University Press, 1990.

Hoyle, R. Birch. *The Holy Spirit in St. Paul.* Garden City, NY: Doubleday, Doran & Company, Inc., 1929.

Hughes, Philip E. "The Christology of Hebrews." *Southwestern Journal of Theology* 28 (1985): 19–27.

Huonder, V. *Israel Sohn Gottes: zur Deutung eines alttestamentlichen Themas in der jüdischen Exegese des Mittelalters.* Oribs Biblicus et Orientalis 6. Freiberg/Schweiz: Universitätsverlag, 1975.

Husbands, Mark, and Daniel J. Treier, eds. *Justification: What's at Stake in the Current Debates.* Downers Grove, IL: InterVarsity Press, 2004.

Irenæus. *The Demonstration of the Apostolic Preaching.* Translated by J. Armitage Robinson. Translations of Christian Literature 4, Oriental Texts. London: Society for Promoting Christian Knowledge, 1920.

Jarrel, W. A. "Adoption Not in the Bible Salvation." *RExp* 15 (1918): 459–69.

Johnson, Marcus Peter. *One with Christ: An Evangelical Theology of Salvation.* Wheaton, IL: Crossway, 2013.

Johnston, Mark G. *Child of a King: What Joining God's Family Means.* Fearn, Ross-shire, UK: Christian Focus, 1997.

Jones, Mark. *Antinomianism: Reformed Theology's Unwelcome Guest?* Phillipsburg, NJ: P&R Publishing, 2013.

Julien, Sarah. "Coming Home: Adoption in Ephesians and Galatians." *Quodlibet Journal* 5.2–3 (2003). http://www.quodlibet.net/articles/murray-adoption.shtml.

Jüngel, Eberhard. *Theological Essays.* Translated by J. B. Webster. Edinburgh: T&T Clark, 1989.

Kaiser, Walter C., Jr. *Exodus.* Expositor's Bible Commentary 2. Grand Rapids: Zondervan, 1990.

Karlberg, Mark W. "Israel and the Eschaton." *WTJ* 52, 1 (1990): 117–30.

―――. "Paul's Letter to the Romans in the New International Commentary on the New Testament and in Contemporary Reformed Thought." *EvQ* 71, 1 (1999): 3–24.

Käsemann, Ernst. *Commentary on Romans*. Translated by Geoffrey W. Bromiley. Grand Rapids: Eerdmans, 1980.

Kaufman, Peter Iver. "Tertullian on Heresy, History, and the Reappropriation of Revelation." *Church History* 60, 2 (1991): 167–79.

Kelly, Douglas F. "Adoption: An Underdeveloped Heritage of the Westminster Standards." *Reformed Theological Review* 52, 3 (1993): 110–20.

―――. *Creation and Change: Genesis 1.1–2.4 in the Light of Changing Scientific Paradigms*. Fearn, Ross-shire, UK: Christian Focus, 1997.

―――. *Systematic Theology: Grounded in Holy Scripture and Understood in the Light of the Church*. Vol. 1. Fearn, Ross-shire, UK: Christian Focus, 2008.

Kent, Homer A., Jr. "The New Covenant and the Church." *Grace Theological Journal* 6, 2 (1985): 289–98.

Kim, Seyoon. *The Origin of Paul's Gospel*. Tübingen: J. C. B. Mohr (Paul Siebeck), 1981.

Kittel, Gerhard, and Gerhard Friedrich, eds. *Theological Dictionary of the New Testament*. Translated by G. W. Bromiley. 10 vols. Grand Rapids: Eerdmans, 1964–76.

Kline, Meredith G. *Images of the Spirit*. N.p.: 1986.

―――. *Kingdom Prologue: Genesis Foundations for a Covenantal Worldview*. Overland Park, KS: Two Age, 2000.

―――. "Primal Parousia." *WTJ* 40, 2 (1978): 245–80.

Knight, George W., III. *The Pastoral Epistles: A Commentary on the Greek Text*. Grand Rapids: Eerdmans, 1992.

Knudsen, Johannes. "Recapitulation Christology and the Church Today." *Dialog* 2, 2 (1963): 126–33.

Ladd, George Eldon. "Eschatology and the Unity of New Testament Theology." *Expository Times* 68 (1957): 268–73.

―――. *A Theology of the New Testament*. Edited by Donald A. Hagner. Rev. ed. Grand Rapids: Eerdmans, 1993.

Laidlaw, John. *The Bible Doctrine of Man*. New rev. and rearranged ed. Edinburgh: T&T Clark, 1895.

Lane, William. *Hebrews 9–13*. WBC 47B. Waco, TX: Word, 1991.

Lash, Nicholas. "Up and Down Christology." In *New Studies in Theology 1*, edited by Stephen Sykes and Derek Holmes, 31–46. London: Duckworth, 1979.

Lawson, John. *The Biblical Theology of Saint Irenaeus*. London: Epworth, 1948.

Leaver, Robin A. *Luther on Justification*. St. Louis: Concordia, 1975.

Leith, John H. *Assembly at Westminster: Reformed Theology in the Making*. Atlanta: John Knox, 1973.

Lenski, R. C. H. *The Interpretation of St. Paul's Epistle to the Romans*. Minneapolis: Augsburg, 1936.

Letham, Robert. *Union with Christ in Scripture, History, and Theology*. Phillipsburg, NJ: P&R Publishing, 2011.

———. *The Work of Christ*. Contours of Christian Theology. Downers Grove, IL: InterVarsity Press, 1993.

Leupold, H. C. *Exposition of Genesis*. Grand Rapids: Baker, 1965.

Leupold, Ulrich S. "Regeneration in the Theology of Paul." *Lutheran Quarterly* 17, 3 (1965): 240–51.

Lewis, Arthur H. "The New Birth under the Old Covenant." *EvQ* 56, 1 (1984): 35–44.

Lewis, Edwin. "A Christian Theodicy: An Exposition of Romans 8:18–39." *Interpretation* 11, 4 (1957): 405–20.

Liddell, Henry George, Robert Scott, and Henry Stuart Jones. *A Greek-English Lexicon*. 9th ed. with rev. supp. Oxford: Clarendon, 1996.

Lidgett, J. Scott. *The Fatherhood of God in Christian Truth and Life*. Edinburgh: T&T Clark, 1902.

Lienhard, Marc. "Luther et Calvin Commentateurs du Notre Père." *Revue d'Histoire et de Philosophie Religieuses* 72 (1992): 73–88.

Lightfoot, J. B. *Colossians and Philemon*. Crossway Classic Commentaries. Wheaton, IL: Crossway, 1997.

———. *Saint Paul's Epistle to the Galatians: A Revised Text with Introduction, Notes, and Dissertations*. London: Macmillan and Co., Limited, 1902.

Lillback, Peter A. *The Binding of God: Calvin's Role in the Development of Covenant Theology*. Edited by Richard A. Muller. Texts and Studies in Reformation and Post-Reformation Thought. Grand Rapids: Baker Academic, 2001.

Lincoln, Andrew T. *Ephesians*. WBC 42. Dallas: Word, 1990.

Löffler, Paul. "The Biblical Concept of Conversion." *Study Encounter* 1 (1965): 93–101.

Longenecker, Richard N. *Galatians.* WBC 41. Dallas: Word, 1990.

Luther, Martin. "Lectures on the First Epistle of St. John." In *The Catholic Epistles*, edited by Jaroslav Pelikan and Walter A. Hansen, 219–327. Vol. 30 of *Luther's Works*. St. Louis: Concordia, 1967.

Lyall, Francis. "Roman Law in the Writings of Paul—Adoption." *JBL* 88, 4 (1969): 458–66.

———. *Slaves, Citizens, Sons: Legal Metaphors in the Epistles.* Grand Rapids: Zondervan, 1984.

Macaskill, Grant. *Union with Christ in the New Testament.* Oxford: Oxford University Press, 2013.

Mackintosh, H. R. *The Christian Apprehension of God.* London: Student Christian Movement, 1929.

Macleod, Donald. *Jesus Is Lord: Christology Yesterday and Today.* Fearn, Ross-shire, UK: Christian Focus, 2000.

———. *The Person of Christ.* Contours of Christian Theology. Downers Grove, IL: InterVarsity Press, 1998.

Macleod, J. *Scottish Theology.* Edinburgh: Banner of Truth, 1974.

Manton, Thomas. *The Complete Works of Thomas Manton.* 22 vols. Worthington, PA: Maranatha, n.d.

Marcel, Pierre. *The Biblical Doctrine of Infant Baptism: Sacrament of the Covenant of Grace.* Translated by Philip Edgcumbe Hughes. London: James Clark & Co. Ltd., 1953.

———. "The Relation between Justification and Sanctification in Calvin's Thought." *EvQ* 27, 3 (1955): 132–45.

Martin, Ralph P. *Colossians and Philemon.* Edited by Matthew Black. New Century Bible. Greenwood, SC: Attic Press, 1974.

———. *James.* WBC 48. Waco, TX: Word, 1988.

Martyn, J. Louis. *Galatians: A New Translation with Introduction and Commentary.* Anchor Bible 33A. New York: Doubleday, 1997.

Marvin, Danny R. "John's Use of *Uios* and *Teknon* Especially in the Constructions *Uios Theou* and *Tekna Theou*." Unpublished master's thesis, Western Conservative Baptist Seminary, Portland, OR, 1979.

Mawhinney, Allen. "Baptism, Servanthood, and Sonship." In *Creator, Redeemer, Consummator: A Festschrift for Meredith G. Kline*, edited by Howard Griffith and John R. Muether, 105–15. Greenville, SC: Reformed Academic, 2000.

———. "*Yiothesia* in the Pauline Epistles: Its Background, Use, and Implications." Ph.D. diss., Baylor University, Waco, TX, 1982.

McCartney, Dan. "Should We Employ the Hermeneutic of the New Testament Writers?" http://www.bible-researcher.com/mccartney1.html.

McCartney, Dan, and Charles Clayton. *Let the Reader Understand: A Guide to Interpreting and Applying the Bible*. Wheaton, IL: Victor, 1994.

McCormack, Bruce L., ed. *Justification in Perspective: Historical Developments and Contemporary Challenges*. Grand Rapids: Baker Academic; Edinburgh: Rutherford House, 2006.

McFague, Sallie. *Models of God: Theology for an Ecological, Nuclear Age*. Philadelphia: Fortress, 1987.

McGrath, James F. "Change in Christology: New Testament Models and the Contemporary Task." *Irish Theological Quarterly* 63, 1 (1998): 39–50.

McKenzie, Steven L. *Covenant*. St. Louis: Chalice, 2000.

McWilliams, Warren. "God the Friend: A Test Case in Metaphorical Theology." *Perspectives in Religious Studies* 16 (1991): 109–20.

Melanchthon, Philipp. *Commentary on Romans*. Translated by Fred Kramer. St. Louis: Concordia, 1992.

———. *Loci Communes (1543)*. Translated by J. A. O. Preus. St. Louis: Concordia, 1992.

Metzger, Bruce Manning. *The Text of the New Testament: Its Transmission, Corruption, and Restoration*. 2nd ed. New York: Oxford University Press, 1968.

———. *A Textual Commentary on the Greek New Testament*. London: United Bible Societies, 1971.

Meyer, Heinrich August Wilhelm. *Critical and Exegetical Hand-Book to the Epistle to the Romans*. Translated by John C. Moore and Edwin Johnson. 5th ed. New York and London: Funk & Wagnalls, 1884.

Miller, John W. *Calling God "Father": Essays on the Bible, Fatherhood and Culture*. New York: Paulist Press, 1999.

Mills, Donald William. "The Concept of Sinlessness in 1 John in Relation to Johannine Eschatology." Ph.D. diss., Westminster Theological Seminary, Philadelphia, 1998.

Minns, Denis. *Irenaeus*. Washington, DC: Georgetown University Press, 1994.

Mitchell, Alex F., and John Struthers, eds. *Minutes of the Sessions of the Westminster Assembly of Divines*. Reprint, Edmonton, AB: Still Waters Revival Books, 1991.

Moessner, Jeanne Stevenson. *The Spirit of Adoption: At Home in God's Family*. Louisville, KY: Westminster John Knox, 2003.

Moffatt, James. *A Critical and Exegetical Commentary on the Epistle to the Hebrews*. ICC. Edinburgh: T&T Clark, 1968.

Moo, Douglas J. *The Epistle to the Romans*. NICNT. Grand Rapids: Eerdmans, 1996.

———. *The Letter of James: An Introduction and Commentary*. TNTC. Leicester: Inter-Varsity Press, 1985.

———. *Romans 1–8*. Wycliffe Exegetical Commentary. Chicago: Moody, 1991.

Moore-Crispin, Derek R. "Galatians 4:1–9: The Use and Abuse of Parallels." *EvQ* 61, 3 (1989): 203–23.

Morris, Leon. *The Epistle to the Romans*. Grand Rapids: Eerdmans, 1988.

———. *Galatians: Paul's Charter of Christian Freedom*. Downers Grove, IL: InterVarsity Press, 1996.

———. *The Gospel according to John*. NICNT. Rev. ed. Grand Rapids: Eerdmans, 1995.

———. *New Testament Theology*. Grand Rapids: Academie Books, 1986.

Morris, Michelle J. "Adoption." In *The Lexham Bible Dictionary*, edited by J. D. Barry, L. Wentz, D. Mangum, C. Sinclair-Wolcott, R. Klippenstein, D. Bomar, and D. R. Brown. Bellingham, WA: Lexham Press, 2012–14.

Mosebrook, Keith Alan. "The Pauline Doctrine of the Adoption of Believers." ThM thesis, Dallas Theological Seminary, 1981.

Moule, C. F. D. "A Neglected Factor in the Interpretation of Johannine Eschatology." In *Studies in John Presented to Professor Dr. J. N. Sevenster on the Occasion of His Seventieth Birthday*, 155–60. Leiden: E. J. Brill, 1970.

———. "'The New Life' in Colossians 3:1–17." *RExp* 70 (1973): 481–87.

Moule, Handley C. G. *The Epistle to the Romans*. Reprint, Minneapolis: Klock & Klock, 1982.

Moulton, James Hope, and George Milligan. *The Vocabulary of the Greek New Testament Illustrated from the Papyri and Other Non-Literary Sources*. London: Hodder & Stoughton, 1930. Reprint, Peabody, MA: Hendrickson, 1997.

Mueller, John Theodore. "Adoption." *Christianity Today* 6 (1962): 22–23.

———. *Christian Dogmatics: A Handbook of Doctrinal Theology for Pastors, Teachers, and Laymen.* St. Louis: Concordia, 1934.

Murray, John. "The Atonement." http://www.graceonlinelibrary.org /doctrine-theology/the-atonement/the-atonement-by-john-murray/.

———. "The Attestation of Scripture." In *The Infallible Word: A Symposium by the Members of the Faculty of Westminster Theological Seminary,* edited by N. B. Stonehouse and Paul Woolley, 1–54. 2nd ed. Phillipsburg, NJ: P&R Publishing, 2002.

———. *The Collected Writings of John Murray.* 4 vols. Edinburgh: Banner of Truth, 1976–82.

———. *The Covenant of Grace: A Biblico-Theological Study.* Philadelphia: Presbyterian and Reformed, 1953.

———. "Definitive Sanctification." *CTJ* 2, 1 (1967): 5–21.

———. *The Epistle to the Romans: The English Text with Introduction, Exposition and Notes.* 2 vols. combined. Reprint, Grand Rapids: Eerdmans, 1997.

———. *The Imputation of Adam's Sin.* Philadelphia: Presbyterian and Reformed, 1959.

———. *Redemption Accomplished and Applied.* Grand Rapids: Eerdmans, 1955.

The New International Dictionary of New Testament Theology. 3 vols. Grand Rapids: Zondervan, 1975.

Neyrey, Jerome H. "John III—A Debate over Johannine Epistemology and Christology." *Novum Testamentum* 23, 2 (1981): 115–27.

Nock, Arthur Darby. "The Vocabulary of the New Testament." *JBL* 52, 2–3 (1933): 131–39.

Norbie, Donald L. "The Washing of Regeneration." *EvQ* 34, 1 (1962): 36–38.

Nygren, Anders. *Commentary on Romans.* Translated by Carl C. Rasmussen. Philadelphia: Muhlenberg, 1949.

O'Brien, Peter T. *Colossians, Philemon.* WBC 44. Waco, TX: Word, 1982.

O'Collins, Gerald. *Christology: A Biblical, Historical, and Systematic Study of Jesus.* 2nd ed. Oxford: Oxford University Press, 2009.

Oke, C. Clare. "A Suggestion with Regard to Romans 8:23." *Interpretation* 11, 4 (1957): 455–60.

Olbricht, Thomas H. "The Stoicheia and the Rhetoric of Colossians: Then and Now." In *Rhetoric, Scripture and Theology*, edited by Stanley E. Porter and Thomas H. Olbricht, 308–28. Sheffield: Sheffield Academic Press, 1996.

Oliphint, K. Scott. *God with Us: Divine Condescension and the Attributes of God*. Wheaton, IL: Crossway, 2012.

———, ed. *Justified in Christ: God's Plan for Us in Justification*. Fearn, Ross-shire, UK: Christian Focus, 2007.

Osler, Margaret J. *Divine Will and the Mechanical Philosophy: Gassendi and Descartes on Contingency and Necessity in the Created World*. Cambridge: Cambridge University Press, 1994.

Owen, John. *The Works of John Owen*. Edited by William H. Goold. 16 vols. N.p.: Johnstone & Hunter, 1850–53. Reprint, Edinburgh: Banner of Truth, 1988.

Packer, J. I. *Keep in Step with the Spirit*. Grand Rapids: Fleming H. Revell, 1984.

———. *Knowing God*. 20th anniversary ed. Downers Grove, IL: InterVarsity Press, 1993.

Palmer, Edwin Hartshorn. *Scheeben's Doctrine of Divine Adoption*. Amsterdam: Kok, 1954.

Pannenberg, Wolfhart. *Jesus—God and Man*. Translated by Lewis L. Wilkins and Duane A. Priebe. Philadelphia: Westminster, 1974.

Partee, Charles. *The Theology of John Calvin*. Louisville, KY: Westminster John Knox, 2008.

Peppard, Michael. *The Son of God in the Roman World: Divine Sonship in Its Social and Political Context*. Oxford: Oxford University Press, 2011.

Peterson, Robert A. *Adopted by God: From Wayward Sinners to Cherished Children*. Phillipsburg, NJ: P&R Publishing, 2001.

———. *Salvation Applied by the Spirit: Union with Christ*. Wheaton, IL: Crossway, 2015.

———. "Toward a Systematic Theology of Adoption." *Presbyterion* 27, 2 (2001): 120–31.

Pieper, Francis. *Christian Dogmatics*. 4 vols. St. Louis: Concordia, 1950–57.

Piper, John. *The Justification of God: An Exegetical and Theological Study of Romans 9:1–13*. 2nd ed. Grand Rapids: Baker, 1993.

Piper, Otto. "The Saviour's Eternal Work: An Exegesis of Col. 1:9–29." *Interpretation* 3, 3 (1949): 286–98.

Poythress, Vern S. *God Centered Biblical Interpretation*. Phillipsburg, NJ: P&R Publishing, 1999.

———. *The Shadow of Christ in the Law of Moses*. Phillipsburg, NJ: Presbyterian and Reformed, 1991.

———. *Symphonic Theology*. Grand Rapids: Academie Books, 1987.

———. "Topics in the Doctrine of Man." ST 763 class notes presented at Westminster Theological Seminary, Philadelphia, 1999.

Proctor, John. Review of *Adoption as Sons of God*, by James M. Scott. *EvQ* 67, 2 (1995): 171–74.

Radoicich, Russell. "'Adoption' in the Pauline Epistles." Unpublished paper, St. Vladimir's Orthodox Theological Seminary, Crestwood, NY, 1999.

Rayburn, Sterling. "Cosmic Transfiguration." *Church Quarterly Review* 168 (1967): 162–67.

Reumann, John. *Creation & New Creation*. Minneapolis: Augsburg, 1973.

Reymond, Robert. *A New Systematic Theology of the Christian Faith*. Nashville, TN: Thomas Nelson, 1998.

Ridderbos, Herman N. *The Coming of the Kingdom*. Edited by Raymond O. Zorn. Translated by H. de Jongste. Philadelphia: Presbyterian and Reformed, 1962.

———. *The Epistle of Paul to the Churches of Galatia*. Translated by Henry Zylstra. NICNT. Grand Rapids: Eerdmans, 1953.

———. *The Gospel according to John: A Theological Commentary*. Translated by John Vriend. Grand Rapids: Eerdmans, 1997.

———. "Israel in het Nieuwe Testament, in het bijzonder volgens Romans 9–11." In *Israel*, 57–64. Rev. informal translation by Richard B. Gaffin Jr., July 1999. Den Haag: Van Keulen, 1955.

———. *Paul and Jesus: Origin and General Character of Paul's Preaching of Christ*. Translated by David H. Freeman. Grand Rapids: Eerdmans, 1958.

———. *Paul: An Outline of His Theology*. Translated by John Richard DeWitt. Grand Rapids: Eerdmans, 1975.

———. *When the Time Had Fully Come: Studies in New Testament Theology*. Grand Rapids: Eerdmans, 1957.

Riffe, Robert Lee. "A Study of the Figure of Adoption in the Pauline Epistles." ThM thesis, Dallas Theological Seminary, 1981.

Robertson, O. Palmer. *The Christ of the Covenants*. Phillipsburg, NJ: Presbyterian and Reformed, 1980.

———. *The Israel of God: Yesterday, Today, and Tomorrow*. Phillipsburg, NJ: P&R Publishing, 2000.

Robson, Edward A. "A Biblical-Theological Exposition of Psalm 2:7 Considering the Sonship of the Messiah." ThM thesis, Westminster Theological Seminary, Philadelphia, 1963.

Rodgers, R. E. L. *The Incarnation of the Antithesis: An Introduction to the Educational Thought and Practice of Abraham Kuyper*. Edinburgh: Pentland Ltd., 1992.

Ruether, Rosemary Radford. "The Liberation of Christology from Patriarchy." In *Feminist Theology: A Reader*, edited by Ann Loades, 138–48. Louisville, KY: Westminster John Knox, 1990.

———. *Sexism and God-Talk: Toward a Feminist Theology*. Boston: Beacon Press, 1983.

Rushdoony, Rousas John. *Systematic Theology*. 2 vols. Vallecito, CA: Ross House Books, 1994.

Rushdoony, Rousas John, and Andrew P. Sandlin. *Infallibility and Interpretation*. Vallecito, CA: Chalcedon Foundation, 2000.

Russell, David M. *The "New Heavens and New Earth": Hope for the Creation in Jewish Apocalyptic and the New Testament*. Studies in Biblical Apocalyptic Literature 1. Philadelphia: Visionary, 1996.

Ryrie, Charles Caldwell. *Dispensationalism*. Rev. and exp. ed. Chicago: Moody, 1995.

Sanday, William, and Arthur C. Headlam. *A Critical and Exegetical Commentary on the Epistle to the Romans*. 5th ed. ICC. Edinburgh: T&T Clark, 1902.

Sarna, Nahum M. *Exodus: The Traditional Hebrew Text with the New JPS Translation*. JPS Torah Commentary. Philadelphia: Jewish Publication Society, 1991.

Schaff, Philip, ed. *The Creeds of Christendom with a History and Critical Notes*. Revised by David S. Schaff. 6th ed. 3 vols. Grand Rapids: Baker, 1998.

———. *Modern Christianity: The Swiss Reformation*. History of the Christian Church 8. Grand Rapids: Eerdmans, 1910.

Schlatter, Adolf. *Romans: The Righteousness of God*. Translated by Siegfried S. Schatzmann. Peabody, MA: Hendrickson, 1995.

Schleiermacher, Friedrich. *The Christian Faith*. Edinburgh: T&T Clark, 1928.

Schlosser, Jacques. Review of *Adoption as Sons of God: An Exegetical Investigation into the Background of* Yiothesia *in the Pauline Corpus*, by J. Scott. *Biblica* 75 (1994): 283–87.

Schnackenburg, Rudolf. *Ephesians: A Commentary*. Edinburgh: T&T Clark, 1991.

———. *The Johannine Epistles: Introduction and Commentary*. Translated by Reginald Fuller and Ilse Fuller. New York: Crossroad, 1992.

Schoenberg, Martin W. "Huiothesia: The Adoptive Sonship of the Israelites." *American Ecclesiastical Review* 143 (1960): 261–73.

———. "*Huiothesia*: The Word and the Institution." *Scripture* 15 (1963): 115–23.

Schreiner, Thomas R. *Galatians*. ZEC 9. Grand Rapids: Zondervan, 2010.

———. *Romans*. BECNT 6. Grand Rapids: Baker, 1998.

Schweizer, Eduard. "Slaves of the Elements and Worshipers of Angels: Gal 4:3, 9 and Col 2:8, 18, 20." *JBL* 107, 3 (1988): 455–68.

Scott, James M. *Adoption as Sons of God: An Exegetical Investigation into the Background of* YIOTHESIA *in the Pauline Corpus*. Wissenschaftliche Untersuchungen Zum Neuen Testament 48. Tübingen: J. C. B. Mohr (Paul Siebeck), 1992.

Seifrid, Mark A. *Christ, Our Righteousness: Paul's Theology of Justification*. NSBT 9. Downers Grove, IL: Apollos/InterVarsity Press, 2000.

Selbie, W. B. *The Fatherhood of God*. New York: Charles Scribner's Sons, 1936.

Shaw, Robert. *An Exposition of the Westminster Confession of Faith*. Fearn, Ross-shire, UK: Christian Focus, 2008.

Shedd, William G. T. *A Critical and Doctrinal Commentary on the Epistle of St. Paul to the Romans*. Reprint, Minneapolis: Klock & Klock, 1978.

———. *Dogmatic Theology*. Classic repr. ed. Grand Rapids: Zondervan, 1950.

Sheldon, Henry C. *System of Christian Doctrine*. Cincinnati: Jennings and Pye, 1903.

Shepard, Samuel G. "The Pauline Doctrine of Sonship." Ph.D. diss., Southern Baptist Theological Seminary, Louisville, KY, 1951.

Shepherd, Norman. *The Call of Grace: How the Covenant Illumines Salvation and Evangelism*. Phillipsburg, NJ: P&R Publishing, 2000.

Sibbes, Richard. *Works of Richard Sibbes*. Edited by Alexander B. Grosart. 7 vols. Edinburgh: Banner of Truth, 1983.

Silva, Moisés. *Biblical Words and Their Meaning: An Introduction to Lexical Semantics*. Grand Rapids: Zondervan, 1983.

Simpson, E. K., and F. F. Bruce. *Commentary on the Epistles to the Ephesians and the Colossians: The English Text with Introduction, Exposition, and Notes*. NICNT. Grand Rapids: Eerdmans, 1957.

Smail, Thomas A. *The Forgotten Father*. Grand Rapids: Eerdmans, 1980.

Smalley, Stephen S. *John: Evangelist and Interpreter*. 2nd ed. Downers Grove, IL: InterVarsity Press, 1998.

Smith, D. Moody. *The Theology of the Gospel of John*. Cambridge: Cambridge University Press, 1995.

Sontag, Frederick. "Metaphorical Non-Sequitur?" *Scottish Journal of Theology* 44, 1 (1991): 1–18.

Sparks, Adam. "Salvation History, Chronology, and Crisis: A Problem with Inclusivist Theology of Religions, Part 1 of 2." *Themelios* 33, 2 (2008): 7–18.

Stacey, W. David. "Paul's Certainties: God's Purpose in Creation—Romans 8:22–23." *Expository Times* 69 (1958): 178–81.

Steele, David N., and Curtis C. Thomas. *Romans: An Interpretive Outline. A Study Manual of Romans, Including a Series of Interpretive Notes and Charts on the Major Doctrines of the Epistle*. Philadelphia: Presbyterian and Reformed, 1963.

Stevenson-Moessner, Jeanne. *The Spirit of Adoption: At Home in God's Family*. Louisville, KY: Westminster John Knox, 2003.

Stibbe, Mark. *From Orphans to Heirs: Celebrating Our Spiritual Adoption*. Oxford: Bible Reading Fellowship, 1999.

Stolt, Birgit. "Martin Luther on God as Father." *Lutheran Quarterly* 8, 4 (1994): 385–95.

Stott, John R. W. *The Cross of Christ*. Downers Grove, IL: InterVarsity Press, 1986.

———. *The Message of Ephesians: God's New Society*. The Bible Speaks Today. Leicester: Inter-Varsity Press, 1986.

Strong, A. H. *Systematic Theology: A Compendium*. Valley Forge, PA: Judson Press, 1907.

Swetnam, James. "On Romans 8:23 and the 'Expectation of Sonship.'" *Biblica* 48 (1967): 102–8.

Swindell, Anthony C. "Abraham and Isaac: An Essay in Biblical Appropriation." *Expository Times* 87 (1975): 50–53.

Tappert, Theodore G., ed. and trans. *The Book of Concord: The Confessions of the Evangelical Lutheran Church*. Philadelphia: Fortress, 1959.

Taylor, Howard. "The Continuity of the People of God in Old and New Testaments." *SBET* 3, 2 (1985): 13–26.

Taylor, Vincent. *The Person of Christ in New Testament Teaching*. London: Macmillan and Co., 1958.

Telford, Andrew. *Subjects of Sovereignty*. Philadelphia: Berachah Church, 1940.

Theron, Daniel J. "'Adoption' in the Pauline Corpus." *EvQ* 28, 1 (1956): 6–14.

Thielman, Frank. *Ephesians*. BECNT. Grand Rapids: Baker Academic, 2010.

Thiessen, Henry Clarence. *Introductory Lectures in Systematic Theology*. Grand Rapids: Eerdmans, 1949.

Tilling, Chris. *Paul's Divine Christology*. Wissenschaftliche Untersuchungen zum Neuen Testament 2 Reihe 323. Tübingen: Mohr Siebeck, 2012.

Tipton, Lane G. "The Covenant Historical Character of Paul's Notion of 'Proof' in Acts 17:29–31: Implications for Van Tillian Apologetics." Unpublished paper, Westminster Theological Seminary, Philadelphia, 2000.

———. "The Gospel and Redemptive-Historical Hermeneutics." In *Confident of Better Things*, edited by John R. Muether and Danny E. Olinger, 185–213. Willow Grove, PA: Committee for the Historian of the Orthodox Presbyterian Church, 2011.

Toon, Peter. *Born Again: A Biblical and Theological Study of Regeneration*. Grand Rapids: Baker, 1987.

Torisu, Yoshifumi. *Gott und Welt: eine Untersuchung zur Gotteslehre des Irenäus von Lyon*. Studia Instituti Missiologici Societatis Verbi Divini 52. Nettetal: Steyler Verlag, 1991.

Torrance, Thomas F. *The Christian Doctrine of God: One Being Three Persons*. Edinburgh: T&T Clark, 1996.

———. *Trinitarian Perspectives: Toward Doctrinal Agreement*. Edinburgh: T&T Clark, 1994.

Trumper, Tim J. R. "Adoption: The Forgotten Doctrine of Westminster Soteriology." In *Reformed Theology in Contemporary Perspective*, edited by Lynn Quigley, 87–123. Edinburgh: Rutherford House, 2006.

———. "Covenant Theology and Constructive Calvinism." *WTJ* 64, 2 (2002): 387–404.

———. "An Historical Study of Adoption in the Calvinistic Tradition." Ph.D. diss., University of Edinburgh, 2001.

———. "The Metaphorical Import of Adoption: A Plea for Realisation I: The Adoption Metaphor in Biblical Usage." *SBET* 14, 2 (1996): 129–45.

———. "The Metaphorical Import of Adoption: A Plea for Realisation II: The Adoption Metaphor in Theological Usage." *SBET* 15, 2 (1997): 98–115.

———. "Theology of Adoption." ST 921 class notes presented at Westminster Theological Seminary, Philadelphia, 1999.

———. "Towards a Westminster Theology of Adoption." Special lecture presented at Westminster Theological Seminary, Philadelphia, October 19, 1998.

———. *When History Teaches Us Nothing: The Recent Reformed Sonship Debate in Context.* Eugene, OR: Wipf and Stock, 2008.

Turner, M. M. B. "The Concept of Receiving the Spirit in John's Gospel." *VE* 10 (1977): 24–42.

———. "The Significance of Spirit Endowment for Paul." *VE* 9 (1975): 56–69.

Turretin, Francis. *Institutes of Elenctic Theology.* Edited by James T. Dennison Jr. Translated by George Musgrave Giger. 3 vols. Phillipsburg, NJ: P&R Publishing, 1992–94.

Twisse, William. *A Briefe Catecheticall Exposition of Christian Doctrine.* London: G. Miller for Robert Bird, 1632.

Ussher, James. *A Body of Divinitie: The Sum and Substance of Christian Religion.* 8th ed. London: R. F. for Jonathan Robinson et al., 1702.

Vallée, Gérard. *A Study in Anti-Gnostic Polemics: Irenaeus, Hippolytus, and Epiphanius.* Edited by J. Ouellette. Studies in Christianity and Judaism 1. Waterloo, ON: Wilfrid Laurier University, 1981.

van den Beld, Antonie. "*Non Posse Peccare*: On the Inability to Sin in Eternal Life." *Religious Studies* 25, 4 (1989): 521–35.

Van Dixhoorn, Chad. "The Sonship Program for Revival: A Summary and Critique." *WTJ* 61, 2 (1999): 227–46.

VanGemeren, Willem A. *The Progress of Redemption: The Story of Salvation from Creation to the New Jerusalem.* Grand Rapids: Baker, 1988.

———. "The Spirit of Restoration." *WTJ* 50, 1 (1988): 81–102.

Van Groningen, Gerard. *From Creation to Consummation*. Sioux Center, IA: Dordt College Press, 1996.

Vanhoozer, Kevin J. "Wrighting the Wrongs of the Reformation? The State of the Union with Christ in St. Paul and Protestant Soteriology." In *Jesus, Paul, and the People of God: A Theological Dialogue with N. T. Wright*, edited by Nicholas Perrin and Richard B. Hays, 235–59. Downers Grove, IL: InterVarsity Press, 2011.

Vanhoye, Albert. "L'Épître Aux Ephésiens et l'Épître Aux Hébreux." *Biblica* 59 (1978): 198–230.

Van Til, Cornelius. *The Defense of the Faith*. 3rd ed. Philadelphia: Presbyterian and Reformed, 1967.

———. *The Great Debate*. 3rd ed. Nutley, NJ: Presbyterian and Reformed, 1971.

———. "The Infallible Word." In *Nature and Scripture: A Symposium by the Members of the Faculty of Westminster Theological Seminary, Philadelphia*, edited by N. B. Stonehouse and Paul Woolley, 263–301. Philadelphia: Presbyterian Guardian, 1946.

———. *An Introduction to Systematic Theology*. Nutley, NJ: Presbyterian and Reformed, 1974.

Vellanickal, Matthew. *The Divine Sonship of Christians in the Johannine Writings*. AnBib: Investigationes Scientificae in Res Biblicas 72. Rome: Biblical Institute, 1977.

Venema, Cornelis. *Accepted and Renewed in Christ: The Twofold Grace of God and the Interpretation of Calvin's Theology*. Göttingen: Vandenhoeck & Ruprecht, 2007.

Vos, Geerhardus. *Biblical Theology: Old and New Testaments*. Grand Rapids: Eerdmans, 1948. Reprint, Edinburgh: Banner of Truth, 1996.

———. *The Eschatology of the Old Testament*. Edited by James T. Dennison Jr. Phillipsburg, NJ: P&R Publishing, 2001.

———. *The Pauline Eschatology*. Princeton, NJ: Princeton University Press, 1930.

———. *Redemptive History and Biblical Interpretation: The Shorter Writings of Geerhardus Vos*. Edited by Richard B. Gaffin Jr. Phillipsburg, NJ: Presbyterian and Reformed, 1980.

———. *Reformed Dogmatics*. Edited by Richard B. Gaffin Jr. and Richard de Witt. Translated by Annemie Godbehere, Roelof van Ijken, Kim

Batteau, Daan van der Kraan, and Harry Boonstra. Vols. 1–3. Bellingham, WA: Lexham Press, 2013.

———. *The Self-Disclosure of Jesus: The Modern Debate about the Messianic Consciousness.* Edited by Johannes G. Vos. Grand Rapids: Eerdmans, 1954.

———. "The Spiritual Resurrection of Believers: A Sermon on Ephesians 2:4, 5." *Kerux* 5, 1 (1990): 3–21.

———. *The Teaching of the Epistle to the Hebrews.* Edited by Johannes G. Vos. Eugene, OR: Wipf and Stock, 1998.

———. *When the Time Had Fully Come.* Grand Rapids: Eerdmans, 1957.

Wall, Robert W. *Colossians and Philemon.* IVP New Testament Commentary Series. Downers Grove, IL: InterVarsity Press, 1993.

Wallace, Ronald S. *Calvin's Doctrine of the Christian Life.* Tyler, TX: Geneva Divinity School, 1982.

Waltke, Bruce K. *An Old Testament Theology: An Exegetical, Canonical, and Thematic Approach.* Grand Rapids: Zondervan, 2007.

Warfield, Benjamin B. *Biblical and Theological Studies.* Philadelphia: Presbyterian and Reformed, 1968.

———. *Biblical Doctrines.* Reprint, Edinburgh: Banner of Truth, 1988.

———. "Calvin as Theologian" (1909). http://www.the-highway.com/caltheo _Warfield.html.

———. *Selected Shorter Writings.* Edited by John E. Meeter. 2 vols. Nutley, NJ: Presbyterian and Reformed, 1973.

———. *Studies in Theology.* Reprint, Edinburgh: Banner of Truth, 1988.

———. *The Works of Benjamin B. Warfield.* 10 vols. Grand Rapids: Baker, 1981.

Waters, Guy Prentiss. *The Federal Vision and Covenant Theology: A Comparative Analysis.* Phillipsburg, NJ: P&R Publishing, 2006.

———. *Justification and the New Perspectives on Paul: A Review and Response.* Phillipsburg, NJ: P&R Publishing, 2004.

Watson, Thomas. *A Body of Divinity in a Series of Sermons on the Shorter Catechism Composed by the Reverend Assembly of Divines at Westminster.* Philadelphia: Thomas Wardle, 1833.

Webb, Robert Alexander. *Christian Salvation: Its Doctrine and Experience.* Richmond, VA: Presbyterian Committee, 1921.

———. *The Reformed Doctrine of Adoption.* Grand Rapids: Eerdmans, 1947.

Weber, Otto. *Foundations of Dogmatics.* Translated by Darrell L. Guder. 2 vols. Grand Rapids: Eerdmans, 1981–83.

Weeks, Noel. *Admonition and Curse: The Ancient Near Eastern Treaty/Covenant Form as a Problem in Inter-Cultural Relationships.* London: T&T Clark, 2004.

Wenham, David. *Paul: Follower of Jesus or Founder of Christianity?* Grand Rapids: Eerdmans, 1995.

Wermuth, Robert E. "The Doctrine of Adoption in Paul's Ephesian Letter." Unpublished master's thesis. Covenant Theological Seminary, St. Louis, 1985.

Westcott, Brooke Foss. *Saint Paul's Epistle to the Ephesians: The Greek Text with Notes and Addenda.* London: Macmillan, 1906. Reprint, Minneapolis: Klock & Klock, 1978.

Westermann, Claus. *Genesis 1–11: A Commentary.* Translated by John J. Scullion. Minneapolis: Augsburg, 1984.

Westhead, Nigel. "Adoption in the Thought of John Calvin." *SBET* 13, 2 (1995): 102–15.

Whaling, Thornton. "Adoption." *Princeton Theological Review* 21, 2 (1923): 223–35.

White, James R. *The Potter's Freedom: A Defense of the Reformation and a Rebuttal of Norman Geisler's Chosen but Free.* Amityville, NY: Calvary Press, 2000.

White, John L. *The Apostle of God: Paul and the Promise of Abraham.* Peabody, MA: Hendrickson, 1999.

Widdicombe, Peter. *The Fatherhood of God from Origen to Athanasius.* Oxford: Clarendon, 1994.

Williams, Michael D. "Regeneration in Cosmic Context." *Presbyterian & Reformed Review* 7 (1989): 68–80.

Wilterdink, Garret A. "The Fatherhood of God in Calvin's Thought." In *Articles on Calvin and Calvinism*, 175–88. Vol. 9 of *Calvin's Theology, Theology Proper, Eschatology.* Edited by Richard C. Gamble. New York and London: Garland Publishing, 1992.

Winslow, Octavius. *No Condemnation in Christ Jesus: As Unfolded in the Eighth Chapter of the Epistle to the Romans.* Edinburgh: Banner of Truth, 1991.

Witherington, Ben, III. *Grace in Galatia: A Commentary on St. Paul's Letter to the Galatians.* T&T Clark Academic Paperbacks. London and New York: T&T Clark, 2004.

―――. "The Waters of Birth: John 3:5 and 1 John 5:6–8." *New Testament Studies* 35, 1 (1989): 155–60.

Witsius, Herman. *The Economy of the Covenants between God and Man: Comprehending a Complete Body of Divinity.* Translated by William Crookshank. Reprint, Kingsburg, CA: den Dulk Christian Foundation, 1990.

Wolters, Albert M. *Creation Regained: Biblical Basics for a Reformational Worldview.* Grand Rapids: Eerdmans, 1985.

Wood, A. Skevington. *Ephesians.* Expositor's Bible Commentary 11. Grand Rapids: Zondervan, 1978.

Wright, N. T. *The Climax of the Covenant: Christ and the Law in Pauline Theology.* Minneapolis: Fortress, 1993.

―――. *The Resurrection of the Son of God.* Christian Origins and the Question of God 3. Minneapolis: Fortress, 1992.

―――. *What Saint Paul Really Said: Was Paul of Tarsus the Real Founder of Christianity?* Grand Rapids: Eerdmans, 1997.

Wright, Scott R. "Regeneration and Redemptive History." Ph.D. diss., Westminster Theological Seminary, Philadelphia, 1999.

Wuest, Kenneth S. *Untranslatable Riches from the Greek New Testament for the English Reader.* Grand Rapids: Eerdmans, 1942.

Wynne, Carlton. "History and Trinity Reconsidered: A Reformed Evaluation of Wolfhart Pannenberg's Retroactive Eschatology." Ph.D. diss., Westminster Theological Seminary, Philadelphia, 2015.

Young, E. J. *Thy Word Is Truth: Some Thoughts on the Biblical Doctrine of Inspiration.* Edinburgh: Banner of Truth, 1963.

Index of Scripture

INDEX OF SUBJECTS AND NAMES